WITH LIBERTY AND JUSTICE FOR WHOM?

WITH LIBERTY AND JUSTICE FOR WHOM?

The Recent Evangelical Debate over Capitalism

by

CRAIG M. GAY

William B. Eerdmans Publishing Company
Grand Rapids, Michigan

Copyright © 1991 by Wm. B. Eerdmans Publishing Co.
255 Jefferson Ave. S E., Grand Rapids, Mich. 49503

Printed in the United States of America

Library of Congress Cataloging-in-Publication Data

Gay, Craig M.
    With liberty and justice for whom?: the recent evangelical debate over
capitalism / by Craig M. Gay.
        p.   cm.
    Revision of the author's thesis (Ph.D.)—Boston University.
    Includes bibliographical references.
    ISBN 0-8028-0289-3
    1. Capitalism—Religious aspects—Christianity.
2. Evangelicalism. I. Title.
BR115.C3G39   1991
261.8′5—dc20   91-9781
                                            CIP

for Julie

Contents

Acknowledgments

Of course a number of people helped to make the following study, which was originally a doctoral dissertation, possible. In the first instance, I want to thank my primary dissertation advisor, Peter Berger, for his help and encouragement. While Peter is well known for his intellectual accomplishments—accomplishments to which I am very much indebted—I am perhaps most grateful to him for the integrity of his friendship. Peter is truly a man whose No means no and whose Yes means yes.

In addition, I want to thank the John M. Olin Foundation for funding three very fruitful years of study and research at Boston University by way of the university's Institute for the Study of Economic Culture, a research center committed to systematic study of the relationships between economic development and sociocultural change. I hope that this study contributes something to our understanding of these relationships.

Also with regard to research, I am very grateful to William Zimpfer, late head librarian at Boston University's School of Theology Library, who taught me how to organize and keep track of large amounts of information. I look forward to that day when I can tell him how well his system worked. I would also like to thank Ms. Dorothy Moore, librarian at Andover Newton Theological School. I practically lived in the A.N.T.S. library for a couple of years, and Dorothy never complained.

For constructive critical comment on the completed project, I am very grateful to Professors Loren Wilkinson (Regent College) and Peter J. Hill (Wheaton College), both of whom took time out of busy schedules to give my dissertation a close reading prior to its final revision. Special thanks also to Dr. Carl F. H. Henry, who not only figures prominently in the following study but who read and commented on several parts of it.

Of course, I am also grateful to James Davison Hunter of the University of Virginia for seconding Peter Berger's supervision of my dissertation, and to Robert Neville and the other members of my dissertation committee at Boston University's Graduate School for deciding to pass it.

For their assistance in translating the study into book form, I want to thank two of my students at Regent College, Jeffrey Hopwood and Ronald Rittgers. They helped proofread the manuscript and kept me current on the evangelical debate.

I would also like to thank Bill Eerdmans, Jr., Professor Robert Goudzwaard (Free University of Amsterdam), and the Rev. Richard John Neuhaus (Institute on Religion and Public Life), all of whom commented insightfully and helpfully on the manuscript.

Finally, I would like to thank my wife, Julie, who has been asked to read and comment on parts of this study quite a few times and still loves me anyway.

Of course, for all of the help I have received, I thank the God and Father of our Lord Jesus Christ.

—CRAIG M. GAY

Foreword

Evangelical Protestants constitute the largest or second-largest segment of organized religion in America (either just before or just after Roman Catholics, depending on how one counts), and arguably its most dynamic segment. What is more, American evangelicals are part of a worldwide community that is rapidly expanding, especially in Latin America, sub-Saharan Africa, and Eastern Asia; the immense social, economic, and political consequences of this expansion are only beginning to be felt. Given these facts, the ignorance about evangelicalism in the general public and in the mass media is astonishing. Ignorance is only part of it. There are also widespread stereotypes, most of them distortive, as to the beliefs and practices of this population. Among these stereotypes is the notion that all or most evangelicals are politically on the right, staunch defenders of the status quo in general and of capitalism in particular. The stereotype, incidentally, may be found on both sides of the political spectrum, though obviously what is greeted as good news on the right is perceived as an ominous threat on the left.

Craig Gay's book is an important, highly useful corrective against this particular simplification of reality. Readers of this book will discover that the facts are much more complicated. Those on the right will be somewhat disappointed; those on the left, somewhat relieved. In either case they will derive not only instruction but pleasure from perusing the book. Gay is a careful, disciplined scholar; he is also lucidly articulate.

Gay shows in considerable detail that the evangelical debate over capitalism is carried on between and among three distinct groups — a left, a right, and a center. These political divisions are not very different from those characteristic of the overall society. The debate, however, is distinctive because it is carried on within the universe of discourse of the evangelical faith, and, needless to say, the sources of this faith are employed to validate very different, indeed contradictory ideological positions. (Also needless to say, not for one moment should one suppose that evangelicals are the only ones who thus employ religion as a political weapon.) Capitalism is one of the central realities of contemporary society; consequently, the debate is over a very important subject, and even nonevangelicals should be interested in what a sizable group of American citizens think about it. But Gay's analysis has implications that go far beyond the debate over capitalism. In covering this debate he must also deal with the much larger topic of the encounter between religious orthodoxy (this one, but also any other one) and the modern world. Looming over the debate over capitalism is the specter of secularization, which of course has loomed for a long time over all reflection concerning the fate of religion in the modern world. Thus Gay's book is not just about how evangelicals think about capitalism; it is also about the prospects of evangelicalism surviving in the pluralistic pressure cooker of modern America.

Gay adopts the so-called "New Class theory" to explain current cultural conflicts in America — that is, the view that there are now two middle classes competing for power and influence, the old middle class centered in business and the old professions, and the new middle class based on the "knowledge industry." This perspective makes clear that the same forces affect evangelicals that have reshaped and to some extent polarized the larger society. Put a little crudely, this means that evangelicals are not protected by their faith against a more or less Pavlovian response to the ideological stimuli in their respective class milieus. But this sociological commonplace has particularly sinister implications for evangelicals. The New Class is not only the purveyor of (broadly speaking) left ideological values; it is also the most secularized group in American society, and the institutions it controls, notably higher education and the media, are primary "carriers" of secularization. As is well known, education and social mobility are closely linked phenomena in a modern society. As evangelicals aspire upward in society, they must pass through the educational rites of passage, and these are firmly in the hands of the New Class. This leads to a painful paradox, which has previously been shown in the work of James Hunter about the same group: the capacity of evangelicals to resist the forces of secularization stands in an inverse relation to their success in achieving education and social mobility.

One of Gay's most interesting observations concerns the relation of the debate over capitalism and the struggle against secularization. On the face of it, there is no reason why quite discrepant views on capitalism could not be held by people with the same orthodox views in religion. And, as Gay shows, this is indeed the case. But there is an important aspect of this that must also be understood: the anticapitalist (or at least generally left-leaning) position is associated with higher education and entry into the new college-educated, knowledge-driven middle class — the same middle class that leads in secularity. When evangelicals adopt the political positions and agendas of this class, they do not of course thereby intend to give up their religious orthodoxy; on the contrary, they usually announce very emphatically that they continue to hold the same orthodox views when it comes to religion. These political agendas, however, put these people squarely into a social and cultural milieu that is hostile to religious orthodoxy. Inevitably, there takes place what I have elsewhere called "cognitive contamination" — a gradual, typically unconscious process of adaptation to the prevailing worldview. In this instance, what happens is that the old theological formulations and pious practices continue for a while as the new political agendas are acted out. But slowly, imperceptibly, it is the new agendas that are deemed most important, deemed to be "where it's at." At this point the old religious contents acquire a merely ritual quality — one goes through the motions, as it were; they fade toward irrelevance. In this way, as Gay shows very clearly, the social and political agendas of the left serve as instruments of "back door" secularization. (Of course, in theory, agendas of the right could play the same role; in fact they don't, precisely because of the aforementioned class locations of American politics: it is the left, not the right, that sits in the midst of the most potent secularizing forces.)

Gay is himself a committed evangelical, and he does not pretend to engage in an analysis *sine ira et studio.* Evidently, therefore, he is not very happy with his conclusions. On the capitalism issue, I suppose, he could be described as a sensible centrist — convinced of the socioeconomic superiority of capitalism but cognizant of some of its "cultural contradictions" (as Daniel Bell put it). His concluding comments, a sort of sermonette in which he recommends a "Sabbath attitude" in Christians' relation to the economy, are original and interesting. His general position is one of both acceptance of and resistance to the modern world, neither believing in modern progress nor harking back to some allegedly better premodern past. Gay wants to be open to the modern world; he also wants to retain his faith in evangelical orthodoxy. He cannot be blamed for failing to tell us just how such a stance can be empirically maintained. He knows that the odds are not very good; he also sees no alternative to trying. In this he is not alone, and neither are evangelicals. All of us who accept the modern world and yet reject its secularity face the same quandary. Craig Gay has written a remarkably honest account of how this quandary plays itself out as an important group within American religion grapples with an important institution of modern life. The book should certainly be read by evangelicals and by observers of evangelicalism; it will also be of profit to others who try to face up to the aforementioned quandary.

Finally, a more personal note: Craig Gay worked on this book while an Olin Fellow at the Institute for the Study of Economic Culture at Boston University, a research center concerned with the relations between culture (including religion) and economic processes. It is very gratifying to all of us connected with the Institute that work of this caliber is coming out under its auspices.

—Peter L. Berger

Introduction

For well over a century now, capitalism has stood as *the* preeminent social issue. Recent events in Eastern Europe and the Soviet Union attest to this very well, for they remind us that communism and socialism were themselves developed as "solutions" to the problems posed by modern capitalism. The rejection of these solutions is propelling the nations involved either back toward a more market-oriented system or toward yet other solutions. Less spectacularly but closer to home, the issue of capitalism has tended to lurk just beneath the surface of any number of social and economic policy debates. Should such basic things as employment and health care be left to big business and the vagaries of the market? Should they be politicized and bureaucratized? These are difficult questions, and along with issues of democracy and self-determination, they are inextricably interwoven with the issue of capitalism in the modern situation.

It is not surprising, then, that capitalism has been of considerable interest to American evangelicals. Yet while evangelicals may once have been unified firmly to the right of center as defenders of capitalism, this has not been the case for some time now. To be sure, an evangelical right has continued to defend capitalism as a natural outgrowth of biblical Christianity. But a vociferous evangelical left, contending that capitalism is responsible for a great many of the world's ills, has become increasingly influential over the last twenty years. While those on the right have tended to defend capitalism under the banner of liberty, those on the left have condemned it under the banner of social justice. Even the evangelical mainstream, so often associated with political and economic conservatism in America, has become troubled by the issue of capitalism, confused over the natures of liberty and justice, and increasingly torn between right and left on social and economic policy matters. Not content merely to draw contradictory conclusions about modern capitalism, representatives of competing factions have impugned each other's moral and intellectual integrity in the process. It is no exaggeration to say that capitalism has

1

been one of the most divisive issues within American evangelicalism in recent decades.

Understandably, evangelicals have tended to think about the conflict over capitalism in theological terms, and they have for the most part sought theo- logical solutions to it. Yet while it is not implausible that the evangelical conflict might ultimately be attributable to theological differences of opinion, there does appear to be more going on within this debate than theological wrangling. Those evangelicals who defend capitalism differ with those who condemn it on so many issues—economic, political, moral, and ethical as well as theological—that the two groups appear to be contending for entirely different visions of American society, with theology often seeming to be something of an afterthought. That the conflict within evangelicalism appears to mirror a larger secular disagreement over social and economic policy pro- vides another indication that theology is probably not the only thing at issue in this debate. Just what *is* at issue within this debate is one of the things I try to uncover in this study. I am interested in the larger social context of the recent evangelical debate over capitalism, for once we recognize its shape, we will be better able to determine the extent to which the recent evangelical conflict may simply be a reflection of this context.

So this book stands apart from other evangelical assessments of economics and theology in the extent to which it steps back from both economics and theology to look a little more closely at the evangelical debate itself. In a sense, it represents an attempt to get to the bottom of the evangelical debate over capitalism, an attempt to determine just how it is that evangelicals, who share a fairly broad range of theological commitments, can have arrived at such radically different assessments of one of the more central institutions in modern American society. For if we can determine how this has happened and why evangelicals have become so polarized over the issue of capitalism in recent years, then we may well be able to move forward, not simply toward a more balanced appraisal of modern capitalism but toward a more constructive evan- gelical theology of economics as well.

Approaching the Evangelical Debate

This study is largely descriptive, but insofar as it explores the relation of recent evangelical appraisals of capitalism to their social contexts or locations, it is an exercise in what has been called the sociology of knowledge, a discipline organized around the insight that all knowledge is *social* knowledge and thus functions within socially constructed constraints. In keeping with this, I will argue that evangelical positions on social and economic policy issues reflect tensions that have been generated within a particular contemporary cultural conflict, a conflict that has been described in terms of the "New Class" thesis. Stated simply, the New Class thesis holds that at least since the end of the Second World War the predominant class conflict within American society (and within other advanced industrial societies as well) has been between two relatively privileged segments of what was once a largely unified middle class—namely, an "old" or "traditional" middle class generally associated with business and basic material production and distribution, and a "new" middle class associated with the production and distribution of knowledge and information. These two classes have slightly different interests with respect to modern capitalism. For example, the New Class owes a good deal of its power and prestige to the regulatory and welfare apparatus of the modern welfare state, and so it naturally has an interest in expanding this apparatus. By far the easiest way to legitimate this expansion has been to highlight the inadequacies of capitalism and business to provide for any number of social needs. The interests of the traditional middle class, on the other hand, are not necessarily served by the expansion of the welfare state; and when this class has chosen to resist state expansion, it has tended to do so by way of the defending capitalism's ability to produce and to distribute prosperity. The contemporary conflict has been further complicated, however, by the fact that members of the New Class have tended to be, for a variety of interesting reasons, much more highly secularized than members of the traditional middle class. Hence the conflict involves not only issues of capitalism and the welfare state but also the issue of whether religion should be allowed to have any place in American public life.

As we will see, evangelical intellectuals have found themselves in a curious position with respect to the competing class factions because they share a number of interests with both the old and the new classes. That they have become polarized over the issue of capitalism seems to suggest that some of them may have chosen to identify with the interests of the traditional middle class in the contemporary cultural conflict while others have chosen to voice the interests of the New Class instead.

Now to say this is not to suggest that evangelical positions on social and economic policy issues are nothing more than expressions of evangelical participation on either side of the contemporary cultural conflict. Still, the evangelical debate does appear to reflect a particular social context, and an exploration of that fact may serve to make the debate more intelligible and offer insights into the ways in which evangelical theology is subtly being affected as it is brought to bear on political-economic questions. The socio-logical notion of "elective affinity" is instructive in this connection. It suggests that groups of persons with common interests will tend to "elect" ideas and opinions with which they have an "affinity" and will tend to ignore or discount other ideas and opinions with which they do not. In other words, while soci-ological factors may not explain the positive content of an idea—its truth or falsehood—they may well explain the success of certain ideas and opinions in certain social contexts. In this respect, it is important to realize that the ideological abuse of knowledge tends not so much to be a matter of corruption per se as it is a matter of selectivity. One of the chief points of interest in this study is the extent to which different evangelical appraisals of capitalism show affinities to the class factions on either side of the contemporary cultural conflict. Also of interest is the extent to which these appraisals have been selective both economically and theologically.

The Scope of the Study

Throughout this study, I use the term *evangelical* to refer to conservative Protestants generally, but it should be noted that evangelicalism is currently divided into two broad streams or coalitions: the evangelical proper and the fundamentalist.[1] Both have formulated a conservative theology. Both are committed to addressing and engaging modern American culture and have developed overlapping organizational and educational infrastructures dedicated to that task. Both are perplexed by the increasing secularity of American society and are opposed to what has been called secular humanism. But the two can be distinguished to the extent that they have developed different visions for the revitalization of American society. Fundamentalists have tended to take a confrontational approach to contemporary American culture in the hopes of reestablishing the broad conservative Protestant consensus of the mid-nineteenth century. Evangelicals have tended to be less confrontational, but they have also been much less uniform in their assessments of the American cultural problem. Indeed, the theological and cultural boundaries of evangelicalism have become increasingly flexible and porous. In part this has been due to the expansion of evangelicalism since the 1940s and to such factors as the commitment of evangelicals to educational excellence and cultural engagement.[2] Whatever the reasons, this broadening has been most noticeable among

1. This kind of scheme was proposed by C. Norman Kraus in "Evangelicalism: The Great Coalition," in *Evangelicalism and Anabaptism,* ed. C. Norman Kraus (Scottdale, PA: Herald Press, 1979), p. 40; and also more recently by Nancy Tatom Ammerman in *Bible Believers: Fundamentalists in the Modern World* (New Brunswick, NJ: Rutgers University Press, 1987).

2. George Marsden has noted that "since mid-century there have been something like 'card-carrying' evangelicals. These people, like their nineteenth-century forebears, have some sense of belonging to a complicated fellowship and infrastructure of transdenominational evangelical organizations for evangelism, missions, social services, publications, and education. Typically, those who have the strongest sense of being 'evangelicals' are persons with directly fundamentalist background, although persons from other traditions—Pentecostal, holiness, Reformed, Anabaptist, and others—are often deeply involved as well. Sometimes the people, groups, and organizations that make up 'evangelicalism' in this sense are rivals; but even in

what Richard Quebedeaux called the "young evangelicals," the generation of evangelical leaders that has arisen since the 1950s.[3] The young evangelicals have grown increasingly critical not only of conservative fundamentalism but also of the more conservative elements within mainstream evangelicalism itself. Tending to be less insistent on issues of strict inerrancy and biblical literalism, the young evangelicals have explored (albeit in a limited way) the use of biblical criticism in interpreting the biblical texts. They have grown impatient with the political and economic conservatism still characterizing fundamentalism and what they have called "establishment" evangelicalism. And they have been much less suspicious of broad ecumenical cooperation, especially in the social and political-economic arena. Yet the multiplying disagreements within the evangelical camp and the movement of many younger evangelicals to the left politically (and apparently theologically as well) has not gone unnoticed in more conservative and self-consciously fundamentalist circles. The emergence of New Christian Right in the late 1970s, along with the resurrection of the word *fundamentalism* in association with cultural militancy, has at least in part been a conservative reaction to the perceived failure of evangelicalism to defend the faith adequately and to develop a thoroughly Christian and distinctively conservative cultural vision.

Most of the subjects of our study come from within the community of those who describe themselves as evangelicals, though some might call themselves fundamentalists. Many are teachers in evangelical seminaries, some are lobbyists or publicists, and a few are scholars in specifically evangelical think tanks. This study is limited to a consideration of the opinions of evangelical *intellectuals*—those who have published books or articles that explicitly deal with the assessment of existing political-economic systems and/or make suggestions for their reform. I do not assess the opinions of the evangelical rank and file, and I take up evangelical political thought only insofar as it is related to matters of political economy in articles and books written primarily to address economic questions. And while there are isolated evangelical voices within many of the so-called "mainline" Protestant denominations, very few of these voices have been included in this study.

"Capitalism" has a considerable range of meanings among the subjects of this study, and so it will not be particularly useful to attempt to define the term

---

rivalry they manifest the connectedness of a family grouping that is quite concerned about its immediate relatives" ("The Evangelical Denomination," in *Evangelicalism in Modern America,* ed. George Marsden [Grand Rapids: William B. Eerdmans, 1984], p. xiv).

3. Quebedeaux, *The Young Evangelicals: The Story of the Emergence of a New Generation of Evangelicals* (New York: Harper & Row, 1974). This group is also described under the headings of "progressive" and "radical" evangelicalism in James Alden Hedstrom, "The Evangelical Program in the United States, 1945-1980: The Morphology of Establishment, Progressive, and Radical Platforms," Ph.D. diss., Vanderbilt University, 1982.

before considering their positions. I will note here, however, that while a few evangelicals have written technical and theoretical works on the subject of political economy, most evangelical appraisals of capitalism have been written at a more popular level. Evangelicals have been more concerned to communicate existing theory than to develop it.

The Significance of the Recent Debate

The significance of my analysis of the evangelical debate over capitalism is twofold. While a number of articles and books have described evangelical social thought, the full range of evangelical opinion on the subject of capitalism, which has been perhaps *the* critical social issue of this last century, simply has not been adequately surveyed as yet.[4] In addition to providing such a survey, this study seeks to illustrate a process that American sociologist Peter Berger has called "cognitive bargaining," whereby competing understandings of the world come to terms with each other by means of strategic compromise.[5] "Mainline" or "liberal" Protestantism provides an instructive example of this process. Among mainline Protestants, who have been seeking to modernize the Christian faith since at least the end of the last century, the process of cognitive bargaining appears to have begun when the social location of the theological enterprise was shifted away from the church per se and toward an increasingly secular academic setting. Describing this shift within liberal Protestantism, Berger has noted that "the theological enterprise now takes place with constant regard for a reference group of secular intellectuals—precisely the 'cultured despisers' of religion. . . . This theology can, indeed, be described as an immense bargaining process with secular thought."[6] This process has

4. There have been two studies covering the entire range of evangelical opinion that touch on the matters we will be considering. Robert K. Johnston's *Evangelicals at an Impasse: Biblical Authority in Practice* (Atlanta: John Knox Press, 1979) contains a chapter describing the range of positions evangelicals are currently taking on "social ethics." Johnston concludes that "the present divergences in social thought throughout contemporary evangelicalism stem largely from . . . differing theological traditions that provide conflicting models for social ethics today" (pp. 79-80). In addition, Robert Booth Fowler describes the range of evangelical political orientations in *A New Engagement: Evangelical Political Thought, 1966-1976* (Grand Rapids: William B. Eerdmans, 1982). Fowler notes a general trend away from political and economic conservatism within evangelicalism (something he welcomes) and wonders if diversity on social and political issues will give way to diversity in theological issues as well, but he does not attempt to provide any theoretical basis for understanding this trend.

5. Berger, *The Heretical Imperative: Contemporary Possibilities of Religious Affirmation* (Garden City, NY: Doubleday-Anchor, 1980), pp. 90ff.

6. Berger, *The Sacred Canopy: Elements of a Sociological Theory of Religion* (Garden City, NY: Doubleday-Anchor, 1969), p. 159.

continued within mainline Protestantism to the point that its leadership is at present quite closely aligned with the highly secularized New Class.

One of the questions I want to raise in this study is whether the range of recent appraisals of capitalism by evangelicals does not suggest that they are in the process of striking a similar bargain with modernity and secularity. Are certain elements of evangelical orthodoxy being discarded or modified in exchange for a broader cultural legitimacy and for the recognition of evangelicalism's social relevance? Has the shift of many evangelical intellectuals to the left politically and economically portended their shift to the left theologically as well? And what have the theological effects of the staunch defense of capitalism been? Has this defense had the effect of secularizing those on the evangelical right as well, and, if so, in what ways?

It was commonly assumed that having once retreated from the centers of American culture during the early decades of this century, conservative Protestantism would not reemerge as a cultural force. Yet beginning in the 1940s and especially since the mid-1970s, evangelicals and fundamentalists alike have repudiated the sectarianism of the early fundamentalist movement and successfully reentered the American cultural mainstream intent upon reforming it and recovering their lost cultural legitimacy. Has this reentry come at the cost of theological enculturation? Richard Quebedeaux thought so in 1978:

> The evangelical right and center has been affected by one set of values of the wider American culture—upward social mobility, financial success, . . . popularity, . . . social respectability, . . . and allegiance to the political status quo. . . . The evangelical left, for the most part, has been influenced by *another* set of values of the wider American culture—education and intellectual respectability, relativism, pluralism, political and cultural liberalism, socialism (traditionally valued by academics and church bureaucrats), and revolution.[7]

While he offered no theoretical explanation for these tendencies, Quebedeaux contended that both the evangelical right and left, albeit in different ways, had succumbed to making a kind of idolatrous compromise with modern American culture.

In a more recent study, however, sociologist of religion James Davison Hunter has suggested that while evangelicalism has indeed been culturally transformed by its reentry into the American mainstream, its theology remains relatively intact.[8] Hunter argues that the reason for this seems to be that evangelicals continue, for the most part, to be located on the margins of American society and that this has insulated them from its secularity to some extent. Noting their desire to recapture a measure of cultural legitimacy through

7. Quebedeaux, *The Worldly Evangelicals* (New York: Harper & Row, 1978), p. 167.
8. Hunter, *American Evangelicalism: Conservative Religion and the Quandary of Modernity* (New Brunswick, NJ: Rutgers University Press, 1983).

educational achievement and political activity, however, Hunter doubted that evangelicalism's theological purity could be maintained for very long.

In a subsequent study Hunter has focused on the evangelical educational elite, suggesting that the "coming generation" of evangelical leadership (i.e., those studying in evangelical colleges and seminaries at present) is accommodating itself to modernity in essentially the same way mainline Protestant leadership did at the end of the last century.[9] He arrives at this conclusion after examining the results of an attitudinal survey conducted within sixteen American evangelical colleges and seminaries between 1982 and 1985. The survey focused on four major areas: theology; views of work, morality, and the self; family ideals; and politics. In each of these areas Hunter detects a softening of older evangelical boundaries, and he concludes that evangelicalism's collective sense of identity is in the process of breaking down.[10]

My work here may be viewed as a follow-up to Quebedeaux's initial insights, and the analysis follows very closely upon Hunter's work. Whereas Hunter has covered evangelical opinion on a broad range of topics, however, I focus on a single issue, but in great detail. And while Hunter's analysis tends to indicate *that* evangelicalism is changing both culturally and theologically as it regains a measure of legitimacy within American culture, I hope to shed light on *where* the process begins and *how* it actually occurs.

Along this line, what seems to happen theologically when evangelicals actively take up issues of social concern in the contemporary situation is that the more transcendent, or "other-worldly" elements of evangelical faith, though not directly threatened by secular political-economic policy proposals, become subject to compromise. At first they are simply displaced by "this-worldly" social and economic concerns. Eventually, however, these transcendent elements seem either to drop out of the picture altogether or to require rather radical reinterpretation

9. Hunter, *Evangelicalism: The Coming Generation* (Chicago: University of Chicago Press, 1987).

10. If the number of books written on the subject of evangelical identity is any indication, evangelicals have indeed been struggling with their identity in recent years. In addition to other titles mentioned in this book, the following are significant in this regard: Donald Bloesch, *The Evangelical Renaissance* (Grand Rapids, MI: Eerdmans, 1973); Donald Bloesch, *The Future of Evangelical Christianity* (Garden City, NY: Doubleday, 1983); Donald Dayton, *Discovering an Evangelical Heritage* (New York: Harper & Row, 1976); Millard Erickson, *The New Evangelical Theology* (Westwood: Revell, 1968); David Allan Hubbard, *What We Evangelicals Believe* (Pasadena: Fuller Theological Seminary, 1979); Morris A. Inch, *The Evangelical Challenge* (Philadelphia: Westminster, 1978); Jon Johnston, *Will Evangelicalism Survive Its Own Popularity?* (Grand Rapids: Zondervan, 1980); Ronald Nash, *The New Evangelicalism* (Grand Rapids: n.p., 1963); C. René Padilla, *The New Face of Evangelicalism* (Downers Grove, IL: InterVarsity, 1976); Bernard Ramm, *The Evangelical Heritage* (Waco, TX: Word, 1973); Jack Rogers, *Confessions of a Conservative Evangelical* (Philadelphia: Westminster, 1974); Bruce Shelley, *Evangelicalism in America* (Grand Rapids: William B. Eerdmans, 1967); and Robert Webber and Donald Bloesch, *The Orthodox Evangelicals* (Nashville: Thomas Nelson, 1978).

along the lines of immanence. This process is nicely illustrated by the development of the "evangelism vs. social action" debate that first surfaced within evangelical circles in the 1950s.[11] Initially the evangelical position was resolute and proclaimed evangelism *as* social action. Then a number of evangelicals began to speak about evangelism *and* social action. Presently, and for not a few evangelicals, the slogan has been almost entirely reversed to become social action *as* evangelism. Liberation theology, though not really an evangelical phenomenon yet, epitomizes the end product of this process—that is, a theological system almost completely devoid of transcendence as traditionally understood.

As we will see, the theological shift away from transcendence has always been most visible on the evangelical left, but something similar has apparently been occurring on the evangelical right as well. The theological compromise has not been quite as obvious on the right as it has been on the left, but those on the right appear to have adopted, for reasons that we will want to examine, an equally "this-worldly" orientation that has amounted to a de facto confession of the ultimacy of economic life. This has been particularly true of the ultraconservative development of "theonomy" or "Christian reconstructionism," a system that is essentially identical to liberation theology except that a kind of libertarian social analysis (ostensibly postmillennial) has been substituted for the Marxist.

Theologically, the implications of ideological captivity on either side of the contemporary cultural conflict are enormous. Maintaining the balance between theological transcendence and immanence is crucial to conservative Protestant orthodoxy, and a shift in the center of gravity away from the transcendent and toward the immanent or vice versa signals a move away from orthodoxy and toward secularity. In this connection, I hope that this study will shed some light on the process of cultural accommodation in such a way as to help evangelical intellectuals avoid the ideological pitfalls that currently surround the debate over social and economic policy. Although they have prepared themselves reasonably well to deal with direct intellectual assaults to their faith, evangelicals have not always been very astute at recognizing the theologically dangerous ideas embedded within socioeconomic policies and structures, something that only confirms the celebrated observation of John Maynard Keynes that "the ideas of economists and political philosophers, both when they are right and when they are wrong, are more powerful than is commonly understood. Indeed the world is ruled by little else. Practical men, who believe themselves to be quite exempt from any intellectual influences, are usually the slaves of some defunct economist."[12]

11. See Arthur P. Johnston, *The Battle for World Evangelism* (Carol Stream, IL: Tyndale House, 1978).

12. Keynes, quoted by Robert L. Heilbroner in *The Worldly Philosophers* (New York: Simon & Schuster, 1980), p. 12.

Evangelicals and Capitalism: A Historical Overview

Capitalism has become a problem for American evangelicals in several differ-ent but related ways. For some the problem has been that of capitalism's continued harmful existence. For others the problem has not been with capi-talism as such but with the unfair and dangerous criticism capitalism has attracted. For still others, the crucial problem has been that the debate over capitalism has directed evangelical energy away from more essential tasks. Interestingly, advocates of all of these positions claim to stand in continuity with American Protestantism historically. Before considering the range of recent evangelical appraisals of capitalism in any detail, then, it will be helpful to determine just when capitalism first became a problem for American Prot-estants and how advocates of the various and conflicting positions have sub-sequently related to each other.

Commenting on the state of "religion and economics" in nineteenth-century America, sociologist J. Milton Yinger has commented that "there was scarcely a doubt in the established Protestant churches that the 'Gilded Age' was solving most of man's problems, that the economic theories of the middle and upper classes [= capitalist] were religiously valid—and that those who opposed the prevailing distribution of power and wealth, therefore, were anti-Christian."[13] Similarly, evangelical historian George Marsden has observed that prior to 1890, economic individualism, success orientation, a strong work ethic, and other things now normally associated with the defense of capitalism were advocated by almost all Protestant churchmen—both the theologically liberal *and* the theologically conservative.[14] Marsden has also noted that these same churchmen exhibited an energetic and generally liberal emphasis on social reform. Prior to the end of the nineteenth century, then, most American Protestants appear to have taken what seems now to have been a highly unlikely position: they advocated ambitious reform programs aimed precisely at the social problems associated with the rise of industrial capitalism while refusing to criticize capitalism itself. Whatever Christianity was held to have been about prior to the advent of the Social Gospel (and, of course, there were increasingly heated debates between liberals and conservatives on this question), it was not principally about politics or economics.[15] Put differently, by the closing de-

13. Yinger, *Religion, Society, and the Individual: An Introduction to the Sociology of Religion* (New York: Macmillan, 1957), p. 218.

14. Marsden, "The Gospel of Wealth, the Social Gospel, and the Salvation of Souls in Nineteenth Century America," *Fides et Historia* 5 (Spring 1973): 10-21.

15. Of course, one could argue that capitalism did not actually *become* a social problem prior to the closing decades of the nineteenth century, but this begs an important question. The capitalist political economy certainly existed prior to the end of the nineteenth century, and if we concede that social conditions worsened at this time as a result of such things as industrial-

cades of the nineteenth century, capitalism had not yet become a problem for American Protestants.

But by the early decades of the twentieth century, capitalism had become a very pressing problem for a number of American churchmen. Indeed, for advocates of the Social Gospel, capitalism had become *the* social problem. As evinced in such works as Walter Rauschenbusch's *Theology for the Social Gospel,* capitalism had come to be regarded by many as an autocratic system that exploited and oppressed its victims and skewed the entire social order toward private accumulation and away from human need. The chaotic social situation wrought by the rapid urbanization and industrialization of the late nineteenth and early twentieth centuries led a number of Protestant "modernists" and advocates of the Social Gospel to call for a modification of traditional Christian orthodoxy such that its social relevance would be demonstrated principally in its prophetic denunciation of the evils of modern capitalism.

Of course not everyone was convinced of the merits of the modernist social and theological project. The early fundamentalist movement, representing a rather odd coalition of conservative scholars and popular revivalist leaders, was formed largely in reaction to theological modernism and to the Social Gospel.[16] One early fundamentalist assessment of the problem posed by the Social Gospel was given in volume 12 of *The Fundamentals* (1914), in an essay entitled "The

---

ization, urbanization, and other sociostructural causes, then these factors need to be analytically disaggregated from a consideration of capitalism per se. It should also be noted that the failure of conservative Protestants to appreciate the "problematic" nature of capitalism during this period may have been due to their understanding of the nature of society. Evangelical historian Douglas W. Frank has written, "one is especially struck by the absence of any serious critique of the free enterprise system as a whole. It was not too early for evangelicals to see the tragic human results of child labor, machine-related accidents or illness, starvation wages, and periodic unemployment. Yet it was assumed that the evils of capitalism were side effects, not systemic and inherent in the very operation of the economy. They would be remedied by the same voluntary and essentially paternalistic processes—by employers being fair and solicitous of their workers' welfare, by workers being patient during hard times, by the rich channeling their excess wealth to worthy programs of charity for the poor" (*Less Than Conquerors: How Evangelicals Entered the Twentieth Century* [Grand Rapids: William B. Eerdmans, 1986], pp. 35-36). While Frank's bias is not difficult to detect here, his observations do suggest that the reason capitalism had not yet become a "problem" for conservative Protestants by the end of the nineteenth century had less to do with the nature of capitalism as such than with their particular understanding of the nature of social change.

16. "The passing of time has obscured how remarkable the alliance between conservative scholars and popular revivalism, the main ingredient in the making of fundamentalism, really was," writes Mark A. Noll. "In nineteenth-century evangelical America such a close alliance had been unthinkable. . . . It was the pressure of events, the expanding terrain of modernism in the churches and of naturalistic scholarship in the academy, that drove conservative scholars and revivalist populists together into a fundamentalist movement" (*Between Faith and Criticism: Evangelicals, Scholarship, and the Bible in America* [San Francisco: Harper & Row, 1986], pp. 37-38).

Church and Socialism" by Princeton theologian Charles Erdman. Erdman stressed that mankind's final hope could not be located in immanent social change and hence that the identification of Christianity with any particular political-economic system represented a serious error. Another assessment of liberal Protestant attacks upon capitalism was given somewhat later by Carl McIntire in *The Rise of the Tyrant: Controlled Economy vs. Private Enterprise* (1945). McIntire sketched the conflict between capitalism and socialism in truly apocalyptic dimensions. He insisted not only that the Bible taught capitalism but that the collectivist attack on capitalism represented an attack on the American way of life, or Christianity, and ultimately on God's eternal ordinances for the governance of human society. That such criticism had been generated from within the church itself, he felt, suggested that the apocalypse must be near at hand and that the "beast" (or "tyrant") mentioned in Revelation 13 was on the rise. Thus while observers such as Erdman had simply insisted on the error of granting ultimacy to economic life, McIntire all but equated modern industrial capitalism with the will of God in the world. Ironically, in his impatience to combat the liberal critics of capitalism, McIntire was forced to emphasize Christianity's "this-worldly" relevance to such an extent that his position amounted, in a manner strikingly similar to the position he was attacking, to a reduction of Christian concerns to those of politics and economics.

During the 1930s and 1940s a number of more moderate fundamentalists began to have serious doubts about the movement's confrontational style. By the early 1950s these moderates had effectively separated themselves from fundamentalism proper and begun to refer to themselves as "neo-evangelicals." Carl F. H. Henry's *The Uneasy Conscience of Modern Fundamentalism* (1947) is often acknowledged to have been the manifesto of this neo-evangelical movement. Henry felt that fundamentalism's nearly exclusive focus on personal sin, its cultural pessimism (born of a dispensational premillennial eschatology), its anti-intellectualism, and its excessive suspicion of all nonevangelical solutions to social problems had in effect rendered the movement impotent in the face of a host of pressing social problems. He called for an energetic conservative Protestant reentry into the modern debate over social and economic policy issues, especially by means of educational attainment. Henry stressed that evangelicals needed to formulate alternatives to both secular socialism and secular capitalism, in order to restore the proper temporal focus of Christianity and reestablish its cultural relevance in the modern situation.

"If there was ever a day when evangelicals were concerned only with evangelization, that day has passed," J. D. Murch wrote in 1956, describing the progress the National Association of Evangelicals had made in addressing social issues.[17] The neo-evangelical position on social and economic policy

17. Murch, *Cooperation without Compromise: A History of the National Association of Evangelicals* (Grand Rapids: William B. Eerdmans, 1956), p. 167.

issues during the 1950s and 1960s, outlined in the N.A.E.'s official monthly publication *United Evangelical Action* and in such periodicals as *Christianity Today*, was generally conservative. The major debate over economic policy issues appears not to have been over whether socialism represented a better economic alternative to capitalism (no one took this position) but over just how strongly capitalism ought to be defended and just how closely evangelicalism ought to be linked with this defense. While most conservatives saw no problem in identifying evangelicalism with the advocacy of a conservative social and economic platform, others insisted that the church ought to stay away from social policy matters altogether. Moderates such as Henry wanted to see individual evangelicals actively involved in the social and economic policy arena but stressed that the church *as* church ought to remain above the debate.[18]

Evangelical opinion during the 1950s and 1960s was also voiced in a periodical entitled *Christian Economics* published by the Christian Freedom Foundation.[19] The manifest purpose of *Christian Economics* was to extol the benefits of capitalism and free enterprise over against the problems of socialism, but one senses that what really moved its editorial staff was their horror at the growth of the American welfare state.[20] *Christian Economics* envisioned America as an example to the rest of the world of the value of voluntary association and as a model of a high standard of personal responsibility before both man and God against all "statist" attempts to limit such responsibility. The church's role within this vision was to remain on a spiritual plane, converting individuals to high ethical standards in Christ and avoiding any interference in civil affairs. "The Church has been known as an institution that proclaims the infallible truth of God," evangelical businessman J. Howard Pew argued in *Christian Economics* in 1968, "but when she issues pronouncements in fields outside her sphere, this can only bring shame, confusion and disillusionment."[21] Interestingly, while Pew apparently had the pronouncements of the National Council of Churches (N.C.C.) in mind here, he obviously did not feel that advocating capitalism in a periodical entitled *Christian Economics* created the same kind of problem.

18. See Carl F. H. Henry, "Evangelicals in the Social Struggle," *Christianity Today*, 19 January 1959, pp. 9-11; and 2 February 1959, pp. 13-16.

19. The Christian Freedom Foundation was organized in 1950 by Howard E. Kershner and Norman Vincent Peale and backed financially by J. Howard Pew. The C.F.F. published *Christian Economics* until 1973. Subsequently, the magazine was renamed *Applied Christianity*, and the organization came under the control of John Conlan and Richard DeVos (of Amway Corporation) who intended to use it to help elect conservative Christians to political office.

20. See James Christensen, "What America Stands For," *Christian Economics*, 17 November 1953, pp. 1-4.

21. J. Howard Pew, "The Mission of the Church," *Christian Economics*, 6 February 1968, p. 3.

While few if any of the specific issues concerning the relation of theology and economics were actually settled during the 1950s and 1960s, Carl Henry and others apparently felt that the foundations for the resolution of these issues had been laid and that the next generation of evangelical leaders, by continuing along more or less the same track, would soon develop a distinctively Christian social and economic policy. As it turned out, of course, the next generation had ideas of its own. Indeed, even as the evangelical mainstream was discussing the extent to which capitalism could be defended without theological compromise, a new generation of younger evangelicals had begun to look askance at American culture, capitalism, and establishment evangelicalism itself.

In his recent book *Reforming Fundamentalism: Fuller Seminary and the New Evangelicalism* (1987), George Marsden has noted that by the late 1960s and early 1970s there had been a substantial increase in the number of evangelicals who had attained college and graduate degrees. While this represented the fruition of the neo-evangelical determination to achieve intellectual credibility, it also signaled a broadening and diversification within what had once been a relatively unified movement. Marsden argues that the increased level of educational attainment, in combination with the social ferment of the period, led to a new kind of conflict within evangelicalism in which "political and theological dispositions coalesced" on either side of a range of questions.[22] Theologically conservative "strict inerrantists" such as Harold Lindsell began to champion conservative cultural and social causes as well. Younger evangelical scholars, more open with regard to the inerrancy question and ecumenical issues, tended also to be increasingly progressive and even radical on issues of social and economic policy.[23] Most vocal and visible in their rejection of American conservatism, of course, were the so-called radical evangelicals.

22. Marsden, *Reforming Fundamentalism: Fuller Seminary and the New Evangelicalism* (Grand Rapids: William B. Eerdmans, 1987), p. 260.
23. "Perhaps most revealing of both the degree and limits of the change," writes Marsden, "concerned the question of the importance of social justice in relation to evangelism. Throughout the 1950s fewer than 10 percent of Fuller students would have said that social, economic, and political justice was 'just as important' as evangelism, and just an additional 15 percent would have said it was 'almost as important.' Three quarters of the students would have said that social justice was simply 'less important' than evangelism. Similar percentages of entering students in the 1960s held these views. By the time the sixties students had left, however, only a little more than half still said social justice was clearly less important. About 20 percent of these mid-sixties students had changed their views while at Fuller" (*Reforming Fundamentalism*, p. 254). The interrelationship of progressive theological and social views at this time has also been noted by James A. Hedstrom in a recent doctoral dissertation entitled "Evangelical Program in the United States, 1945-1980" (Vanderbilt University, 1982): "Although Evangelical Progressivism had no common mind as that of its parent evangelical establishment, the chances were good that those taking a progressive viewpoint on one or more of the larger issues of the community—such as social ethics or biblical inerrancy—would also be found on the 'liberal' side of a host of other questions" (pp. 354-55).

Nurtured within the protest movements of the 1960s, self-described radical evangelicals sought to rediscover a costly and truly biblical discipleship by utterly renouncing what they considered to be a thoroughly decadent American culture. Yet instead of simply withdrawing from such a culture, radical evangelicals chose instead to adopt a vocal and activistic "prophetic" stance over against it in such journals as *The Other Side* (established in 1965) and *Post American* (established in 1971 and renamed *Sojourners* in 1974). Analytically central to their indictment of an oppressive American culture was the assertion that capitalism was largely to blame. "To be more specific," several contributors to *The Other Side* explained, "the system which creates and sustains much of the hunger, underdevelopment, unemployment, and other social ills in the world today is capitalism. Capitalism is by its very nature a system which promotes individualism, competition, and profit-making with little or no regard for social costs. It puts profits and private gain before social services and human needs. As such, it is an unjust system which should be replaced."[24]

While the number of radical evangelicals was not large, a number of other younger evangelical intellectuals became convinced that the radical analysis of American culture had warrant and were similarly repulsed by the cultural conservatism of the evangelical mainstream. Just as Carl Henry had criticized fundamentalism for its neglect of social concerns at mid-century, so these younger progressive evangelicals leveled the same argument at Henry and establishment evangelicalism a generation later. Whereas progressives felt that fundamentalists had turned away from social concerns in their mistaken but understandable reaction to the errors of theological modernism, they argued that mainstream evangelicals had neglected social issues largely because they had become ideologically ensnared within bourgeois culture.[25] Henry's efforts, along with those of other neo-evangelicals who had attempted to address social and economic issues during the 1950s and 1960s, were discounted by these progressives as poor examples of social concern because they were not premised on an adequate criticism of American capitalist culture. "The social impress of evangelical Christianity between 1860 and 1960," Sherwood Wirt

24. Eugene Toland, Thomas Fenton, and Lawrence McCulloch, "World Justice and Peace: A Radical Analysis for American Christians," *The Other Side* 12 (January-February 1976): 50.

25. A host of books came out between 1965 and 1976 making essentially this claim, including the following: David O. Moberg, *Inasmuch: Christian Social Responsibility in Twentieth Century America* (1965) and *The Great Reversal: Evangelism and Social Concern* (1972); Sherwood Wirt, *The Social Conscience of the Evangelical* (1968); Richard V. Pierard, *Evangelical Christianity and Political Conservatism* (1970) and *The Unequal Yoke: Evangelical Christianity and Political Conservatism* (1970); Robert Clouse, Robert Linder, and Richard Pierard, *The Cross and the Flag* (1972); Charles Y. Furness, *The Christian and Social Action* (1972); Paul B. Henry, *Politics for Evangelicals* (1974); and Donald W. Dayton, *Discovering an Evangelical Heritage* (1976).

stated frankly in a book entitled *The Social Conscience of the Evangelical*, "must be judged a failure."[26]

By the 1970s the neo-evangelical project aimed at reengaging American culture had met with considerable success. Yet its successes placed the movement in the position of having to cope not only with an increasing diversity of opinion on social questions within its own ranks but also with countering the liberal social and theological positions of the National and World Councils of Churches, a task they had inherited from the fundamentalists. In response to ecumenical Protestant suggestions that the church ought to celebrate cultural and religious pluralism and foster radical social ferment, evangelicals organized a series of conferences during the 1970s aimed at upholding the priority of the task of evangelism in the church's global mission.[27] "We have one task," Billy Graham insisted at the International Congress on World Evangelization held in Lausanne, Switzerland, in 1974—"to proclaim the message of salvation in Jesus Christ. In rich countries and in poor, among the educated and uneducated, in freedom or oppression, we are determined to proclaim Jesus Christ in the power of the Holy Spirit that men may put their trust in him as Savior, follow him obediently, and serve him in the fellowship of the Church, of which he alone is King and head."[28]

Issued in conjunction with the Lausanne Congress was a confessional statement entitled "The Lausanne Covenant: An Exposition and Commentary." This document, which was signed by the delegates and was intended to strengthen their subsequent commitment to the task of world evangelization, contained several articles that dealt specifically with evangelical social responsibility. Ironically, however, the Lausanne Covenant has been subsequently heralded as having raised social action on a par with evangelism in the church's mission.[29] Hence it appears that the Lausanne Congress may

26. Wirt, *The Social Conscience of the Evangelical* (New York: Harper & Row, 1968), p. 50.

27. See Johnston, *The Battle for World Evangelism.*

28. Billy Graham, "Why Lausanne?" in *Let the Earth Hear His Voice: Official Reference Volume of the International Congress on World Evangelization, Lausanne, Switzerland,* ed. J. D. Douglas (Minneapolis: World Wide Publications, 1975), p. 28.

29. See Johnston, *The Battle for World Evangelism,* pp. 324-25. This trend is evident in the following comments made by C. René Padilla: "If the relationship between evangelism and social responsibility is defined in [terms of "partnership"], it is obvious that the primacy of evangelism mentioned in the Lausanne Covenant (section 6) could not mean that evangelism is to be regarded as more important than its partner *every time* and *everywhere.* If that were the case, something would be wrong with the marriage! One of the values of the Grand Rapids Report [a subsequent report specifically dealing with the question of evangelism and social responsibility] is that, in contrast with all the previous documents produced by evangelicals in the last few years, it clarified that the primacy of evangelism can be stated only in a relative, not in an absolute, sense" ("Evangelism and Social Responsibility: From Wheaton '66 to Wheaton '83," in *The Best in Theology,* vol. 1, ed. Paul Fromer [Carol Stream, IL: Christianity Today, 1988], pp. 246-47).

actually have achieved the opposite of the result intended by its organizers: it may have served to blur further the distinction between evangelism and social action in the church's mission.

On a slightly different front, by the end of the 1970s the evangelical mainstream had grown somewhat impatient with radical evangelicalism. Admired initially for their energy and sense of commitment, the radicals were increasingly criticized for their legalistic and essentially gnostic attitude.[30] Progressive positions were viewed with increasing suspicion from within the mainstream as well.[31] In addition, mainstream evangelicals remained convinced that a Christian-Marxist dialogue was impossible and so were quite critical of the theologies of liberation that had emerged within ecumenical circles since the late 1960s.[32] By way of reaction to liberation theology's harsh criticism of capitalism, some of those within the mainstream became much more vocal in its defense, while others continued to insist that some distance be kept between Christianity and political-economic advocacy.[33]

But evangelical confusion on a number of fronts, combined with the perceived liberal drift of the nation as a whole, had by the early 1970s created a situation ripe for the public revival of American fundamentalism. "Neofundamentalism," as it has been called, has subsequently embraced not only the older militants such as Carl McIntire but many evangelicals as well. Indeed, the movement has provided an opportunity for any number of theological conservatives to give public expression to their cultural and political conservatism. In a sense, the movement has provided conservatives with an opportunity to reassert a kind of "countermythology," or cultural vision, over and against that of what has been perceived to be a highly secularized knowl-

30. See the following by Carl Henry: "Revolt on Evangelical Frontiers," *Christianity Today,* 26 April 1974, pp. 4-8; "The Judgement of America," *Christianity Today,* 8 November 1974, pp. 22-24; *Evangelicals in Search of Identity* (Waco, TX: Word, 1976), p. 61; and *God, Revelation, and Authority,* vol. 4 (Waco, TX: Word, 1979), p. 524.

31. Ronald J. Sider's *Rich Christians in an Age of Hunger* (1977) seems especially to have provoked a number of angry responses from within the evangelical mainstream. "Widely trumpeted calls for Christians to feed the world's hungry," Robert E. Frykenberg suggested, ". . . are useless and even harmful when they do not address the real problems of how this can be done. Moral obligation and Christian stewardship do not end with the act of simple giving, or merely divesting oneself of material surpluses" ("World Hunger: Food Is Not the Answer," *Christianity Today,* 11 December 1981, p. 37).

32. See "The Marxist Never-Never Land," *Christianity Today,* 20 December 1974, p. 20. See also the editorial "Jesus, Marx and Co.," *Christianity Today,* 8 June 1973, p. 28; and Ira Gallaway, "Liberation and Revolution," *Christianity Today,* 25 August 1972, p. 20.

33. One editorial in *Christianity Today* entitled "Capitalism: Basically Unjust?" declared, "The time has come for Christians who believe in capitalism . . . to make themselves heard" (25 October 1975, p. 32), and Harold Lindsell, editor of *Christianity Today* from 1968 to 1978, published an apology for capitalism (and a corresponding attack on "statism") in 1982 entitled *Free Enterprise: A Judeo-Christian Defense* (Tyndale House, 1982).

edge elite in American society.[34] Although neo-fundamentalism's social
agenda has been quite broad and has focused on a number of issues not directly
related to political-economic policy (e.g., the breakdown of the traditional
family, gay rights and feminist legislation, abortion, pornography, the banning
of prayer in public schools), the neofundamentalist position on a number of
social and economic policy issues (e.g., welfare issues, unemployment, education) has been informed chiefly by its opposition to the expansion of the
welfare state and what it has pejoratively labeled "statism." The neofundamentalists contend that while the welfare state may initially have represented a
reasonable attempt to rectify social ills, its growth has become irresponsible
and has usurped what ought to be the roles of the church, the community, and
the family in modern society.[35] The defense of capitalism, then, has provided
neofundamentalists with their chief intellectual line of defense against the
ever-encroaching state. John Eidsmoe, for example, has asserted that

> It is the free enterprise system—people producing for profit—that has made
> America the prosperous nation it is today. It is the free enterprise system—people
> looking for a better way to do things for profit—that has produced the marvelous
> technology of American society. It is the free enterprise system—each man working
> for himself—that has enabled Americans of all classes to enjoy luxuries unknown
> to kings a century ago. And the reason free enterprise works so well is that it is based
> on solid biblical principles. Let us think twice before abandoning it.[36]

Others on the evangelical right have similarly contended that capitalism has
direct biblical warrant. Indeed, at the extreme right, in what is called
"theonomy" or "Christian reconstructionism," modern capitalism is held to be
instrumental to the coming of God's kingdom.

The State of the Debate at Present

The state of the evangelical debate over capitalism at present is somewhat
uncertain. Self-styled radical evangelicals continue to issue their harsh denunciations of capitalism and bourgeois culture, although they have tended to identify
less and less with American evangelicalism as such and increasingly with other
groups that tend to share their particular interests and outlook. This new alignment,

---

34. On the conservative "countermythology," see Donald Heinz, "The Struggle to
Define America," in *The New Christian Right: Mobilization and Legitimation,* ed. Robert C.
Liebman and Robert Wuthnow (New York: Aldine, 1983), pp. 133-48.

35. See Jerry Falwell, *Listen America* (Garden City, NY: Doubleday, 1980), p. 12; and
Larry Burkett, "Is Welfare Scriptural?" *Fundamentalist Journal* 4 (April 1985): 21-23.

36. John Eidsmoe, *God and Caesar: Christian Faith and Political Action* (Westchester,
IL: Crossway, 1984), p. 112.

which includes Latin American liberation movements, the sanctuary movement, antiapartheid activities, feminist interests, the antinuclear movement, and numerous other causes, has been interpreted by radicals as an international "rise of Christian conscience" (as in Jim Wallis's book of that title [1987]) and has been defined by and large in contradistinction to American evangelicalism.

But while it is doubtful that the influence of radical social analysis is gaining much ground within American evangelicalism at present, it is almost certainly the case that the progressive viewpoint is having an increased impact on the movement, especially on its leadership. Ronald Sider and others associated with the World Evangelical Fellowship (WEF), for example, have organized a number of conferences and have issued numerous articles, books, and statements in recent years decrying the existence of oppressive social and economic structures and encouraging evangelicals to show their concern for the poor by adopting simpler lifestyles.[37] In addition, scholars affiliated with the Christian Reformed Church, who have to a considerable extent assumed the intellectual leadership of the evangelical movement, have continued to advocate moderately interventionist social and economic policy.

Yet despite the doubts voiced by radicals and progressives, neofundamentalists and others on the evangelical right continue to defend capitalism. Indeed, those on the right have been encouraged intellectually in recent years by neoconservative social analysis, even to the extent that they have begun to hold conferences and issue statements of their own championing free enterprise against the threat of statism.[38] The recent political-economic developments in Eastern Europe have proven particularly satisfying to those on the evangelical right who have interpreted these developments as a spectacular vindication of their defense of capitalism.

Along these lines, there are indications of a convergence of evangelical

37. The "Wheaton '83 Statement," for example, was issued in conjunction with a conference sponsored by the WEF held in Wheaton, Illinois. The text of the statement appears in "Social Transformation: The Church in Response to Human Need," *Transformation* 1 (January-March 1894): 23-28. It renounces utopianism, denounces multinational corporations, suggests that noninvolvement in social issues simply lends tacit support to the existing sociopolitical order, and stresses (again) that evangelicals are only just beginning to understand the social and political implications of the gospel. Similarly, in 1986 and 1987 international conferences sponsored by the WEF to address the relationship of Christian faith to economics. A new evangelical publication entitled *Transformation: An International Dialogue on Evangelical Social Ethics* emerged out of these conferences, as did plans for subsequent regional and international conferences and for a series of international study projects.

38. An international conference of conservative scholars entitled "Biblical Mandates for Relief and Development," for example, was held in Villars, Switzerland, in the spring of 1987. The "Villars Statement on Relief and Development" issued subsequently was intended to provide a contrast to those issued by the more progressive WEF. See *Freedom, Justice, and Hope: Toward a Strategy for the Poor and Oppressed,* Turning Point Christian Worldview Series #3, ed. Marvin Olasky (Westchester, IL: Crossway, 1988), pp. 141-48.

opinion at the conservative end of the political-economic spectrum. At a recent conference held at Oxford, for example, a number of evangelical economists, theologians, and economic development experts produced a rather extraordinary document entitled the "Oxford Declaration on Christian Faith and Economics."[39] Far more comprehensive than earlier statements, the Oxford Declaration reflects concerns for both production and distribution, stewardship of the environment, the limits of technological development, work and leisure, human rights, democracy and limited government, and a number of related issues. The remarkable cooperation of progressives and conservatives at this conference, combined with the intellectual impact of recent political-economic developments in Eastern Europe and elsewhere, appear to have led to the drafting of a uniquely balanced statement. As Ronald Sider put it, the conference witnessed "liberation-oriented theologians affirming free-market strategies" and "conservative market economists demanding a special focus on justice for the poor."[40] It remains to be seen, however, how this statement will be received by the various evangelical factions and how lasting the hopeful convergence will prove to be. An investigation of the social context of the recent debate should provide us with some significant clues in this regard.

Outline of the Study

The first three chapters of this study provide detailed descriptions of the range of recent evangelical appraisals of capitalism. Their organization in terms of left, right, and center reflects an observation Peter Berger made some years ago:

> The different theories seeking to explain the facts of the wealth and poverty of nations may today be broadly divided into two competing paradigms or models of theoretical understanding. They are the theory of modernization and the theory of imperialism (though these are not always the exact titles used by their respective advocates). Each paradigm has what may be called "clue concepts"—key explanatory categories, the use of which readily identifies adherents of the two rival schemes. Modernization theorists already give themselves away by the very term "modern" and its permutations, and by categories such as "development," "economic growth," "institutional differentiation," and "nation-building." The other camp employs "clue concepts" such as "dependency," "exploitation," "neo-colonialism," and "liberation."[41]

39. See *Transformation* 7 (April-June 1990): 1-9; see also "Ideology Succumbs to Unity in Oxford," *Christianity Today,* 19 March 1990, p. 52; and David Neff, "When Economists Pray," *Christianity Today,* 9 April 1990, p. 13.

40. Sider, "Trickle-Up Economics," *Advocate,* March 1990, p. 2.

41. Peter L. Berger, *Pyramids of Sacrifice: Political Ethics and Social Change* (Garden City, NY: Doubleday-Anchor, 1976), p. 13.

Chapter 1 covers the positions of those on the evangelical "left," who have analyzed capitalism in terms of oppression and imperialism. In Chapter 2 I discuss the defense of capitalism and modernization that has been offered by those on the evangelical "right." Chapter 3 covers those positions that have exhibited elements of both paradigms and have been articulated by those who have self-consciously sought to steer a middle course between the extremes of left and right.

Of course, as Berger's comments indicate, while recent observers have tended toward either of two competing positions, these positions are rarely if ever espoused in their pure forms. Instead, the situation has been and continues to be one in which positions are arranged along a continuum between the poles of oppression and modernization. For this reason, when I use the terms "left," "right," and "center," I am not necessarily referring to identifiable groups of persons. These are simply the rather arbitrary designations I have used to give order to a fairly complex debate.

In Chapter 4 I interpret the material presented in the previous three chapters, summarizing the political-economic, cultural, ethical and moral, and theological issues raised within the evangelical debate over capitalism. I also deal with the New Class thesis here, outlining the cultural characteristics of the New Class and the social location of opposition to its socio-political agenda. I then take up the relationship of evangelical intellectuals (as defined by their appraisals of capitalism) to the contemporary cultural conflict described by the New Class thesis.

It seems clear that a number of the issues raised within the evangelical debate over capitalism deserve serious evangelical reflection, reflection that seems to have been hampered of late by evangelical advocacy on behalf of one or another of the class factions engaged in the contemporary cultural conflict. While such advocacy has seemed to both sides to display the relevance of evangelicalism within the contemporary situation, it has actually undermined evangelicalism's relevance by reducing or threatening to reduce the domain of Christian concerns to those of politics and economics. I hope that exploring the ideological dimensions of the recent evangelical debate will help clear a way for this debate to move constructively forward such that evangelicals will be able to take issues of political-economy seriously while refusing to take them with ultimate seriousness. To this end, the study concludes with an epilogue in which I offer a more balanced evangelical appraisal of modern capitalism.

CHAPTER ONE

Capitalism as Oppression: The Evangelical Left

The debate over capitalism among American Protestants in general and evangelicals in particular began on the "left"—that is, among those who identified capitalism as an economic system essentially at odds with Christian theology and ethics. And so this survey of recent evangelical appraisals of capitalism begins with a discussion of the positions taken by those on the evangelical left. Several groups fall into this category: radical evangelicals, such as Jim Wallis and others who contribute to such publications as *Sojourners* (formerly *Post American*) and *The Other Side;* those at the left end of the progressive evangelical spectrum who are interested in issues of global economic development, such as Ronald Sider and Waldron Scott; and those who have been engaged in an attempt to formulate what might be called an "evangelical theology of liberation," such as Andrew Kirk, Samuel Escobar, and C. René Padilla. To make an analysis of these categories practicable, it will be necessary to synthesize the various arguments into one more or less unified position. Admittedly, this ideal-typical procedure entails neglecting the nuances of individual arguments and minimizing the differences of opinion between individuals on certain issues, but in large part these differences are not crucial to the matter at hand. My sole criterion for including these individuals and groups on the evangelical left is their largely negative assessment of modern capitalism either domestically or globally (usually both), and not the particular theological orientations they exhibit. I place on the evangelical left all those who view capitalism as a system of oppression.

The Nature of the Capitalist System

The evangelical left's understanding of what capitalism is and how it actually functions may be summarized briefly as follows: capitalism is a comprehensive system, encompassing economic, political, and social realities globally, in which a relatively small elite exploits and oppresses the majority of mankind.[1] As such, it is principally responsible for a great many of the economic, political, cultural, and environmental evils in the modern world. While this basic appraisal of capitalism is shared by all of those on the evangelical left, the different directions their analyses have taken makes it possible to distinguish between the groups mentioned above. Development-oriented evangelicals and the evangelical theologians of liberation tend to direct their attention toward issues of global economic development. Radical evangelicals, while interested in global issues, tend to focus instead on the American situation, underscoring the role capitalism plays in fostering American economic, political, and cultural decadence. As Jim Wallis put it in the first issue of *Post American* in 1971,

> We have become disillusioned, alienated, and angered by an American system that we regard as oppressive; a society whose values are corrupt and destructive. We have unmasked the myth of the American Dream by exposing the reality of the American Nightmare. . . . Our ethical revolt against systematic injustice, militarism, and the imperialism of a "power elite" is accompanied by our protest of a technocratic society and a materialistic profit-culture where human values are out of place. . . . The ulcerating drive for air-conditioned affluence has not given satisfaction or fulfillment, but has instead, produced lives that are hollow, plastic, and superficial; characterized by economic surplus and spiritual starvation.[2]

Capitalist Economics

Undoubtedly the most critical theme running through radical evangelical appraisals of the American capitalist system is that of greed. "Covetousness," Art

---

1. The evangelical left's understanding of capitalism, like the evangelical right's understanding, has been derived almost entirely from nonevangelical sources. Neo-Marxist analyses have perhaps figured most prominently in their cognitive estimation of capitalism, especially as popularly translated in various American "New Left" classics. C. Wright Mills's *The White Collar* (1951) and *The Power Elite* (1945) appear to have been quite influential in this regard. Other New Left sources include Herbert Marcuse's *One Dimensional Man* (1964), David Riesman's *The Lonely Crowd* (1950), Eric Fromm's *The Sane Society* (1955), Jack Newfield's *A Prophetic Minority* (1966), and the work of Michael Harrington, William Appleman Williams, and Joyce and Gabriel Kolko. Thus while those on the evangelical left have strenuously resisted the suggestion that they are Marxists, their understanding of capitalism has undeniably been shaped by Marxist thought. Various "world-systems" approaches to capitalism's global impact should be mentioned here as well. Richard Barnet and Ronald Muller's *Global Reach: The Power of Multinational Corporations* (1974) has been quite influential on the evangelical left, as has Immanuel Wallerstein's work. Other material commonly cited with reference to global economic development by those on the left includes the work of Robert Heilbroner, Robert McNamara, and Barbara Ward; various reports issued by the Club of Rome; Gunnar Myrdal's *The Challenge of World Poverty* (1970); the Brandt Commission report *North and South: A Program for Survival* (1980); Wassily Leontif's *The Future of the World Economy* (1977); Mahbub Al Haq's *The Poverty Curtain* (1976); and Samir Amin's *Unequal Development* (1976).

2. Wallis, "Post American Christianity," *Post American* 1 (Fall 1971): 2.

Gish commented, "is the engine of the capitalist economy."[3] Wes Michaelson has asserted that capitalism "depends on and fosters human selfishness."[4] And John Howard Yoder has insisted that capitalism is "a political economy based on personal accumulation."[5] Notions of capital and profit, in other words, are held by those on the left to be synonymous with personal accumulation and consumption. Even those who understand capital accumulation as a specific kind of economic activity directed toward reinvestment and growth nevertheless consider it activity geared toward personal profit, motivated chiefly by personal greed, and hence necessarily destructive of the social good. Jim Wallis, for example, has stated that capitalist "economic institutions act to make profit, accumulate wealth, and exploit the poor, workers, and consumers, while ravaging the environment instead of providing for the equitable distribution of goods and services."[6]

Given the assumption that capitalism depends on purely private accumulation, those on the evangelical left are naturally averse to suggestions that capitalism promotes free and competitive enterprise within the context of a market. Indeed, those on the left stress that "competition" and "the market," and hence true economic freedom, do not really exist in the capitalist situation.[7] "Free enterprise economics is often defended on the basis that it promotes freedom and an open society," Andrew Kirk has written. "This idea, however, is a fallacy. It certainly increases the freedom of some, but always and inevitably at the expense of the freedom of others."[8] Instead, those on the left insist that real economic freedom (and hence freedom per se) in a capitalist economy is possessed only by the small elite that controls the productive process and manipulates the economic behavior of most other members of society toward the maximization of its own profit. "Our society prides itself on its competitive

3. Gish, "A Decentralist Response," in *Wealth and Poverty: Four Christian Views of Economics,* ed. Robert G. Clouse (Downers Grove, IL: InterVarsity Press, 1984), p. 76.

4. Michaelson, "Evangelicalism and Radical Discipleship," in *Evangelicalism and Anabaptism,* ed. C. Norman Kraus (Scottdale, PA: Herald Press, 1979), p. 78.

5. Yoder, "A Critique of North American Evangelical Ethics," *Transformation* 2 (January-March 1985): 29.

6. Wallis, *Agenda for Biblical People* (San Francisco: Harper & Row, 1976), p. 63.

7. See Bill Tabb, "The Demise of Our Free Enterprise System," *The Other Side* 15 (December 1979): 44-49. Tabb suggests that while there may be a truly competitive sector (e.g., small businesses) in the U.S. economy, it is rapidly disappearing. "To suppose that corporate decisions are subject to the forces of the 'free market' . . . is to engage in illusion," writes Jim Wallis (*Agenda for Biblical People,* p. 85)

8. Kirk, *The Good News of the Kingdom Coming: The Marriage of Evangelism and Social Responsibility* (Downers Grove, IL: InterVarsity Press, 1983), p. 77; Fred Pearson expresses this same sentiment in *They Dare to Hope: Student Protest and Christian Response* (Grand Rapids: William B. Eerdmans, 1969): "We do not have a perfect society in the United States, but we do have 'one best way.' We believe in a system of individual competition which automatically, so we suppose, produces the most satisfaction for all of us. . . . But a win-lose system requires losers" (pp. 97-98).

economy," Eddy Hall has commented. "Amidst an ocean of businesses designed to exploit customers and employees for the profit of the owners."[9]
Similarly, Danny Collum of *Sojourners* has insisted that "the gross inequalities
of wealth and poverty in the U.S. are the natural result of a social, political,
and economic system that places the maximization of private profit above all
other social goals. The human, social, cultural, and spiritual benefits that would
result from a more just distribution of wealth and power will never show up
on the all-important quarterly profit and loss statement."[10]

In addition, those on the left contend that this capitalist elite has grown
progressively smaller and so has become increasingly powerful in American
society. Referring to a variety of social ills, Jim Wallis argues in *Agenda for
Biblical People* that "all of this is aggravated and intensified by the growing
concentration of economic and political power in the hands of a few persons
and institutions. Certain people, classes, and institutions possess an enormous
and illegitimate amount of power which is exercised for their own benefit and
against social justice and especially against the poor. . . . In the United States,
such power is centered in the small number of large corporations which shape
the political economy. The decision making of these large corporations is in
the hands of the very few and the very rich."[11]

Thus a second critical theme that runs through the evangelical left's appraisal
of capitalism is that of concentration. That economic power has become increasingly concentrated, those on the left contend, is evident in the increasingly
uneven distribution of product and income in contemporary American society, a
situation that has essentially amounted to an "assault on the poor" by a wealthy
business elite.[12] They argue that the adverse effects of capitalism spread well
beyond those who are actually poor. They hold the American business elite
responsible for treating employees as "one more resource to be cheaply
exploited,"[13] for requiring "near depression-level unemployment,"[14] for foist-
ing largely useless products on consumers,[15] for producing frequent periods
of inflation and recession in which only the illusion of affluence is pre-

9. Hall, "Living Cooperatively in a Competitive World," *The Other Side* (January 1983):
12.

10. Collum, "Assault on the Poor," *Sojourners* 10 (July 1981): 16.

11. Wallis, *Agenda for Biblical People,* p. 85. See also Richard K. Taylor, *Economics
and the Gospel* (Philadelphia: United Church Press, 1973), p. 73.

12. See Collum, "Assault on the Poor," an article specifically critical of the Reagan
administration's plan the cut the federal budget in 1982.

13. John Bookser-Feister, "The Struggle for Work Place Justice," *The Other Side* 21
(April-May 1985): 48.

14. Danny Collum, "Assumptions from on High: The Assaults of Capitalism," review
of *The Spirit of Democratic Capitalism,* by Michael Novak, *Sojourners* 12 (May 1983): 40.

15. John Alexander, *Your Money or Your Life: A New Look at Jesus' View of Wealth
and Power* (San Francisco: Harper & Row, 1986), p. 103.

served,[16] for neglecting the modernization of basic industries,[17] for developing what has been called the "national security state,"[18] for squandering valuable natural resources,[19] and for the general deterioration of the economic process. Rather than focusing on the expansion of human potential, Danny Collum suggested recently, the capitalist system is creating a situation in which only two classes of persons will eventually exist in American society: "an increasingly wealthy and isolated managerial and professional elite and an ever-larger class of the permanently left-behind who will either be unemployed or channeled into low-pay and low-dignity 'service' jobs."[20]

Furthermore, those on the left insist that capitalist economic growth cannot be sustained indefinitely. "The reality is that the eighties and nineties will mark the end not only of the Western dream of unrestrained growth," Tom Sine predicted in 1981, "but also of the American Dream of unrestrained affluence. As a consequence of the rapid depletion of nonrenewable resources, the United States is entering a major transitional period from a time of high growth and prosperity to a future of scarcity and limits."[21]

16. Danny Collum, "Economics: The Way America Does Business," *Sojourners* 14 (November 1985): 14. Of all of those on the evangelical left, Collum has been the most specific on matters of economic policy. In this article he suggests that the American economy is increasingly at the mercy of transnational corporations which no longer consider domestic interests to be particularly important. The American economy has been sustained in the short run with massive military expenditures (and, consequently, reductions in social spending), he argues, but the growing federal deficit will render this solution disastrous in the long run. He offers a similar analysis in "The Crash of '87," *Sojourners* (January 1988): "This long-term downward [economic] trend," he writes, "is the result of an international economic order created to benefit multinational corporations and investment institutions, with little consideration for workers at home or abroad" (p. 4). See also "The Big Picture: Where We Are and How We Got Here," in *The Rise of Christian Conscience,* ed. Jim Wallis (San Francisco: Harper & Row, 1987), pp. 3-16.

17. John Zingaro and Philip Harnden, "Since Steel Went Down," *The Other Side* 21 (April-May 1985): 30-36.

18. "The Failure of Conventional Wisdom: Economic Realities in the '80's," *Sojourners* 10 (January 1981): 13-18, excerpts from a "Forum on Economics" held by *Sojourners* in November 1980. The participants (Richard Barnet, Larry Rasmussen, Jeremy Rifkin, and Robert Hamlin) argue that the U.S. economy cannot continue to grow as rapidly as it did between 1950 and 1970, and this makes redistributive questions crucial and calls military expenditures into question. They also contend that America has shifted from a "social welfare state" to a "national security state"—i.e., from an economy that emphasized social harmony to one that has become disastrously competitive.

19. Those on the evangelical left have tended to assume that productive resources are fixed and limited and hence that one nation's use of natural resources necessarily comes at the expense of all other nations. "In a world where resources are finite," Wes Michaelson has asserted, "the rich nations' monopoly of wealth is the prime . . . cause of the poor's plight" ("Evangelicalism and Radical Discipleship," p. 77).

20. Collum, "Economics: The Way America Does Business," p. 15.

21. Sine, *The Mustard Seed Conspiracy* (Waco, TX: Word, 1981), pp. 45-46.

Capitalist Politics

While the themes of greed and concentration are critical to the evangelical left's appraisal of capitalist economics, the notion of conspiracy is central to the left's understanding of American capitalist politics. The same tiny elite that has conspired to control the economy, they argue, has also successfully conspired to control the American political process and manipulate this process to its own advantage. This is especially true of the large American corporations, next to which they see politicians as essentially helpless.[22] Danny Collum has argued, for example, that Jimmy Carter's presidency was basically created and marketed by the corporate business elite simply because he "could potentially ameliorate the dangerous anger and alienation of black America."[23]

To speak of democracy in such a situation, those on the evangelical left feel, is misleading at best. "In fact," several contributors to *The Other Side* have suggested, "capitalism is the opposite of democracy, since it is an economic system not owned by the people and run for the people, but owned and run by a plutocracy, that is, by the rich and super-rich."[24] In the eyes of the evangelical left, contemporary rhetoric about such things as "democracy," "freedom," "growth," and "opportunity" simply reflects a political ideology that has been created and promulgated by the ruling elite. While political liberals and conservatives have both been guilty of advocating this kind of ideology, those on the evangelical left contend that the New Religious Right has completely succumbed to it, especially to its anticommunist component, which serves only to legitimate the interests of the military-industrial complex and of the "national security state."[25] Danny Collum has recently written that

> [the] error of being blinded to the truth because of an obsession with political ideology is one that can be made on the Left as well as the Right. But obscuring biblical faith behind anti-communist or pro-capitalist ideology has particularly dangerous consequences when it results in Christians . . . placing their intellectual and rhetorical skills at the service of the rulers of the richest, most powerful, and most heavily armed nation in the world. At a time when this nation has the poor under such heavy attack at home and in the Third World, the consequences are especially striking.[26]

22. See Tabb, "The Demise of Our Free Enterprise System," pp. 47-48.
23. Collum, "The Big Picture," p. 7.
24. Eugene Toland, Thomas Fenton, and Lawrence McCulloch, "World Justice and Peace: A Radical Analysis for American Christians," *The Other Side* 12 (January-February 1976): 57.
25. See, for example, Collum, "The Big Picture."
26. Collum, "Assumptions from on High," p. 42.

Capitalist Culture

Those on the evangelical left believe that in addition to dominating American political life, the business elite also dominates contemporary American culture. The media, the schools and universities, the arts, the conservative churches—virtually all of the major cultural institutions are held to be "under the sway of corporate power."[27] This inordinate influence of business has resulted in cultural decadence, they say, decadence that has been evinced chiefly in a kind of consumerism that results from the artificial stimulation, by means of manipulative advertising, of ever-increasing "needs" for largely useless and even harmful things.[28] This manipulation appeals to such base human drives as greed, envy, and fear, and it fosters selfishness and individualism at the expense of any kind of social or communal spirit. "It's hard to expect people to give of their own resources to meet the needs of poor people," Collum says, "when the schools, the work process, and the relentless cry of advertising are encouraging them every day of their lives to be greedy, competitive, and conspicuously consumptive."[29]

Those on the left suggest that the intensely competitive, and hence anti-cooperative, capitalist spirit also nurtures racism and sexism and that it is principally responsible for the break-up of the family and of the community. The capitalist spirit has created a situation in which such things as abortion are acceptable,[30] and it has manifested itself as a materialistic, individualistic, and exclusivistic social pathos. "My own view," John Alexander has recently written, "is that our [capitalist] system is a juggernaut. It crushes forty thousand kids a day, grows fat selling cigarettes and bombs, installs mind-numbing programs on television, and encourages a climate that destroys marriages."[31] Following observers such as Herbert Marcuse, those on the evangelical left insist that the end-product of capitalist culture is "one-dimensional" people—people who are so oriented toward personal consumption that they have no sense of communal or social responsibility.[32]

Capitalism Globally

While radical evangelicals have tended to focus on the harmful impact of capitalism on American culture, they have also become increasingly concerned with

27. See Collum, "Assumptions from on High," p. 41.
28. See Kirk, *The Good News of the Kingdom Coming,* p. 63; and Ronald J. Sider, *Rich Christians in an Age of Hunger* (Downers Grove, IL: InterVarsity Press, 1977), pp. 46-49.
29. Collum, "Assault on the Poor," p. 16.
30. Kirk, *The Good News of the Kingdom Coming,* pp. 35ff.
31. Alexander, *Your Money or Your Life,* p. 204.
32. See Marcuse, *One Dimensional Man: Studies in the Ideology of Advanced Industrial Society* (Boston: Beacon Press, 1962).

capitalism's global impact, and it is on issues of global economic development that radical evangelical analysis has linked up with that of development-oriented evangelicals such as Ronald Sider and with the positions of the evangelical theologians of liberation. The evangelical left's assessment of capitalism's global impact is on the whole simply an expansion of their assessment of the American system so as to include the entire planet. Using such terms as "economic imperialism," "the monopolization of world capital," and "neocolonialism," they argue that the extraordinary economic development of the West can be attributed more or less directly to its exploitation of the Third World. As W. Stanley Mooneyham has suggested, the international "system" is one in which resources are taken from the poor and given to the rich.[33] While similar in its effects to the exploitative colonialism of earlier centuries, recent Western economic exploitation has occurred "invisibly," under the guise of the world market.[34] "Direct colonialism has virtually ended," Mark Hatfield has noted in *Post American,* "but it has been replaced by this more subtle and insidious form of exploitation, which primarily rests on the monopolization of capital by the multinational enterprises of the rich, developed countries be they market economies or centrally planned."[35]

Although, as Hatfield indicates, the socialist world has been partially responsible for global underdevelopment, the real burden of guilt is judged to lie in the capitalist West, and especially in the United States. Jim Wallis has written, for example, that

> though all the wealthy and powerful nations are deeply implicated in this alliance against the poor and powerless, the clear leader of this oppressive world order is the United States. American policy has become dominated by the vested interests of an increasingly concentrated corporate power structure which seeks greater control, profit, and power throughout the world with a coherent global strategy to help create and stabilize a system of "open societies" where United States economic, political, and military interests can operate more or less freely.[36]

33. Mooneyham, *What Do You Say to a Hungry World?* (Waco, TX: Word Books, 1975), pp. 115ff.; see also Sine, *The Mustard Seed Conspiracy,* p. 26.

34. See Jim Wallis, "The Invisible Empire," *Post American* 2 (November-December 1973): 1, 14.

35. Hatfield, "An Economics for Sustaining Humanity," *Post American* 4 (January 1975): 16.

36. Wallis, *Agenda for Biblical People,* pp. 80-81. Those on the left flatly reject the suggestion that Western economic development has occurred independently of the exploitation of the Third World, because of some genius inherent in modern capitalism or in modern Western culture. They hold that such suggestions are simply ideological myths that need to be exploded. "Why is the United States the richest nation on earth?" Jim Wallis asks rhetorically. "The answer is due neither to Yankee ingenuity nor to God's special blessing. It is starkly material. As our nation grew, resources were always cheap. We built our country on land taken from Native Americans and the labor of black slaves and, later, ethnic immigrants"—and later still, Wallis goes on to suggest, by international economic imperialism (*The Call to Conversion* [San Francisco: Harper & Row, 1981], pp. 46-47).

More specifically, the culprits in this pattern of international imperialism and exploitation are the multinational corporations, and those on the evangelical left have issued harsh denunciations of this type of business enterprise.[37] By its own internal logic, the multinational corporation must continually seek new markets for its products,[38] new sources of raw materials, a regular flow of needed commodities, the utilization of cheap labor, and new opportunities for highly profitable investment—and it must seek all of these without any real regard for the interests of the various host nations within which it operates.[39] Indeed, the evangelical left accuses multinational operations of contributing to the concentration of wealth and income by local elites in their host countries, changing the consumption patterns of local populations, dumping faulty and dangerous products on these populations, and in general inhibiting the process of indigenous economic development.[40] In addition, it is charged that since the activities of these corporations are "transnational" and have not been subject to any political authority, the multinationals are able to pursue their exploitative global program largely with impunity.[41]

Those on the left commonly contend that global capitalist imperialism is being sustained by the manipulation of the international political process. Such manipulation is evident in international commodity pricing controls, which have depressed the prices of raw materials, and in preferential trade agreements, various barriers to imports, uneven international currency liquidity, the monopolization of international transport, and international banking policies that charge the developing world high rates of interest. In short, manipulation is evident in any number of policies that tend to benefit the developed West at the expense of the Third World.[42]

But if the West has attained its economic stranglehold on the developing

---

37. See Taylor, *Economics and the Gospel,* pp. 98ff.

38. Products, it should be noted, that those on the evangelical left generally consider either useless or harmful. Tom Sine has argued that the intention of the multinational corporations "is to redefine the nature of the good life for persons in all cultures in order to expand the global market for Coke, Twinkies, Nabisco crackers and a host of other western consumer products" ("Development: Its Secular Past and Its Uncertain Future," in *Evangelicals and Development: Toward a Theology of Social Change,* ed. Ronald J. Sider [Philadelphia: Westminster Press, 1981], p. 81).

39. See Waldron Scott, *Bring Forth Justice: A Contemporary Perspective on Mission* (Grand Rapids: William B. Eerdmans, 1980), pp. 137ff.

40. See Scott, *Bring Forth Justice,* pp. 141-42.

41. See Scott, *Bring Forth Justice,* p. 140.

42. See Toland, Fenton, and McCulloch, "World Justice and Peace"; Kirk, *The Good News of the Kingdom Coming,* p. 65; Mooneyham, *What Do You Say?* p. 129; George DeVries Jr., "Trade on the High Seize," *The Other Side* 12 (January-February 1976): 59-62; and Ronald J. Sider, "Mischief by Statute: How We Oppress the Poor," *Christianity Today,* 16 July 1976, pp. 14-19.

world by means of the manipulation of international trade policy, it has ultimately maintained its position through the use of force. Danny Collum has
asserted,

> it is certainly the case that the people who run America think globally and system-
> atically about their course of action. They are, after all, sitting astride an empire that
> requires trade, raw materials, labor, and markets from across the planet. Protecting
> that economic reach, of course, requires a global projection of military power. And
> the maintenance of a global military capacity ultimately requires that the citizens of
> the mother country be convinced, through a combination of material rewards and
> cultural conditioning, that the whole imperial enterprise is worth the cost.[43]

Collum goes on to suggest that the "consolidation and management of the
global system" went largely unnoticed between 1945 and 1965 but that the
protest movements of the late 1960s, triggered especially by the Vietnam War,
finally revealed the insidious nature of the global project and led to what he
and others have called a "rise of Christian conscience" directed primarily
against the oppressive global capitalist system.[44]

Those on the left argue that ultimately the global capitalist system is driven
by consumerism and particularly by the consumerism of the wealthy West. Jim
Wallis has stated, for example, that "overconsumption is theft,"[45] and Ronald
Sider has insisted that "an affluent minority devours most of the earth's nonrenewable resources. Food consumption patterns are grossly lopsided. Unless
you have retreated to some isolated valley where you produce everything you
use, you benefit from unjust structures that contribute directly to the hunger
of a billion unhappy neighbors."[46] Similarly, Waldron Scott has observed that
"the western or northern minority of mankind, numbering no more than 20

43. Collum, "The Big Picture," pp. 4-5.
44. Collum, "The Big Picture," p. 5. Jim Wallis describes this movement as follows:
"the rise of Christian conscience around the world is a search for social, political, and
economic alternatives based on more human values than the solutions offered by the present
ideological competitors. . . . [It is] politically independent. It is neither right nor left, nor
liberal nor conservative" (*The Rise of Christian Conscience,* ed. Jim Wallis [San Francisco:
Harper & Row, 1987], p. xxviii).
45. Wallis, "Of Rich and Poor," *Post American* 3 (February-March 1974): 13.
46. Sider, "Mischief by Statute," p. 18. He goes on to say, "we are participants in a
system that dooms even more people to agony and death than the slave system did" (p. 19).
In *Rich Christians in an Age of Hunger* he says that "Our standard of living is at least as
luxurious in comparison with that of a billion hungry neighbors as was the lifestyle of the
medieval aristocracy in comparison with the serfs" (p. 39). He also occasionally includes
statistics comparing the amount of money Americans spend on such things as pet food relative
to the amount American Christians spend on world development missions—e.g., in "Living
More Simply for Evangelism and Justice," in *Lifestyles in the Eighties: An Evangelical
Commitment to Simple Lifestyle,* ed. Ronald J. Sider (Philadelphia: Westminster Press, 1982),
p. 26.

percent of the world's population, has garnered fully 65 percent of the world's total production of goods and services. . . . This North/South division between the 'haves' and 'have nots' is both incredible and intolerable."[47] And Jim Wallis concluded in *Post American* in 1974 that "we privileged people are the major source of the world's problems and they will not be solved before we give up our privileged position."[48]

Interpretations of exactly what "giving up our privileged position" means have varied somewhat from one author to the next, but on the whole those on the evangelical left agree that the key to redressing the problem of uneven global development lies in the redistribution of wealth and resources. This is especially true, they feel, given the fact that we have almost reached the limits to global industrial development.[49] In other words, they reject the thesis that the global problem is a matter of inadequate production, as "development" or "modernization" theory has suggested.[50] And while some authors (e.g., Sider) argue that global redistribution might be accomplished in part voluntarily by means of charity, it is more common for those on the evangelical left to argue that such redistribution necessitates fundamental structural changes in the world economic system. "We think structures need to be changed," John Alexander commented recently. "The reason kids starve is not shortage of food; there's plenty of food for all of us to eat. The reason kids starve is the economic system—the way food is distributed."[51]

Policy Prescriptions on the Evangelical Left

While those on the evangelical left tend to be rather vague on the subject of economic policy per se, they occasionally advocate specific economic policy measures. Domestically, they tend to argue that the only way to redress existing distributional injustice is through enhanced government regulation of economic life and increased social spending. Put differently, the left's solutions to domestic social and economic problems focus almost exclusively on redistributive policies.

On the regulatory side, they insist that the power of corporate capitalism

47. Scott, *Bring Forth Justice,* pp. 125-26.
48. Wallis, "Of Rich and Poor," p. 13.
49. See Sine, *The Mustard Seed Conspiracy,* p. 26.
50. On modernization theory, see Peter L. Berger, *Pyramids of Sacrifice* (Garden City, NY: Doubleday-Anchor, 1974), p. 12. The evangelical left's rejection of modernization theory is reflected in their avoidance of such terms as "development," "economic growth," "modernization," and the like. They feel that these concepts merely obfuscate the real problems of economic imperialism, exploitation, and inequitable global distribution.
51. Alexander, *Your Money or Your Life,* p. 101.

is such that only the regulatory apparatus of the modern state is capable of redirecting corporate energies toward the social good.[52] Andrew Kirk, for example, has advocated the socialization of basic industries, the adoption of what he has called a "social wage," steeply progressive income taxes, and other measures aimed at redressing existing material inequality and preventing the development of such "grievous imbalances" in the future.[53]

On the spending side, those on the evangelical left suggest that the solutions to many of our most pressing social problems lie in increased social spending, and they contend that the state should guarantee such things as employment, housing, food, and medicine through an expanded welfare system.[54] Increased social spending could be easily funded, they argue, simply by cutting the defense budget, which ultimately only facilitates the exploitation of the Third World and serves to enrich the military-industrial corporate elite. "Social programs," Danny Collum has argued, are "the least inflationary, most productive kind of government spending. . . . Government funds spent on poor people go directly into purchasing the necessities of life: food, clothing, shelter—thus subsidizing production and employment in those basic industries."[55]

While those on the evangelical left are aware that welfare programs have been criticized for perpetuating dependency and inhibiting market solutions to the problems they address, they insist that these programs have failed not in principle but only in practice, and that because they have not been adequately funded. "It is not government generosity which has created the incentive for recipients of welfare programs to remain dependent," Stephen Mott has insisted, "but the timidity of government and the failure of a full-employment policy."[56] Citing Michael Harrington, Mott has also argued that such programs

52. There is a deep ambivalence concerning the state among those in the evangelical left. On the one hand they perceive it to be dominated by the capitalist elite, but on the other hand they view it as the only institution powerful enough to challenge corporate power. This ambivalence is evident in the fact that they denounce the state as perhaps the chief "principality and power" while at the same time devoting a great deal of energy to public policy issues and trying to forge a grass-roots political power base (e.g., see Collum, "Assault on the Poor"). It is also evident in the fact that they call for "participatory democracy" and less bureaucracy while at the same time advocating redistributive schemes that could only be carried out by massive bureaucracies.

53. Kirk, *The Good News of the Kingdom Coming,* pp. 82ff. Kirk describes a "social wage" as follows: "The worth of different jobs, training and experience would be assessed collectively and each would receive according to their respective grading. This already happens, to a certain degree, in government employment" (p. 83). See also Alexander, *Your Money or Your Life,* p. 103; and Taylor, *Economics and the Gospel,* p. 86.

54. Alexander, *Your Money or Your Life,* p. 103; see also Taylor, *Economics and the Gospel,* p. 61.

55. Collum, "Assault on the Poor," p. 13.

56. Mott, *Biblical Ethics and Social Change* (New York: Oxford University Press, 1982), p. 202; see also Collum, "Assault on the Poor," p. 15.

"have never included a pervasive governmental intrusion into the private sphere."[57]

The policies favored by the evangelical left to correct global problems are again almost entirely redistributive, for the most part after the fashion of the New International Economic Order proposals issued by Third World representatives to the United Nations in 1974. These proposals call on the West to transfer more capital abroad, offer concessionary trading terms to developing countries, increase development aid, and so on. They also call for the strict regulation of multinational corporations.[58] Curiously, inasmuch as such global proposals necessarily entail the distribution of wealth away from the developed West, they are in conflict with the left's domestic recommendations. The practice of transferring capital abroad, for example, is precisely what many of those on the evangelical left have blamed for domestic unemployment,[59] and reverse-preferential trading policies would almost certainly increase such unemployment. While Ronald Sider has argued that the developed nations should be willing to accept increased levels of domestic unemployment as a consequence of helping people abroad who are relatively much poorer than we are,[60] many others on the evangelical left have advocated guaranteeing full domestic employment. The evangelical left's advocacy of essentially mercantilist domestic policies, combined with their stress on greatly increased development assistance, then, is problematic and may account, at least in part, for the fact that they have tended to avoid discussions of policy implementation. They appear to assume that if global military expenditures were eliminated, there would be more than enough surplus in the world economy to pay for what might otherwise be mutually exclusive policies.

Capitalism and Social Change

Since society, in the opinion of the evangelical left, is an integrated system organized primarily around economic institutions, and since such institutions cannot be changed simply by changing the attitudes of the individuals involved within them, efforts toward effecting social change must be directed principally toward the political economy.[61] But simply reforming the existing political

57. Mott, *Biblical Ethics and Social Change,* p. 202.

58. For a list of very specific proposals for restricting the activities of corporations, including multinationals, see Walter Wink, "Unmasking the Powers: A Biblical View of Roman and American Economics," *Sojourners* (October 1978): 9-15.

59. See Zingaro and Harnden, "Since Steel Went Down."

60. Sider, *Rich Christians in an Age of Hunger,* p. 212.

61. Mott states that "one cannot deal with the problems posed by capitalism merely by getting enough good people into the system" (*Biblical Ethics and Social Change,* p. 120).

economy is not the answer either, according to George DeVries, Jr.: "We cannot
. . . rely upon the workings of the international market system if we wish to
rectify the present bad situation, for that system is designed to preserve the
status quo and is wrong, all wrong."[62] Similarly, Orlando Costas has asserted
that "Capitalism is not something that can be transformed and reformed. The
very root of capitalism is the process of enslaving people, exploiting their
resources. . . . The only alternative I know to capitalism is to reverse the whole
thing and begin a proper distribution of the wealth."[63] Moreover, those on the
evangelical left contend that it is well within our capabilities to reverse the
capitalist system if only we will exert the moral will to do so. "To the extent
we think of the 'economy' as 'out there' or as a machine functioning automatically without real guidance, it is not 'ours.' When we recognize that the
fundamental terms of reference of the 'economy' begin with public decisions,
it becomes eminently clear that what we choose or do not choose to do to alter
these decisions in a democracy is the fundamental economic question."[64]

Those on the left argue that they have come to understand the "real"
workings of the capitalist system only recently. Wallis and Collum date the
beginnings of this realization to the 1960s but suggest that it is only now
coming to fruition in a "rise of Christian conscience" around the world. In a
small booklet entitled *An Evangelical Commitment to Simple Life-Style,* Alan
Nichols argues that there has been a "great shift in thinking about world poverty
and Christian affluence since 1974,"[65] presumably referring to the Lausanne
Congress. Gar Alperowitz has offered a more sociological view, suggesting
that a new "post-materialist" or "post-affluent" segment of the middle class
has emerged in recent years that has been increasingly alienated by the utter
lack of community in capitalist culture. This class, he argues, will be able to
wrest control of the economic process back from the corporations and direct
the process toward a fundamental restructuring, thereby "altering the culture
so as to encourage a less materialistic approach to life [and] a sense of

---

See also Scott, *Bring Forth Justice.* The evangelical left self-consciously contrasts its emphasis on "structural" social change with the more conservative view that social change is
primarily a function of changing individuals.

62. DeVries, "Trade on the High Seize," p. 61.

63. Costas, *The Other Side* 12 (January-February 1976): 30.

64. Gar Alperowitz, "Economics: Putting a Value on Values," *Sojourners* 14 (November
1985): 18. Alperowitz has maintained that such things as the economic growth rate and the
unemployment rate can be planned if we so desire, a view that is self-consciously contrasted
with the core proposition of all conservative defenses of capitalism—namely, that it is indeed
a system that functions "automatically without real guidance" and yet results in the social
good.

65. Nichols, *An Evangelical Commitment to Simple Life-Style: Exposition and Commentary,* Lausanne Occasional Papers, no. 20 (Wheaton, IL: Lausanne Committee for World
Evangelization, 1980): p. 7; see also Sine, *The Mustard Seed Conspiracy,* p. 14.

community."[66] Yet however they describe their understanding, it is clear that those on the evangelical left feel themselves to be on the forefront of a historical movement that has found its focus in the protest against modern capitalism.

Most of those on the evangelical left assume that their understanding of capitalism is more or less self-evident, and there is a certain "taken-for-granted-ness" in this part of their overall argument against capitalism. Reflecting on his experience within radical evangelicalism, Clark Pinnock, who has since become quite conservative, recently commented,

> I remember being asked if I realized the Marxist content of what we were saying in the *Post American* and being puzzled by the question. . . . It seemed reasonable to think of the rich as oppressors, and the poor as their victims. The Bible often seemed to do the same thing. It was obvious to me that the welfare state needed to be extended, that wealth ought to be forcibly redistributed through taxation, that the third world deserved reparations from us, that our defense spending was in order to protect our privilege, and the like. I did not require proof of such propositions—they all seemed obvious and self evident.[67]

That those of the evangelical left have considered capitalism to be self-evidently conspiratorial and oppressive explains their incredulity with assertions to the contrary and their great impatience with conservative evangelical

66. Alperowitz, "Economics: Putting a Value on Values," p. 22.

67. Pinnock, "A Pilgrimage in Political Theology," in *Liberation Theology*, ed. Ronald H. Nash (Milford, MI: Mott Media, 1984), pp. 110-11. There have been several defections of prominent radicals back toward and even back into the evangelical mainstream. Pinnock was an early member of the People's Christian Coalition and writer for *Post American,* but more recently he has criticized the evangelical left rather harshly for its ideological captivity to radical secular analysis. In an article entitled "Pursuit of Utopia, Betrayal of the Poor," he writes, "The point I am driving at here is that in a quite parallel way, many churchmen are now supporting the Marxist ideology in one version or another in much the same way as others had supported the Nazi ideology in the Third Reich. . . . And what may make [this] even worse is the distinct possibility that their support, coming at a time when Marxism has lost most of its legitimacy and mythical appeal, owing to its brutality and colossal failures, may prove to be the factor which actually prolongs the life of this evil empire. What a supreme irony it would be if Christians were to give Marxism the religious legitimacy which it could never have generated for itself as a secular doctrine and were to give it an extension to its life as a deadly totalitarian force" (*Crux* 23 [December 1987]: 7). Somewhat less spectacularly, John Alexander, editor until recently of *The Other Side,* has commented, "It is time those of us with sensitive consciences showed our bleeding hearts by wondering aloud why fewer people are hungry in South Korea and Singapore than in Burma and Tanzania. . . . It is also time that we admitted that when it comes to producing material goods (like food) then the market does quite a job. In fact, it would be easier to make a case against the market for generating too many material goods than too few. Its ability to do that is strewn across the face of North America, Western Europe, and Japan. Whether you call it consumerism, environmental degradation, or serving the public, its 'productivity' cannot be questioned" (quoted in "On the Other Side of the Other Side," *Religion and Society Report* 4 [August 1987]: 2-3).

attempts to defend capitalism. It also explains why the evangelical left focuses its analytical effort almost exclusively on countries where capitalism has apparently failed while almost entirely neglecting nations where capitalist economic development has been successful. In the opinion of the evangelical left, capitalism is a system from which by definition only bad things can be expected.

Debunking the Opposition

Given these assumptions about the workings of capitalism both domestically and globally, it is no wonder that the evangelical left has drawn the conclusion that capitalism is an immoral and essentially anti-Christian system. "The dehumanizing nature of modern American corporate capitalism ought to compel Christians to cry out in protest," Richard Pierard has suggested. "It forces the individual into the mold of conformity . . . and places the free worker in the chains of wage slavery. The average citizen is manipulated by unscrupulous advertising and thrust into the never ending cycle of consumerism that keeps him spiritually and economically impoverished."[68] George McClain has stated that

> judged on the basis of God's revelation through the Bible, American capitalism is an abomination. . . . It requires that a host of people be unemployed, simply because there aren't enough jobs. It enables some to gain and retain great amounts of wealth at the expense of others. It leaves most people pretty much on their own to scrape for a living under conditions they can't control, like inflation and recession. Capitalism almost forces us to act in a selfish, un-Christian way in order to provide for our loved ones.[69]

Why more Christians are not, in fact, crying out in protest against American capitalism has puzzled those on the evangelical left, and they have tended to suggest two explanations for this state of affairs. The first, less common explanation, is that their opponents on the right are simply immoral. The second explanation, which has been a good deal more common, is that those on the right have become ideologically blinded within the capitalist system.

Although the rhetoric of the evangelical left implies that there is a group of evil persons in positions of power who are responsible for directing the exploitative capitalist enterprise, such persons have rarely if ever been specifically identified. More commonly, it is assumed that whoever its directors may ultimately be, the capitalist system is held together largely by people who are

68. Pierard, "Where America Missed the Way," *Journal of the American Scientific Affiliation* 29 (March 1977): 19.
69. McClain, "Money Trouble," *The Other Side* 14 (March 1978): 20.

simply unaware of its true nature. "I suspect," John Alexander has written recently, "that more harm is done by good people quietly doing their jobs for such groups [corporations] and doing them well than by all the crime and malice in the world."[70] "How is it that perfectly nice people can let hundreds of thousands starve?" Alexander asks. "Freud and Marx explain how it's done. Class interest, the unconscious, ego-defense mechanisms, and ideology allow us not to acknowledge almost anything we choose."[71]

Thus the notion of ideology is central to the evangelical left's understanding of conservatism in general and its assessment of American evangelicalism in particular.[72] On the domestic front, the evangelical left views "establishment" Christianity—American Christianity in both its liberal and conservative expressions—as having succumbed to the great temptation to conformity within the American capitalist system.[73] The liberals have succumbed to the secularization of the Christian faith within a materialistic culture,

70. Alexander, *Your Money or Your Life,* p. 182.

71. Alexander, *Your Money or Your Life,* pp. 9-10.

72. In 1965, evangelical sociologist David Moberg suggested that in addition to the explanations commonly given for evangelical social inactivity in this century (reaction to the Social Gospel, separatism, pietism, etc.), there was the matter of evangelicalism's success within American culture. The increased affluence and rising status of evangelicals created a situation in which they had come to "identify themselves with the interests of wealth and power" within American society. For evangelicals to posture neutrality on social policy issues (e.g., to suggest that the church should not endorse specific social policies), he argued, simply reflected this identification. "Sanctioning the status quo by refusing to work for the reformation of society is the equivalent of saying that society is already 'Christian' or that the gospel is powerless to change it" (*Inasmuch: Christian Social Responsibility in Twentieth-Century America* [Grand Rapids: William B. Eerdmans, 1965], pp. 21-22). Whereas Moberg was somewhat vague as to just exactly what evangelicalism's captivity to cultural conservatism entailed, other progressive evangelicals have spelled it out more clearly. Richard Pierard, for example, has insisted that economic and political conservatism (as evidenced in such things as the defense of capitalism and resistance to expansion of the welfare state) are the chief problems. He contends that the evangelical "right wing" (e.g., the Christian Freedom Foundation) emphasizes selfish individualism at the expense of social justice, is closely aligned with the military-industrial complex, and is responsible for the increasing likelihood of a "fascist revolution" in America ("Evangelical Christianity and the Radical Right," in *The Cross and the Flag,* ed. Robert Clouse, Robert Linder, and Richard V. Pierard [Carol Stream, IL: Creation House, 1972], pp. 116-17). "It is my sincere conviction," Pierard has written, "that, if the trend toward political, economic, and social conservatism is not reversed, evangelical Christianity will soon be facing a crisis of disastrous proportions. In fact, its very survival in the 1970s may well depend on whether it can escape from the Unequal Yoke [of theological and cultural conservatism]" (*The Unequal Yoke: Evangelical Christianity and Political Conservatism* [Philadelphia: J. B. Lippincott, 1970], p. 10).

73. See Wallis, *Agenda for Biblical People,* pp. 47ff. Interestingly, Andrew Kirk, himself an evangelical theologian of liberation, suggests that radical evangelicals have become ideologically captive to "a particular passing view of reality" as well (*The Good News of the Kingdom Coming,* p. 13). It would seem that no one is immune to this kind of criticism.

while the conservatives, with their individualistic emphasis on personal faith and their tendency toward a dualistic separation of the material from the spiritual, have essentially rendered the gospel into a commodity and reduced the Christian faith to a purely personalistic and hence socially irrelevant affair.[74] Those on the left feel that the connection between such tendencies and modern capitalism is obvious. Wes Michaelson has stated that "Evangelicalism has been part and parcel of this economic system, dominated by it in deed as well as thought. Note how much of Evangelicalism's framework of thinking is determined by the values and modes of our economic order, in, for example, the idolization of church growth, the selling of Jesus in various kinds of evangelism, the reduction of the gospel to sales slogans that can be marketed."[75] John Alexander has gone so far as to suggest that "many of the most visible [evangelical] evangelists are franchising death."[76] Critics such as these dismiss the conservative evangelical defense of capitalism out of hand as an expression of the class interests of the largely affluent, middle-class, white, male leadership of the movement.[77] Indeed, the conservative evangelical defense of capitalism represents what some of those on the left feel is perhaps "the major heresy of our time";[78] Jim Wallis has predicted that the present period may well "come to be regarded as one of the most shallow and self-serving periods in U.S. church history."[79]

This assessment of evangelicalism's ideological captivity is much the same in treatments of the global context. It has been charged that American evangelical missionary efforts overseas are "nothing but the reflection of the commercial and imperial practices of the *Pax Americana*."[80] Andrew Kirk has written about those not actively protesting capitalist oppression, suggesting that "particularly in North America, Western Europe, and Australasia there are many evangelical Christians who support (some directly, many unwittingly) the economic dominations of the poor nations of the world by the economic policies of the developed nations and the activities of multinational corporations. Those evangelicals that lend their support to these practices are a great scandal to the evangelical witness in general and to the evangelisation of the poor of the earth in particular."[81]

74. See Kirk, *The Good News of the Kingdom Coming*, pp. 85ff.

75. Michaelson, "Evangelicalism and Radical Discipleship," p. 79.

76. Alexander, *Your Money or Your Life*, p. 93.

77. See Boyd Reese, "Christ and Capitalism: Evangelicals Look at the Free Market System," *Sojourners* 13 (May 1984): 36-37.

78. Thomas P. Hanks, "Why People Are Poor," *Sojourners* 10 (January 1981): 22.

79. Wallis, *The Call to Conversion*, p. 27.

80. Samuel Escobar and John Driver, *Christian Mission and Social Justice* (Scottdale, PA: Herald Press, 1978), p. 76.

81. Kirk, *The Good News of the Kingdom Coming*, p. 149.

And so those on the evangelical left view the present as "one of the great turning points in history,"[82] in which the question of evangelicalism's stance on political-economic issues is crucial. The credibility of the Christian faith in the modern world and especially in the Third World, they feel, is at stake, as are any realistic prospects for global peace and justice.[83] "It is evident," Waldron Scott insisted in 1980, "that the biggest issue of our time, the point at which the world and the devil are subverting the Kingdom of God, is social justice in a global context."[84] Alerting fellow evangelicals to the nature of the present situation has become an exceedingly urgent task, and the evangelical left tends to see its mission in terms of educating and "sensitizing" those in the evangelical mainstream and those on the evangelical right to the problem of global capitalist oppression.

Along these lines, those on the evangelical left emphasize trying to help their fellow evangelicals to see their "complicity" in, and hence their culpability for, the destructive capitalist global order.[85] This would appear to explain the acutely confessional tone of many of the documents and statements that have been issued on the left. Consider the much-heralded "Chicago Declaration," a statement issued by a group of progressive evangelical leaders at a Thanksgiving Day workshop held in Chicago in 1973, for example:

> We acknowledge that God requires justice. But we have not proclaimed or demonstrated his justice to an unjust American society. . . . Further, we have failed to condemn the exploitation of racism at home and abroad by our economic system. . . .
> We must attack the materialism of our culture and the maldistribution of the nation's wealth and services. We recognize that as a nation we play a crucial role in the imbalance and injustice of international trade and development.[86]

82. Sider, *Rich Christians in an Age of Hunger*, p. 225.

83. Ronald J. Sider, "An Evangelical Theology of Liberation," *The Christian Century*, 19 March 1980, p. 318.

84. Scott, *Bring Forth Justice*, p. 155.

85. Waldron Scott has suggested that part of the task of evangelism is to "point out the individual's complicity in structural evil, institutionalized sin, and national unrighteousness" (*Bring Forth Justice*, p. 214).

86. "A Declaration of Evangelical Social Concern," *International Review of Missions* 63 (April 1974). See also Ronald J. Sider, *The Chicago Declaration* (Carol Stream, IL: Creation House, 1974). Interestingly, Richard Quebedeaux noted that a unit committee of the N.C.C.'s "Division of Church and Society" drafted a very favorable response to the Chicago Declaration in 1974 (*The Worldly Evangelicals* [New York: Harper & Row, 1978], p. 135). Apparently evangelicals were finally beginning to understand the root of America's problem. It is also interesting to note that, already by 1975, the "workshop" was paralyzed by a series of rather bitter disagreements—blacks distrusting whites, women distrusting men, activists distrusting academics, and so on. Access to cognitive or analytical privilege, first claimed for anyone simply "identifying" with the "poor and oppressed," appears to have

In this same vein, George DeVries, Jr., has asserted that "we sin grievously when we sanction and participate unquestioningly in exploitive, manipulative systems and policies. The idea that we could all be participating in such a public, collective sin is still foreign to most of us, but it may well represent our greatest condemnation before God."[87] Others take a dim view of suggestions that the church not involve itself directly in policy matters on the grounds that silence simply supports the political-economic status quo.

Those on the left also argue that contemporary American evangelical stances on social and economic policy issues are far removed from those of their ancestors. Instead of emulating the likes of Wesley and Wilberforce, Ronald Sider commented in 1980, "the evangelical community [today] is largely on the side of the rich oppressors rather than that of the oppressed poor . . . [and so] has been profoundly unorthodox."[88] To correct these serious errors, the evangelical left is calling for American evangelicalism to recover a truly biblical faith, a faith that is able to address decisively issues of political-economic injustice, or, as Andrew Kirk has put it, "the real circumstances of today's world."[89]

The Biblical Case against Capitalism

Following closely on the assumptions outlined above, the evangelical left's theological case against capitalism suggests that the Bible more or less explicitly condemns capitalism as an oppressive political-economic system in which private accumulation is allowed to occur at the expense of the poor. Interestingly, the left's argument encompasses two kinds of assertions. The first are ethical and propositional—for example, that the Scriptures condemn private accumulation, that they teach that wealth is necessarily gained at the expense of the poor, that they do in fact address such things as "structural" injustice. The second kind of assertions are historical and eschatological, suggesting that God is at work in history progressively liberating those who, as a result of such things as capitalist domination, have become poor and oppressed. As the evangelical left has matured, its theological condemnation of capitalism has increasingly drifted away from merely ethical and propositional assertions and toward an incorporation of such assertions into an overarching view of history and eschatology. Exactly why this shift has

---

required some further specification (e.g., *which* poor, *which* oppressed, and *how* to correctly identify with them), which the participants were not able to agree on. See Richard V. Pierard, "Floundering in the Rain," *The Reformed Journal* 25 (October 1975): 6-8.

87. DeVries, "Trade on the High Seize," p. 60.

88. Sider, "An Evangelical Theology of Liberation," p. 318.

89. Kirk, *The Good News of the Kingdom Coming*, p. 12.

occurred is something we will want to explore after we have taken a closer look at the assertions themselves.

Ethical and Propositional Assertions

The evangelical left commonly begins to make its theological case against capitalism by asserting that the subject of wealth and poverty is perhaps the single most important theme in the Bible.[90] Those on the left stress that the private accumulation of wealth that they hold to be at the heart of the capitalist enterprise is roundly prohibited in both the Old and the New Testaments. For example, Andrew Kirk cites the Mosaic legislation concerning the release of Hebrew slaves (Exod. 21:2-6; Deut. 15:12-18), the Sabbatical Year (Exod. 23:10-11; Lev. 25:1-7), the periodic cancellation of debt (Deut. 15:1-11), and especially the Year of Jubilee (Lev. 25:8-17) as clear indications that the Old Testament sanctions the "ideal of equality among brethren" and prohibits private accumulation for any purpose other than that of "meeting of basic needs." "The capitalist economic system . . . ," he concludes, "cannot be justified as an ideal."[91] Similarly, John Alexander cites Proverbs 8:10 ("Choose my instruction instead of silver") to suggest that the pursuit of wealth and the knowledge of God are mutually exclusive.[92]

In the New Testament, Jesus' announcement "Blessed are you who are poor" (Luke 6:20) and the corresponding "But woe to you who are rich" (v. 24), along with Jesus' encounter with the rich young ruler (Mark 10:17-31; Matt. 19:16-30; Luke 18:18-30), are often cited by those on the left to illustrate not simply that Jesus commands a certain attitude toward wealth but that he rejects its accumulation altogether.[93] John Alexander has suggested that Jesus "con-

90. Having counted the number of verses that he felt touched on the subject of wealth and poverty, Bob Sabath announced that it "is the second most dominant motif in the Bible, the most dominant being idolatry" ("The Bible and the Poor," *Post American* [February-March 1974]: 1). Jim Wallis has asserted that "questions concerning wealth, poverty, and economic justice take a central place throughout the Bible" (*Agenda for Biblical People,* p. 88).

91. Kirk, *The Good News of the Kingdom Coming,* pp. 71, 73.

92. Alexander, *Your Money or Your Life,* p. 45. The title of his book also suggests this basic position.

93. Sabath has argued that "the New Testament condemns not just improper attitudes toward wealth, but also the mere possession of undistributed wealth. . . . If we really had the 'right' attitude toward wealth, then we would no longer be wealthy. Many wealthy Christians believe that their break from attachment to possessions is most clearly and visibly shown in their willingness to give large proportions of their income to Christian causes. In this connection, it is well to remember that the mark of sacrificial giving in the New Testament is not how much is given, but how much is left over after the giving is finished" ("The Bible and the Poor," p. 3).

demn[s] the profit motive and completely reject[s] acquisitiveness" and also that Jesus' insistence that "any of you who does not give up everything he has cannot be my disciple" (Luke 14:33) means that "one of the conditions of being [Jesus'] disciple is to get rid of your possessions, and unless you're going to do it, don't bother to start following him."[94] "We can hardly avoid the conclusion," C. René Padilla has argued recently, "that Jesus regarded poverty to be essential to Christian discipleship."[95] Any number of examples of this point of view could be cited, but the point is nicely summarized by Andrew Kirk: "The overwhelming weight of biblical evidence suggests that private accumulation of wealth is not to be tolerated beyond the enjoyment of a frugal, adequate lifestyle when substantial sectors of society (in our world hundreds of millions) do not have the basic necessities of their existence met."[96]

In general, the evangelical left claims biblical warrant for the premise that poverty is primarily a result of private accumulation. Peter Davids has insisted, for example, that "wealth, in [the prophets'] eyes, is the result of violence and oppression, for without taking advantage of the unfavorable situation of the poor (driving advantageous bargains), and without withholding generous assistance (refusing loans or foreclosing mortgages) the wealthy would not have obtained their wealth. The rich worked within the law and followed accepted business practices, but God calls that violence and oppression."[97] Similarly, Thomas Hanks has argued not only that the biblical authors insist that wealth is gained at the expense of the poor but that the oppression of the poor by the rich "is a major category in the Bible's understanding and approach to reality."[98] In the conflict between rich and poor, God is "especially [on] the side of the poor and oppressed," says Davids.[99] The mark of the true people of God

See also Peter Davids, "God and Mammon: Part 1," *Sojourners* 7 (February 1978): 11-17, and "God and Mammon: Part 7," *Sojourners* 7 (March 1978): 25-29; and Walter Wink, "Unmasking the Powers," *Sojourners* reprint (October 1978). Despite the fact that Jesus insisted that no rich person could enter the kingdom of heaven, says Wink, already by the time 1 Timothy 6:17-19 was written ("Commend those who are rich . . . to be rich in good deeds, to be generous and willing to share"), "the wealthy were being courted, coddled, and coaxed to be generous with wealth they were no longer required to renounce."

94. Alexander, *Your Money or Your Life,* pp. 103, 64.

95. Padilla, *Mission between the Times: Essays on the Kingdom* (Grand Rapids: William B. Eerdmans, 1985), p. 178.

96. Kirk, *The Good News of the Kingdom Coming,* p. 74.

97. Davids, "God and Mammon: Part 1," p. 14.

98. Hanks, "Why People Are Poor," *Sojourners* 10 (January 1981): 19; see also Hanks's *God So Loved the Third World* (Maryknoll, NY: Orbis Books, 1983).

99. Davids, "God and Mammon: Part 1," p. 12; see also Wallis, *Agenda for Biblical People,* p. 3; and Taylor, *Economics and the Gospel,* p. 15. It is difficult to know exactly what this phrase means. Ronald Sider insists that God is on the side of the poor and oppressed, but adds, "I do not mean that material poverty is a biblical ideal. . . . I do not mean that the poor and oppressed are, because they are poor and oppressed, to be idealized or automatically

is that they also identify with the interests of those who have been oppressed by economic exploitation.[100]

It may be worth noting that the impression given by the evangelical left on the subject of wealth is somewhat paradoxical. One the one hand it is argued that the accumulation of wealth should be entirely avoided, but on the other it is suggested that God's creation (and hence wealth) should be enjoyed, that material concerns are central to human existence, and that the Christian's handling of wealth is a critical indicator of spiritual health. Bob Sabath, for example, has written that "Jesus knew that money and possessions were one of the central issues of human experience and revealed more about individuals than almost any other single aspect of their existence. Jesus was not just talking 'economics': money to him was a deeply spiritual issue that was closely tied to the central core of an individual."[101] Similarly, Bill Faw has suggested that "our economic choices are central, not peripheral, to discipleship. The ways our congregations make these choices will show the extent to which we have understood and accepted the message of Jesus."[102]

It may also be worth noting that the evangelical left has tended to assume that the production of wealth in any given situation will be adequate for the provision of basic material needs. Speaking in the context of the creation account in Genesis, Donald Hay says, "We would not therefore expect to find that world shortages of resources are the sources of international inequality."[103] Instead, the problem of inequality must lie in the way resources are distributed, and the biblical ideal in this regard is held to be distributional equality. The Mosaic legislation, for example, "contains regulations tending to minimize capital accumulation and actualize relative social equality,"[104] and this is especially true of the legislation of the Jubilee Year (Lev. 25:8-17), which some

---

included in the church. . . . I do not mean that God cares more about the salvation of the poor than the salvation of the rich or that the poor have a special claim to the gospel. . . . To say that God is on the side of the poor is not to say that knowing God is nothing more than seeking justice for the poor and oppressed. . . . I do not mean that hermeneutically we must start with some ideologically interpreted context of oppression (for instance, a Marxist definition of the poor and their oppressed situation) and then reinterpret Scripture from that ideological perspective" ("An Evangelical Theology of Liberation," pp. 314-15). Since the phrase "God is on the side of the poor and oppressed" would on the face of it seem to connote many if not all of the meanings Sider rules out, I cannot help but wonder why he would continue to use it.

100. See Wallis, *Agenda for Biblical People,* p. 94. "To live in radical obedience to Jesus Christ," Wallis insists, "means to be identified with the poor and oppressed. If that is not clear in the New Testament, then nothing is."

101. Sabath, "The Bible and the Poor," p. 1.

102. Faw, "Our Daily Bread: Biblical Themes of Economics," *Sojourners* 9 (January 1980): 24.

103. Hay, quoted by Nichols, in *An Evangelical Commitment to Simple Life-Style,* p. 8.

104. Davids, "God and Mammon: Part 1," p. 12.

understand to mandate the periodic equalization of capital.[105] "Regardless of its antiquity or implementation," Ronald Sider argues in *Rich Christians in an Age of Hunger,* "Leviticus 25 remains a part of God's authoritative Word. Because he disapproves of extremes of wealth among his people, God ordains equalizing mechanisms like the year of Jubilee."[106]

Similarly, those on the evangelical left often cite the example of the early church's communism described in Acts 4 and 5 as a warrant for the equalization of capital today. Peter Davids has argued that all of the churches Paul founded "apparently had a system of sharing similar to that which Acts reports was practiced in Jerusalem."[107] Bill Faw sees in Paul's determination to return to Jerusalem (Acts 20) an indication that income redistribution was his chief concern.[108] In any event, those on the evangelical left urge a contemporary recovery of the New Testament ideal of simple and communal lifestyles.[109]

> Over and over again God specifically commanded his people to live together in community in such a way that they would avoid extremes of wealth and poverty. . . . Compare that with the contemporary church. Present economic relationships in the worldwide body of Christ are unbiblical, sinful, a hindrance to evangelism and a desecration of the body and blood of Jesus Christ. . . . It is a sinful abomination for a small fraction of the world's Christians living in the Northern Hemisphere to grow richer year by year while our brothers and sisters in Christ in the Third World ache and suffer for lack of minimal health care, minimal education, and even . . . just enough food to escape starvation.[110]

105. See, for example, John Howard Yoder, *The Politics of Jesus* (Grand Rapids: William B. Eerdmans, 1972), p. 74; Alfred Krass, "The Land of Angel Food Cake: Adam Smith and the Biblical Jubilee," *The Other Side* 24 (September 1988): 41-42; and John Alexander, "Back at the Family Farm: Economics as if God Mattered," *The Other Side* 23 (September 1987): 14-15.

106. Sider, *Rich Christians in an Age of Hunger,* p. 90; see also Merold Westphal, "Sing Jubilee," *The Other Side* 14 (March 1978): 28-35.

107. Davids, "God and Mammon: Part 2," p. 26; see also Virgil Vogt, "Economic Koinonia," *Post American* (June-July 1975), pp. 22-27.

108. Faw, "Our Daily Bread," p. 24.

109. See Sine, *The Mustard Seed Conspiracy,* pp. 111ff.; and Padilla, *Mission between the Times,* pp. 170ff. Descriptions of various Christian communities are given in *Living More Simply: Biblical Principles and Practical Models,* ed. Ronald J. Sider (Downers Grove, IL: InterVarsity Press, 1980), pp. 108-44. See also Virgil Vogt, "Economic Koinonia." In "Our Daily Bread," p. 24, Bill Faw notes that "the congregation could move toward incorporating equality by agreeing that those who have more surplus income should tithe a higher percentage of their money. Fuller equality could be reached if a per capita standard of living were decided upon and all the money above that amount were pooled together in the church. If that common standard of living were set to correspond with the welfare standards of one's area, a life of simplicity and poverty together would be possible" (p. 24).

110. Ronald J. Sider, "Living More Simply for Evangelism and Justice," in *Lifestyle in the Eighties: An Evangelical Commitment to Simple Lifestyle,* ed. Ronald J. Sider (Philadelphia: Westminster Press, 1982), p. 30.

Proponents contend that the adoption of simple communal lifestyles would not only create an appropriate identification with the poor and oppressed but would also place the Christian community in the position of having to trust God for its ongoing provision.[111] It is worth noting that those on the left tend to minimize the voluntary character of redistribution in the early church. The redistribution of wealth, they insist, is a matter not of charity but of economic justice.

Interestingly, the evangelical left draws a close connection between freedom, material equality, and justice. Those on the left tend to define freedom as a function of the measure of economic opportunity or power one has relative to others in society. True freedom, then, depends on the equalization of economic goods and opportunities, and real democracy cannot exist in a situation of material inequality. This understanding of freedom forms the foundation for the left's conception of social, or economic, justice. If there is to be genuine social justice and if the poor and oppressed are to be truly liberated, they must be enabled to achieve a position of relative material equality vis-à-vis their oppressors, a position that will enable them to exercise as much socioeconomic power as their oppressors.[112] The sort of help for the poor that fails to correct the imbalance of wealth in society is misguided: it does not accomplish social justice. This is why the evangelical left tends to reject the utilitarian defense of capitalism out of hand.[113] Utilitarian reasoning fails to appreciate that the crucial social problem is not poverty per se but the imbalance of economic power (and hence the imbalance of freedom and justice) in society.[114] Those on the left, then, tend to view relative poverty as a much more basic social problem than poverty in an absolute sense.

111. See Kirk, *The Good News of the Kingdom Coming,* p. 74. Vogt has commented that "The Christian does not accumulate, does not insure against the future, does not borrow and pledge, in order that brotherly love can function realistically. Instead of accumulating and insuring believers share what they have with those who need it now. . . . Resources are set free for immediate use" ("Economic Koinonia," p. 2).

112. See Mott, *Biblical Ethics and Social Change,* p. 67.

113. This is also why the evangelical left has been generally suspicious of economic modeling and calculation—as, e.g., in "The Failure of Conventional Wisdom: Economic Realities in the 80's," *Sojourners* 10 (January 1981): 13-18. They argue that such modeling is not specific enough to be able to identify exactly the kinds of effects various policies may be expected to have on the poor, and yet the whole point of policy analysis in their view should be to determine these effects. Social justice depends on the ability to improve the relative position of the poor, not on the ability to improve the lot of society as an abstracted whole.

114. Of course almost anyone may be said to be "relatively" poor, and it is interesting to note that definitions of the "poor" have varied a great deal from one argument to the next among those on the evangelical left. Some consider all North Americans to be "wealthy," while others categorize most North Americans as an immiserated majority dominated by a tiny capitalist elite, and so forth.

The left also expresses its concern for relative material equality in society in terms of human rights. Each person is said to have a right to more or less equal participation in the life of the community, participation mandating relative material equality for the reasons cited above. And those on the evangelical left recognize the persuasive force of the language of human rights in the context of modern democracies. Stephen Mott has asserted that "the language of rights is the language of political criticism. . . . A social program can be built upon rights but not on a vague conception of the worth of the individual alone. One must draw out the broader implications of this worth in order to have a social ethic."[115]

In connection with their understanding of capitalism as an oppressive sociopolitical-economic system calling for a fundamental structural overhaul, the evangelical left insists that the Bible has a great deal to say about structural injustice and sociopolitical action. Indeed, those on the left contend that the centrality of sociopolitical reform in Scripture has been obscured only recently by the competitiveness and individualism of capitalist culture. For this reason, they argue that Christians desperately need to recover a holistic understanding of their faith today, an understanding encompassing both social and structural realities. "For too long Christians of most traditions have accepted and communicated a deficient message," Andrew Kirk has written. "Neither theologically, nor practically, do they seem to have been able to make much sense of the relationship between social and personal salvation, between spiritual life and the material world, between God's action in the present and in the future, between evangelism as the communication of words and as compassionate caring for the physical welfare of people."[116] And Jim Wallis has gone so far as to suggest that, given the circumstances of today's world, "the gospel must be preached as a social and economic revolution."[117]

In this regard, those on the left commonly suggest that the exodus of God's people from Egypt provides a paradigm for understanding his desire to liberate the economically oppressed and that the denunciation of economic exploitation was the chief concern of the prophets. "The explosive message of the prophets," Ronald Sider has argued, for example, "is that God destroyed Israel because of mistreatment of the poor! The Word of the Lord is this: Economic exploitation sent the chosen people into captivity."[118]

In addition, the life and work of Jesus are interpreted in political- economic terms. Jesus's announcement in Luke 4:18-21 that "the Spirit of the Lord is upon me, because he has anointed me to preach good news to the poor . . . ,

---

115. Mott, *Biblical Ethics and Social Change*, p. 53.
116. Kirk, *The Good News of the Kingdom Coming*, p. 57.
117. Wallis, *Agenda for Biblical People*, p. 22.
118. Sider, *Rich Christians in an Age of Hunger*, p. 62.

to proclaim freedom for prisoners . . . , to release the oppressed" is perhaps the most frequently cited passage in all of Scripture by those on the evangelical left. There is simply no question, they insist, but that Jesus was referring to material oppression and that he saw his principal task as releasing those oppressed by economic and political exploitation.[119] John Howard Yoder, an Anabaptist theologian very influential on the evangelical left, has stated,

> We must conclude that in the ordinary sense of his words Jesus . . . was announcing the imminent *entrée en vigueur* of a new regime whose marks would be that rich would give to the poor, the captives would be freed. . . . We may have great difficulty in knowing in what sense this event came to pass or could have come to pass; but what the event was supposed to be is clear: it is a visible socio-political, economic restructuring of relations among the people of God, achieved by his intervention in the person of Jesus as the one Anointed and endued with the Spirit.[120]

Those on the evangelical left tend to understand evil in sociostructural terms as well, and they frequently cite capitalism as an example of the quasi-demonic "principalities and powers" mentioned in the New Testament (Rom. 8:38; 1 Cor. 2:8; 15:24-26; Eph. 1:20ff.; 2:1ff.; 3:10; 6:12; Col. 1:16; 2:15). Wallis and others have contended that modern theological scholarship has finally recovered an understanding of what these references to the "principalities and powers" mean—references that are largely neglected by conservative evangelicals.[121] Hendrikus Berkhof's *Christ and the Powers* (1962) has often been cited as an example of this recovery.

Berkhof argues that Paul used the terms "principalities and powers" to refer to the many suprapersonal social structures—including "the state, politics, class, social struggle, national interest, public opinion, accepted morality, the ideas of decency, humanity, democracy"[122]—that were originally created by God to give order to human existence but that have since become demonic and now rebel against both God and man. Berkhof contends that Christ defeated these "powers" and that it is now the church's job to discern and to expose their illusory claims to divinity.

In two recent studies entitled *Naming the Powers* (1984) and *Unmasking the Powers* (1986), Walter Wink has taken Berkhof's analysis several steps further, arguing that

119. See Wallis, *The Call to Conversion*, p. 55.

120. Yoder, *The Politics of Jesus*, p. 39.

121. The application of this analysis to capitalism has been quite prominent in works such as Yoder's *Politics of Jesus* (pp. 135ff.) and Wallis's *Agenda for Biblical People* (pp. 63ff.). It has also been evident in Sider's work (see, e.g., "Evangelism, Salvation, and Social Justice," *International Review of Mission* 4 [July 1975]: 251-67).

122. Berkhof, *Christ and the Powers* (Scottdale, PA: Herald, 1962), p. 32.

the "principalities and powers" are the inner and outer aspects of any given manifestation of power. As the inner aspect they are the spirituality of institutions. . . . As the outer aspect, they are political systems . . . , all the tangible manifestations which power takes. . . . Both come into existence together and cease to exist together. When a particular power becomes idolatrous, placing itself above God's purposes for the good of the whole, then that power becomes demonic. The church's task is to unmask this idolatry and to recall the Powers to their created purposes in the world.[123]

Of the institutional powers Wink deems to have become demonic, modern capitalism, and especially multinational corporate capitalism, provides perhaps the most outstanding example. "We are contending," he says, "against the greed, including our own, reified into systemic solidity [e.g., in monopoly capitalism] by a host of persons over a long span of time. . . . It is precisely this institutionalization of greed that Jesus called 'Mammon.' "[124] Similarly, Jim Wallis has asserted that the demonic powers institutionalized in the present global economic order "hurt and destroy more people than the worst of wars and do it all in the name of business as usual."[125] And Stephen Mott has written that "the struggle against the demonic in general becomes concrete in the struggles against the oppression exerted by the power structures of our day. These can be discerned through a spiritual awareness of the existence of social evil and the injustices through which they work. Stalinism, capitalism, racism, nationalism, and tyranny over the human body and spirit on both the political right and the left are identifiable foci of such oppressive powers in our century."[126]

All of this is not to suggest that those on the evangelical left deny the reality of personal evil.[127] But there is no question that the focus of their

123. Walter Wink, *Naming the Powers: The Language of Power in the New Testament* (Philadelphia: Fortress Press, 1984), p. 5. See also "The Powers Behind the Throne," *Sojourners* 13 (September 1984): 22-25. Wink's project in both *Naming the Powers* and *Unmasking the Powers* is basically the "demythologization" of the concept of evil in the New Testament. "In the final analysis," he says, "Satan is not even a 'personality' at all, but rather a function in the divine process, a dialectical movement in God's purpose" (*Unmasking the Powers: The Invisible Forces That Determine Human Existence* [Philadelphia: Fortress Press, 1986], p. 33). See also his *Sojourners* article "Unmasking the Powers."

124. Wink, "Unmasking the Powers," p. 14.

125. Wallis, *Agenda for Biblical People* p. 104.

126. Mott, *Biblical Ethics and Social Change*, p. 96.

127. Ronald Sider, for example, has stated that "we reject humanistic and Marxist views that naively suppose that if we could just create good social structures, a new humanity would automatically emerge. To be sure, the social sciences clearly demonstrate that societal structures profoundly shape our lives. But the human predicament lies deeper than our frequently oppressive, unjust environments. Since the Fall, persons are selfish and wicked at the core of their being" ("Introducing *Transformation*," *Transformation* 1 [January-March 1984]: 2).

concern and analysis has shifted away from the personal and individual and toward the social and structural, a shift evident in their insistence that a new theological discipline called Christian social ethics is needed to supplement traditional ethical study, which presumably has to do with the merely personal and individual.[128]

Of course, those on the left also tend to understand salvation socially and structurally. John Howard Yoder, for example, has argued that the message of Paul's epistle to the Galatians is not the salvation of individuals by grace through faith, as most Protestants have assumed since the sixteenth century, but rather that "the fundamental issue was that of the social form of the church"—specifically, that the church ought to be socially inclusive in terms of race, class, sex, and the like.[129] While few of those on the evangelical left would go this far, they do stress that salvation encompasses the social order, and essentially all of their expositional effort has been spent stressing the social and structural relevance of the gospel. For Jim Wallis and others, this incorporation of social and structural concerns into the traditional evangelical message has been so important that they have spoken of it in terms of "conversion."

> Neither evangelicals nor liberals have adequately grasped the meaning of conversion for these times. Both movements are floundering without an understanding of discipleship that is historically relevant. . . . Biblical conversion is never an ahistorical, metaphysical transaction affecting only God and the particular sinner involved. Conversion happens in individuals in history; it affects history and is affected by history. . . . Conversion marks the birth of the movement out of a merely private existence into a public consciousness. Conversion is the beginning of active solidarity with the purposes of the kingdom of God in the world.[130]

128. Regarding this shift away from merely personal ethics and toward "social" ethics, it is interesting to note that its proponents still use personal pronouns (especially "we" and "they") to refer to structural social realities. Such usage adds to the force of their rhetoric of course, and it has been made plausible by their use of the logic of "implication" as well as the "principalities and powers" argument. Still, I suspect that it may also be the result of problems they have encountered in trying to bridge the gap between the biblical ethics and our peculiarly modern understanding of what society is—i.e., something operating independently, or "behind," the official or normative definitions attached to it. Applying ethical categories to society as a reality *sui generis,* in other words, has turned out to be quite difficult.

129. Yoder, *The Politics of Jesus,* p. 220.

130. Wallis, *The Call to Conversion,* pp. xviii, 8, 9. Similarly, Ronald Sider has argued that "too often in this century . . . [evangelical Protestants] have failed to add [to their notion of conversion] that coming to Jesus necessarily involves repentance of and conversion from the sin of involvement in structural evils such as economic injustice and institutional racism" ("Evangelism, Salvation, and Social Justice," *International Review of Missions* 4 [July 1975]: 265). This sort of conversion is essentially a conversion to a particular kind of analysis, analysis that has then been given theological support. Here again, the confessional tone of many of the documents and statements the evangelical left has issued is an indication of how significant they feel this kind of conversion is.

By almost all accounts, those on the evangelical left hold that the church, consisting of relatively small gathered communities of those converted in the sense just indicated, should model a new human reality, an essential aspect of which is economic. Ronald Sider has written that "The new community of the redeemed begins to display an entirely new set of personal, social, and economic relationships. The present quality of life among the people of God is to be a sign of that coming perfection and justice which will be revealed when the kingdoms of this world finally and completely become the kingdom of our Lord."[131] Eddy Hall has argued that "in an economy where meeting people's needs (or wants) is a means to the end of profit-making, God's people must reverse that trend. We must create servant-businesses where business income is the means, and ministry providing products or services is the end. . . . This will often require rejecting business structures (such as the shareholder corporation) designed to serve the profit-seekers in favor of structures better suited to servanthood objectives (such as cooperatives and employee-owned businesses)."[132]

Curiously, the new order that the evangelical left encourages the church to model is defined for the most part negatively, as the antithesis of the capitalist order. Imagining the societal ideal, for example, John Alexander commented recently,

> There would be no one to buy the junk that our economic system pours out—and no one to make it, promote it, or retail it. The economy would turn more toward human services and human products: food, health maintenance, home care, education, family enrichment. And more money would be available for spiritual concerns and for the oppressed and the sick. Consumers would be transformed into servants, and the entrepreneurs and executives now driven by the desire for money or power would be freed to serve others. We would find better things to do, and capitalism as we know it would be unthinkable.[133]

Indeed, those on the left maintain that the church must assume a primarily marginal and adversarial relation to the larger culture and in fact that it derives its strength from its negative and nonconforming stance.[134] In the contem-

---

131. Sider, *Rich Christians in an Age of Hunger,* p. 87.
132. Hall, "Living Cooperatively in a Competitive World," pp. 12-13.
133. Alexander, *Your Money or Your Life,* pp. 103-4.
134. Wallis, *Agenda for Biblical People,* p. 69. In terms of H. Richard Niebuhr's analysis in *Christ and Culture* (New York: Harper & Row, 1951), the evangelical left's position on the relation of the church to the larger society has obviously been that of "Christ against culture," and just as Niebuhr suggested, the position has had several theological problems. First, it has tended to be "gnostic," something clearly evident in the evangelical left's conception of conversion and in its insistence that spiritual discernment is a function of negativity vis-à-vis the status quo. Niebuhr also noted that the "Christ against culture" position tends to be characteristically uncritical of itself and somewhat legalistic. Lastly,

porary situation in which the culture is deemed to be dominated by capitalistic consumerism, the left contends that the church must exhibit, at the least, "a visible, outward break with the power of money and possessions."[135] An affluent church, it is charged, will simply not have anything to say either to our own culture or to the "dispossessed majority of this globe."[136]

As a result of its adversarial stance, however, the church should expect to experience resistance and persecution. Indeed, persecution is an important indication that the church is fulfilling its "prophetic" (i.e., adversarial) function within the larger culture and that it has correctly discerned the will of God. Andrew Kirk has stated that persecution "is as strong a sign of the reality of reconciliation with God as is humility, mercy, purity, peacemaking, and right relationships."[137] Jim Wallis has similarly asserted that "we may measure our obedience to the gospel by the degree of tension and conflict with the world that is present in our lives."[138]

At first glance, it appears that those on the evangelical left have taken a characteristically Anabaptist approach to theology and ethics, both in their advocacy of an adversarial stance vis-à-vis the larger culture and their views concerning the nature of Christian obedience.[139] Note the Anabaptist reso-

---

Niebuhr noted that the position has a very difficult time relating God's redemption of the world to his creation of the world, a problem that tends to surface in the position's understanding of the relation of the church to the state and the relation of the ethics of Jesus to the other ethical material in Scripture.

135. Wallis, *Agenda for Biblical People,* p. 93.

136. Sabath, "The Bible and the Poor," p. 4.

137. Kirk, *The Good News of the Kingdom Coming,* p. 136.

138. Wallis, *Agenda for Biblical People,* p. 96. See also Yoder, *The Politics of Jesus,* p. 97; and Alexander, *Your Money or Your Life,* p. 30. There has been a tendency, understandable given this kind of position, for the evangelical left actually to seek persecution in an attempt to authenticate its own position—a strategy Richard John Neuhaus has wryly referred to as "repression envy" (*The Religion and Society Report* 5 [March 1988]: 6). Such persecution has not been difficult to generate. The use by those of the left of harshly judgmental and highly moralistic rhetoric has easily provoked a negative reaction from those not convinced by their arguments, a reaction that they have interpreted as a substantiation of their position.

139. Insofar as the relation of church and state is concerned, John Howard Yoder's *The Politics of Jesus* has been quite influential on the evangelical left. Yoder's position in this volume is distinctively Anabaptist: he contends that there should not be any relation between the two. On the subject of ethics, Yoder insists that Jesus' teaching, especially as given in the Sermon on the Mount (Matt. 5–7), is literally normative and calls for absolute obedience, which entails among other things that in determining ethical strategies, attempts to assess the likely consequences of our actions are inappropriate. He argues that the uniquely Christian form of pacifism "is one in which the calculating link between our obedience and ultimate efficacy has been broken" (*The Politics of Jesus,* p. 246). An attempt to defend capitalism (or any other political-economic system for that matter) on the basis of its performance constitutes a move away from the Christian position of arguing on the basis of moral absolutes.

nances in Arthur G. Gish's assertion that "obedience to Christ means that one does not make decisions on the basis of consequences, expediency, or effectiveness. It means that one does what is right regardless of the result. . . . It is wrong to use effectiveness as the criterion for action."[140] In the same vein, Dale W. Brown has argued that "since no one can predict accurately the result of his actions, he needs to be faithful to what he believes is right and leave the results to the working of the Holy Spirit. The Christian radical . . . is not obliged to demonstrate the pragmatic feasibility of all of his actions because he is freed by his confidence in the present and future reality of God's kingdom to formulate ethical responses based on the righteousness of this kingdom."[141]

Yet the sophisticated use of media resources undertaken by those on the evangelical left and their increasing willingness to take sides on specific issues of public policy raise doubts as to just how consistently adversarial, radical, and Anabaptist they actually are. In fact, they seem to incorporate a rather odd mixture of Anabaptist rhetoric and calculated political pragmatism.[142] While this is probably attributable in part to the historical strength of the tradition of activism and reform within American evangelicalism, it may also reflect an appreciation for the neo-Marxist notion that utopian thought is the engine of historical progress.[143]

Historical and Eschatological Assertions

I have argued that the evangelical left's theological case against capitalism has tended to drift away from the simple propositional condemnation of the accumulation of wealth and toward the inclusion of this proposition in an overarching understanding of history and eschatology. This shift represents a move away from the traditional Christian understanding of history and toward the adoption of a peculiarly modern historical paradigm, in this case the Marxist.

The Marxist paradigm holds that history describes the progressive mastery

140. Gish, *The New Left and Christian Radicalism* (Grand Rapids: William B. Eerdmans, 1970), p. 108.

141. Brown, *The Christian Revolutionary* (Grand Rapids: William B. Eerdmans, 1971), p. 127.

142. Yoder was apparently referring to the evangelical left when he noted that true Anabaptist pacifism "is significantly different from that kind of 'pacifism' which would say that it is wrong to kill but that with proper nonviolent techniques you can obtain without killing everything you really want or have a right to ask for. In this context it seems that sometimes the rejection of violence is offered only because it is a cheaper or less dangerous or more shrewd way to impose one's will upon someone else, a kind of coercion which is harder to resist" (*The Politics of Jesus,* p. 243).

143. See Karl Mannheim, *Ideology and Utopia: An Introduction to the Sociology of Knowledge* (New York: Harcourt, Brace & World, 1968).

of nature by mankind, a mastery summarized in the notion of "praxis," which involves the comprehensive manner in which people have responded to the problems of material existence. Unfortunately, because of the dynamics of the practical economic process, this progress has been difficult. As new praxes have emerged, violent conflicts have erupted between classes with different relations to the means of production and hence with competing practical and material interests. Those benefiting from the existing (and hence, by definition, passing) state of affairs have commonly sought both consciously and unconsciously to legitimate and to stabilize the status quo by means of ideology. Those who are oppressed by the existing social order have naturally been interested in moving beyond it, and their desire to do so has generated utopian thought. While Marx seems to have suggested that human thought simply mirrors competing practical and material interests, subsequent theorists such as Karl Mannheim have argued that the relation between theory and praxis is dialectical—that is, ideas *and* economic practices together drive the historical process forward. Thus, from the neo-Marxist perspective, historical social change results from the interaction of utopian and ideological thought. Put differently, human existence in the context of the continuous struggle with material scarcity has exhibited the regular and repeated "transcendence" of utopian visions generated by the oppressed over and against the inhibiting influence of ideologies perpetrated by those in positions of power and privilege.

While obviously a great deal more could be said about the Marxist vision, the important point in this context is that it understands history primarily in terms of the conflict between those currently in positions of power within the existing political-economic order and those oppressed by this order. We should also note that the Marxist vision suggests that those oppressed within the existing political-economic order have, precisely for that reason, a special ability to understand and appreciate where the historical process is going. Put differently, the poor and oppressed possess a kind of "epistemological privilege" to the future, and their vision of this future reality cannot be judged by assumptions about what is "realistic" at present. Conversely, those in positions of power and privilege within the existing social order are held to be epistemologically handicapped. Because they have vested interests in the status quo, they are ipso facto at odds with the historical process and therefore unable to make valid judgments about society.

Of course, it is on this issue of epistemological privilege that the Marxist vision contrasts most sharply with the traditional Christian understanding of historical progress. Christian orthodoxy holds that God's direction of history toward its fulfillment is intimately linked with the believing church and that history's movement toward this fulfillment is something affirmed primarily in faith, quite often in spite of appearances to the contrary. The Marxist view not only uncouples the historical process from the church (indeed, it typically charges that the church is a primary agent of ideological resistance) but it suggests that the "real" understanding of history is available only to those correctly positioned to receive it—that is, those positioned in adversarial relation to the political-economic status quo. The Marxist view also suggests that this understanding is available only to those willing consciously to participate in historical development.

There is evidence that the evangelical left has begun to incorporate elements of the Marxist vision into its understanding of Christian theology. This synthesis is perhaps most obvious in its assessments of the secular "New Left" in the 1960s and 1970s and in its continuing attraction to the various "theologies of liberation." Expressed in works such as Art Gish's *The New Left and Christian Radicalism* (1970), the evangelical left's theological assessment of the New Left suggests that despite its secularity, the movement's radical criticism of the existing political-economic order was actually an expression of God's ongoing revolutionary activity in history. Gish, himself of Anabaptist heritage, inferred that the secular New Left was really Anabaptist without knowing it, and he also suggested that the Anabaptist community could learn a great deal about its own tradition from the movement: "Out of personal involvement with the New Left has come a new appreciation for the radical heritage of the Christian faith in general and the Anabaptist tradition in particular. Although raised in the Church of the Brethren, I was unaware of the radical nature of this tradition until I had contact with the New Left."[144] Though not an Anabaptist, Dale Brown made a similar observation in *The Christian Revolutionary* (1971): "though it would, of course, be mistaken to equate the outlook of the [secular] radical community with the vision of the Christian community, many Christians do

---

144. Gish, *New Left and Christian Radicalism*, p. 49. Many of those on the evangelical left appear to have had similar experiences. Having been raised in Christian traditions, they became involved in the New Left during the 1960s and 1970s and then returned to their traditions to attempt to integrate the radical social agenda of the New Left back into them. Even a cursory reading of such works as Jack Newfield and Jeff Greenfield's *A Populist Manifesto: The Making of a New Majority* (New York: Warner, 1972), a book that presents the vision of the New Left largely in secular terms, reveals that the platforms of groups such as *Sojourners* do not exhibit any significant differences from their secular counterparts. The analysis of capitalism, the cultural diagnosis, the advocacy of an adversarial stance against the status quo, the emphases on grass-roots political organization and "community," the advocacy of identification with the poor and oppressed, and even the emphasis on voluntary poverty are all secular New Left themes. The only differences between the New Left and the evangelical left are that the latter has attempted to justify these emphases biblically and has survived into the present. Of course, if Gish is correct, these emphases are universal characteristics of the Spirit's ongoing generation of radical, or Anabaptist, social ferment. One senses, however, that the coincidence of emphases between the evangelical left and the secular left is such that it would be far easier to argue that the evangelical left has really been "secularized" without realizing it.

feel that they can discern the Spirit moving in many of the manifestations of community in our time."[145]

Thus, while it is unclear just what was involved in this process of discernment, many of those on the evangelical left testify to having discerned the movement of God's Spirit within the secular New Left. They suggest that the New Left failed not in its social and historical analysis (which they assume to have been correct) but in its refusal to recognize its spiritual source. What remains to be done, Brown and others have urged, is to "Christianize" such movements for radical social change and to bring them into full consciousness of their role in God's revolutionary historical plan.[146] Nonradical Christians, meanwhile, have to be taught to discern how God is in fact working within such movements and have to be made aware of the social implications of the Christian faith. Fred Pearson suggested that that participation in radical social movements, which constitute the loci of God's historical activity, represented an "opportunity to cooperate in the redemption of the world which is our society. In other words, to help God create a new heaven and a new earth."[147]

This understanding of history, which identifies the purposes of God in the world with radical social ferment, has been given full expression in the various theologies of liberation that have emerged chiefly in Latin America since the late 1960s.[148] It is interesting that while proponents of these theologies of liberation concur with the secular Marxist contention that history is essentially a human project, they have made explicit what remains implicit in secular analysis—namely, that the utopian thought critical for historical movement is essentially religious and so falls within the purview of theology. Just as Marx stood Hegel on his head by attempting to fully secularize the discussion of historical social change, so the theologians of liberation resacralize history by bringing the notion of Spirit back into the discussion.[149] In addition, the

145. Brown, *The Christian Revolutionary*, p. 76.

146. Brown, *The Christian Revolutionary*, p. 139.

147. Pearson, *They Dare to Hope*, p. 102.

148. For examples of these theologies, see Hugo Assmann, *Theology for a Nomad Church* (Maryknoll, NY: Orbis, 1975); José Míguez Bonino, *Christians and Marxists* (Grand Rapids: William B. Eerdmans, 1976), and *Theology in a Revolutionary Situation* (Philadelphia: Fortress Press, 1975); Enrique Dussel, *History and Theology of Liberation: A Latin American Perspective* (Maryknoll, NY: Orbis, 1976); Alfredo Fierro, *The Militant Gospel* (Maryknoll, NY: Orbis Books, 1975); Gustavo Gutiérrez, *A Theology of Liberation* (Maryknoll, NY: Orbis Books, 1973); and José Porfirio Miranda, *Marx and the Bible* (Maryknoll, NY: Orbis Books, 1974).

149. "There are not two histories, one sacred and one profane . . . ," writes Gustavo Gutiérrez. "Rather there is only one human destiny. . . . The salvific action of God underlies all human existence. The historical destiny of humanity must be placed definitely in the salvific horizon" (*A Theology of Liberation*, p. 86). Of course, Gutiérrez is not advocating a return to traditional orthodoxy but rather a retranslation of orthodoxy to render it useful to the immanent historical project.

theologies of liberation suggest that the historical situation is revealed only by Marxist socioeconomic analysis and hence only to those who are either "poor and oppressed" themselves or who have been able to correctly identify with the poor and oppressed by adopting Marxist socioeconomic analysis. Along these lines, liberation theologians insist that the contemporary theological project must reflect essentially and primarily upon the present historical moment and hence that theology must turn away from transcendence, at least as traditionally understood, and toward the transformation of "this world." Of course this necessitates a rather drastic reinterpretation of Christian orthodoxy, a reinterpretation that is legitimated on the grounds that orthodoxy has become ideologically perverted. It also requires liberation theologians to take sides within the present world-historical struggle against capitalist oppression. Finally, we should note that the theologies of liberation tend to expand the notion of "church" to include all of those movements, Christian and otherwise, that actively seek to overcome the exploitation and oppression of global capitalism. If the institutional churches hinder the liberating activity of the Spirit in history, then they effectively renounce their churchly status in spite of any claims they may still make to theological orthodoxy.

The analysis of global capitalist oppression given in the theologies of liberation has obviously proven attractive to those on the evangelical left. It is identical to their own, after all. Theologically, however, liberation theology raises a number of perplexing problems for the evangelical left. Early on, for example, those on the left tended to be quite critical of liberation theology's insistence that "revolutionary praxis" be viewed as authoritative for theology. "One is left with the impression," C. René Padilla wrote in 1973, "that the whole question of the kind of action expected of the Christian in a revolutionary situation has been settled *a priori* and that the role of theology is then merely to provide a facade for this particular political option."[150] Liberation theology's radical secularization of the gospel, its deemphasis of personal and individual salvation, and its complete realization of eschatology have also troubled those on the evangelical left.[151] Elsewhere Padilla noted that

> The 'theology of revolution' is in essence a new version of the 'other gospel' that Paul combatted so vigorously in the first century. . . . It is basically a negation of the gospel of grace. It puts man in the place of God. . . . It ignores the Bible's diagnosis of human nature and takes as its basis the simplistic thesis that evil is external to man and consequently can be eradicated through change in social structures. . . . The 'theology of revolution' idealizes man and consequently con-

150. Padilla, "The Theology of Liberation," *Christianity Today*, 9 November 1973, p. 69.

151. See Thomas Finger, "Christians and Marxists: The Debate Goes On . . . ," *Sojourners* 6 (April 1977): 33-36.

verts the gospel into a utopian ideology that employs theological terminology but has little relation to the eschatological message of the Bible.[152]

Still, those on the evangelical left tend to insist that Marxist socioeconomic analysis is such an indispensable tool for understanding contemporary economic realities that it is worth the theological risk posed by Marxist philosophical presuppositions. Even C. René Padilla has departed from his early opinions and more recently encouraged mainstream evangelicals to view liberation theology as an essentially "orthodox" movement.[153] And Thomas Finger has suggested that

> Marxist analysis challenges the individualism of American Christians, probes their deepest economic and social assumptions, and opens their eyes to the Third World's misery. Insofar as capitalism is founded on selfish individualism and monetary motives, Marxist critiques can help flesh out, in economic and social terms, biblical indignation against these things. Marxist analysis, understood in the light of scripture and Christian praxis, can help shake one lose [sic] from the idolatries of one's culture. It can help forge a true revolutionary—not of Marxist vintage, but one challenging that primal struggle for power and control pervading Marxism and capitalism alike.[154]

Thus the evangelical left argues that it is possible to utilize Marxist socioeconomic analysis without necessarily adopting Marxist philosophical presuppositions. Just how successful they have been in maintaining this delicate balance is debatable, however. The same sorts of historical assumptions we have noted with respect to the evangelical left's assessment of the radical social movements of the 1960s appear in their more recent assessments of international revolutionary movements. Waldron Scott, for example, has wondered "if any of the bloody revolutions of the twentieth century are, in some way, evidences of the strong arm of the Lord working on behalf of the

152. Padilla, "Revolution and Revelation," in *Is Revolution Change?* ed. Brian Griffiths (Downers Grove, IL: InterVarsity Press, 1972), pp. 80-81.

153. See Padilla, "Liberation Theology Is Remarkably Protestant," *Christianity Today*, 15 May 1987, p. 12.

154. Finger, "Christians and Marxists," p. 36. Finger's position is basically similar to that of José Míguez Bonino, whose book *Christians and Marxists: The Mutual Challenge to Revolution* (Grand Rapids: William B. Eerdmans, 1976) he is reviewing in this article. Míguez Bonino writes, "The crux of the matter is that Christian ethics has lacked—quite understandably until recent times and quite ideologically at present—an instrument for analyzing the real dynamics of society and assessing the churches' active role in it. . . . It is in this respect, I think, where a Christian ethics can—and indeed I would say must—take Marxism seriously. It offers a scientific, verifiable, and efficacious way to articulate love historically" (pp. 114-15). The irony here is that it has been precisely those aspects of Marxist theory available to empirical verification that have proven, in almost every instance, to be false. Theologians such as Míguez Bonino may be among the last persons in the modern world to believe the "scientific" claims of Marxist analysis.

oppressed in the absence of evangelical action."[155] More specifically, by way of contrast to suggestions that some distance be maintained between God's sustenance of creation and his work of redemption in Christ, Vinay Samuel and Chris Sugden, both of the World Evangelical Fellowship, have asserted that

> we are beginning to see that the scope of the kingdom of God extends not just to the community of the King that consciously acknowledges Jesus as Lord, but is also seen in God's kingdom activity in the world beyond the church . . . as the just relationships that belong to the kingdom are established in society. . . . Thus all of history becomes the arena where God can be discerned at work, and all of history is moving toward fulfilment in Christ. We assert that this is true not only of those activities where Christ is consciously acknowledged, but also of those areas where 'ground-breaking' is going on, where structures of justice are being established, where opportunities of choice are being increased so that people can also choose Christ; here also God's grace can be seen at work. God's redemptive activity is also at work, even though it is not consciously acknowledged as such.[156]

In terms of the evangelical debate over evangelism versus social action, it appears that for individuals such as Samuel and Sugden, social action has become at least as important as evangelism and, to the extent that social action is held to break the ground for evangelism, it may actually be considered more important.

Furthermore, those on the evangelical left suggest that this expanded view of God's redemptive activity in history is in fact what the Bible has been saying all along. The exodus, for example, is paradigmatic for each nation's experience of "integral liberation-salvation."[157] The Mosaic law, the message of the prophets, Jesus' teaching, and so on all find their focus in such things as the "just redistribution of possessions [which] is not merely a future apocalyptic element, but an essential part of eschatology that is realizable 'in this present age.' "[158] "The liberation from oppression," Thomas Hanks has written, ". . . is not relegated to the second coming but to the Messiah's birth, which is to mark the beginning of a kingdom characterized by liberation from oppression, continual growth, and the final triumph of true justice."[159]

155. Scott, *Bring Forth Justice*, p. 206.

156. Samuel and Sugden, "Toward a Theology of Social Change," in *Evangelicals and Development: Toward a Theology of Social Change*, ed. Ronald J. Sider (Philadelphia: Westminster Press, 1981), pp. 52-53, 57. In this case Samuel and Sugden are responding to the position of evangelical theologian John Stott, who has insisted that the Christian perspective on redemption needs to include—and indeed needs to begin with—the conscious confession of Christ. One who adopts such a position, they suggest, is thereby an "unwitting ally of the status quo" (pp. 51-52).

157. Hanks, "Why People Are Poor," p. 20.

158. Thomas P. Hanks, "The Evangelical Witness to the Poor and Oppressed," *TSF Bulletin* 10 (September-October 1986): 18.

159. Hanks, "Why People Are Poor," p. 21.

Yet apart from this reinterpretation of God's activity in history, those on the evangelical left also suggest that the modern situation calls for several other modifications of evangelical orthodoxy. The most basic modification, understandable given the left's view of the nature of God's redemptive activity, is the reorientation of evangelical theology and ethics toward praxis. Practically, of course, this has translated into such things as the denunciation of global capitalist imperialism. Many of those on the evangelical left also insist, on the basis of the "epistemological privilege of the poor," that so long as wealthy Western evangelicals refuse to identify with the poor and oppressed, they simply will not be capable of understanding the biblical message.[160] Thomas Hanks has suggested that "most of the Bible makes a lot more sense when read from the perspective of the oppressed-poor in the Third World. Latin American theologians like to point out that after the conversion of Constantine, the church (Catholic and Protestant alike) stopped reading the Bible from the perspective of the oppressed-poor, aligning itself instead with the wealthy and powerful, or at best with the middle-class. That would explain why we search in vain in our multivolumes of systematic theologies and Bible encyclopedias for articles on oppression."[161] Similarly, John Howard Yoder has argued that wealthy North American evangelicals are simply not in the right "posture to be able to reflect ethically from the perspective of Jesus."[162] Those on the evangelical left attribute their own ability to develop "sensitivity" to the poor and oppressed to their having adopted simpler lifestyles, but ultimately they understand this sensitivity as a spiritual gift of discernment.[163]

Finally, it is important to note that the evangelical left's understanding of theological authority has expanded to include socioeconomic analysis as well as Scripture. They have argued that socioeconomic analysis is a hermeneutical necessity because the realities of the present historical moment must be correctly assessed in order to understand Scripture adequately. Despite his early warnings about the tendency of theology to become a mere facade for particular political options, C. René Padilla made the following comments more recently:

160. The phrase "epistemological privilege of the poor" was apparently coined by Hugo Assmann in *A Theology of the Americas,* ed. Sergio Torres and John Eagleson (Maryknoll, NY: Orbis, 1976). The psychological pressure to "identify" with the poor and oppressed, and hence to be able to make a claim to this epistemological privilege, has grown as this category has expanded to include women, minorities, the "physically challenged," the old, the young, service-sector employees, trade unions—and, in short, just about everyone in modern societies except for the very small group of persons presumed to dominate the economic process. This tendency has been reinforced by the evangelical left's assumption that epistemological privilege is authenticated by persecution.

161. Hanks, "Why People Are Poor," pp. 19-20; see also Thomas D. Hanks, *God So Loved the Third World* (Maryknoll, NY: Orbis Books, 1983), p. 105.

162. Yoder, "A Critique of North American Evangelical Ethics," p. 30.

163. See Stephen Mott, *Biblical Ethics and Social Change,* p. 80.

> The answer to both a rationalistic theology concerned with orthodoxy [e.g., traditional evangelicalism] and a pragmatic theology concerned with orthopraxis [e.g., liberation theology] is a contextual theology concerned with faithfulness to the Word of God and relevance to the historical situation at the same time. . . . Theology is the reflection on praxis in the light of faith for the sake of obedience to the whole counsel of God. It represents, therefore, a real merging of the horizons of the Biblical text and the horizons of our historical context. Neither our understanding of Scripture nor our understanding of our concrete situation is adequate unless both of them constantly interact and are mutually corrected.[164]

Thus the hermeneutical process has increasingly come to be understood by those on the evangelical left as a two-stage process in which first the concrete historical situation is assessed in terms of Marxist analysis and then the perspective revealed by this analysis is used to reinterpret Scripture and to find, for example, "its abundant but often ignored teaching on the poor."[165]

"Cognitive Bargaining" and the Evangelical Left's Theological Case against Capitalism

The evangelical left's attempted modification of orthodoxy illustrates a process that sociologist Peter Berger has called "cognitive bargaining," a process in which competing understandings of reality come to terms with each other by means of a kind of negotiated exchange.[166] In this case, the competing understandings of reality have been provided by Christianity on the one hand and Marxism on the other. The chief point at issue is whether human reality ultimately transcends this world, as Christians have traditionally maintained, or does not, as the Marxists argue. The two understandings are good candidates for the bargaining process for at least two reasons. First, Marxist thought continues to be very influential in the intellectual academic arenas that evangelicals have been trying to reenter in recent years. Second, Christianity and Marxism, while mutually exclusive on a number of crucial points, are still similar enough—for example, in their linear conceptions of history and in their denunciation of oppression and concern for human liberation—that some sort of synthesis ought arguably to be possible between them.

164. Padilla, "Liberation Theology," in *The Challenge of Marxist and Neo-Marxist Ideologies for Christian Scholarship,* ed. John C. Vander Stelt (Sioux Center, IA: Dordt College Press, 1982), pp. 96, 101.

165. Scott, *Bring Forth Justice,* p. 242. Scott suggests that such a procedure, called "reading through the eyes of the poor," will reveal a number of things that evangelicals, blinded by ideology, have overlooked for many years.

166. See Berger, *The Heretical Imperative: Contemporary Possibilities of Religious Affirmation* (Garden City, NY: Doubleday-Anchor, 1980), pp. 90ff.

Initially (and this is still true to a large extent) the evangelical left managed to hold the two conflicting understandings apart, adopting an ahistorical version of Marxist socioeconomic analysis and linking it to certain biblical propositions. But the historical, philosophical, and eschatological elements of Marxism that ultimately account for its tremendous mythopoetic appeal in the modern world[167] have apparently begun to influence the evangelical left's understanding of orthodoxy more significantly, as they themselves acknowledge. While those on the evangelical left have not yet gone as far in this direction as the various theologians of liberation have, it would appear to be only a matter of time before they do so. There is a clear tendency among them to link theological categories to economics, for example. They have increasingly centered their theological anthropology, their notion of evil and of the human condition, and their views of salvation, history, eschatology, and other crucial theological concepts in the economic life. James Davison Hunter has described this trend, using Weberian terminology, as "a shift in varying degrees from other-worldly interests to inner-worldly interests; from the transcendent to the immanent."[168] Evangelical philosopher Bernard Zylstra has referred to the process as "immanentization."

> By *immanentization* I mean the absorption of the God of the Bible—Father, Son, and Holy Spirit—and of His transcendent Word or law into the realm of human culture. Within this realm, *human creativity* is identified with deity; and the goals of *human willing* take the place of the Word and will of God. This immanentization of the transcendent components of the religion of the Bible entails a radically new conception of what is described as creation in the Scriptures. Creation becomes *nature,* not in the classical Greek sense in which nature is the source of *limits* to human action ("natural law"), but in the modern sense, in which nature is the *object for the self-realization of the deified human will.*[169]

Though characterizing modern thought generally, Zylstra argues that this process of immanentization had been epitomized in Marxism—in the very intellectual tradition, in other words, with which the left would have the larger evangelical community come to terms.

We might say, then, that in exchange for Marxism's dynamic and attractive model for understanding social reality, and also for recognition from the liberal intellectual community and hence a claim to relevance in the modern situation, the evangelical left has begun to negotiate away some of the elements of traditional orthodoxy more offensive to secular theorists—especially orthodoxy's insistence that the kingdom of God radically transcends "this-

167. On the mythopoetic appeal of Marxism, see Lesek Kolakowski, *Main Currents of Marxism: Its Origin, Growth, and Dissolution,* vol. 3 (Oxford: Clarendon Press, 1978), pp. 525-26.

168. Hunter, *Evangelicalism: The Coming Generation* (Chicago: University of Chicago Press, 1987), p. 48.

169. Zylstra, "Marxism and Education: Some Observations," in *The Challenge of Marxist and Neo-Marxist Ideologies for Christian Scholarship,* p. 246.

worldly" reality and hence radically relativizes the present sociopolitical situation. Traditional orthodoxy's "exclusivistic" view of redemption and its understanding of salvation as requiring the conscious acknowledgment and confession of Jesus Christ as Lord appear to have been brought to the bargaining table as well. While having to forfeit radical atheism and a strict dialectical materialism, those on the secular side of the exchange have apparently been in a stronger bargaining position and have gained a degree of religious legitimation for Marxism that it could never have succeeded in generating for itself.

The Evangelical Left and Capitalism: Concluding Remarks

The case the evangelical left makes against capitalism is impressive. Indeed, it is quite compelling, as all of the various elements of the argument, which is at times quite complex, eventually fall into place within a simple and eminently plausible scheme depicting an ongoing conflict between oppressors and oppressed. Yet in spite of the argument's elegance, the left's denunciation of capitalism is surprisingly "uneconomic." In fact, it might be described as "anti-economic" in the sense that those on the left not only refuse to think economically but condemn capitalist culture precisely for its preoccupation with economics.

The left's case against capitalism is also quite abstract. Many of the argument's crucial concepts—for example, "oppression," "poverty," and "justice"—remain largely undefined, and Western readers are asked simply to suspend critical and empirical judgment and accept responsibility for oppression by means of the notions of "implication" and "complicity." The true nature of capitalism, it is asserted, is confirmed only by the experience of those who have an epistemological privilege to such knowledge, and Western readers must take the word of the poor and oppressed on these matters, or at least the word of those who have learned to identify correctly with the poor and oppressed. In addition, the left's case is constructed in such a way that it is virtually impossible to object to it without automatically becoming guilty of ideological captivity. According to the left, capitalism is oppressive by definition, and assertions to the contrary simply confirm its corrosive ability to continually generate self-legitimating ideologies.

Finally, it should be noted that the theological case that those on the evangelical left make against capitalism, where so much of their rhetorical energy is focused, essentially collapses if their basic assumptions about the way capitalism actually functions are refuted. The left assumes that in the capitalist political economy virtually all social power is concentrated in the hands of a tiny business elite and that the rest of society, including what is ostensibly a democratic polity, is manipulated to the advantage of this elite. Not surprisingly, then, it is precisely this assumption to which those on the evangelical right take exception.

CHAPTER TWO

In Defense of Capitalism: The Evangelical Right

While the evangelical left links a great many of the world's problems to the existence of capitalism, an evangelical right reacts by insisting that capitalism offers the only real hope of solving these problems. Not only has capitalism provided for the economic liberation of modern humanity, those on this evangelical right argue, but the market economy has also formed the foundation for the political and cultural liberation of modern societies. In this chapter we will explore the positions of those evangelicals who have recently come to capitalism's defense.

Just as the sole criterion for my inclusion of persons and groups on the evangelical left is their predominantly negative assessment of modern capitalism, so the persons and groups I categorize as belonging on the right are those who have made a largely positive assessment of it. Specifically, I will be reviewing the opinions of older conservative neo-evangelicals such as Harold Lindsell and various contributors to *Christian Economics;* neofundamentalists such as Jerry Falwell and the editors of the *Fundamentalist Journal;* younger neo-evangelical authors such as Ronald H. Nash, John Jefferson Davis, Franky Schaeffer, Herbert Schlossberg, and E. Calvin Beisner; conservative evangelical economists such as Peter J. Hill and Brian Griffiths;[1] and the advocates of what has been called "theonomy" or "Christian reconstruction." By placing these groups together under the heading "evangelical right" I do not mean to suggest anything beyond the fact that they are economically conservative and tend to take a rather dim view of the proposals that have been offered by the evangelical left. Indeed, to an even greater extent than on the left, those on the evangelical right have significant differences of opinion among themselves

---

1. While Griffiths is not an American evangelical, his work—especially *The Creation of Wealth: A Christian's Case for Capitalism* (Downers Grove, IL: InterVarsity Press, 1984)—has been published and widely read in North America, and so I have included it in this discussion.

on a number of theological and cultural issues. The evangelical right, in other words, is more of a coalition than a movement as such.

The Nature of Capitalism and Free Enterprise

The evangelical right's understanding of capitalism may be summarized briefly as follows: capitalism, understood as a system of production by private producers for a market, represents an extraordinarily efficient method of producing wealth, and it has transformed the world largely for the better.[2] While it is not a perfect economic system, capitalism has drawn unfair and dangerous criticism from certain quarters—unfair because the critics of capitalism have misunderstood and misrepresented it, and dangerous because the alternatives that these critics have proposed, all calling for more political intervention in the economy, are potentially disastrous. Since the critics of capitalism level charges against it in the areas of economics, politics, and culture, the evangelical right's defense of capitalism tends to focus on these three areas as well.

2. Like the evangelical left, the evangelical right has relied heavily on nonevangelical sources for its understanding of the nature of modern capitalism and contemporary culture. While the evangelical right's defense of capitalism has stood generally in the tradition of classical liberalism, it has shown definite affinities to the three strands of recent American conservatism identified by George H. Nash in *The Conservative Intellectual Movement in America since 1945* (New York: Basic Books, 1976): libertarianism, anticommunism, and traditionalism. In the libertarian vein, representatives of the so-called "Austrian school" of economics have been particularly influential on the evangelical right. Austrian school works commonly cited by those on the right include Ludwig Von Mises' *Human Action: A Treatise on Economics* (1949), *The Free and Prosperous Commonwealth* (1962), and *Socialism: An Economic and Sociological Analysis* (1922); Friedrich Hayeck's *The Road to Serfdom* (1944); and Wilhelm Ropke's *A Humane Economy: The Social Framework of the Free Market* (1960). The Austrian school position has been popularized in America by groups such as the Foundation for Economic Education (Irvington-on-Hudson, New York) and in books such as Henry Hazlitt's *Economics in One Lesson* (1979). In addition, Joseph A. Schumpeter's classic *Capitalism, Socialism, and Democracy* (1950) has often been cited by those on the evangelical right, as have Milton Friedman's *Capitalism and Freedom* (1962) and *Free to Choose* (1979), the latter cowritten with Rose Friedman. P. T. Bauer's works *Dissent on Development* (1972), *Equality, the Third World, and Economic Delusion* (1981), and *Reality and Rhetoric: Studies in the Economics of Development* (1984) have also been particularly crucial to the right's understanding of Third World development issues. Antistatist/anticommunist authors such as Albert Jay Nock (*Our Enemy the State* [1983]) and James Burnham (*The Suicide of the West* [1964]) have been popular on the evangelical right, and neoconservative authors have provided the evangelical right with a good deal of ammunition in their battle with the left on the issue of the decadence of contemporary liberal culture. See, e.g., Eduard Banfield's *The Unheavenly City Revisited* (1974), Charles Murray's *Losing Ground: American Social Policy: 1950-1980* (1981), Thomas Sowell's *Race and Economics* (1975), George Gilder's *Wealth and Poverty* (1981), Michael Novak's *The Spirit of Democratic Capitalism* (1982), and, most recently, Peter L. Berger's *The Capitalist Revolution* (1986).

Capitalist Economics

As indicated in Chapter 1, the evangelical left's basic criticism of capitalism
is that it represents a comprehensive sociopolitical-economic system in which
a small business elite exploits and oppresses the majority of people in modern
societies. Strenuously objecting to this characterization, those on the evangelical right respond to it in several ways. First, they insist that capitalism is not
a comprehensive system at all. There is much more to social life than the
economic, they argue, and while capitalism does represent the institutionalization of economic relationships, it must be considered in conjunction with
other primary social institutions (e.g., the state, the church, the family) insofar
as social problems are concerned. The market system is not, Peter J. Hill has
argued, an institutional order capable of offering meaning and purpose in life.[3]
Those on the right contend to the contrary that the market system is simply
one of a number of institutions that together constitute the social order.

Those on the evangelical right also insist that by equating the profit motive
with greed, the critics of capitalism confuse human selfishness with legitimate
self-interest and as a result entirely misunderstand how capitalism actually
functions. Precisely what constitutes legitimate self-interest is, of course, a
matter of some debate. At one extreme Brian Griffiths has argued, following
Bernard of Clairvaux, that self-interest is ultimately legitimate only when it is
an expression of the "love of self for God's sake."[4] Somewhat less idealisti-
cally, however, he has also suggested that, while the notion of profit is a
technical accounting concept, the motivation toward profit is basic to human
rationality.[5] At what might be said to be the other extreme, profit has been
defended as the appropriate reward for satisfying the desires of consumers,
whatever those desires might be.[6] Theonomist Gary North, for example, has
argued in *The Freeman* that every person has the "right to become rich, if he
chooses and if he has the ability to do so in competitive markets." There will

3. Hill, "An Analysis of the Market Economy: Strengths, Weaknesses, and the Future,"
Transformation 4 (June-September/October-December 1987): 41.

4. Griffiths, *The Creation of Wealth*, p. 68.

5. Griffiths, *The Creation of Wealth*, pp. 64ff. Similarly, Paul Heyne has written, "I
believe that 'capitalism' is simply a pejorative synonym for 'economy,' and that capitalism
consequently cannot be rejected without simultaneously repudiating the basis of contemporary life. Christians who want to reject capitalism ought to know what else they are rejecting
at the same time: the coordination of complex cooperative activities in the only way they
can be coordinated [i.e., rationally]. The cost would not just be the loss of some luxuries; it
would be famine, disease, and a new dark age as the communities of science, literature, and
art disintegrated right along with the institutions that provide our 'necessaries and con-
veniences'" ("Christianity and 'the Economy,'" *This World* 20 [Winter 1988]: 38).

6. See Tom Rose, *Economics: Principles and Policy from a Christian Perspective*, 2nd
ed. (Mercer, PA: American Enterprise Publications, 1986), pp. 176-77.

always be an "apex" or political-economic elite, North argues, and so the crucial political-economic question is simply how one is allowed to achieve this apex.[7] Along similar lines, those on the evangelical right commonly argue that it is fundamentally mistaken to imagine that greed and human selfishness are somehow more crucial to capitalism than to capitalism's reasonable alternatives. "Greed and human selfishness," Harold Lindsell has suggested, "are part of the human given, constituting a weak link in the chain of life and conduct. Therefore the question must be asked which of the two systems, socialism or free enterprise, is more likely to prove beneficial to the greater number of people? In this regard free enterprise is far and away the better economic system to contain human greed."[8]

Far from creating or encouraging greed and selfishness, which they hold to be problematic in any situation, those on the right contend that capitalism has actually managed to contain greed and selfishness better than its alternatives and that it has channeled this potentially harmful behavior toward the social good.[9] Stated positively, those on the evangelical right hold that capitalism is best characterized as a system of voluntary economic exchange in which both producers and consumers are enabled to satisfy their legitimate self-interests in a peaceful fashion,[10] and indeed in a manner that actually "encourages respect for other human beings."[11] By way of contrast, those on the evangelical right view socialism as a system of "violent economic exchange" in which the state forcibly determines and mandates economic activity.[12]

Those on the evangelical right also dispute the left's charge that capitalism benefits only a tiny business elite. Clearly capitalism benefits some more than others, but those on the right reason that a degree of inequality characterizes all societies and that some inequality is a small price to pay for economic freedom. More specifically, those on the right argue that, on the demand side, capitalism is a system singularly oriented toward the need of the average consumer.[13] In fact, the free-market economy has been the only system to permit "consumer sovereignty,"[14] a concept those on the right cite in contrast

7. North, "Trickle-Down Economics," *The Freeman* 32 (May 1982): 280, 276.

8. Lindsell, *Free Enterprise: A Judeo-Christian Defense* (Wheaton, IL: Tyndale House, 1982), p. 21.

9. See Ronald H. Nash, *Poverty and Wealth: The Christian Debate over Capitalism* (Westchester, IL: Crossway Books, 1986), pp. 72ff.

10. Nash, *Poverty and Wealth,* p. 66.

11. Ronald H. Nash, "The Christian Choice between Capitalism and Socialism," in *Liberation Theology,* ed. Ronald H. Nash (Milford, MI: Mott Media, 1984), p. 61.

12. Nash, *Poverty and Wealth,* p. 63.

13. Rose, *Economics: Principles and Policy,* p. 277.

14. Rose, *Economics: Principles and Policy,* p. 178. The notion of "consumer sovereignty" assumes that demand cannot be created or manipulated as the evangelical left has maintained. In this regard, the evangelical right has commonly defended advertising as

to the left's suggestion that producers dominate consumers in capitalist societies. On the supply side, furthermore, capitalism is acclaimed for providing
unequaled opportunities for the economic advancement of all classes. Evangelical economist James D. Gwartney recently stated that "capitalism provides
opportunity for achievers of all socio-economic backgrounds to move up the
economic ladder. It is no coincidence that poor people around the world flow
toward capitalist countries rather than away from them. Poor Mexican laborers
risk their lives for work opportunities in the U.S. In Europe, the Soviets built
a wall to keep people from the capitalist West. In Southeast Asia, people are
drawn to Hong Kong, Taiwan, Thailand, and other capitalist countries. Why?
Because capitalism provides opportunity for those who want to achieve."[15]

Regarding the left's insistence that capitalism is oppressive, those on the
evangelical right maintain that this is simply not the case. Capitalism is a
system in which wealth is efficiently created, not stolen. In fact, far from being
the cause of poverty, capitalism has been largely responsible for the ameliora-
tion of a great deal of poverty in the modern period.[16] And while relative
poverty remains something of a problem even in capitalist societies, hindering
productivity by attempting to regulate the economy politically would not help
the poor; in all likelihood it would make matters worse for them. E. Calvin
Beisner has suggested that "The inescapable conclusion of a competent analysis of the factors determining economic value and price is that permitting
markets to function freely (without coercion, either governmental or private,
by fraud, theft, or violence) results in prices and availabilities of goods and
services that are most beneficial to the most people in society, particularly to
those most in need and least able to pay for the satisfaction of their needs and
to defend themselves against fraud, theft, and violence: the poor."[17]

In accusing capitalism of oppression, those on the evangelical right argue,
the critics make several fundamental mistakes. First, they take productivity for
granted and fail to appreciate the historical novelty of the market system's
ability, made possible by the mechanism of price, to coordinate economic
activity efficiently.[18] With reference to the evangelical left's position, Herbert
Schlossberg has written that "The one-sided focus on poverty makes it seem

---

an important channel for the distribution of product information to consumers. See Ronald H.
Nash, *Freedom, Justice, and the State* (Lanham, MD: University Press of America, 1980),
p. 173.

15. Gwartney, "A Christian Speaks up for Capitalism," *The Freeman* 36 (August 1986):
284-85.

16. Hill, "An Analysis of the Market Economy," p. 41.

17. Beisner, *Prosperity and Poverty: The Compassionate Use of Resources in a World
of Scarcity,* Turning Point Christian Worldview Series, no. 5, ed. Marvin Olasky (Westchester,
IL: Crossway Books, 1988), p. 119.

18. Hill, "An Analysis of the Market Economy," p. 42.

as if economic health is as natural as breathing, and that if it is not there we have to find out which lever to push to set things right. It makes it seem as if wealth is just lying around to be picked up, and that if it is not distributed in the way that we like, all we have to do is redistribute it."[19]

On the other hand, those on the right also contend that the left's oppression argument rests on faulty "neo-Malthusian" premises concerning the availability of resources.[20] While certain resources may indeed be scarce, the right tends to be optimistic about modern technology's potential for generating new ways to use whatever resources are available.[21] In addition, Brian Griffiths and others have asserted that the wealth of the developed West must be credited more to efficiency of production techniques than to the consumption of resources.[22] And those on the right argue that to insist that capitalism is oppressive is to mistakenly employ the Marxist assumption that economic value is primarily a function of labor and hence that relative inequality is explicable only in terms of exploitation. Not only is this labor theory of value mistaken, Tom Rose has written, but it is one of the chief culprits in "worldwide industrial conflict" and political unrest.[23] By way of contrast to the labor theory of value, many of those on the evangelical right and especially those influenced by Austrian school economists insist that economic value is actually a function of imputation in which economic goods become valuable simply as they become desirable within the entire framework of economic activity.[24] Percy L. Greaves

19. Schlossberg, "A Response to Nicholas Wolterstorff," *Transformation* 4 (June-September/October-December 1987): 21. "The key question, then, when confronted by the disparity between rich and poor individuals and societies," Beisner has suggested, "is 'How did this man, or this society, become rich?' It is not 'How did this man, or this society, become poor?' Poverty is the natural condition of mankind, a condition from which some have risen from time to time, from which many have yet to rise, and into which many will fall back if they ignore, misunderstand, or fail to apply the causes of wealth" (*Prosperity and Poverty,* p. 194).

20. See Schlossberg, "Imperatives for Economic Development," in *Freedom, Justice, and Hope: Toward a Strategy for the Poor and Oppressed,* ed. Marvin Olasky (Westchester, IL: Crossway Books, 1988), pp. 99-117.

21. See John Jefferson Davis, "Profits and Pollution," *The Freeman* 32 (June 1982): 323-31.

22. Griffiths, *The Creation of Wealth,* p. 23.

23. Rose, *Economics: Principles and Policy,* p. 98.

24. This is perhaps especially true of Ronald Nash, who devotes an entire chapter of *Poverty and Wealth* (pp. 33ff.) to the theory of subjective economic value as developed by the Austrian school. Similarly, Tom Rose has written that "it wasn't until economists in the latter 19th century [viz., the Austrian School] discovered that value exists only in the mind . . . that the mystery of how man chooses began to be unveiled" (*Economics,* p. 21). Interestingly, the subjective theory of value has obviated the need for the defenders of the market to show that such things as "market equilibrium" and "perfect competition" are actually possible. Instead, it has been suggested that since human subjectivity and evaluation are constantly changing, the market becomes necessary as the only mechanism capable of responding efficiently to such changes.

explained some years ago that "No one can make a profit or receive an income in a free society unless he contributes something which his fellow men consider an improvement over previous circumstances. No one in a free economy, operating in accordance with Christian principles, can become rich unless he raises the standards of the poor. In such an economy, no man becomes rich by oppressing another but rather by helping others. That some become rich means that others become less poor."[25] More recently, Ronald Nash has written,

> the myth about exploitation lends support to a related claim that often functions as a ground for rejections of capitalism. Capitalism is denounced because of the mistaken belief that market exchanges are examples of what is called a zero-sum game. . . . On the contrary, market exchanges illustrate what is called a positive-sum game. A positive-sum game is one in which both players may win. . . . In voluntary economic exchanges, both parties may leave the exchanges in better economic shape than would otherwise have been the case. Both parties to a voluntary exchange believe that they gain through the trade. If they did not perceive the exchange as beneficial, they would not continue to take part in it.[26]

Whereas capitalism's critics insist that monopoly and a relatively high rate of unemployment are intrinsic to the capitalistic process, those on the evangelical right argue that while such things as monopoly and unemployment are serious problems in modern societies, they are not the product of capitalism per se. Instead, authors such as Herbert Schlossberg have suggested that monopolies commonly result from the attempts of big businesses, often in collusion with the state, to avoid competition, and Schlossberg has advocated stiff enforcement of antitrust legislation as a solution.[27] As far as unemployment is concerned, Brian Griffiths has argued that while some level of unemployment is probably unavoidable in a market system, declining productivity combined with wage inflation, minimum wage and other benefit requirements, and the disincentives to employment created by government welfare programs have created a situation in which it is simply unfair to blame all unemployment on capitalism.[28]

Along similar lines, those on the evangelical right insist that capitalism cannot be blamed for poverty and underdevelopment in the Third World. The

25. Greaves, "Economic Equality," *Christian Economics* 5 (27 January 1953): 3.
26. Nash, *Poverty and Wealth*, pp. 71-72.
27. Schlossberg, *Idols for Destruction: Christian Faith and Its Confrontation with American Society* (Nashville: Thomas Nelson, 1983), pp. 111ff.; see also Marvin N. Olasky, "Unholy Alliance," *Eternity* 36 (June 1985): 19-23. Apart from Schlossberg and Olasky, however, few others on the evangelical right have suggested that large corporations are responsible for manipulating the political process to their own advantage. Most of those on the right are either silent on this point or imply that businesses cannot be blamed for taking advantage of the opportunities for monopoly created for them by the state.
28. Griffiths, *The Creation of Wealth*, pp. 84ff.

charge that Western development has come at the expense of the Third World, Brian Griffiths has maintained, is almost completely untrue.[29] Nor does neo-colonialist rhetoric adequately explain the Third World's present predicament, say those on the right; the poverty of Third World nations can be attributed primarily to internal factors such as political instability, population growth, and cultural patterns that inhibit successful business enterprise.[30] For the evangelical left to continue to propose redistributive solutions to Third World poverty, those on the right insist, simply indicates their fundamental misunderstanding of the problem and "totally distorts and undermines a Christian perspective on global poverty."[31] Insofar as the left's harsh criticism of multinational corporations is concerned, those on the evangelical right contend that only increased productive capacity will ultimately be able to solve global poverty problems, and multinational corporations may well be the most effective means by which such capacity is created in the Third World.[32] Multinational profits have not been exorbitant, those on the right argue,[33] and in any event they are justified on the grounds that they induce corporations to transfer vital capital and skill from the First to the Third World.

But this is not to say that all those on the evangelical right support capitalism unreservedly. While those on the far right do tend to imply, in a manner quite similar to the left's appraisal of socialism, that capitalism's present difficulties stem from its not having been properly implemented as yet, most of those on the right are willing to admit (albeit begrudgingly) that capitalism has its problems. The economists tend to be most acutely aware of such problems. P. J. Hill, for example, has assessed the weaknesses of the market system as follows: (1) relative poverty and unequal income distribution pose problems for market economies; (2) private property rights are subject to abuse,[34] and prosperity has a tendency to become an end in and of itself;

29. Griffiths, *Morality and the Market Place: Christian Alternatives to Capitalism and Socialism* (London: Hodder & Stoughton, 1982), p. 130.

30. See Griffiths, *Morality and the Market Place,* p. 138. See also Nash, *Poverty and Wealth,* pp. 184ff.; and John Jefferson Davis, *Your Wealth in God's World: Does the Bible Support the Free Market?* (Phillipsburg, NJ: Presbyterian & Reformed, 1984), p. 33. Those on the evangelical right commonly cite the work of P. T. Bauer in this regard.

31. Griffiths, *Morality and the Market Place,* p. 136.

32. Griffiths, *Morality and the Market Place,* p. 150; see also Lindsell, *Free Enterprise,* p. 23.

33. Griffiths, *Morality and the Market Place,* p. 131; see also Lindsell, *Free Enterprise,* p. 86.

34. On the subject of the abuses of private property, it should be noted that those on the right, including Hill, commonly suggest that public ownership often results in similar if not worse abuses. In "The Christian and Creation" (*Chronicles* 12 [February 1988]: 19-25), for example, Hill argues that federal mismanagement of forest lands in the Western U.S. has resulted in unnecessary resource depletion and wastage. "It is common ownership—bureaucratic ownership," Gary North has contended in a more extreme fashion, "which

(3) because the market mechanism is largely impersonal and abstract, it needs to be balanced with more personal structures, such as family, church, and community; and (4) the market's inability to value certain public goods probably necessitates some degree of public intervention.[35] In a recent work entitled *The Samaritan Strategy*, Colonel Doner, an early organizer of the Moral Majority, even speaks out against multinational enterprise. "Around the globe," writes Doner, "large American corporations aggressively exploit Third World nations by either taking unfair advantage of local labor or by keeping in power reprehensible dictatorships that safeguard a handsome return on American corporate investments."[36]

Capitalism and Politics

As far as the relation of capitalism to politics is concerned, those on the evangelical right reject the suggestion that a small business elite somehow dominates the political process and directs the political agenda toward the maximization of its own profit at the expense of the public good. Indeed, those on the right argue that capitalism and the private ownership of productive resources work strenuously to prevent the collusion of economic and political power. Capitalism promotes peaceful and voluntary social interaction, they argue, and the private ownership of property permitted within the market system provides an important defense against the agglomeration of power and the best line of defense against inappropriate uses of political power.[37] P. J. Hill has asserted that "it is difficult to overemphasize the importance of private property rights and individual freedom of choice in furthering workers' control over their own lives. The right to use one's capital and labor in the manner that one wishes means that numerous options are available, ranging from self-employment to working for a large corporate entity. . . . It is the removal of that right that is at the basis of much worker exploitation in Communist countries."[38]

---

creates most of the economic incentives to pollute and exploit the environment" ("Pollution Control and Biblical Justice," *The Freeman* 36 [September 1986]: 338). Similarly, Ronald Nash has argued that because a system of private ownership permits costs to be borne by property owners, it encourages the responsible use of resources (*Poverty and Wealth*, pp. 78ff.)

35. See Hill, "An Analysis of the Market Economy."

36. Colonel V. Doner, *The Samaritan Strategy: A New Agenda for Christian Activism* (Brentwood, TN: Wolgemuth & Hyatt, 1988), p. 82.

37. Doner, *The Samaritan Strategy*, p. 44.

38. Hill, "Appropriate Intervention in a Market System: A Critique of the Literature," paper prepared for a conference entitled "Biblical Perspectives on a Mixed Market Economy," 18-20 September 1987, Wheaton College, Wheaton, IL.

In a similar vein, James Gwartney has suggested that it is the capitalist society, a society in which the demands of all consumers are taken into account in the marketplace, that provides for the expression of minority viewpoints most generously.[39] Since evangelicals are themselves a minority in most modern societies, writes Gwartney, they should appreciate the merits of the market environment if only for this reason. In addition, those on the right contend that capitalism actually eases social tensions by minimizing the need for collective decision making in the highly pluralistic modern setting.[40]

Thus while the evangelical left contends that capitalism is incompatible with freedom and democracy, those on the evangelical right insist that the economic freedom permitted by capitalism has formed the foundation for personal and political liberty, and hence for democracy.[41] "A market economy," Ronald Nash has written, "begins by assuming a system of human rights such as the right to make decisions and the right to hold and exchange property."[42] Similarly, Franky Schaeffer has asserted that "civil and religious freedom, progress, and the preservation of human rights are inextricably linked with economic freedom, with the right to own property, and with a minimum of state interference in economic affairs."[43]

Far from being dominated by a business elite, those on the right insist, modern governments tend to be controlled instead by bureaucratic political elites that are largely unaccountable to the electorate and that have grown increasingly hostile to business activity. While moderates on the right tend to view such hostility as a natural feature of bureaucracy, those on the far right have suspected a conspiracy. Gary North, for example, has stated that "by abandoning the free market, consumers transfer a portion of their sovereignty as economic actors to the elite corps of bureaucrats who exercise monopolistic power as officials of the civil government. . . . *The 'amateur' politician, who may be out of office after the next election, is no match for the entrenched power of the Civil-Service-protected lifetime career bureaucrat.*"[44] Thus just as the evangelical left contends that modern capitalism has made democracy something of an illusion, those on the evangelical right contend that the bureaucratization of political life has had a similar result. At least business activity is held in check by consumer sovereignty and competition, say those on the right, but the activities of the welfare-state

39. Gwartney, "A Christian Speaks up for Capitalism," p. 285.
40. See Hill, "An Analysis of the Market Economy," p. 42.
41. See, e.g., Jake Barnett, *Wealth and Wisdom: A Biblical Perspective on Possessions* (Colorado Springs: Navpress, 1987), p. 60.
42. Nash, *Freedom, Justice, and the State,* p. 131.
43. Schaeffer, in the introduction to *Is Capitalism Christian?* ed. Franky Schaeffer (Westchester, IL: Crossway Books, 1985), p. xvii.
44. North, "Trickle-Down Economics," pp. 277-78.

bureaucracy are not subject to the same kind of self-regulating constraints and so tend to be irresponsible.

Capitalism, Culture, and Social Change

On the relation of capitalism to culture, those on the evangelical right tend to be just as concerned about decadence in the modern situation as those on the left, albeit, as one might expect, for entirely different reasons. Contemporary decadence is not the fault of capitalism, they insist; rather, the prevailing intellectual climate of materialism and secularism has led to the failure of other primary social institutions, such as the church, to provide adequate standards and values. Indeed, those on the right insist that most of the economic problems with which the evangelical left is concerned stem from this intellectual and ultimately spiritual failure. They argue that moral and ethical behavior is not the result of proper economic relationships, as the left implies, but is instead presupposed by such relationships. "What transpires in the market," Ronald Nash has suggested, "will be as moral or immoral as the human beings who are active in the market."[45] Similarly, Herbert Schlossberg has predicted that "if Europe and North America continue departing from the faith that built their civilization, they will also continue the [economic] decline that is already under way." Describing the connection between morality and economic health, Schlossberg goes on to say,

> it is a world in which there is [a] tremendous abundance of resources that can be tapped only by the application of hard work and intelligence. But it is also a world in which the ethical and spiritual dimensions are far more central to economic well-being than the various materialisms understand; in which economic life is closely allied with culture, so that the lack of certain moral and spiritual attributes ensures the failure of economic performance; and in which institutions that try to exact production by means of force, rather than allowing the citizens to keep the fruit of their efforts, are condemned to futility.[46]

The moral and spiritual attributes to which Schlossberg refers are those of conservative Protestantism, and those on the evangelical right commonly defend modern capitalism on the grounds that it is a product of Christian (read *Protestant*) civilization. While authors such as Brian Griffiths have recognized that the connection between Protestantism and capitalism is not one of simple causality, others have been much less reluctant to equate economic prosperity with the influence of Protestantism.[47] "Nations that have been significantly

45. Nash, *Social Justice and the Christian Church* (Milford, MI: Mott Media, 1983), p. 57.
46. Schlossberg, "A Response to Nicholas Wolterstorff," p. 25.
47. Griffiths, *The Creation of Wealth,* p. 27. Those who see a stronger connnection than

influenced by biblical teaching, such as the lands of the Protestant Reformation," John J. Davis has noted, for example, "have tended to be more prosperous than nations such as India."[48] And Harold Lindsell has gone so far as to
suggest that to denounce capitalism is essentially to denounce the "Judeo-
Christian tradition."[49]

Given their assumption that cultural and economic well-being presupposes
moral and spiritual vitality, it is not at all surprising that those on the evangelical
right do not perceive social change primarily in sociostructural terms. Instead,
they insist that the solutions to contemporary social and economic problems
require the moral and spiritual renewal of individuals, a renewal necessitating
the task of evangelism.[50] Brian Griffiths has written, for example,

> Christianity starts with faith in Christ and it finishes with service in the world.
> Although not its object, it is nevertheless, its inevitable consequence. Because of
> this I believe that evangelism has an indispensable part to play in the establishment
> of a more just economic order. . . . I believe that more than anything else this is
> what people the world over are looking for. It will not be found in either capitalism
> or Marxism but only through humility and obedience to Christ. But having found
> it in the most personal and intimate of all encounters, the most remarkable thing
> is that it is relevant to the social, political, and economic problems even of the
> late twentieth century.[51]

The Case against Statism

While those on the evangelical left say that they do not advocate a planned
economy so much as a middle path between capitalism and socialism, those
on the evangelical right argue that no such middle path is possible. Following
Ludwig Von Mises, authors such as Ronald Nash have argued that a "mixed

Griffiths does often cite Max Weber's "Protestant ethic" hypothesis. See, e.g., Irving E.
Howard, "Christianity: Parent of Modern Capitalism," in *Christian Economics,* 17 May 1966,
p. 4. Interestingly, those who refer to Weber generally fail to see the irony in Weber's
analysis—i.e., that while capitalism may indeed have resulted from the Protestant ethic, it
was at best an unintended result. Indeed, in a recent paper entitled "The Cultural Roots of
Economic Development" presented at the "Oxford Conference on Christian Faith and
Economics," Oxford, 3-9 January 1990, Herbert Schlossberg argues that Japan's spectacular
economic success in recent years has been due to the influence of Christianity on Japanese
culture. "Surprisingly," says Schlossberg, "given the lack of widespread acceptance of Christianity in Japan, Western influence there was to a large extent Christian influence."

48. Davis, *Your Wealth in God's World,* p. 22.
49. Lindsell, *Free Enterprise,* p. 36.
50. See Davis, *Your Wealth in God's World,* p. 71; see also A. Robert Hemmingson,
"The American Economic System in the Light of Christian Teachings," *Journal of the
American Scientific Affiliation* 13 (March 1961): 10-11.
51. Griffiths, *Morality and the Market Place,* pp. 154-55.

economy," in which only part of the economy is state-regulated, is inherently unstable and must necessarily tend toward increased state intervention until such intervention is total.[52] For this reason, those on the right generally view the left's position as a de facto advocacy of statism. "The interventionist literature makes several caveats to the dangers of concentrated government power," P. J. Hill has noted, "but those seem to be simply a form of obligatory recognition that government is not always a beneficent force. When it comes time to make policy proposals little reference is made to the possibility that government action will achieve anything other than the stated goals."[53] The evangelical right, in other words, tends to feel that however much those on the left may object to being characterized as socialists, they are socialists nonetheless, or at least statists.

And socialist economies, those on the right have insisted, simply do not work. They are economically inefficient, they have tended to be politically totalitarian, and they have often been culturally repressive as well. Tom Rose has asserted that "history shows—to those who are willing to read her lessons—that societies which use the agency of government as a vehicle for redistributing wealth embark on the road to social upheaval and certain ruin."[54] Along these lines, those on the right argue that the evangelical left is simply not empirical enough in its analysis, that it arrives at its conclusions and policy prescriptions after simplistically comparing real capitalism with ideal socialism. In comparing capitalism to socialism, Brian Griffiths has warned, "It is vital that . . . fact should be compared with fact, and ideal with ideal. It is wrong to judge the facts of capitalism with the ideals of socialism, much as it is wrong to judge the facts about socialism with the ideals of capitalism."[55] Similarly, Franky Schaeffer has stated that

> No economic plan, solution, or type of political arrangement will ever be perfect. Yet, having accepted man's fallen state as the only natural limit to the possibilities of man's creativity, we must then look about us and decide on the basis of evidence, not ideology, what economic systems presently and realistically available best provide for the needs of most people. Not just in one area, but in all areas, from free speech to the price of oatmeal. From the diversity represented in art galleries and movie theaters to the state of farm technology. From the freedom of worship of the most obscure sect to individual mobility.[56]

52. Nash, "The Christian Choice between Capitalism and Socialism," p. 59; see also Nash, *Poverty and Wealth,* pp. 115ff.

53. Hill, "Appropriate Intervention in a Market System," pp. 18-19.

54. Rose, "Anarchy: Fruit of Government 'Charity,'" *Christian Economics* 23 (May 1971): 5.

55. Griffiths, *The Creation of Wealth,* p. 89.

56. Schaeffer, *Is Capitalism Christian?* p. xxvii.

Of course it is true that many on the evangelical right violate this principle by contrasting the facts of socialism with the ideals of capitalism. This is especially true of those on the far right, who, like Rose, equate socialism with certain ruin. Indeed, they are disinclined to say anything positive about existing socialism or about the potential social and economic role of the state in Western democracies.

As to why they believe socialism does not and cannot work, those on the evangelical right offer two kinds of reasoning, the first having to do with socialist economics per se and the second having to do with the economic requirements of the socialist polity. Socialist economics focuses almost entirely on the redistribution of existing wealth, those on the right argue, and it neglects any consideration of how wealth is produced. It fails to appreciate the nature of what motivates people to produce things as well as the amount of information necessary for people to make reasonable decisions as to what to produce.[57] Some critics have characterized redistributive economic policies as essentially a form of legalized theft.[58] Others charge that at the very least such policies discourage potential producers from taking the entrepreneurial risks necessary for successful economic enterprise.[59] Moreover, these policies encourage consumers to wait for the state to provide for their needs, thus reducing their incentives to work and save: "Men will not do things for themselves or for others if they once believe that such things can come without exertion on their own part. There is not sufficient motive."[60] Second, those on the right contend that in the absence of the market's price signals, there is no effective way for producers and consumers to communicate.[61] While socialist economies appear to substitute planning for the market, it is argued, in fact they have to rely on the price information generated by capitalist economies.[62]

Those on the right are not at all surprised that socialist societies have been politically repressive, given the socialist state's need to plan and manage the economic activities of its citizens.[63] It is precisely because economics has been collapsed into politics in such societies, they say, that producers and consumers have been forced to cope with political as well as economic uncertainty, and political uncertainties have ultimately been much more paralyzing than those of the marketplace.[64]

57. Nash, *Freedom, Justice, and the State,* p. 63.
58. See, e.g., Schlossberg, *Idols for Destruction,* p. 118.
59. See, e.g., Griffiths, *The Creation of Wealth,* p. 32.
60. David Chilton, *Productive Christians in an Age of Guilt Manipulators* (Tyler, TX: Institute for Christian Economics, 1981), p. 51.
61. See Nash, *Poverty and Wealth,* pp. 82ff. Here again, Nash has relied on Von Mises' *Socialism: An Economic and Sociological Analysis.*
62. See Nash, *Poverty and Wealth,* p. 84.
63. See Schlossberg, *Idols for Destruction,* pp. 188ff.
64. Griffiths, *The Creation of Wealth,* pp. 32ff.

In addition, those on the evangelical right have commonly argued that the harmful legacy of statist policy is painfully evident in the United States at present. Ronald Nash has gone so far as to assert that "the economy of the United States is interventionist, not capitalist."[65] The right suggests that this has been the case at least since the New Deal programs of the 1930s, and especially since the Great Society programs of the 1960s. Yet those on the right insist that it was interventionist policy that caused the Great Depression[66] and that has been largely responsible for the problem of contemporary poverty. Indeed, they argue that government intervention in the economy almost always has negative effects.[67] Interventionism commonly creates the very monopoly situations with which those on the left are so concerned.[68] Interventionism also interferes with the information function of the market and so reduces productivity and efficiency.[69] In addition, the two chief instruments of intervention in the United States—fiscal and monetary policy—have actually exacerbated inflation and unemployment. While taxation is manifestly redistributive, those on the right commonly argue that expansionary monetary policy has a similar effect in that the inflation it causes is essentially redistributive.[70] Nor are such policies equitable: the burdens they produce fall most heavily on the middle class. "In a *modern welfare State*," Gary North has written, "there is only one class with sufficient resources to pay for all of the government programs: *the middle-class.*"[71]

In addition, those on the right are averse to statist economic policy because they feel that most of the money redistributed by the state is either wasted or actually serves to perpetuate the problems it is meant to solve. In America this problem is evident to some extent in the Social Security system but more egregiously in federal welfare programs, which they say have in effect created and sustained an entire culture of poverty.[72] "Centralized government welfare . . . is a bumbling, fumbling, uncoordinated monster," George Grant has ar-

65. Nash, *Poverty and Wealth,* p. 62.

66. Nash, for example, devotes chaps. 12 and 13 of *Poverty and Wealth* to a consideration of the Great Depression, insisting that interventionist economic policies were the chief culprit in this period of economic downturn. See also Davis, *Your Wealth in God's World,* pp. 92-93.

67. See Lindsell, *Free Enterprise,* p. 105.

68. See Nash, "The Christian Choice," p. 55; Rose, *Economics,* p. 348; and Davis, *Your Wealth in God's World,* pp. 89-92.

69. Nash, "The Christian Choice," p. 56.

70. See Griffiths, *The Creation of Wealth,* p. 17; and Schlossberg, *Idols for Destruction,* p. 98. See also Beisner, *Prosperity and Poverty,* pp. 121ff.

71. North, "Trickle-Down Economics," p. 273.

72. Ronald Nash devotes an entire chapter in *Poverty and Wealth* to discussing Social Security, calling it "an elaborate pyramid scheme in which late joiners are forcibly taxed to meet the cost of benefits assigned to earlier joiners." For criticism of federal welfare programs, see John Eidsmoe, *God and Caesar: Christian Faith and Political Action* (Westchester, IL: Crossway, 1984), pp. 91ff.; and Doner, *The Samaritan Strategy,* p. 141.

gued. "It blunders its way along, splintering families, crushing incentive, decimating pride, and foiling productivity. It naturally falls into the traps of blatant mismanagement, fiscal irresponsibility, and misapportioned authority."[73] Similarly, Larry Burkett recently commented that "when society tries to make up for previous wrongs by providing government welfare, the result will be permanent dependence and poverty. With the best of intentions, our welfare system traps people at the lowest economic level by indiscriminate giving."[74] The only real beneficiaries of welfare programs, insist those on the right, are the bureaucrats who administer them.[75] "It pays to serve the poor," Ronald Nash has suggested, "under the aegis of the liberal state."[76]

Those on the right express fears that despite all these problems, statism is on the rise, and it is threatening the future of the market system.[77] "It is discouraging to know," Harold Lindsell has written, "that the free enterprise system will be interfered with and strangulated by government intervention in the near future."[78] Along this line the right sees capitalism in the midst of a crisis of moral legitimacy.[79] It appears unable to defend itself against the heightened material expectations it has created,[80] and it simply does not have the same quasireligious appeal as socialism.[81] And the combination of capitalism's crisis of legitimacy with the inexorable growth of the welfare state creates a dilemma. "From the point of view of social and economic policy," Brian Griffiths has stated, "I believe we face a choice: *either* we accept the present trends which will lead inevitably to a decline in individual freedom and responsibility and the restriction of opportunities for our children and grandchildren, *or else* we face the seemingly impossible task of dismantling the corporate [i.e., welfare] state. This is not an attempt to return to a nineteenth-century form of laissez-faire but to change the structures of our society in a direction more consonant with our Christian principles."[82]

73. Grant, *In the Shadow of Plenty: Biblical Principles of Welfare and Poverty,* Biblical Blueprint Series, no. 4 (Fort Worth: Dominion, 1986), p. 76.

74. Burkett, "Is Welfare Scriptural?" *Fundamentalist Journal* 4 (April 1985): 22. See also Judy Hammersmark, "Grandmother Was a Capitalist," *Fundamentalist Journal* 4 (September 1985): 32-33.

75. See Nash, *Poverty and Wealth*, p. 177; and Davis, *Your Wealth in God's World*, p. 59.

76. Nash, "The Economics of Justice: A Conservative's View," *Christianity Today*, 23 March 1979, p. 29. Welfare and other "programs are necessary to the statist," Nash says in *Freedom, Justice, and the State*, "not as a means of aiding the poor, but as a means to his possession of power; and that is what the Liberal State is all about" (p. 67).

77. See Hill, "An Analysis of the Market Economy," p. 47.

78. Lindsell, *Free Enterprise*, p. 112.

79. Griffiths, *Morality and the Market Place*, p. 20.

80. Davis, *Your Wealth in God's World*, pp. 87ff.

81. Hill, "An Analysis of the Market Economy," p. 47.

82. Griffiths, *Morality and the Market Place*, p. 124.

Policy Prescriptions on the Evangelical Right

We have seen that those on the evangelical left are less than specific about policy prescription, and those on the evangelical right tend to be vague in this area as well. Whereas the left focuses almost exclusively on questions of distribution, the right focuses largely on issues of production. Curiously, while the policies proposed by those on the right are very nearly the opposite of those proposed on the left, both contend that support for their respective proposals will need to be generated at the grass-roots level and will probably encounter stiff resistance from the political and cultural elites.[83]

Just as one might expect, the evangelical right generally supports policies aimed at reducing the size and scope of the welfare state and opposes policies that enhance state power. In terms of social welfare, Ronald Nash has summarized the right's view of the problem as follows: "America has been spending more than enough money on poverty, [but] it has not spent that money very wisely."[84] For this reason those on the evangelical right commonly advocate such things as welfare reform and the restructuring of the Social Security system. While conceding that federal subsidies appear to be necessary in the cases of Social Security and welfare, those on the right feel that such subsidies should be administered much more directly and efficiently and, where possible, in such a way as to permit maximum individual choice. Most importantly, federal assistance should not be handled in such a way as to discourage welfare recipients from working. In this regard, those on the evangelical right often cite proposals such as Milton Friedman's "negative income tax" as a feasible alternative to the current system of welfare provision.[85] It has also been suggested that Social Security ought to be administered as a true insurance program and that as much of the program as possible should be privatized and eliminated from the federal budget.[86] Those on the right also argue against using progressive income taxation and inflationary monetary policy as methods for funding federal subsidies such as welfare and Social Security on the grounds that they jeopardize the continued creation of wealth by reducing the incentives to invest and produce. John J. Davis has suggested, for example, that "During the last several years it has become increasingly clear that American tax policies have discouraged the degree of savings and investment necessary to create new jobs and increase productivity. . . . Lagging

---

83. On the need for grass-roots involvement, see George Grant, *The Changing of the Guard: Biblical Principles for Political Action*, Biblical Blueprint Series, no. 8 (Fort Worth: Dominion, 1987), pp. 145ff.

84. Nash, *Poverty and Wealth*, p. 177.

85. For a description of this concept, see Friedman, *Capitalism and Freedom* (Chicago: University of Chicago Press, 1962), pp. 190-95.

86. Nash, *Poverty and Wealth*, p. 153.

American productivity has demonstrated that punitive attitudes toward wealth and its creation in the long run only serve to make society as a whole less prosperous."[87]

Some proposals have been more extreme, calling for the complete elimination of federally funded welfare and entitlement programs in favor of church- and community-based social services. "In order for us to fully implement the Biblical blueprint for charity," George Grant has written, "we must get the government *out* of the way. Government welfare is inefficient, unproductive, and destructive. . . . Government welfare, because it is *completely out of line* with God's plan and purpose, inevitably does *more harm than good.*"[88]

Specifically regarding domestic economic policy, the evangelical right consistently advocates the elimination of any impediment to a freely competitive market in the form of either public or private sector institutions. On the public side, the right opposes such things as minimum-wage legislation, rent control, wage and price controls, special industry subsidies and bail-outs, and the like.[89] On the private side, many of those on the right advocate vigorous antitrust legislation and the elimination of closed-shop unions.[90] In addition, those on the evangelical right tend to favor strictly limited monetary policy. Christian reconstructionists have even called for a return to the gold standard. "Debasement of currency is the practice of falsely increasing the money supply by cheapening the monetary unit," David Chilton has argued. "When private persons do this, it is called counterfeiting. When governments do this, it is called progressive monetary policy. The Bible calls it theft no matter who does it."[91]

On the question of international economic development, those on the evangelical right advocate market solutions to development problems. "The Third World does not need more socialism," Ronald Nash has written; "what it needs is more capitalism."[92] Working from this assumption, those on the right are critical of the no-growth mentality of many of those on the left. Such an attitude, they contend, can only harm those in the underdeveloped regions most in need of economic growth.[93] What the Third World needs, they argue, is quite the opposite of "no growth." "Churches can help alleviate Third World

87. Davis, *Your Wealth in God's World,* p. 47.

88. Grant, *In the Shadow of Plenty,* p. 135.

89. See Nash, *Poverty and Wealth,* pp. 114ff. See also Chilton, *Productive Christians in an Age of Guilt Manipulators,* p. 224; and Grant, *In the Shadow of Plenty,* p. 134.

90. See Griffiths, *Morality and the Market Place,* pp. 121ff. See also Chilton, *Productive Christians,* p. 388.

91. Chilton, *Productive Christians,* p. 380. See also Tom Rose and Robert M. Metcalf, "Inflation Is Immoral," *The Journal of Christian Reconstruction* 7 (Summer 1980): 31-39.

92. Nash, *Poverty and Wealth,* p. 198.

93. Davis, "Profits and Pollution," p. 331.

poverty in two distinct ways," Mark Amstutz has suggested: "first, they can respond in a humanitarian way to immediate human needs domestically and internationally; second, they can help establish the preconditions for long-term economic expansion. . . . [This] involves the sending of missionaries and volunteers to teach and to model practices and values essential to economic expansion. By seeking to model values such as organization, savings, planning, and rationality, Christian workers can contribute to the preconditions for job creation."[94]

In addition, and again in contradistinction to the left, Brian Griffiths and others have contended that multinational enterprise is crucial for Third World development and should be actively encouraged. While agreeing that multinational corporations should abide by the guidelines set by the United Nations, Griffiths has argued that the transfer of skills and capital made possible by multinational corporations is far superior to direct government aid, which is easily politicized and so tends to serve as a "tax levied on the poor in rich countries to subsidize the rich in poor countries."[95] He has even suggested that Christian missionary endeavors might be usefully integrated into multinational corporate activity.[96]

Assessing Capitalism's Critics

As we have seen, the evangelical left has a difficult time understanding how and why anyone would actually support what they consider to be the self-evidently exploitative and oppressive capitalist system. Those on the evangelical right face the same problem in reverse. Given their understanding of how capitalism performs economically, and of how socialism fails to perform, those on the right have concluded not only that capitalism is the best economic system in terms of efficiency but that it is the most just and moral system as well. Ronald Nash has asserted that "capitalism is quite simply the most moral system, the most effective system, and the most equitable system of economic exchange. When capitalism, the system of free economic exchange, is described fairly, there can be no question that it, rather than socialism, comes closer to matching the demands of the biblical ethic."[97] John J. Davis has

94. Amstutz, "The Churches and Third World Poverty," *Missiology* 17 (October 1989): 462; see also Mark R. Amstutz, "The Bishops and Third World Poverty," in *Prophetic Visions and Economic Realities: Protestants, Jews and Catholics Confront the Bishops' Letter on the Economy,* ed. Charles R. Strain (Grand Rapids: William B. Eerdmans, 1989), pp. 61-80.

95. Griffiths, *Morality and the Market Place,* p. 153; see also Nash, *Poverty and Wealth,* pp. 190ff.

96. Griffiths, *Morality and the Market Place,* p. 151.

97. Nash, "Does Capitalism Pass the Moral Test?" p. 43.

commented similarly that "basic biblical principles . . . point to the free market as the most desirable economic system."[98]

The question of why capitalism has attracted such harsh criticism has been a matter of great concern for those on the right, and they have produced three basic kinds of answers. Following economist Joseph Schumpeter, Brian Griffiths and others have suggested that capitalism fosters intellectual hostility ironically—in part because the apparently chaotic market mechanism begs to be planned, and in part because the modern intellectual enterprise, itself a product of modern capitalism, finds criticism of the status quo more marketable than a positive assessment of it.[99]

Next, those on the right contend that much of the contemporary hostility toward capitalism, especially that of the evangelical left, is the result of ignorance and misunderstanding. Many of capitalism's critics, in other words, may be well-intentioned but simply do not understand economics. "Leaders have emerged whose gullibility is made dangerous by their popularity," Franky Schaeffer has argued. "Though perhaps sincere in their Christian concern for the poor, Ronald Sider, Tony Campolo, Jim Wallis, and John Alexander, for example, have allowed their zeal for a socially conscientious gospel to lead them towards leftist dogma in one guise or another. Their common stock in trade is to nourish a kind of wallowing guilt and self-recrimination against the United States, capitalism, and prosperity."[100]

Part of this problem is attributed to critics wrongly blaming capitalism for what have in fact been the failures of interventionism. Another source of confusion, those on the right believe, is that the economic policy debate among evangelicals tends to proceed on a normative plane in spite of the fact that there is really very little disagreement about the ends the advocates of the various positions feel ought to be pursued, such as the elimination of poverty, the equitable distribution of resources, and so forth. Those on the right stress that the real issues concern differences of opinion over how best to reach these ends.[101] This is one of the reasons those on the right tend to be suspicious of the language of human rights: they hold that more often than not the moral and rhetorical force of this language is simply used to legitimate state intervention in social and economic affairs—intervention that in truth harms those whose rights are ostensibly being protected.

At another level, those on the evangelical right view the left's confusion as the natural result of secularization. Indeed, the central theme of Herbert

98. Davis, *Your Wealth in God's World,* p. 80.

99. See Nash, *Poverty and Wealth,* p. 124; and Griffiths, *Morality and the Market Place,* pp. 20ff.

100. Schaeffer, *Is Capitalism Christian?* p. xxii.

101. Nash, *Social Justice and the Christian Church,* p. 166; see also Hill, "An Analysis of the Market Economy," p. 40.

Schlossberg's recent book *Idols for Destruction* is "the displacement of the biblical faith that once informed Western Society by the Enlightenment faith."[102] Schlossberg catalogues the various idolatries (e.g., statism) that he believes have resulted from this displacement. Along these same lines, Ronald Nash has suggested that "a capitalism that is cut loose from traditional values is a capitalism that is headed for trouble. . . . The West's continued movement in the direction of secularism and humanism holds disturbing implications for economic life."[103] Similarly, Brian Griffiths has argued that secular humanism is at the root of the modern economic crisis: "However good the intentions it is possible in retrospect to see that the drift towards the modern corporatist state [i.e., the welfare state] has been dominated by secular humanism. The prevailing ethos today is that the state not the individual, is responsible for his welfare, that the erosion of private property rights and the control by the state of many areas of our lives is legitimate and welcome and that the distribution of wealth must take precedence over its creation."[104] Those on the right argue that secular humanism has produced an outlook that values material possessions as the greatest good.[105] Udo Middelman has suggested that this outlook is quite evident on the evangelical left as well: "By reducing poverty to the result of class conflict, and remedies to systems of redistribution, one caters to expectations of salvation in material structures."[106]

Statism, then, is viewed by those on the evangelical right as the natural outgrowth of secularism and, as Tom Rose has suggested, as "an indication that humanists are in a more prominent position of making policy recommendations than are Christians who recognize man's true nature."[107] Rose has argued that in the battle to determine whether the biblical or humanist vision will prevail in determining the contours of modern society, the crucial point at issue is "who shall have active control over the spending streams generated

102. Schlossberg, *Idols for Destruction*, p. 262; see also Lindsell, *Free Enterprise*, p. 24.

103. Nash, *Poverty and Wealth*, p. 199.

104. Griffiths, *Morality and the Market Place*, pp. 106-7.

105. Schlossberg, *Idols for Destruction*, p. 61.

106. Middelman, "A Response to Stephen Mott," *Transformation* 4 (June-September/October-December 1987): 40.

107. Rose, *Economics: Principles and Policy*, p. 41. In speaking of "man's true nature," Rose refers to what he has called man's "absolute moral depravity" (p. 40). He assumes that there is ultimately no basis for individual freedom and dignity in humanist thought and hence that all humanist aspirations are necessarily directed toward the deified state. According to humanist thought, he writes, "Man's first duty, indeed his whole duty, is to the state because the state is the source of law. . . . Man exists for the good of the state. . . . The end goal of government is to build an earthly utopia which is guided and directed by philosopher-king types" (pp. 78-79). See also Rose, *Economics: The American Economy from a Christian Perspective* (Mercer, PA: American Enterprise Publications, 1985), p. 144.

by the people's work and their private wealth? Will it be the people themselves as they freely go about ministering to each other's needs? Or will it be the elected politicians and their appointed bureaucrats who gain and hold control of people and property through a 'legally wielded' power to tax."[108]

The archetypical expression of modern secular humanism is Marxism. Brian Griffiths has asserted that "for modern secular Western man, severed from his cultural roots by the processes of industrialisation and secularisation, Marxism makes a real appeal. It offers the qualities of religion without rejecting any of the fixed points of modernity—science, progress, agnosticism."[109] Working from these sorts of assumptions, those on the evangelical right view attempts to synthesize Marxism and Christianity in the various theologies of liberation as nothing short of disastrous.[110] Atheism is not incidental to Marxism, they argue; it is essential to it. "Marxism and the Judeo-Christian faith," Harold Lindsell has stated, "are and ever must be antithetical."[111] Raymond C. Hundley has written that "far from being an attempt to affirm and refine orthodox Christianity, Liberation Theology is a premeditated attempt to destroy biblical faith and replace it with a secular humanist perspective based on Marxism which promotes violent revolution and the establishment of a socialist society as the primary tasks of the Christian Church."[112]

The revolutionary character of liberation theology, along with the faulty understanding of economics on which it is based, has created a situation that Ronald Nash has argued "is both tragic and ironic. It is tragic because they [liberation theologians] have rejected the one system that offers real economic hope for the masses they wish to assist. It is ironic because, in promoting the violent means of exchange, they have taken a path that will not only deny their people bread, but also deprive them of liberty. That such a movement should call itself 'liberation theology' truly is ironic."[113] That evangelical intellectuals are attracted to the various theologies of liberation is viewed by those on the right as a sobering development indeed. Such persons, they feel, are not only mistaken economically and theologically but also play unwittingly into the hands of whichever elite happens to control the state.[114]

108. Tom Rose, *Economics: The American Economy*, p. 51.

109. Griffiths, *Morality and the Market Place*, pp. 57-58.

110. A group called the National Citizens Action Network in Costa Mesa, California, recently published a special edition of its *Family Protection Scoreboard* (1989) stressing the dangers of liberation theology. The publication details the impact of liberation theology in such places as Nicaragua and South Africa, its impact on black and feminist theology in the United States, the connections between Marxism and Satanism, and so on.

111. Lindsell, *Free Enterprise*, p. 41.

112. Hundley, "Dangers of Liberation Theology," *Family Protection Scoreboard*, special ed. (Costa Mesa, CA: National Citizens Action Network, 1989), p. 7.

113. Nash, "The Christian Choice," p. 66.

114. See Nash, *Poverty and Wealth*, p. 157.

The third type of explanation those on the right offer for the existence of hostility to capitalism, similar to the left's explanation of the existence of support for capitalism, is that of ideology. They argue that the critics of capitalism oppose it either out of an acute sense of guilt or because such opposition legitimates the expansion of a welfare state in which they have a vested interest. As we have noted, some on the evangelical right claim that the only real beneficiaries of federal welfare programs are those who administer them. That publicly employed bureaucrats are critical of the market system, they argue, is to be expected. "Manipulation of economic matters by bureaucrats can lead only to disaster," Angus MacDonald has argued with some passion; ". . . they believe neither in God nor divine law. . . . They believe in themselves. They are filled with greed. They are lovers of power. They are content to live from the labor of others. They are talkers and deceivers in whom there is no truth but falsehood covered with sweetness."[115] And Colonel Doner has suggested more recently that "America is bankrupt because our intellectuals, our philosophers, our cultural trendsetters, are disillusioned with America—with themselves. Those who tell us what to think about, when, and how to think about it—who mold our culture through our universities and the media, who run think tanks founded by giant tax-exempt foundations, who provide the bureaucracy its intellectual capital—they are all tired and bewildered."[116]

Herbert Schlossberg's *Idols for Destruction* is perhaps the most articulate statement of the evangelical right's ideological analysis of left-liberal opposition to capitalism. Schlossberg draws on the New Class thesis to suggest that a "publicly employed middle class [currently] uses the redistribution process to despoil the privately employed middle class." He goes on to argue that "in the redistributory society, the main redistribution that takes place is the flow of power from the periphery [i.e., business] to the center [i.e., the state] where the new class awaits. The despoiled are the possessors of private power, against whom the elite still warn us, while they quietly accrue that power to themselves. But the former power was decentralized and to some extent self-neutralizing, because competitive. Power that is concentrated is to a much greater extent inescapable."[117] The process of redistribution is legitimated on the grounds capitalism is oppressive, and so has ostensibly been motivated out of concern for those who have been oppressed by it. But the real motivation behind the criticism of the market economy, Schlossberg contends, is envy, or *ressentement*. Quoting Max Scheler, Schlossberg argues that "the 'altruistic'

115. MacDonald, "God and Economics," *Christian Economics* 24 (December 1972): 27-28.
116. Doner, *Samaritan Strategy*, pp. 203-4.
117. Schlossberg, *Idols for Destruction*, pp. 110, 200. See also Davis, *Your Wealth in God's World*, p. 108.

urge is really a form of hatred, of self-hatred, *posing* as its opposite ('Love') in the false perspective of consciousness. In the same way, in ressentiment morality, love for 'the small,' the 'poor,' the 'weak,' and the 'oppressed' is really disguised hatred, repressed envy, and impulse to distract . . . directed against the opposite phenomena: 'wealth,' 'strength,' 'power.' "[118]

Those even more conservative take the New Class analysis several steps further and suggest that the bureaucratic elite currently dominating American public policy is self-consciously using guilt and envy to manipulate the electorate and accrue political power. "The political cultivation of guilt," Rousas John Rushdoony argues in *Politics of Guilt and Pity*, "is a central means to power, for guilty men are slaves; their conscience is in bondage, and hence they are easily made objects of control."[119] Similarly, in a volume entitled *Productive Christians in an Age of Guilt* (a response to Ronald Sider's *Rich Christians in an Age of Hunger*), David Chilton argues that "the captivity of the church is essential to the strategy of the statists. If the church can be persuaded to abandon its calling [in this context, presumably including its calling to defend capitalism], nothing on earth can prevent the domination of power-mad government."[120] In addition, George Grant has written that "ultimately the sinful men who dominate our society, those who have encumbered the poor with the bondage of welfarism, must be ousted from their places of influence and power."[121]

But however differently those on the evangelical right have understood and assessed capitalism's critics, they are united in suggesting that what is desperately needed at present is a recovery both of our ability to judge capitalism's performance objectively and of the Christian values that have made capitalism's remarkable economic performance possible. As Ronald Nash has put it,

> The poor and oppressed peoples of the world need the help of committed Christians who will become involved in social and political action. But what they really need is a new liberation theology that will recognize the irrelevance and falseness of socialist attacks upon capitalism, that will unmask the threats that socialism poses to liberty and economic recovery, and that will act to move existing economic institutions and practices closer to the principles of a free market system that alone offers the hope of economic progress.[122]

118. Schlossberg, *Idols for Destruction*, p. 53.
119. Rushdoony, *Politics of Guilt and Pity* (Fairfax, VA: Thoburn Press, 1978), p. 19.
120. Chilton, *Productive Christians*, p. 210.
121. Grant, *In the Shadow of Plenty*, pp. 132-33.
122. Nash, "The Christian Choice," p. 49.

The Biblical Case for Capitalism

As one might expect, all of those on the evangelical right insist that the Scriptures provide norms for the ordering of economic life. While moderates tend to argue that the Bible offers only general economic principles, however, those on the far right have contended that the Bible offers a virtual blueprint for the construction of political economy. Yet in spite of their differences of opinion as to the economic relevance of Scripture, those on the right are just as concerned as those on the evangelical left to ground their appraisals of capitalism biblically.

In organizing their biblical defense of capitalism, those on the evangelical right have argued, in the first instance, that Scripture in no way rules capitalism out. That those on the left have reached such a conclusion is simply an indication that their position only appears to be based on Scripture, that in fact its conclusions have been arrived at a priori along extrabiblical (e.g., Marxist) lines. For this reason, the evangelical right expends a great deal of theological energy refuting the interpretations the left attaches to certain Scriptural passages and reinterpreting these passages in such a way that they support capitalism instead of condemning it. Ronald Nash, for example, has suggested that "one of the more surprising things about the current interest in finding biblical passages that support a collectivist ideology is this: while people exhibit great ingenuity in discovering hitherto unrecognized implications in ambiguous Old Testament passages, hardly anyone bothers to look at several clear texts in the New Testament."[123] He then cites 2 Thessalonians 3:6ff. as an example: "if anyone will not work . . . let him not eat." The implication here, of course, is not only that such passages support capitalism but that they are neglected by those on the left for just that reason.

In spite of the fact that the word is used in the Old Testament, those on the right argue that "oppression" is not a biblical-theological category.[124] In addition, those on the right contend that it is a mistake to view such things as the exodus of Israel from Egypt as paradigmatic for socioeconomic liberation.[125] The exodus, they argue, was an event in which God fulfilled a specific promise to the nation of Israel. And while God certainly cares for the weak and helpless, he is not "on the side of the poor and oppressed" in the sense that he perverts justice in their favor.[126] Furthermore, the Jubilee legislation could not have been intended as a scheme for expropriating the rich, for that

123. Nash, *Social Justice and the Christian Church,* p. 78.
124. See Harold O. J. Brown, "What is Liberation Theology? A Hermeneutical Battlefield," in *Liberation Theology,* p. 10.
125. Middelman, "A Response to Stephen Mott," p. 37.
126. Davis, *Your Wealth in God's World,* p. 31.

would contradict the eighth commandment, which prohibits theft and expressly legitimates private ownership. Instead, as John J. Davis has argued, the Jubilee was intended to "safeguard equal *opportunity* for Israelites to earn income without destroying the *incentives* to work and invest through normal economic activities."[127] "The major objectives of this system," Brian Griffiths has written, referring to the Jubilee, "were to guarantee the individual a measure of economic security and to insure that each family was not permanently debarred from participating in the economic life of the nation through temporary misfortune."[128]

Those on the right also object to the left's use of the prophetic literature. "The prophets," Herbert Schlossberg has argued, "were concerned neither about social analysis as such, nor about the issues of relative incomes that are the preoccupation of so much governmental and academic analysis; but rather about the ethical lapses that took place in their societies and the impact of those lapses on the innocent."[129] Similarly, Pierre Berthoud has contended that "to read Amos as an attack on the wealthy or a call for class warfare is not only superficial, but wrong and perverse: It is turning God's message of compassion into a sermon of hatred."[130]

As far as Jesus' teaching on economic matters is concerned, those on the evangelical right argue that it has been almost completely distorted by those on the left. It is impossible, Brian Griffiths has asserted, "to deduce any economic system from Jesus' teaching on the Kingdom."[131] In addition, Jesus' announcement in Luke 4:18 of God's desire that he "preach good news to the poor" does not imply, as those on the left argue, that Jesus viewed his mission primarily in sociopolitical terms. Instead, those on the right insist that the poverty spoken of in this passage is spiritual poverty and that Jesus' mission was "to give us spiritual sight and to end our spiritual poverty by making available the righteousness that God demands and that only God can provide."[132] And while they admit that wealth can be an obstacle to one's entrance into the kingdom of God, those on the evangelical right contend that Jesus never said that there was anything intrinsically wrong with private ownership.[133] Jesus condemned the "improper acquisition and use of wealth" but not

127. Davis, *Your Wealth in God's World,* p. 41; see also Lindsell, *Free Enterprise,* p. 57; and Beisner, *Prosperity and Poverty,* pp. 57ff.

128. Griffiths, *Morality and the Market Place,* p. 84.

129. Schlossberg, "A Response to Nicholas Wolterstorff," p. 20; see also Griffiths, *The Creation of Wealth,* p. 60.

130. Berthoud, "Prophet and Covenant," in *Freedom, Justice, and Hope,* p. 39.

131. Griffiths, *The Creation of Wealth,* p. 63.

132. Nash, *Poverty and Wealth,* p. 170.

133. See Griffiths, *Morality and the Market Place,* p. 87; and *The Creation of Wealth,* pp. 43ff. See also Nash, *Poverty and Wealth,* pp. 163ff.

the mere possession of it.[134] "There is no socialism and no equalitarianism," Harold Lindsell has stated, "in [the] words of Jesus."[135]

Indeed, those on the right feel that many of Jesus' parables actually support the free enterprise system.[136] Ronald Nash has suggested that "those who draw attention only to passages in which Jesus indicted prosperous people are presenting only a part of His teaching. Jesus also praised those who through wise management and careful stewardship created wealth. We must avoid the temptation of selecting a few passages from the Gospels and attempting to show that Jesus' views conformed to our preferred opinions and lifestyle. Jesus' teaching about money, wealth, and poverty is extremely diverse."[137]

Those on the evangelical right also question the left's insistence that the early church's communalism is somehow normative for the life of the contemporary church. The communalism described in Acts 4 and 5, they insist, was only temporary; while it should encourage gracious generosity, it was not made mandatory by the apostles for the other first-century churches, and hence it is not mandatory for the church today.[138]

There are any number of examples of the evangelical right's objections to the left's abuse of Scripture, which is itself somewhat telling. It appears that the exegetical agenda has been set largely by those on the left and hence that the evangelical right has been forced to spend most of its energies refuting the left's interpretations and far less developing a positive biblical case for capitalism. When those on the right do defend capitalism biblically, however, they almost always do so with reference to the creation. For example, it is argued that because man is created "after God's image" (Gen. 1:26), the capacity to create wealth is basic to human nature. "This God-given ability to create and to see new possibilities for products, services, and labor-saving devices lies at the very heart of a strong and growing economy," John J. Davis has suggested. "Economic productivity that can produce a better quality of life for all is not just a matter of discovering new deposits of iron, coal, oil, and other physical resources, but is primarily a matter of new ideas, new insights, new leaps of the human imagination."[139] Similarly, Brian Griffiths has written,

> we bear an integral relationship to the material world and it is because of this that the business of creating and using wealth is a natural activity for mankind. Life itself demands that we be continually involved in the process of wealth creation.

134. Nash, *Poverty and Wealth,* p. 164.
135. Lindsell, *Free Enterprise,* p. 60.
136. See, e.g., *Free Enterprise,* p. 61.
137. Nash, *Poverty and Wealth,* p. 164.
138. See Davis, *Your Wealth in God's World,* p. 20. See also Griffiths, *Morality and the Market Place,* p. 89.
139. Davis, *Your Wealth in God's World,* pp. 4-5. See also Rose, *Economics: Principles and Policy,* pp. 99-100.

The basic necessities for living are not provided like manna; the land has to be cultivated, the sea has to be harvested, minerals have to be extracted, the city has to be supplied with services. God created us with the capacity and the desire to do all these things. Life itself, therefore, demands that we use what God has given us to provide the necessities.[140]

Furthermore, those on the right argue that God's command to have dominion over the earth (Gen. 1:28) reflects his economic expectations of humanity. While the evangelical left believes that this passage mandates collective dominion, those on the evangelical right interpret it individualistically.[141] They contend that responsible human dominion of the earth requires the private and individual ownership of resources. "The Scriptures call all people to assume personal responsibility for their own lives and circumstances," John J. Davis has insisted, "rather than depend on government for their basic needs."[142] Those on the right contend that private ownership, which necessarily implies some degree of economic freedom, has naturally given rise to market-oriented economic systems, and such systems in turn have fostered and encouraged individual responsibility.[143]

Still, those on the evangelical right do not want to suggest that the rights associated with private ownership are absolute. Rather, they maintain that these rights are limited by the concept of stewardship, which they define as the responsible use of resources by individuals in a manner that best serves the objectives of the kingdom of God.[144] Summarizing the biblical teaching about wealth and possessions, Ronald Nash has written,

> Christians should remember that whatever they have, they possess it temporarily as a steward of God. They should share with those less fortunate than themselves; they should practice economic justice, encourage economic justice on the part of others, and seek to correct instances of economic injustice. But none of this implies that Christians are to shun money and wealth as necessary evils. In spite of the dangers that accompany money and wealth, Christians are called to create wealth and then make certain that they use it in ways that are consistent with their other Christian obligations.[145]

140. Griffiths, *The Creation of Wealth,* pp. 60-61.
141. It should be noted that not all of those on the right are happy with this emphasis on individualism. Jake Barnett has suggested, for example, that "perhaps the greatest weakness within capitalism is the tendency toward excessive individualism. If this is true, Christians need to apply the biblical teaching on community to counteract this tendency. Individualism, coupled with economic freedom, provides the opportunities for exploitation and injustice" (*Wealth and Wisdom,* p. 305). See also Griffiths, *The Creation of Wealth,* pp. 80ff.
142. Davis, *Your Wealth in God's World,* p. 35.
143. Davis, *Your Wealth in God's World,* p. 77.
144. Nash, *Poverty and Wealth,* p. 166.
145. Nash, *Poverty and Wealth,* p. 169.

Thus the ethic those on the evangelical right associate with stewardship might be termed an "ethic of production," in contrast to the "ethic of consumption," or the right to consume various things, that they suggest has been advocated on the evangelical left. They typically list such things as hard work, diligence, thrift, prudence, sobriety, and honesty as characteristic of this ethic of production. John J. Davis has written that the "New Testament virtue of diligence in work helped to undergird the economic development of the West. That same biblical virtue must be cultivated anew if the American economy is to remain competitive in our time."[146]

Those on the evangelical right are also united in insisting that Scripture mandates a strictly limited state. The fallen nature of man, P. J. Hill has argued, virtually ensures that concentrated political power will be abused.[147] Others cite the warnings about the dangers of kingship in 1 Samuel 8 and the limitations to state power implied in Romans 13.[148] Those on the right insist that the Bible limits the appropriate role of the state to such areas as national defense, the adjudication of disputes, the defense of private property, and the monitoring of certain public goods. "The worldly goal of civil government, from the Christian viewpoint," Tom Rose has suggested, "is not to build an earthly utopia, but only to establish a *workable justice* that will serve to restrain man's evil heart, on the one hand, and to free him from the evil inclinations of others, on the other, so that he can be free and self-responsible to his Creator and Lord."[149]

In terms of social welfare, while they are willing to admit that some kind of limited safety net is warranted in Scripture, those on the evangelical right are quick to point out that the biblical approach to welfare is largely voluntary and relies chiefly upon "moral suasion."[150] They note that love cannot be legislated or enforced.[151] And since its accumulation of various kinds of power (significantly, military power) has rendered the modern state an enormous and impersonal institution of coercion, it is misguided to suggest that it undertake errands of mercy. Indeed, say those on the right, people who argue that the state should be engaged in such activities have confused its responsibility for justice with the responsibility of individuals to love one another. They maintain that the prevailing statism of the age has apparently prevented many from recognizing this serious conceptual error. As Ronald Nash has put it, "when the evangelical liberal confuses love with justice, he is doing more than simply

146. Davis, *Your Wealth in God's World*, p. 11. See also Beisner, *Prosperity and Poverty*, pp. 78ff.

147. Hill, "An Analysis of the Market Economy," p. 44.

148. See, e.g., Davis, *Your Wealth in God's World*, p. 52.

149. Rose, *Economics: Principles and Policy*, p. 80.

150. See, e.g., Davis, *Your Wealth in God's World*, pp. 51-52.

151. Beisner, *Prosperity and Poverty*, p. 152.

urging others in his society to manifest a compassionate love for the needy. He is in effect demanding that the state get out its weapons and force people to fulfill the demands of love. And how does the state do this? The state does this by becoming an institutionalized Robin Hood . . . [stealing] primarily from innocent individuals whose only crime was some measure of success or good fortune in life."[152] And those on the right feel that the language of benefit rights only contributes to this confusion. They object to its use for the same reason the evangelical left has been drawn to it: its utility in generating support for redistributive social and economic policy. Such language, they feel, only serves to further empower the welfare and regulatory apparatus of the modern state.

From the perspective of the evangelical right, then, redistributive taxation is essentially theft and so is prohibited by the eight commandment. They believe that such things as wage and price controls also violate the spirit of this commandment.[153] For these and other reasons, many of those on the evangelical right have concluded that, from a biblical perspective, the redistributive welfare state is inherently immoral.

One of the chief reasons the welfare state has expanded so disastrously in recent years, those on the right insist, is that the church has neglected its social role. "Prior to the Great Depression of the 1930s," Larry Burkett has argued in the *Fundamentalist Journal,* "providing welfare was the function of the church. . . . The function of the government was to protect our freedom from external attack. . . . It was acknowledged that welfare was a responsibility of the church. The New Deal administration ended that principle once and for all in American politics. Once the government got involved in social programs . . . , welfare became a political tool."[154] While others (most often neo-evangelical conservatives) suggest that the social role of the church was lost somewhat earlier and actually began to be recovered during the late 1940s, all of those on the right stress that the church's social role desperately needs to be reclaimed today. It is not only that the church can deal more effectively with social problems than the state, they feel, but also that the reentry of the church into the social arena would serve to delegitimate the state's claims there. Larry Burkett has suggested that the church should handle "health and child care centers, vocational training centers, employment agencies, and the like, so that when faced with needs from the Christian or secular community, we could respond without relying on government 'help.' "[155]

On the other hand, those on the right have been careful to distinguish the

152. Nash, "The Economics of Justice," p. 27.
153. See, e.g., Beisner, *Prosperity and Poverty,* p. 174.
154. Burkett, "Is Welfare Scriptural?" p. 22.
155. Burkett, "Is Welfare Scriptural?" p. 23.

church's recovery of social concern from direct political involvement on the part of Christians, and especially the Christian advocacy of revolution. Brian Griffiths has argued, for example, that "in his specific concern with political issues such as industrial relations, fiscal policy, foreign affairs, education, welfare and so forth, the contribution of the Christian is not as a political revolutionary. This would be in outright contradiction of the life of our Lord as well as of the whole of biblical teaching. Based on the principle that we are to render to Caesar what is Caesar's, the distinctive contribution of the Christian will be that of a reformer, a proponent of gradual change, who seeks to alter and modify the system from within."[156]

Interestingly, many of those on the evangelical right tend to see themselves within the church in much the same way that those on the evangelical left see themselves: as a beleaguered minority. Herbert Schlossberg, for example, has stated,

> it is absurd that the name "Christian" should be taken by so many as synonymous with respectable, middle class, or conventional. It was first used to refer to *disciples* . . . and it was coined in the midst of persecution (Acts 11:26). Should we stop accommodating ourselves to the prevailing norms, we can expect to be treated in the same fashion. . . . If the ancient precedents are repeated, we can expect the new persecution of Christians to be led by the social and religious elite, in conjunction with the authorities of the state. . . . The state is never amused at being defied, and Christians who take their responsibilities seriously are not likely to remain within the pale of what its functionaries regard as socially responsible.[157]

The similarities between Schlossberg's perspective and that of radical evangelicalism are striking. Both the evangelical left and right, it seems, have become quite anxious about the power of the modern state. While those on the left equate the concentration of political power with the concentration of capital and hold that the state is controlled by business interests aligned with conservative church leaders, those on the right attribute the concentration of political power to bureaucratization and contend that the state is under the control of secular bureaucrats in conjunction with a social and religious elite.

The Defense of Capitalism and the Opposition to State Expansion

In their theological defense of capitalism, those on the evangelical right have produced three somewhat different approaches, each corresponding to an intellectual strand that has characterized American conservatism since 1945:

156. Griffiths, "Conclusion: The Christian Way," in *Is Revolution Change?* ed. Brian Griffiths (Downers Grove, IL: InterVarsity Press, 1972), pp. 109-10.

157. Schlossberg, *Idols for Destruction,* pp. 330-31.

anticommunism, libertarianism, and what might be called traditionalism, or the notion that contemporary culture, including capitalism, is the fruit of a long development and reflects basic human nature in such a way that it ought not be tampered with.[158]

Insofar as the anticommunist strand is concerned, it should be clear that many of those on the evangelical right defend capitalism principally as a means to the end of opposing the expansion of the state. This is particularly true of the neofundamentalists. While Jerry Falwell and his compatriots assume that capitalism has scriptural warrant, they have not been concerned to make a detailed theological case for it. Of course this may be simply because they have taken the value of capitalism for granted, but they may also have chosen not to do so because they are reluctant to attempt to fit the market economy into any sort of eschatological framework that is at all realizable. "Why did Paul not fight slavery?" asks Paul T. Meadows, an author critical of neo-evangelical social activism. "Why did he not attack Rome and its many inequalities between the royal and the working class? Because Paul had a greater task to perform and he was a realist concerning the post-lapse world. Jesus did not call Paul or present day Christians to a primary task of changing the world system, but to evangelize individuals, to teach them all the things He commanded, and to recognize that Satan is the 'god of this world' and that our only hope for ultimate political correction is Jesus' second advent."[159]

Clearly, if one views the prospects for "this world" as minimal at best, it will be difficult to generate a great deal of enthusiasm over issues of political economy. However evil the expansion of the state may be for those holding such views, the dispensational premillennial schema makes it difficult to hope that resistance, as expressed in various alternatives to state expansion (e.g., unencumbered free enterprise, church-sponsored voluntary welfare systems), will actually work. Ironically, then, while neofundamentalists are most commonly associated with the conservative defense of free enterprise, their theological defense of capitalism is actually much less developed than that of neo-evangelicals and others who have not inherited the culturally pessimistic understanding of dispensational premillennialism.[160] Colonel Doner's recent

158. These three intellectual strands are described in some detail by George H. Nash in *The Conservative Intellectual Movement in America since 1945* (New York: Basic Books, 1976).

159. Meadows, "John R. W. Stott on Social Action," *Grace Theological Journal* 1 (Fall 1980): 146.

160. Eschatology is notoriously vulnerable to ideological abuse. Thus, while the rise of dispensational premillennialism can be understood as an evangelical reaction to disestablishment from the centers of American culture during the early decades of this century, a "rediscovery" of postmillennialism might be expected to have accompanied the heightened cultural aspirations of American evangelicals in recent years. As neofundamentalist opposi-

book *The Samaritan Strategy* (1988) provides some indication that neofundamentalists have themselves begun to recognize this problem. The New
Christian Right failed, Doner argues, because it failed to develop a "Christian
worldview" and a clear and coherent understanding of culture.[161]

The Libertarian Defense of Capitalism

A more positive theological case for capitalism has been made along libertarian
lines. Many of the contributors to *Christian Economics* defended capitalism
in this manner in the 1950s and 1960s, and the libertarian case has been made
more recently by P. J. Hill, James D. Gwartney, Ronald Nash, George Roche,
and others. From the perspective of the evangelical libertarians, capitalism is
defensible on the basis of the context it has created for the exercise of individual
freedom. Their case rests on three basic assumptions: (1) freedom is essential
to humanity, (2) all human endeavors are plagued by the effects of original
sin, and (3) human actions are always undertaken in the context of limited
knowledge.

That libertarians value freedom is, of course, a commonplace. "The central
idea of capitalism," George Roche has written, "does not lie in the miracle of
the market or even in the ingenuity of the entrepreneur. It rests, rather, on the
fundamental principle of freedom. . . . It is here that the free market, private
property, private institutions—that whole private sector idea—has special
validity, because it does leave people free to build their own voluntary associations, to be uniquely self-transcending, to get on with the dignity of leading
their own lives."[162] Yet even while stressing the primacy of freedom, evangelical libertarians are quick to add that freedom makes responsibility before God
intelligible, and so it must be understood from within the sobering context of
God's judgment.

Evangelical libertarians also contend that the unavoidable reality of original sin makes it necessary to limit not only the power of the state but the
power of individual economic agents as well. "Deviations from the market
ideal," Ronald Nash has argued, apparently referring to situations calling for
government interference, "occur because of defects in human nature. This can
hardly come as news to Christians who are supposed to know about sin. Human
beings naturally crave security and guaranteed success, values not found

---

tion to the expansion of the welfare state builds—opposition that would be greatly aided by
the full eschatological legitimation of capitalism—perhaps there will be an increasing number
of "conversions" in the direction of postmillennialism.

161. Doner, *The Samaritan Strategy,* p. 37.

162. Roche, "Capitalism and the Future of America," *Imprimus,* special ed. (Hillsdale,
MI: Hillsdale College, 1988).

readily in a free market."[163] He goes on to suggest that the state should not pander to this craving after security and guaranteed success but should seek instead to maintain a truly competitive marketplace in which such sinful inclinations are effectively held in check.

In addition, evangelical libertarians insist that human behavior is so complex that the effects of radical social change simply cannot be anticipated except insofar as, given the assumption of original sin, they are more likely to be bad than good. Specifically with reference to economics, the libertarian assumption of limited knowledge suggests that economic planning is fraught with so many uncertainties that it is best left to individual economic agents, agents who are best acquainted with their own needs and who will suffer the consequences (or reap the rewards) of their own decisions. The assumption of limited knowledge also explains the retroactive and empirical approach that libertarians take with respect to the evaluation of economic policy. Since capitalism has historically permitted relatively free economic activity and also appears to have produced certain social benefits, the libertarians argue, it may therefore be assessed positively. "Christians would do well to settle for an economic system that reinforces Christian virtues, improves living standards, and provides for minority views," James D. Gwartney has suggested, and "capitalism is such a system."[164] Similarly, libertarians contend that redistributive policies should be judged not on the merits of their intended ends but on the basis of what they actually accomplish, and by such standards they are failures. Says Gwartney,

> it does seem clear that the structure of the current transfer policies in the United States is unscriptural. Current transfers encourage people not to work, while the Scriptures condemn idleness and honor work. Current policies undermine both voluntary charity and the family, the two major Scriptural defenses against poverty. Current policies oppress both the poor and the taxpayer. They make it extremely difficult for the poor to help themselves. Simultaneously, they take the fruit of the taxpayer's labor without providing a compensating good or service. Surely a God who despises oppression and values human freedom would disapprove of such policies.[165]

Of course, the libertarian assumption of limited knowledge is closely linked to the subjective theory of value mentioned above. Economic calculation, from this perspective, depends on the assessment of economic values, but such values are subjectively determined and hence subject to constant

163. Nash, "The Christian Choice," p. 55.
164. Gwartney, "A Christian Speaks Up for Capitalism," p. 285.
165. Gwartney, "Human Freedom and the Bible," a paper prepared for a conference entitled "Biblical Perspectives on a Mixed Market Economy," 18-20 September 1987, Wheaton College, Wheaton, IL.

change. For this reason, libertarians consider centralized economic planning impossible in principle as well as in practice; they believe that only the market mechanism, in which individual economic agents are allowed to express their determinations of value freely by means of price signals, can adequately keep pace with the unpredictable shifting of value determinations:

> Austrian economics takes as its starting point the behavior of people with incomplete knowledge, who have not only to "economize" in the situations in which they find themselves, but also to be on the alert for better opportunities "just around the corner." . . . From a "normative" point of view (of what policy should be), the adequacy of an economic system is judged not by the efficiency with which it allocates given resources at a point in time, but by the speed with which it discovers and responds to new opportunities over time.[166]

Similarly, P. J. Hill has written, "we do not know the future, nor is there a consensus about resource values. Therefore it is beneficial for a society to provide a mechanism for diverse preferences and projections about resource uses to be expressed. The private property system, based on individual decision making, expresses that diversity much better than a system of public ownership under collective decisions rule."[167]

The assumption of limited knowledge has important implications for the understanding of social justice as well. As mentioned above, Ronald Nash has argued that those on the evangelical left confuse the concept of social justice with the concept of love. Nash has contended that while this confusion is understandable given the fact that the biblical authors use the word *justice* in conjunction with such things as "love, charity, kindness to the poor, and help for the hungry," the left's use of the term is seriously mistaken nonetheless.[168] When those on the evangelical left speak of social justice, Nash has insisted, they do not refer to love and charity generally, but more specifically to a kind of distributive justice that has to do with the fairness of economic distribution and that requires the "necessary support and active intervention of a large, powerful and paternalistic state."[169] He has argued that distributive justice must be distinguished from commercial (or procedural) justice on the one hand, and from remedial justice on the other.[170] The problem with distributive justice is that those who would execute it must have a legitimate right to the goods being distributed, and they must also know specifically who has a legitimate right to receive these goods. While it may be possible to meet these conditions in

---

166. Stephen Littlechild, quoted by Nash in *Poverty and Wealth*, p. 46. Nash contrasts this position to that of mainstream neoclassical economics. Since neoclassical theory still assumes that value inheres, at least in part, in objects, it has been unable to show that economic planning is impossible in principle as well as in practice.

167. Hill, "The Christian and Creation," p. 24.

168. Nash, "The Economics of Justice," p. 30.

169. Nash, *Social Justice and the Christian Church*, p. 27.

170. Nash, "The Economics of Justice," p. 24.

certain limited situations, Nash has asserted, "a massive leap is required to get from the limited and controlled situations where considerations of distributive justice are obviously relevant to the unlimited and *spontaneous situations* found in society as a whole." And so he has argued that the chances that distributive justice can be accomplished on a society-wide basis are very slim indeed: "Liberal devotees to social justice fail to recognize how their theory enslaves them to the state. They overlook the massive threat the institution of the state poses to human liberty and values."[171] Far better, he has argued, for the state to focus on issues of commercial or procedural justice.[172] Similarly, E. Calvin Beisner has suggested that

> just as personal justice is individual conformity with the standards of rightness, so social justice is societal conformity with the standards of rightness. Understanding this should prevent our falling into the mistaken idea that social justice has something to do with a particular distribution of goods, privileges, or powers in society. Real social justice, on the contrary, attends only to the question whether goods, privileges, and powers are distributed in conformity with the standards of rightness. Whatever factual distribution results from conformity with those standards is just regardless how far it strays from conditional equality—the real idea behind many uses of the term *social justice* today.[173]

Finally, it should be noted that the assumptions of original sin and limited knowledge serve to attenuate any emphasis the evangelical libertarians place on the dominion mandate. While all of those on the evangelical right interpret this mandate individualistically, the libertarians take the most individualistic position. Consequently, libertarian evangelicals tend to hold a high view of providence and contend that it is not man's responsibility to bring order out of the seemingly chaotic market process, but God's. All of the evidence, they feel, suggests that this is well within God's capabilities. Indeed, they argue that this is precisely how God's providence is made manifest.[174] Those who advocate economic planning, Irving Howard wrote in *Christian Economics* in 1966, "refuse to accept the Christian doctrine of the providence of God. . . . To accept [this doctrine] . . . would give their whole case away for a Big Brother government."[175]

171. Nash, "The Economics of Justice," pp. 25, 26.

172. Interestingly, in his discussion of social justice, Nash understands the left's position to suggest that economic equality is the goal of "social justice." While this may be true in part, the left's understanding of the connection between economic equality and democracy is such that economic equality is not viewed as an end in itself but as a kind of minimum precondition for a kind of human freedom that does not yet exist.

173. Beisner, *Prosperity and Poverty,* p. 47.

174. See, e.g., Irving E. Howard, "Christian Approach to Economics," *Christianity Today,* 18 August 1958, p. 9.

175. Howard, "The Providence of God and Economics," *Christian Economics,* 22 February 1966, p. 4.

Capitalism as Natural Law

A number of those on the evangelical right also suggest that the market economy embodies a number of keen insights into the human condition. Indeed, some argue that capitalism is consonant with natural law and represents part of God's design for human society. Brian Griffiths has employed this kind of argument in what is perhaps its mildest form, simply suggesting that while capitalism is consistent with certain aspects of human nature, it still needs to be informed by a Christian view of justice. He has been critical of the purely libertarian position, arguing that "both the [in]justice and inhumanity of capitalist societies result inevitably from the failure to assert certain absolutes and so place proper limits on the use of freedom."[176]

Harold Lindsell takes the "capitalism as natural law" argument several steps further in *Free Enterprise: A Judeo-Christian Defense* (1982). "The case for free enterprise presented here is based on the authority of God mediated through his divine revelation to man in the Old and the New Testaments and is binding on all men everywhere. Because it [free enterprise] comes from God it is normative, it will work, and it will prove itself to be superior to socialism, which can only be validated by denying what God has revealed and can only function by destroying the foundations on which Western culture has been built."[177] He goes on to say that the "laws" of free enterprise are "writ large in the affairs of men by way of natural revelation" and so are actually empirically available.[178] "The observed social phenomenon we call the market system," Tom Rose has contended similarly, "is simply the natural outworking of God's design for man expressed in economic terms."[179] And John J. Davis has argued that "just as God providentially works through the laws of nature by which he has ordered the physical universe, so he also has established laws and principles for our social and economic life. The law of supply and demand, for example. . . . God has ordained basic economic principles just as surely as he has ordained the law of gravity, and we ignore such principles only at our own peril."[180]

Interestingly, proponents of this position seem to suggest that basic economic laws are so explicit and accessible that the economic task is simply to discover them and put them to use. E. Calvin Beisner, for example, has

---

176. Griffiths, *Morality and the Market Place,* p. 29.

177. Lindsell, *Free Enterprise,* p. 51.

178. Lindsell, *Free Enterprise,* p. 67; similarly, George Roche has insisted that "our message must not be that the free market is good because it works, but rather that it works because it is good—because it is the fundamentally proper view of human nature" ("Capitalism and the Future of America").

179. Rose, *Economics: Principles and Policy,* p. 224.

180. Davis, *Your Wealth in God's World,* p. 7.

urged us to "test numerous economic regulations . . . by the twin standards of Biblical justice and economic efficiency. These two standards always yield the same results because God made spiritual and material reality consistent with each other. Anything unjust is ultimately economically inefficient, and anything just is ultimately economically efficient (though it may appear otherwise in the short run)."[181]

Tom Rose has argued that only Christian civilization has really been able to uncover these great economic truths and profit from them. "Western man has found the secret of wresting an ever-increasing harvest from parsimonious mother earth. This secret has a twofold aspect: (1) The scientific discovery of preexistent cause-and-effect patterns (economic laws), and (2) The consistent subjection of man-made institutions within society to the rule of such laws. . . . It is my contention that without the shining light of the Gospel of Christ, Western man's mind would not have been enlightened, and Western nations would be as economically underdeveloped today as many non-Western nations are."[182] The Christian, Rose continues, is at a decided advantage in the current economic debate because the Bible is the ultimate compendium of these cause-and-effect economic laws. The truth, he insists, has not only made us free but has made us rich as well.

The "capitalism as natural law" argument has been taken to its logical conclusion by the so-called "theonomists"—advocates of what has been called "dominion theology" and/or "Christian reconstruction." In the view of this small but very prolific group, capitalism is not only in harmony with natural law[183] but is actually the vehicle of eschatological fulfillment. Indeed, capitalism is the economic system by which the faithful will be "blessed with increasing dominion over the earth," a blessing that will culminate in the return of Christ to earth.[184]

Formulated in response to liberation theology,[185] dominion theology specifies that the Bible embodies God's will for his faithful—in fact, that it provides blueprints for the proper structuring of every aspect of society—and that as

181. Beisner, *Prosperity and Poverty,* p. xiii.

182. Rose, *Economics: Principles and Policy,* pp. 34-36.

183. Gary North has stated, for example, that "Biblical Christianity can only lead to a society which is necessarily capitalistic" (*Inherit the Earth: Biblical Principles for Economics* [Fort Worth: Dominion, 1987], p. 134). See also Gary North, *The Sinai Strategy: Economics and the Ten Commandments* (Tyler, TX: Institute for Christian Economics, 1986), p. 11.

184. Chilton, *Productive Christians,* p. 378.

185. Speaking of *Liberating Planet Earth: An Introduction to Biblical Blueprints* (Fort Worth: Dominion, 1987), Gary North notes, "I originally wrote this book as an evangelical tool to be used primarily by Spanish-speaking Christians in their struggles against atheism, Communism, and the popular socialist religion known as liberation theology. . . . Marxism is the most consistent and powerful secular religion of all time; it can only be successfully challenged by an even more consistent and more powerful Biblical religion" (p. 1).

Christians come to a better understanding of the Bible they will progressively take dominion over nature and over society, a process that will eventually usher in the kingdom of God.[186] Theonomist Gary North has described four covenants outlined in Scripture, one personal and three institutional—ecclesiastical, civil, and family. "All other human institutions (business, educational, charitable, etc.) are . . . under the jurisdiction of these four covenants. . . . Christian people are required to take dominion over the earth by means of all these God-ordained institutions, not just the church, or just the state, or just the family. *The kingdom of God includes every human institution, and every aspect of life, for all of life is under God and is governed by His unchanging principles.*"[187]

In a manner strikingly similar to that of the radical evangelicals, the advocates of Christian reconstruction contend that their position simply represents the rediscovery of orthodoxy. "A growing minority of Christian activists," Gary North has suggested, "have at last begun to turn to the long abandoned theology that was the foundation of the Christian West until the late nineteenth century."[188] In a sense North is correct. Dominion theology does appear to stand in the tradition of postmillennial cultural optimism, a tradition that was quite strong in American Protestantism until the end of the nineteenth century. What sets dominion theology apart from this earlier tradition, however, is the highly rationalistic manner in which it approaches theology and salvation history and the fact that it understands the focus of the church's progressive cultural conquest to be primarily economic. In sociological terms, dominion theology represents the full rationalization of Christian

186. In an article entitled "Democracy as Heresy" (*Christianity Today*, 20 February 1987, pp. 17-23), Rodney Clapp notes that dominion theology was formulated in the early 1960s, and while there are only a handful of reconstructionist authors, they have produced an enormous amount of literature during the past twenty years. Uncertain about how many adherents the reconstructionists have, Clapp contends that they are to be found mostly among neopentecostal evangelicals and evangelicals connected with the Orthodox Presbyterian Church. Clapp also says that reconstructionism appears to be a mixture of Van Tilian presuppositional apologetics (i.e., the belief that there is no valid knowledge outside that contained in Scripture—see Cornelius Van Til, *A Christian Theory of Knowledge* [Phillipsburg, NJ: Presbyterian & Reformed, 1969]), "theonomy" (the assumption that although the Mosaic ceremonial legislation has been abrogated, Israel's moral and civil legislation, along with all of the other prescriptive material in the Bible, is comprehensive and valid not just in principle but literally in every detail), and postmillennial eschatology (the conviction that the church will progressively conquer human society until Christ's return). In a more recent article entitled "The Theonomic Urge" (*Christianity Today*, 21 April 1989, pp. 38-40), Randy Frame suggests that the influence of Christian reconstructionism is on the rise at present, especially in Reformed theological circles.

187. North, *Inherit the Earth*, pp. 188-89.

188. North, introduction to George Grant's *The Changing of the Guard: Biblical Principles for Political Action* (Fort Worth: Dominion, 1987), p. xxii.

theology: Christians are to achieve global dominion by voluntarily adopting the socioeconomic principles or "blueprint" detailed in Scripture.[189] It has been argued that utilizing these principles over time will naturally make Christians affluent and so will enable them to procreate effectively and prolifically.[190] Eventually, as Christians become increasingly affluent, increasingly numerous, and hence increasingly powerful, they will assume control of society.[191] "The industrious meek," David Chilton has commented, summing this process up, "shall inherit the earth."[192] "The capital base of righteousness," Gary North has suggested similarly, "will grow to fill the earth over time."[193]

The dominion schema is also used to explain the economic failure and underdevelopment in the non-Christian world and to predict the economic demise of formerly Christian nations that have succumbed to secular humanism. Referring to the inexorable effects of failing to adhere to biblical socio-economic law, David Chilton has stated that "The curse devours productivity in every area, and the ungodly culture perishes (Dt. 28:15-26). They suffer terrible disease (Dt. 28:27) and are politically oppressed (Dt. 28:28-34). This is how God controls heathen cultures: they must spend so much time

189. The reconstructionists take this "blueprint" idea very seriously and attempt to follow it through consistently, even to the extent of suggesting that because there are certain regulations in Scripture having to do with the treatment of slaves, slavery ought to be reintroduced into modern culture. David Chilton, for example, devotes several pages of *Productive Christians* to such matters as how slaves ought to be obtained, cared for, and the like (pp. 59ff.).

190. Advocates of Christian dominion acknowledge that this process may take centuries. A single individual, North has written, "cannot hope to build up his family's capital base in his own lifetime sufficient to achieve conquest . . . [but] if he looks two or more centuries into the future, it becomes a conceivable task" (*Liberating Planet Earth*, p. 81).

191. In "Democracy as Heresy," Rodney Clapp asserts that dominion theology is most popular among neopentecostal Christians. While no data exist to support his contention (and it would be slightly ironic, given the reconstructionists' disdain for neopentecostalism), the theonomist's legitimation of personal affluence is consonant with the so-called "health and wealth gospel" popular in neopentecostal circles. Proponents of the health and wealth gospel believe that God wants all Christians to be both healthy and wealthy and that there are certain "laws of prosperity" that, when applied correctly, invariably produce these results. See, e.g., Bruce Barton, *The Health and Wealth Gospel* (Downers Grove, IL: InterVarsity Press, 1987). In a sense, then, dominion theology takes this position several steps further, suggesting that individual aspirations to wealth fit into an eschatological framework that further legitimates them. From the perspective of Christian reconstructionism, the failure of Christians to become wealthy is not simply an indication of a lack of faith but actually postpones the coming of the kingdom of God.

Regarding the eventual cultural supremacy of Christians, North writes, "Let us make no mistake: Christian dominion necessarily involves the exclusion of anti-Christians from positions of public power" (*Inherit the Earth*, p. 79).

192. Chilton, *Productive Christians*, p. 36.

193. North, *The Sinai Strategy*, p. 44.

surviving that they are unable to exercise ungodly dominion over the earth. In the long run, this is the history of every culture that departs from God's word."[194]

Theonomists argue that the chief impediment to this progressive Christian dominion is the welfare state. Financed by redistributive taxation and ir- responsible and inflationary monetary policies, they argue, the welfare state prevents the faithful from accumulating the capital necessary for successful dominion. Gary North has written,

> The modern State promises to support its citizens from womb to tomb. It educates children, cares for the aged, and steadily transfers power to the government officials by taking on new responsibilities. It taxes our labor, it taxes our profits, and it taxes our children's inheritance. . . . We can see the drift of twentieth-century socialist societies. The State intends to seize the wealth of the just. The State is acting as the political agent of the envious, the incompetent, and the misled. . . . Until families recapture control over the wealth of the family, and lay up capital for godly children and grandchildren to inherit, the socialist State will continue to extract the wealth of the population and waste it.[195]

The "envious, incompetent, and misled" are those whom North elsewhere describes as "guilt-ridden intellectuals, politicians, and sons of the rich."[196] He states that they are in collusion with a bureaucratic elite to dispossess the entrepreneurial middle class—the class that constitutes the backbone of West- ern society, the class upon which capitalist development most depends.[197] "The modern welfare state has imposed tax burdens on the wage-earning, middle- class citizenry that are systematically decapitalizing the modern world."[198] And the project is being carried out by means of a combination of legislated theft and psychological manipulation. As Rousas John Rushdoony has put it, "The politics of the anti-Christian will . . . inescapably be *the politics of guilt.* In the politics of guilt, man is perpetually drained in his social energy and cultural activity by his over-riding sense of guilt and his masochistic activity. He will progressively demand of the state a redemptive role . . . so that the state, as man enlarged, becomes the human saviour of man."[199]

Advocates of Christian reconstruction view the expansion of the welfare state as a reflection of the philosophy of humanism that took root in Western culture at the Enlightenment, especially at the level of the educated elite. Rushdoony has suggested that culture is essentially religion externalized, and

194. Chilton, *Productive Christians*, p. 92.
195. North, *Inherit the Earth*, pp. 71-72.
196. North, *Liberating Planet Earth*, p. 126.
197. North, *Inherit the Earth*, pp. 52ff.
198. North, *The Sinai Strategy*, p. 174.
199. Rushdoony, *Politics of Guilt and Pity*, p. 9.

the totalitarian welfare state is the externalization of a humanist religion predicated on the autonomy of secular man.[200] "Until truth and law are again located in the sovereign God of Scripture and all regulation and predestination ascribed to God and his laws for men," he has argued, "until then we will continue to have the totalitarian regulatory state. We will have predestination by state planners, and cradle to grave, or womb to tomb, government by the new hand of 'providence,' a statist agency. Men act out of their faith in history, and historical problems are enactments of faulty and erroneous faiths. To clean up society, we must clean up its presuppositions. This, clearly, is a religious task."[201]

The reconstructionists also view the expansion of the welfare state as a reflection of God's judgment on the Western church for having abandoned its dominion mandate.[202] Not surprisingly, they place the burden of guilt for this problem squarely on the theological left. George Grant, for example, has argued that "when the church and her leaders call for more government interference in the economy, more programs to 'help the poor,' and more legislation to provide entitlements, benefits, and affirmative action, the work of the Kingdom is inevitably compromised and paralyzed. An unholy alliance has been forged . . . [and] dominion is subverted."[203] Yet the "escapist religion" of neofundamentalism, expressed in terms of personal piety and in the cultural pessimism of dispensational premillennialism, has been severely criticized by dominion theologians as well.[204] North has denounced it as "cultural retreatism" and a de facto abdication of the control of culture to the statists.[205] Interestingly, the theonomists also reject neofundamentalism's political activism on the grounds that it represents a kind of "power religion" only too willing to compromise with the existing political status quo.[206]

Theologically, proponents of Christian reconstruction have suggested that the dominion of the earth, understood in terms of private property rights, was

200. Rushdoony, *The Foundations of Social Order: Studies in the Creeds and Councils of the Early Church* (Fairfax, VA: Thoburn Press, 1978), p. 219.

201. Rushdoony, *The Roots of Inflation* (Vallecito, CA: Ross House Books, 1982), p. 84.

202. See Grant, *In the Shadow of Plenty,* pp. 140ff.; and *Bringing in the Sheaves: Transforming Poverty into Productivity* (Brentwood, TN: Wolgemuth & Hyatt, 1988).

203. Grant, *In the Shadow of Plenty,* p. 45.

204. North, *Liberating Planet Earth,* p. 188. Fundamentalist theologians have responded to this criticism by rejecting the theonomists' use of the Mosaic law. See Norman L. Geisler, "Dispensationalism and Ethics," *Transformation* 6 (January/March 1989): 7-14. See also Wayne H. House and Thomas Ice, *Dominion Theology—Blessing or Curse: An Analysis of Christian Reconstructionism* (Portland: Multnomah Press, 1988).

205. North, introduction to Grant, *The Changing of the Guard,* p. xvii; see also Grant, *In the Shadow of Plenty,* pp. 140ff.

206. See North, *Liberating Planet Earth,* pp. 42-43.

conferred to man just after the creation. "God doesn't directly control the earth," Gary North has stated, "apart from those he has chosen to manage his property. He directly controlled all of it during the first week of creation, but he no longer does. . . . He has decided to delegate control over his property to mankind throughout history."[207] God had intended human dominion to proceed in accordance with the divinely established laws of justice and economics, but Adam violated his property rights by stealing the fruit of the forbidden tree, thereby forfeiting his inheritance and his right to earthly dominion.[208] This first act of theft set in motion the fundamental heresy of statism—the ultimate violation of God's property rights. Christ reclaimed Adam's inheritance of earthly dominion in principle and subsequently passed this inheritance on to the church to be reclaimed in practice. Specifically, this inheritance will be reclaimed in accordance with the socioeconomic laws provided in the Bible—and it will be reclaimed despite the demonic opposition marshaled by the statists.[209]

> When men are taught that the capitalist (free market, meaning voluntary exchange) system is rigged against them, that they have a legal and moral right to welfare payments, and that those who live well as a result of their own labor, effort, and forecasting skills are immoral and owe the bulk of their wealth to the poor, we must recognize the source of these teachings: the pits of hell. This is Satan's counter-philosophy, which is expressly intended to thwart godly men in their efforts to subdue the earth to the glory of God. . . . It is a *conscious philosophy of destruction,* a systematically anti-Biblical framework which is calculated to undercut successful Christians by means of false guilt and paralysis. That such teachings are popular among Christian intellectuals in the latter years of the twentieth century only testifies to their abysmal ignorance. . . . We live in an age of guilt manipulators, and some of them use Scripture to their evil ends.[210]

What is urgently required at present, North and other theonomists have argued, is the complete "decapitalization" of the welfare state, presumably coupled with the recapitalization of the church and of the family.[211] The state should be brought into conformity with the strictly limited pattern provided in

207. North, *Inherit the Earth,* p. 23.
208. In *Inherit the Earth* North implies that the original sin was simple theft (pp. 37ff.). He goes on to suggest that the fact that God prohibited Adam and Eve from eating of the tree of the knowledge of good and evil was significant only insofar as it was a test of their respect for the rights of property.
209. North has written that "the Bible offers . . . a dominion concept of long-term scientific, economic, and intellectual progress which can overcome most (though not all) of the limits placed by God on His creation as a part of His curse" (*Liberating Planet Earth,* p. 47).
210. North, *Liberating Planet Earth,* p. 121.
211. North, *Liberating Planet Earth,* p. 86. See also North, *The Sinai Strategy,* p. 115.

Scripture, its authority restricted to such things as defending the rights of property, maintaining just weights and measures, ensuring civil justice and national defense, establishing quarantines for contagious diseases, defending Christianity from public attack, and so forth.[212] "Outside those areas where God's law prescribes their intervention and application of penal redress," Greg Bahnsen has asserted, "civil rulers are not authorized to legislate or use coercion (e.g. in the economic marketplace)."[213] Most importantly, theonomists stress that government has no legitimate authority to provide many of the services the welfare state currently provides. They insist that God's law prescribes that most if not all of the social problems currently under the jurisdiction of various state agencies should be redressed "by means of voluntary and charitable enterprises, or the censures of the home, church, and marketplace."[214] The reconstructionists also insist that the notion of social justice, which is so often used to legitimate the expansion of the welfare state, is entirely mistaken. James Sauer has flatly stated that "social justice is a myth. . . . It is not something of this world; but a thing that has descended from the imaginary realms of idealistic wishes. It is the enshrinement of ideals which are in part Hebrew-Christian—but which are incarnated in our time among the collectivist liberals, especially among the Marxists."[215]

The reconstructionists argue that Christianity is at war with humanism, and Christians can win it if they will only utilize the weapon of the biblical law which prescribes exactly how society is to be structured. In this regard, North and others anticipate the biblical reconstruction of the United States and hope that the American example will be emulated around the world.[216] Rushdoony has written that "the humanistic city still has its worst days ahead probably. However, out of its decay, the City of God will emerge. We are beginning to see the stirrings of a strong faith, among minority and majority groups alike. We are seeing the rise of Christian schools and agencies, manifesting a renewed literacy, and a greater Christian compassion than we have seen in years. We are witnessing on all sides the growth of Christian reconstruction, and the application of God's law-word to every area of life and thought."[217]

212. See Gary DeMar, *Ruler of the Nations: Biblical Principles of Government* (Ft. Worth: Dominion, 1987), pp. 77ff.

213. Bahnsen, "Christ and the Role of Civil Government: The Theonomic Perspective," part 1, *Transformation* 5 (April-June): 25.

214. Bahnsen, "Christ and the Role of Civil Government," part 1, p. 25. George Grant offers a book-length exposition of the "biblical principles for welfare" in *In the Shadow of Plenty*.

215. Sauer, "The Myth of Social Justice," *Chalcedon Report,* no. 273, April 1988, p. 2.

216. See North, *Inherit the Earth,* p. 182.

217. Rushdoony, "Wealth and the City," Position Paper no. 28 (Vallecito, CA: Chalcedon), p. 2.

The church's role in the recovery of what Douglas Kelly has called a "new medievalism" is to apply the biblical law prophetically to contemporary political-economic problems.[218] If this law is fully implemented, it will inevitably result in the conversion of culture, and such conversion is the goal of evangelism.[219] Indeed, the reconstructionists have insisted that carrying this theonomic socioeconomic perspective to other cultures is a critical first step in the evangelistic process.[220] "God is continually at work," David Chilton has written, "to destroy unbelieving cultures and to give the world over to the dominion of his people."[221]

One can easily see why dominion theology has been described as the liberation theology of the far right. Here, once again, human existence is reduced to the material and the economic. The doctrines of the Trinity, the *imago Dei*, original sin, the person and work of Christ, the nature of salvation and the eschaton—in sum, all of the major doctrines of the Christian faith—are reinterpreted along wholly this-worldly and merely economic lines.[222] Divine agency in history is collapsed into historical social conflict, and so is fully immanentized. Social action becomes evangelism. Eschatology becomes an essentially realizable human project. Scripture is distorted by means of highly selective exegesis, and so forth.[223] Indeed, the only real difference between dominion theology

218. Kelly, "The Present Struggle for Christian Reconstruction in the United States," *The Journal of Christian Reconstruction* 9 (1982-83): 23.

219. Chilton, *Productive Christians,* p. 96.

220. Grant, *In the Shadow of Plenty,* pp. 109ff. See also North, *Inherit the Earth,* p. 24.

221. Chilton, *Productive Christians,* p. 94.

222. Tom Rose, who is apparently on the edge of the reconstructionist movement, has argued that man is essentially (i.e., not just for the purposes of economic modeling) a "welfare maximizer" and that greed is not necessarily a result of the man's fall into sin (*Economics: Principles and Policy,* pp. 38-39). North has suggested that the right to private property is indicated by the trinitarian nature of God (*Inherit the Earth,* pp. 12-13), and he has also argued that the original and still most heinous sin is the theft of property, that the restoration of economic dominion was the point of Christ's redeeming work, that salvation is essentially economic, and that the Christian hope is for a laissez-faire eschaton in which the last of the left-wing intellectuals and federal bureaucrats will finally be thrown into the lake of fire along with the devil and his evil angels.

223. In *Inherit the Earth,* for example, North interprets God's command to man to "keep" the garden (Gen. 2:15) to mean that he should keep it away from others—i.e., as a legitimation of private property (p. 76). He interprets Paul's exhortation to the Roman Christians "to present yourselves as living sacrifices" (Rom. 12:1) to mean that one "should be allowed to enter any market and offer his goods or services to consumers" (p. 99). He interprets the Jubilee legislation as a kind of intentional disincentive for the people of Israel to remain in the promised land, since it made capital accumulation over time difficult. Along this line, Chilton cites North as having suggested that "if the Jubilee Year worked at all in the land of covenantally faithful Israel, or in any land that came under the rule of God's law, it worked as a *disincentive* to remain in the land of one's fathers. . . . [The children] must

and the theologies of liberation (leaving aside the fact that the reconstruction-ists' argument is much less sophisticated) is that the reconstructionists substi-tute a procapitalist analysis for Marxist analysis. Beyond this, however, they both suggest that God's will in history is for the progressive realization of a particular kind of political-economic order.[224]

Cognitive Bargaining and the Evangelical Right's Theological Defense of Capitalism

Just as it was possible to detect the process of cognitive bargaining in the evangelical left's denunciation of capitalism, so there are indications of cogni-tive bargaining in the evangelical right's staunch defense of capitalism. Whereas those on the evangelical left are tempted to bargain with Marxist analysis and retranslate evangelical orthodoxy along the lines of what might be called the "ideology of the intelligentsia," those on the right are tempted to interpret Christian theology and ethics through the lens of bourgeois liber-alism or what might be called the "ideology of commerce."

As any number of observers have noted, modern capitalism has produced a distinctive culture, especially in Protestant countries—a culture featuring a unique kind of person typically labeled *bourgeois.* Such people tend both to value and to exhibit a high degree of individual autonomy, a specific kind of rationality, and at least practically speaking a materialistic or this-worldly orientation. Peter Berger has suggested that the bourgeois individual is characterized

> by functional rationality, by a sober, no-nonsense, problem-solving attitude to life in general and, of course, to economic life in particular. . . . Put differently, what we have here is a "calculating" individual—not, or not necessarily, in the sense that all human relations are perceived in terms of some sort of economic costs/benefits analysis (that is the anticapitalist stereotype)—but rather in the sense that specific sectors of life, and notably the sector of economic activity, are approached in a rationally calculating and planning manner. This individual is also animated by a strong sense of ambition and the goals of this ambition are to be reached by way of competitive achievement. Finally, here is an individual who is open to innovation, as against one bound by the past. Indeed, there is a tendency within this individual to regard anything as better just because it is new. This trait, of course, is highly relevant to the "creative destruction" of capitalism.[225]

---

make plans to move outward, bringing the whole world under God's law" (*Productive Christians,* p. 162).

224. See Richard John Neuhaus, "Why Wait for the Kingdom? The Theonomist Temp-tation," *First Things* 1 (May 1990): 13-21.

225. Berger, *The Capitalist Revolution: Fifty Propositions about Prosperity, Equality, and Liberty* (New York: Basic Books, 1986), pp. 107-8.

The economic agent envisioned in the evangelical right's defense of capitalism is obviously this sort of bourgeois individual. Indeed, those on the evangelical right perceive man primarily as *homo faber*—as a wealth-producer who views the dominion of the natural world to be his or her chief end. Furthermore, they perceive this "productive dominion" individualistically, or at least in terms of individuals cooperating on a contractual basis. In this regard, we might note that such terms as *solidarity* and *community* are conspicuously absent from the evangelical right's arguments in defense of capitalism. Those on the right tend to leave the impression that while such things are important and may well complement the capitalist economy, we cannot necessarily expect them from the market. In addition, the evangelical right tends to imply that productive dominion can be achieved simply by applying functional rationality or technique to the problems of material existence.

It is important to stress here, however, that the habit of rationality easily gives way to a kind of practical materialism and, just as on the evangelical left, to the process of theological immanentization. Indeed, Bernard Zylstra has suggested that the process takes two forms. Those on the left grant ultimacy to social labor, as in Marxism, while those on the right grant ultimacy to individual labor. "The tragedy of Christian scholars with respect to the issue at hand [immanentization] lies in their acceptance of the underlying framework of reference as posited by the proponents of Renaissance-Enlightenment humanism. Concretely this means that Christian scholars in Europe and South America tend to accept the Marxian pole of the dialectic while most Christian scholars in North America accept the liberal-individualist pole."[226]

While Zylstra's remarks are most relevant with reference to those on the far right, who have almost entirely collapsed the kingdom of God into the bourgeois vision of progressive technological mastery by means of capital accumulation, the process of cognitive bargaining with this peculiarly modern understanding is widely evident elsewhere on the evangelical right as well. Ironically, the result of this process on the right has been identical to that which we observed on the evangelical left—namely, that the more transcendent elements of evangelical orthodoxy have been increasingly bargained away in exchange for a claim to relevance in the contemporary political-economic struggle, in this case in the struggle against statism. Economic and material existence, in other words, have increasingly come to be understood by many of those on the evangelical right as being of ultimate importance.

Still, it should be noted that the process of cognitive bargaining is somewhat more complicated on the evangelical right than on the evangelical left.

226. Zylstra, "Marxism and Education: Some Observations," in *The Challenge of Marxist and Neo-Marxist Ideologies for Christian Scholarship,* ed. John C. Vander Stelt (Sioux Center, IA: Dordt College Press, 1982), p. 250.

Returning to the distinction between the libertarian and the traditionalist (natural law) defenses of capitalism, for example, it is evident that while elements of both defenses are included in many of the positions of those on the right, there is a distinct tension between them. In dominion theology, where the natural-law approach is taken to a rationalized extreme, freedom is obviously very limited.[227] We are "free" either to obey the pre-existent laws governing every aspect of human existence on the one hand or to perish on the other. Yet the reconstructionists have also incorporated the libertarian theory of subjective value into their system and so have argued that economic values are not as objective as their "biblical law-order" scheme has implied.[228] A similar paradox has characterized American conservatism in general. Citing Frank Meyer's *In Defense of Freedom* (1962), for example, George Nash has observed that

> on one side were the authoritarian conservatives, rightly concerned for virtue and order but wrongly willing to use government to achieve their ends. They confused the moral and political realms. On the other side were the classical liberals [i.e., libertarians], commendably devoted to the limited state, the autonomous individual, and the free economy. But *they* were increasingly indifferent to the "organic moral order" and unable "to distinguish between the *authoritarianism* with which men and institutions suppress the freedom of men, and the *authority* of God and truth."[229]

Nash goes on to describe how these libertarian and authoritarian strands are fused in such works as Wilhelm Ropke's *A Humane Economy: The Social Framework of the Free Market* (1960).[230] Ropke's work is basically a libertarian apology for the free-market economy, but he suggests that market transactions need to be informed by ethical norms instilled by family, church, and community—a position commonly taken by those on the evangelical right.

In an essay entitled "The Normative Framework for Pluralism in America," Robert Bellah provides a historical perspective on the tension between the libertarian and traditionalist strands in American thought. He argues that the libertarian position (which he calls simply "liberalism"), a position granting ontological priority to the individual and tending to view social relationships exclusively in terms of contract, arose out of a bitter conflict with a Puritanism which had insisted that social life needs to be measured against the authoritative

227. Reconstructionists are quite critical of the individualism they feel characterizes the libertarian defense of free enterprise. They contend that economic agency ought to be located in the family unit for two reasons: (1) the family unit is capable of applying the appropriate moral restraint to economic activity, and (2) it is the only unit able to accumulate the capital requisite for dominion over time. See Elizabeth McEachern Miller, "Money, Inheritance, and the Family," in Rushdoony's *The Roots of Inflation*, pp. 91-96.

228. See Chilton, *Productive Christians*, p. 398.

229. Nash, *The Conservative Intellectual Movement*, p. 174.

230. Nash, *The Conservative Intellectual Movement*, p. 181.

standard of Scripture.[231] The Puritan determination that economic activity conform to biblical requirements profoundly threatened the "ideology of commerce" of the early capitalist class; and, indeed, it was this class that first challenged the Puritan hegemony in colonial America. "Already in 1630," Sydney Ahlstrom notes in *A Religious History of the American People,* "the merchants had expressed doubt that the Bible as interpreted by the clergy made adequate allowance for the exigencies of healthy commerce."[232] In a sense, then, it was the victory of liberalism that accounts for the explosion of capitalist enterprise and the triumph of bourgeois civilization in American history. As Bellah suggests, however, the success of liberalism probably also accounts for the loss of collective solidarity that plagues American culture.[233] Among other things, this is because a "liberal" society is by definition a secularized society.

It is somewhat ironic, then, that those on the evangelical right use the libertarian argument to protest the state's interference in economic life, especially given that their view of social life is so thoroughly Puritan otherwise. Indeed, it would seem that in adopting a libertarian defense of capitalism, the evangelical right is taking a position that must undermine its defense of church and family life along traditionalist lines. Of course, those on the evangelical right defend their synthesis of libertarianism and traditionalism by suggesting that God intends different spheres of life to be governed by different laws and that unrestricted freedom in the marketplace is not necessarily in conflict with the restriction of freedom in other areas of life. This may be true, but instead of reflecting a defensible theological position, those on the right may, in their concern to resist the expansion of the welfare state, have simply adopted the most convenient philosophical weapons available to them, regardless of whether they cohere logically.[234] Indeed, I suspect that if conservative evangelicals were ever to recapture their hegemony within American culture, the

231. Robert Bellah, "The Normative Framework for Pluralism in America," *Soundings* 61 (Fall 1978): 364.

232. Ahlstrom, *A Religious History of the American People,* vol. 1 (Garden City, NY: Doubleday-Image, 1975), p. 161.

233. Bellah, "The Normative Framework," p. 364.

234. It should be noted that the ironic combination of libertarian and Puritan reasoning on the evangelical right almost certainly reflects the division of modern life into "public" and "private" spheres of activity. As Robert Bellah and his coauthors argue in *Habits of the Heart: Individualism and Commitment in American Life* (Berkeley and Los Angeles: University of California Press, 1985), p. 43, the public sphere is that area of life suited to the exigencies of the modern economy and to the needs of bureaucratic industrial corporations. It is governed by a kind of rationalized "utilitarian individualist" outlook. The private sphere, on the other hand, has become the domain of individual fulfillment and encompasses such things as religious and family-oriented activities. The private sphere is potentially governed by moral principle, and it is probably true that to a large extent a Puritan attitude toward private existence compensates for the impersonality and abstraction of modern economic life.

libertarian argument, probably championed by capitalist entrepreneurs, would almost certainly be used against them and would just as certainly be rejected by them as a result.

The Evangelical Right and Capitalism: Concluding Remarks

Commenting on American intellectual conservatism generally, George Nash has suggested that "above all, the most noteworthy feature of this body of thought is the simple fact that it was overwhelmingly *intellectual* history. In nearly all these accounts of the decline of the West, relatively little attention was paid to 'material' or 'social' forces. Instead, ideas were alleged to have been decisive; *ideas* had had consequences. Evil thoughts had generated evil deeds. At the root of modernity was *intellectual error.*"[235]

Nash goes on to note that this primarily intellectual understanding of history and modernity has driven conservative intellectuals to search for those crucial *ideas* that might serve to reverse the trend toward decadence in the modern situation. Of course, these observations apply quite well to the evangelical defenders of capitalism. Modern social and economic structures, those on the right argue, are more or less direct reflections of certain ideas. The modern trend toward statism, for example, is the predictable result of the deification of humanity incipient in secular humanism. Modern capitalism, meanwhile, is deemed the fruition of a number of very good ideas, most if not all of them found in Scripture. In other words, those on the right tend not to appreciate the irony of history or the fact that while ideas may well have social consequences, many of these consequences—capitalism among them—have been largely unintended. And in spite of the fact that the evangelical right points to such things as capitalism's economic efficiency relative to that of the statist alternatives, I suspect that their appraisal of capitalism rests principally on ideational grounds and that they have tended to use the empirical evidence simply to buttress what they had already determined ought to be the case.

Of course, the crucial issue for those on the evangelical right is not capitalism per se but the appropriate role of the modern state. Yet in spite of this, they tend to be curiously vague on matters of political philosophy, and they seem to have serious differences of opinion among themselves as to just what the problem with the modern state is. On the one hand, the evangelical libertarians argue that the problem lies not with any particular government but with the inevitable tendency of any centralized social authority to impinge on the ability of individuals to realize their creative potential and act freely and hence responsibly before God. The traditionalists, on the other hand, contend

235. Nash, *The Conservative Intellectual Movement,* pp. 55-56.

that the problem does not involve centralized social authority per se but is rather a matter of who is allowed to exercise this authority. For traditionalists, then, the problem is that social and political authority have fallen into the hands of a secular elite and must be recaptured by Christians so that authority can henceforth be exercised in accordance with biblical guidelines and on behalf of God's kingdom.

The libertarian understanding, of course, is much better suited to legitimate what economist Joseph Schumpeter has called the "creative destruction" of the capitalist process, a process that essentially institutionalizes novelty.[236] One must have a high view of providence, in other words, to be completely comfortable with capitalism. In fact, in considering the position of the evangelical traditionalists, I wonder if they would continue to advocate free enterprise so enthusiastically if they really appreciated the revolutionary character of the capitalist process. There can be no blueprint, biblical or otherwise, for such a process, for it is as unpredictable as the entrepreneurial spirit that incessantly moves it forward. In the case of the traditionalists, then, it appears that they have defended capitalism primarily as a means to the end of opposing the sociopolitical agenda of those currently in positions of social and cultural authority.

I began this chapter by asserting that the appraisals of capitalism made by those on the evangelical right are largely reactive, and it might be helpful to conclude by returning to this point. The reactive character of the right's position is indicated in the fact that it has tended to pose its arguments in the form of point-by-point refutations of the position taken by those on the evangelical left. Its reactive nature is also indicated in the distrust those on the right have evinced of radical social change, which they fear may well be for the worse. Of course the reactive (read *reactionary*) nature of the evangelical right position is commonly noted by those on the evangelical left, who dismiss the position as false by definition. Still, we should not stress the opposition of left and right to the extent that we miss the remarkable similarities between the two.

Both left and right address essentially the same American evangelical audience. Both insist that a correct understanding of the present situation requires a certain amount of abstraction. They differ only concerning which elements of our experience it is safe to ignore—about whether what we are really seeing is the invisible hand of market coordination or that of capitalist oppression. Both left and right tend to understand the present situation as one of crisis, but they disagree as to whether capitalism or statism precipitated the crisis. Both fear the concentration of power in modern society, but they differ

236. Joseph A. Schumpeter, *Capitalism, Socialism, and Democracy,* 2d ed. (New York: Harper, 1942), p. 83.

as to whether this concentration is most acute among the business elite or the bureaucratic political elite. Both left and right insist that the true social relevance of the Christian faith is only now being rediscovered after having been lost, but they differ on whether its relevance is anticapitalist or not. Both feel that American evangelicalism is moving in the wrong direction at present, but they disagree on the matter of which is actually the wrong direction. Both argue that their opponents are either ideologically blind or evil or both. At their extremes, both left and right insist that salvation is essentially economic, but they differ on whether the kingdom will be populated by social workers or entrepreneurs. Both fear that the faithful exercise of Christianity's social relevance will elicit persecution from a powerful anti-Christian cultural elite, but they disagree about who constitutes this elite. Finally, both left and right fail to appreciate fully the character of modern capitalism. The left fails to appreciate the remarkable ability of capitalism to create wealth and hence to alleviate material poverty, and the right fails to appreciate the ability of capitalism to dissolve traditional culture and hence to exacerbate spiritual poverty. It is not difficult to see, then, why a number of other evangelical intellectuals interested in issues of political economy have been concerned to try to steer a path between the extremes of left and right.

CHAPTER THREE

Capitalism as a Cause for Concern: The Evangelical Center

While the evangelical right's ardent defense of free enterprise contrasts neatly with the evangelical left's condemnation of capitalist oppression, there are a number (perhaps the majority) of evangelical authors with an interest in economics whose appraisals of capitalism are neither wholly negative nor entirely positive. Many of these authors seek to balance appreciation of the overall efficiency of the market mechanism with concerns for those the market has apparently left behind. They are also engaged, like all parties to the economic dispute, in trying to determine not just what constitutes good economic policy but also what the church's stance on political-economic issues should be. Reviewing the positions of those evangelicals whose appraisals of capitalism fall roughly in between the left and right, then, is our task in this third chapter. While the competition between left and right within evangel- icalism provides little indication about the general drift of evangelical thought on the subjects of capitalism and social and economic policy at present, a consideration of this evangelical "center" may furnish us with important clues concerning the direction in which evangelical opinion is heading. It may also help to clarify the relation of evangelical political-economic thought to that of the broader intellectual community.

In my treatments of the evangelical left and right, I was able to synthesize the positions to facilitate the analysis. In my treatment of the evangelical center, however, I have felt it necessary to consider each of three groups separately. In the first section I discuss those who have remained in what I call the evangelical "mainstream"—specifically, Carl F. H. Henry and recent contribu- tors to *Christianity Today*. In the second section I take up the work of a number of younger progressive evangelical economists. And in the third section I review the political-economic thought of intellectuals in the Christian Reformed Church. In addition, I have appended an excursus toward the end of the chapter in which I discuss the contributions that several British evangelical scholars have made to the recent American political-economic debate.

Mainstream Evangelical Appraisals of Capitalism

I use the term *mainstream* to describe individuals committed to the neo-evangelical project of reentering the social and economic policy arena while remaining theologically, as well as relatively culturally and politically, conservative. During the 1950s and 1960s, those in the evangelical mainstream refused to identify Christianity with particular political-economic systems and/or policies, and they stressed that social change should be approached from the standpoint of changing the hearts and minds of individuals. Still, they did maintain that capitalism is the best of the available alternatives. In addition, those in the mainstream tended to be suspicious of the sort of suggestions that were voiced by the National Council of Churches during this period—namely, that American churches needed to be more closely aligned with federal welfare provision. "In striving for the total economic security for all men as the supreme goal," wrote Robert James St. Clair, "the churches may get something like desired results through the help of friends, agencies and the patronage of the state, only to discover that one day they are more in debt to them than to Christ, and have lost not only their momentum but also their unique reason for being in existence."[1]

But with the movement, beginning in the late sixties, of many younger evangelicals away from cultural and political conservatism and toward more progressive and even radical positions, and with the reemergence of political fundamentalism more recently, the evangelical mainstream has suffered, at least at the level of intellectual representation, a considerable degree of attrition. It seems that the mainstream has grown confused trying to find a path between the left and the right on matters of social and economic policy. The original neo-evangelical desire to develop a clearly articulated evangelical stance on social and economic policy issues to which all evangelicals could subscribe and behind which they could unite has not materialized. Indeed, as we have noted, the mainstream has not even managed to resolve such foundational issues as that of the relation of evangelism to social action in the church's mission. In many respects the questions facing the evangelical mainstream now are the same questions they faced twenty years ago, and hence it should come as no surprise that representatives of the mainstream are saying

1. St. Clair, "Now It's the Social Welfare Gospel," *United Evangelical Action* 20 (January 1962): 10.

many of the same things they have said for a generation. If mainstream voices are becoming increasingly difficult to hear, it is probably simply because there are fewer of them.

Carl F. H. Henry

"There is a rising tide of reaction in Fundamentalism today," a young Carl F. H. Henry contended in *The Uneasy Conscience of Modern Fundamentalism* (1947), "a reaction born of an uneasy conscience and determined no longer to becloud the challenge of the Gospel to modern times."[2] A crucial element of this challenge was social, Henry felt, and he encouraged an energetic conservative Protestant reentry into the modern debate over social and economic policy. While he emphasized that the correction of social conditions was not the church's primary task, he insisted that individual Christians should model social compassion and should endorse "remedial efforts in any context not specifically anti-redemptive."[3] Among other things, Henry's program called for a concerted evangelical effort directed at education. Evangelical alternatives to secular solutions, he argued, should be developed in the areas of economic and political policy, in the social sciences, and in ethics. Insofar as economic policy was concerned, Henry stressed that

> Evangelicalism must not make the mistake, so common in our day of regarding Communism or state Socialism as the adequate rectification of the errors of totalitarianism or the inadequacies of democracism [*sic*]. . . . No economic reorganization, however much it overcomes the antithesis of absolutism and individualism, is on that account to be identified with the kingdom of God.[4]

Still, Henry's warnings about socialism did not lead him to endorse the capitalist alternative uncritically. The crux, he felt, was the presence or absence of the "redemptive ingredient," or faith ultimately in the necessity of divine redemption within either system. Such faith recognizes that man's deepest needs are not simply economic and hence admits the penultimate status of all economic systems, systems making no provision beyond the needs of economic man. Indeed, in this regard Henry suggested that a "redemptive Communism" would be far more advantageous than an "unredemptive Capitalism" and vice versa.[5]

Though now in his seventies, Henry continues to be actively involved in

2. Henry, *The Uneasy Conscience of Modern Fundamentalism* (Grand Rapids: William B. Eerdmans, 1947), p. 34.

3. Henry, *The Uneasy Conscience of Modern Fundamentalism*, p. 87.

4. Henry, *The Uneasy Conscience of Modern Fundamentalism*, p. 73.

5. Henry, *The Uneasy Conscience of Modern Fundamentalism*, p. 73.

the evangelical debate over social and economic policy issues. He continues to maintain that the Christian is a citizen of two kingdoms simultaneously—the kingdom of God (i.e., the church) and "Caesar's kingdom" (i.e., the realm of secular affairs). While upholding the priority of the church's evangelistic task, Henry continues to chastise fundamentalists and evangelicals alike for their evasion of issues of social justice, and he has continued to advocate the development of a uniquely Christian social policy.[6] Such a policy, he urges, should first be modeled within the church itself, in order to provide a visible alternative to materialistic capitalism and utopian socialism, both of which have led to cultural decadence. In Henry's view, the church *is* a primary instrument of social change, but by example rather than active political participation. "Its task," he has written, "is not to force new structures upon society at large, but to be the new society, to exemplify . . . the way and the will of God."[7]

Specifically with respect to capitalism, Henry has continued to criticize its "sex-and-things promotion of technological gadgets and marvels" and the materialism this promotion has fostered.[8] But when he has contrasted capitalism with socialism, his assessment has been more positive. In a recent work entitled *The Christian Mindset in a Secular Society* he writes,

> I hold no brief for Marxist theory, which has nowhere made good on its promise of economic utopia and never will. Free enterprise has immense values over against the bureaucratically controlled societies. I do not find in the Old Testament a single prophet or in the New Testament a single apostle who considers private property an evil; nor do I find the Christ of the Gospels equalizing the wealth either of the Jews or of the Romans of his day as the path to social or spiritual utopia. Stripped of moral answerability, however, free enterprise soon invites ethical censure by sensitive social critics and by ideologists given to socialist alternatives. More importantly, when free enterprise frees itself of God it invites the judgement of God. As we know, communism and socialism impede rather than help the Christian cause; while Christianity does not depend upon capitalist economics, a truly viable capitalism does depend upon moral principle.[9]

Henry has charged that the church's failure to "Christianize" capitalism has led to the popularity of Marxism among many younger evangelical intellectuals. "Wherever secularism, especially secular capitalism, provides little or no moral stimulus, and readily accommodates and even thrives on a spiritual vacuum," he commented recently, "there Marxism exploits the realities of

---

6. See Henry, *A Plea for Evangelical Demonstration* (Grand Rapids: Baker Book, 1971).

7. Henry, *God, Revelation, and Authority*, vol. 4 (Waco, TX: Word Books, 1979), p. 530.

8. Henry, *God, Revelation, and Authority*, 4:578.

9. Henry, *The Christian Mindset in a Secular Society: Promoting Evangelical Renewal and National Righteousness* (Portland: Multnomah Press, 1984), pp. 21-22.

human discontent; it presents itself to the noncommunist world as a pristine humanism that imparts meaning and worth to individual life."[10] Still, while the attraction to Marxism may be understandable, Henry has been harshly critical of those evangelicals who have attempted to synthesize Marxist analysis and Christian theology. He has not only condemned Marxism as a "cruel economic hoax"[11] but has argued that its encounters with theology always end with the gospel being materialized.

> So-called Marxist exegesis of the Bible perpetuates a materialistic understanding of reality and life. It transmutes the Saviour and Lord of scriptural revelation into a sociopolitical liberator who promotes a modern socioeconomic ideology. For the redemptive conflict with Satan and sin and death at the heart of the gospel, it substitutes the class-struggle; it ignores supernatural aspects of the kingdom of God and substitutes a temporal sociopolitical utopia; it miscasts the promised Messiah as a political-economic liberator and dilutes the content of the new covenant which seeks inscription of God's moral law on man's inner nature, and it does all this in accord with a partisan modern social ideology.[12]

Instead, Henry has noted elsewhere, "evangelical Christianity ought to espouse . . . the liberation of exegesis from prerevolutionary and all other extraneous ideologies, even those whose goal is defined as human liberation."[13]

Henry has also been critical of those who are quick to call for statist solutions to contemporary social and economic problems. To look immediately to the state to fulfill social responsibilities when voluntary responses have not been forthcoming, he has argued, is an "evasive tactic."[14] The state is not suited to exercise the qualities of charity and compassion, and in any event, Christians should not be interested in trying to shift the burden of performing acts of compassion away from individuals and the church.[15] "From a reading of her

10. Henry, *God, Revelation, and Authority*, 4:585. Similarly, in an interview with *Sojourners* (April 1976), Henry commented, "I think there are strengths to capitalism. But our failure to criticize capitalism, in its operation—the shoddy record of production for obsolescence, the reckless depletion of natural resources, the prizing of profit over sensitivity to worker's needs, the bribery by multinational corporations, the big stake in smoking and cigarette production despite the fact that we know it to be harmful, the alcohol traffic—gave a one way street to the Marxists to criticize capitalism, in such a way that our younger generation became enchanted with Marxism as an alternative" (31-32).

11. Henry, *The Christian Mindset in a Secular Society*, p. 22.

12. Henry, "Liberation Theology and the Scriptures," in *Liberation Theology*, ed. Ronald H. Nash (Milford, MI: Mott Media, 1984), pp. 200-201; see also Henry, *God, Revelation, and Authority*, 4:555-77.

13. Henry, *God, Revelation, and Authority*, 4:570.

14. Henry, *God, Revelation, and Authority*, 4:553.

15. In his autobiography, Henry writes that "some evangelicals, writing as if capitalism were intrinsically unjust, promote forced redistribution of wealth as a divine necessity. . . . In this context Christian giving loses status as voluntary compassion and instead becomes a

own past," Henry has suggested, "the regenerate church knows that neither a change of political leadership nor adoption of legislation can assure transformation of a people's moral character. . . . But Christian responsibility on earth does not end [with evangelism]. As citizens of two worlds, Christians know that the penalty for withholding exemplary guidance and involvement for the social common good is to surrender the political arena by default to non-Christian alternatives."[16]

A crucial component of this exemplary social guidance, Henry has insisted, is the church's defense of freedom: "The cardinal concern for evangelicals should be human liberty and its ramifications. Failure to exhibit freedom as a foremost religious, political, and social concern makes it easy for critics to misrepresent the Christian agenda as the subjugation of society by a yoke of tradition."[17]

Christianity Today

Mainstream evangelical opinion on social issues has also been well represented in the pages of *Christianity Today*. This weekly magazine was launched in 1956 with the intent of providing a contrast to the theologically liberal *Christian Century* and of creating a forum for neo-evangelical thought and opinion on a broad range of topics, including those of social import. On the issue of social change, most of the contributors to *Christianity Today* during the 1950s and 1960s (many of whom, it should be noted, were also contributors to *Christian Economics* at this time) took the position that such change is essentially a function of changing individuals.[18] In support of this claim, contributors commonly cited the leadership of conservative Protestantism in the development of hospitals, medical missions, orphanages, and other benevolent social institutions.[19] And since they considered changing individuals the key to social change, they repeatedly stressed the primacy of the church's evangelistic task with respect to social issues during this period. "Faith in God puts courage, compassion, and determination into the hearts of men," wrote Howard E.

---

legal due. Evangelicals in fact increasingly cloud the distinction between justice and charity and compassion" (*Confessions of a Theologian: An Autobiography* [Waco, TX: Word, 1986], p. 399).

16. Henry, "Church and State: Why the Marriage Must Be Saved," *Christianity Today,* 19 April 1985, p. I-13.

17. Henry, "Church and State," p. I-10.

18. See, e.g., Irving E. Howard, "Christ and the Libertarians," *Christianity Today,* 17 March 1958, p. 10.

19. See the editorial "A Better Way to Confront Poverty," *Christianity Today,* 31 January 1969, pp. 24-26.

Kershner. "These are the qualities that conquer poverty and solve other social problems. It is the business of the Church to mobilize spiritual power. By doing so, it can solve our perplexing social and economic ills; but if it deserts its true function [viz., evangelism] the Church will meet with tragic failure."[20]

Insofar as issues of political economy were concerned, *Christianity Today's* editorial policy was to dissuade the institutional church from endorsing specific policies. "The issue before the Church seems to be this," Harold Kuhn observed in 1966: "Are we to accept the New Testament mandate to 'preach the Gospel to every creature,' or are we to accept the revised definition of evangelism proposed by ideologists whose views are conditioned almost entirely by a socio-political creed? . . . Certainly [the evangelist] ought to interest himself . . . in the financial structures that control trade and wealth among nations. But his major concern must be to relate the unchanging Revelation to man's needs in a changing world."[21] On the other hand, individuals were encouraged to become involved in the political-economic debate and to endorse "responsible free enterprise over Marxist collectivism."[22] Most of *Christianity Today's* contributors agreed that capitalism was far superior to socialism in terms of both its actual economic performance and its provision of freedom.[23] Yet it was stressed that freedom must not be seen as an end in itself, but only in terms of responsible stewardship before God. Indeed, it was argued that if freedom is pursued only for its own sake, it must inevitably lapse into nihilism.[24]

While contributors to *Christianity Today* commonly argued that a combination of private charity and economic growth provided the best way to confront the problems of poverty, they also felt that state-sponsored social programs aimed at education and enabling people to participate in the national economy were worth their cost.[25] Beyond such educational efforts, however, the encroachment of the welfare state was viewed with great suspicion. The utopian quest for perfect material security underlying the expansion of the modern state was considered a subtle form of idolatry to which the church should be opposed.[26] Similarly, several articles during the sixties stressed the

20. Kershner, "The Church and Social Problems," *Christianity Today,* 4 March 1966, p. 35.

21. Kuhn, "Twentieth-Century Evangelism," *Christianity Today,* 14 October 1966, p. 62.

22. Henry, *Confessions of a Theologian,* p. 170.

23. See Irving E. Howard, "Christian Approach to Economics," *Christianity Today,* 18 August 1958, pp. 7-9.

24. See Howard, "Christ and the Libertarians"; and Norman C. Hunt, "Christians and the Economic Order," *Christianity Today,* 2 September 1959, pp. 5-8.

25. See the editorials "A Better Way to Confront Poverty" and "The President's Poverty Plan," *Christianity Today,* 12 December 1969, pp. 34-35.

26. See Kershner, "The Church and Social Problems"; and Howard, "Christian Approach to Economics."

impossibility of a Christian-Marxist dialogue and the dangers of the kind of synthesis of Marxism and Christianity that was to surface in the late 1960s in the various theologies of liberation.[27] Contributors to *Christianity Today* subsequently argued that liberation theology is an essentially secular and materialistic philosophy deceptively hidden beneath a biblical veneer and that if it were accepted, it would inevitably pervert historic orthodoxy.[28]

While *Christianity Today* may originally have been envisioned as the forum within which evangelicals would shape a distinctively Christian social policy, this has yet to happen. Especially since Carl Henry resigned the editorship in 1968 and the journal assumed a magazine format oriented increasingly toward a lay readership, articles detailing distinctively evangelical positions on economic and social policy issues have been relatively few and far between. But a recent conference sponsored by and reported in *Christianity Today* did address the question of church-state relations and is perhaps indicative of the kind of course the magazine, and many of those in the evangelical mainstream with it, are trying to steer at present. The report outlines three kinds of errors that should be avoided with respect to social policy. The first of these is "politicized Christian relativism," which is attributed chiefly to those on the evangelical left. The second error is "pietistic Christian absolutism," a kind of separatism with respect to social issues that is attributed chiefly to popular American fundamentalism. The third error is "imperial Christian biblicism," which is attributed chiefly to those on the evangelical far right.[29] It remains an open question what success those in the mainstream are having in avoiding these kinds of errors.

Generally speaking, recent contributors to *Christianity Today* have tended to stress that since our understanding is limited, since our ability to calculate the consequences of specific policy proposals varies a great deal, and since power inevitably corrupts, we would do well to opt for a democratically limited government. Since capitalism has apparently facilitated limited government better than its alternatives, it is worthy of support as a means to this end. Walter W. Benjamin has written, for example,

> Make no mistake: I am not a knee-jerk apologist for capitalism. It is not the Christian economic system—as if any economic system could be. Like all systems,

27. See the editorials "Is Christian-Marxist Dialogue Possible?" *Christianity Today*, 6 January 1967, pp. 26-27; and "The Danger of Christian-Marxist Dialogue," *Christianity Today*, 27 October 1967, pp. 26-27. And see C. Peter Wagner, "Evangelism and Social Action in Latin America," *Christianity Today*, 6 January 1966, pp. 10-12.

28. See "The Marxist Never-Never Land," *Christianity Today*, 20 December 1974, p. 20. See also the editorial "Jesus, Marx and Co." *Christianity Today*, 8 June 1973, p. 28; and Ira Gallaway, "Liberation and Revolution," *Christianity Today*, 25 August 1972, p. 20.

29. James I. Packer, "How to Recognize a Christian Citizen," *Christianity Today*, 19 April 1985, pp. I-4-8.

it forges it own unique chains of enslavement. But the enduring values of free enterprise should not be overlooked: that profit is necessary for economic motivation, and private ownership is requisite for the full development of personality. It often lifts people out of poverty even without equalitarian redistribution. Moreover, Western capitalism keeps economic and political power divided. To whom or what does one repair when all political and economic power is coalesced in the state? When all jobs are dispensed by the state, the dissenter is highly vulnerable.[30]

As these comments suggest, contributors to *Christianity Today* have stressed that some distance needs to be maintained between evangelical Christianity and the defense of capitalism so that systemic economic problems can be frankly admitted and, if possible, corrected. At the same time, however, contributors have not necessarily been ready to admit that a more powerful state offers the only solution to contemporary social and economic problems. A number of contributors to *Christianity Today* have argued that in many cases entitlement programs have become idols for their beneficiaries, and the welfare system has been subject to abuse.[31] "Poverty in America is a stark reality for many," Nelson Bell wrote in 1970, "but now that it has become a political issue there is grave danger that its alleviation will become motivated by other than compassion, and its victims will be pawns in a sociological experiment that can cost billions in waste and bureaucratic management while it destroys initiative and breeds dependence on others."[32] More recently, Charles Colson asserted that "the evidence is mounting . . . that no one is willing to restrain mushrooming government programs, which now provide direct grants to 66 million Americans. And if we have lost self-restraint, one must question if we still have the moral capacity essential for democracy to function."[33] Instead of granting dangerous power to the "monolithic monster of a bloated state," Francis Schaeffer suggested, the church ought to emphasize the "compassionate use of accumulated wealth."[34]

In spite of these sorts of warnings, recent contributors to *Christianity Today* have not been as threatened by the growth of the welfare state as those on the evangelical right have been. Evangelical economist John E. Mulford, for example, has argued that the state has a legitimate role to play in meeting the needs of the truly poor, and indeed that it has a responsibility to redistribute

30. Benjamin, "Liberation Theology: European Hopelessness Exposes Latin Hoax," *Christianity Today,* 5 March 1982, p. 23.

31. See the editorial " 'Sensitive' Security," *Christianity Today,* 10 November 1972, pp. 38-39.

32. Bell, "The Church and Poverty," *Christianity Today,* 27 March 1970, p. 27.

33. Colson, "Budget Cuts and Self-Denial," *Christianity Today,* 20 September 1985, p. 56.

34. Schaeffer, "Race and Economics," *Christianity Today,* 4 January 1974, p. 19.

wealth and income.[35] Similarly, a recent *Christianity Today* editorial urged that "a history of bureaucratic malfeasance must not overshadow the fact that over 30 million Americans depend upon some kind of government subsidy for economic survival. While the so-called government safety net seems secure to assist those who find themselves in destitute poverty, further entitlement cutbacks could prove disastrous to those who are above the government cutoff line for destitute poverty, yet below the national poverty level. These 'nominally poor' could well find themselves in a tailspin heading for an economic abyss from which there would be no return."[36]

It is also interesting to note that the suggestion that social change must result principally from the conversion of individuals has not been emphasized as strongly in recent *Christianity Today* editorials as it was in the 1950s and 1960s. The persistence of a variety of social problems in the face of the resurgence of evangelical Christianity in recent decades may well have called this kind of assumption into question.

Recent Progressive Evangelical Appraisals of Capitalism

As we have seen, Carl Henry and other neo-evangelicals stressed at mid-century that if evangelicals were going to develop a distinctly Christian social policy, they would need to study such things as economics and social science. A number of younger evangelicals acted on Henry's advice, and many of them have since become self-consciously progressive on issues of social and economic policy.

Unlike those on the radical evangelical left, progressive evangelicals have generally appreciated the capacity of capitalism to produce wealth. Still, they believe that the system's problems have had to do with its propensity to abuse both people and resources in the productive process and its failure to distribute wealth equitably. Accordingly, progressive evangelical solutions to social problems tend to include calls for the expansion of the regulatory apparatus of the modern state. Citing the massive scale of modern business and the complexity of modern society, progressives have argued that private initiative and benevolent activity are simply not equal to the task of restraining modern capitalism.[37] Instead, they have urged Christians to view government as a

35. Mulford, "The War on Poverty: A Christian Economist on the Bible and State Involvement," *Christianity Today*, 14 June 1985, p. 30. Mulford also argues that we must take care to ensure that poverty is not institutionalized and that poverty programs stress self-help rather than dependence.

36. "Flesh-and-Blood Priorities," *Christianity Today*, 13 January 1989, pp. 18-19.

37. See Tony Brouwer, "Poor People and the Economic System," *Reformed Journal* 18 (January 1968): 16-18; and John Timmerman, "Greed or Gain," *Reformed Journal* 23 (September 1973): 3.

positive force for social change and to look to the state for solutions to complex social problems.[38] Richard K. Taylor suggested, for example, that "reliance on the economic mechanisms of self-interest, profit-seeking, and market regulation has contributed to many of our problems in ecology and planetary human relations. Economic activity should be guided, at least in part, by institutions that focus on the overall common good, that is, by a democratic planning system that measures goals and activities in ecological and human, not in conventional economic, terms."[39] And William E. Diehl has asserted that "it taxes all credibility to assume that in this highly complex society in which we live the needs of the poor can be met by Christians acting individually or through their churches on a voluntary basis. Even if all Christians had the commitment to care for the poor, how could I or my congregation possibly know where all the unmet needs were, and how could we be certain that there would be an equitable distribution of our benevolence? Some overall agency is needed for such a task, and it is obviously civil government."[40]

Since progressives tend to assume that welfare legislation accomplishes what it sets out to accomplish, they commonly interpret opposition to the expansion of welfare programs as opposition to the stated aims of these programs.[41] In addressing their more conservative cohorts, progressive evangelicals tend to focus on normative issues and stress the need for conservatives to develop compassion and social concern. In addition, they argue that the political economy is a human creation, and as such it can be changed for the better if only we choose to identify the necessary changes and exhibit the moral will to effect them.[42]

Progressives speak of the church's role in social change in terms of its

38. Richard V. Pierard has urged evangelicals to *"view the government as a positive force for the achievement of social and economic justice . . . [for] it is the only agency with enough power to counteract the giant combines which characterize modern capitalism"* (in Edward Coleson and Richard V. Pierard, "Is There a Christian Economic System?" *Journal of the American Scientific Affiliation* 29 [March 1977]: 18). Similarly, David Moberg has urged young Christians to go into social service work instead of business-related occupations: "Christian love can usually be demonstrated most actively by entering church-related vocations or service occupations like social work, psychiatry, clinical counseling, corrections, public health services, child guidance, and institutional administration" (*Inasmuch: Christian Social Responsibility in Twentieth Century America* [Grand Rapids: William B. Eerdmans, 1965], p. 150).

39. Taylor, *Economics and the Gospel* (Philadelphia: United Church Press, 1973), p. 107.

40. Diehl, "A Guided Market Response," in *Wealth and Poverty: Four Christian Views of Economics,* ed. Robert G. Clouse (Downers Grove, IL: InterVarsity Press, 1984), pp. 68-69.

41. The effectiveness of social legislation is axiomatic in much of progressive evangelical social thought, especially its early manifestations. David Moberg has stated, for example, that "Most social legislation can be interpreted as 'love in action'" (*Inasmuch,* p. 129).

42. See Taylor, *Economics and the Gospel,* p. 9; and George DeVries, Jr., "The Business of America," *Reformed Journal* 27 (April 1977): 15-19.

call both to model a new social reality and to act as the "conscience" of society.[43] While this may not appear at first glance to be significantly different from mainstream evangelical views such as those of Carl Henry, the progressive position, due largely to the negative assumptions it has made about the operations of modern capitalism, has suggested much more of an activist political and economic role for the church *as* church. Progressive evangelicals are much less reluctant to argue that the church ought actively to endorse specific (usually left-liberal) socioeconomic policies. They contend that merely changing individuals, and even encouraging such changed individuals to become involved in social action, is wholly inadequate to the task of effecting change in the modern situation.[44] Evangelicalism's evangelistic mission ought also to incorporate a social agenda oriented toward redistributive economic policies. Indeed, the appropriate integration of social and personal concerns in evangelism, progressives insist, was taken for granted within evangelicalism up until its "great reversal" on social concerns at the beginning of this century, and this integrated view urgently needs to be recovered.[45] Not only would this serve to authenticate the spiritual elements of the gospel for evangelicals themselves, but it would also eliminate the hypocrisy of wealthy evangelicals preaching the gospel to a poverty-stricken world.

In spite of the general tendency of many younger evangelical scholars to move toward the left politically and economically, it is important to note that others have become discouraged with the arguments of both left and right and have refused to identify Christianity with any of the present political-economic alternatives. "It is an unfortunate sight," evangelical economist Kenneth Elzinga commented some years ago, "to observe a Christian vehemently defending any economic system, for two reasons: first, any system, viewed abstractly . . . can appear utopian. . . . Second and even more seriously, promoting and hawking an economic system subtly, even invidiously, feeds the notion that man maybe or *does* or *can* live by bread alone."[46] More recently, Elzinga has noted that "the problem in formulating a Christian view of economic order is not so much the ideology we bring to our economics, but rather the ideology we bring to our hermeneutics."[47] Similarly, evangelical

43. See Moberg, *Inasmuch*, p. 52.

44. Richard V. Pierard has characterized as "pitiful" the argument that it is acceptable for individuals to get involved in social action but not for the church *as* church to do so ("Needed: An Evangelical Social Ethic," *Evangelical Quarterly* 44 [April-June 1972]: 87).

45. See David O. Moberg, *The Great Reversal: Evangelism and Social Concern,* (Philadelphia: J. B. Lippincott, 1977).

46. Elzinga, "The Demise of Capitalism and the Christian's Response," *Christianity Today,* 7 July 1972, p. 16.

47. Elzinga, "A Christian View of the Economic Order," *Reformed Journal,* October 1981, p. 16.

economist J. David Richardson has written, "I find much Christian commentary on economics long on ideology and short on integrity, full of unsupported assertion, unsubstantiated allegation, and unrepresentative anecdote. I believe it is needful ministry and needful scholarship for at least some believing economists to cultivate a reputation for definitive, documentary, empirical and historical work."[48]

Of course a number of evangelical scholars have attempted to do just this with the intent of improving the quality of the contemporary evangelical political-economic debate. In a recent study entitled *Counting the Cost: The Economics of Christian Stewardship,* for example, Robin Kendrick Klay, an economist at Hope College, notes that "theological studies tell us either that American-style free enterprise is God's will for every society, or that revolution and socialism are God's plan to liberate the oppressed and unite the human family. All too often we find ourselves assaulted with recitations of distressing problems and then asked to accept a set of purportedly straightforward, biblically informed answers. But where is the prudent, intelligently informed analysis of these complex problems?"[49] *Counting the Cost* is Klay's answer to this question.

Arguing that the biblical notion of stewardship requires us to make "well-intentioned *and* well-informed [economic] choices," Klay suggests that "both efficiency and growth"—key features of capitalism—"are important if we are to responsibly use precious gifts, meet the demand of [distributive] justice, and imitate the selfless love of God, the creative Giver."[50] Along these lines, she argues that Christians should resist the temptation toward protectionism and "urge their governments . . . to assume leadership in international negotiations leading to freer trade." In the interests of economic stability, however, she stresses the necessity of fiscal and monetary policy tools.[51]

Klay is convinced that contemporary economic dilemmas such as "stagflation" and the problems of consistently underfunded domestic social programs and inadequate Third World development aid have ultimately been caused by excessive military expenditures. With reference to Third World development, for example, she argues that "economically well-informed and thoughtful Christians ought to be able to critique the disproportionate emphasis that nations have put on military expenditure compared with development assistance."[52] And regarding domestic social programs, she suggests that "in-

48. Richardson, "Frontiers in Economics and Christian Scholarship," *Christian Scholar's Review* 17 (June 1988): 395.

49. Klay, *Counting the Cost: The Economics of Christian Stewardship* (Grand Rapids: William B. Eerdmans, 1986), p. 1.

50. Klay, *Counting the Cost,* pp. 3, 162.

51. Klay, *Counting the Cost,* pp. 140, 156.

52. Klay, *Counting the Cost,* p. 71; see also p. 186.

come redistribution in favor of the poor could be taken further without having extremely adverse effects on incentives if increased help for the poor were to come out of changes elsewhere in the federal budget, such as a reduction in military spending."[53]

While *Counting the Cost* provides us with a "prudent, intelligently informed analysis" of complex modern economic problems, Klay's analysis is founded on peculiarly optimistic assumptions about our ability to engineer solutions to these problems. These assumptions are most evident in a chapter entitled "Social Responses to the Problem of Scarcity," written by Klay's colleague James B. Heisler. "Societies must choose what will be consumed collectively," insists Heisler.[54] This would seem to indicate a faith in the proposition that we can be more or less certain of achieving specific socio-economic conditions if only we make adequate plans beforehand. While he admits that planning poses a threat to economic efficiency, Heisler implies that this problem is not endemic to the planning process. To the contrary, he argues that inefficient planning is a result of society's failure to be adequately informed about economic realities.[55]

Jim Halteman has made another attempt to steer a course between the evangelical left and right on the issue of capitalism in a study entitled *Market Capitalism and Christianity*. Halteman, a professor of economics at Wheaton College, asserts that while "market capitalism can deliver goods and services in amazing quantities, . . . it cannot guarantee caring communities that sustain body and spirit."[56] He proposes to solve this problem through the creation of small communitarian churches in the midst of the larger market-oriented society, churches in which basic economic decisions could be made on a collectivist basis. He contends that such a system would preserve capitalism's productive efficiency and at the same time minimize the alienation caused by capitalistic individualism.

Halteman offers theological warrant for his proposal in a variation on the Anabaptist "two kingdoms" theme—the idea that the church and the larger culture constitute two separate "kingdoms," each of which functions on the basis of an essentially different value system. He argues that the secular

53. Klay, *Counting the Cost,* p. 48.

54. Heisler, "Social Responses to the Problem of Scarcity," in *Counting the Cost,* p. 14.

55. Heisler, "Social Responses to the Problem of Scarcity," p. 30. While Klay (and Heisler) intend to steer a course between the evangelical left and right, they fail to counter what is perhaps the principal criticism directed at the notion of planning by those on the right. Conservative critics hold that knowledge is much more limited than Klay and Heisler assume it to be. Indeed, they maintain that our knowledge is so limited that attempting to engineer social outcomes is not only mistaken but actually dangerous.

56. Halteman, *Market Capitalism and Christianity* (Grand Rapids: Baker Book, 1988), p. 14.

kingdom values the individual freedom symbolized in private property rights and operates competitively on the basis of self-interest (with some moral restraints). This being the case, capitalism and limited government are particularly well suited to this kingdom. The kingdom of God (i.e., the church, understood as small gathered communities), on the other hand, places less value on individual freedom than on the "total welfare of people," Christian love, and cooperation.[57]

Halteman envisions small church communities making collective economic decisions informed by the values of the kingdom of God—such things as need-based voluntary sharing and collective norm setting and disciplining—rather than simply on the basis of the competitive market mechanism. He specifies that these communities would also exhibit low-consumption standards, a commitment to collectively determined ethical norms that would go "far beyond the legal constraints of society," a genuine concern for the environment, a global consciousness, and an identification with those oppressed by the market mechanism.[58] But Halteman parts ways with traditional Anabaptist two-kingdom thinking in suggesting that the relation of these communities to the larger society would not be one of separation. The churches would model the values of the kingdom of God with an eye toward eventually influencing the values of the larger secular system by "infiltration."[59]

Halteman recognizes that within the kind of system he is proposing individual autonomy in personal consumption and business decisions is, to some degree, sacrificed, but he is convinced that this sacrifice is necessary. For example, he maintains that decisions about employment and investment need to be made collectively "so that individual vested interests take second place to an unbiased search for the will of God in the investment decision."[60] He believes that this loss of individual autonomy would be more than offset by the elimination of the alienating effects of modern individualism.

Halteman also believes that state intervention is necessary in economic life. "Government is not an enemy of the market place but a complementary part of the whole of society. It defines the rules of the system, it operates stabilization policy, it helps correct market allocation difficulties when public goods and natural monopoly conditions exist, and it redistributes income in a manner that is practically and morally acceptable."[61] Indeed, he suggests that one of the ways Christians can effectively infiltrate and influence the larger secular culture is through the advocacy and support of state-supervised corrections of market failures.

In a similar fashion, Charles K. Wilber and Laura Grimes have recently

---

57. Halteman, *Market Capitalism and Christianity*, p. 51.
58. Halteman, *Market Capitalism and Christianity*, p. 151.
59. Halteman, *Market Capitalism and Christianity*, p. 14.
60. Halteman, *Market Capitalism and Christianity*, p. 75.
61. Halteman, *Market Capitalism and Christianity*, p. 133.

argued that market failures not only require state intervention but completely undermine the evangelical right's moral defense of capitalism. Because "the market system underproduces private goods with social benefits and it over-produces private goods with social costs," there is a substantial need for certain kinds of market regulation.[62] "A weakness of [the defense of] free market economics . . . is that it sees the threat to freedom from too much government control, but ignores the diminishing of freedom by an unrestrained market. If some people are free to do whatever they want in the economic sphere—refuse to pay a living wage, pollute the atmosphere, have unsafe working conditions in their business—this impinges upon other people's rights and freedoms. Another lack of freedom is the inequality of opportunity that occurs in a capitalist society when children's opportunities are determined through their parents' race, income, and education level."[63]

Wilber and Grimes have concluded that the defense of market capitalism on the basis of individualism and self-interest is at least partly responsible for individualistic and self-interested behavior in modern societies and also for a great deal of resistance to constructive state intervention.[64] And so they have suggested that it is within the purview of the state, and especially within the purview of the church, to construct social and economic policy in such a way that individuals are effectively encouraged to move beyond considerations of self-interest and toward "a moral consensus wherein we re-learn to internalize habits of non-calculating behavior."[65]

Recent Neo-Calvinist Appraisals of Capitalism

Intellectuals in the Christian Reformed Church have played a particularly influential role in shaping contemporary evangelical social and political-economic thought, especially at the progressive end of the evangelical spectrum. This appears to be the case in large part because of the Reformed tradition of cultural criticism, but it has probably also been due to the difficulties many Reformed scholars have had with American fundamentalism and American cultural conservatism generally.[66] Whatever the reasons, self-consciously Re-

62. Wilber and Grimes, "The Moral Defense of Market Capitalism: A Critique of the Literature," a paper presented at a conference entitled "Christian Perspectives on a Mixed Market Economy," 18-20 September 1987, Wheaton College, Wheaton, IL, p. 20. Wilber is a professor of economics at the University of Notre Dame, and Grimes is a graduate student in theology at that institution.

63. Wilber and Grimes, "The Moral Defense of Market Capitalism," pp. 37-38.

64. Wilber and Grimes, "The Moral Defense of Market Capitalism," pp. 50ff.

65. Wilber and Grimes, "The Moral Defense of Market Capitalism," p. 56.

66. See James D. Bratt, *Dutch Calvinism in Modern America: A History of a Conservative Subculture* (Grand Rapids: William B. Eerdmans, 1984).

formed intellectuals writing in publications such as the *Reformed Journal* have
emerged at the forefront of progressive evangelical social thought of late.

With respect to issues of political economy, Reformed scholars are concerned to avoid what they consider to be the errors of the radical evangelical
left as well as those of the conservative evangelical right.[67] Article 19 of a
document entitled *The Church and Its Social Calling,* issued by the Reformed
Ecumenical Synod in 1980, for example, states,

> the Church should realize . . . that our whole world is burdened with structures
> that create poverty, injustice, and oppression. All systems in our modern age are,
> to a lesser or to a larger degree, at fault on this point. In its prophetic ministry the
> Church should not only reject all totalitarian systems, whether they are of a
> left-wing [Marxist] or a right-wing [fascist] nature, because in such systems in-
> justice is built into the very fabric of the system; but it should also critically
> evaluate and challenge the so-called capitalistic social order by asking the question
> whether a society which considers as its primary value the pursuit of material
> abundance and uses all of its resources for the fulfillment of this pursuit, can be
> a just society.[68]

Christian Reformed scholars have approached the task of "critically eval-
uating and challenging" modern social and economic structures assuming that
"Christ is the transformer of culture," to use H. Richard Niebuhr's typifica-
tion.[69] This assumption is clearly evident in another affirmation of the Reformed Ecumenical Synod:

67. While Christian Reformed intellectuals have been perhaps most embarrassed by
popular perceptions associating theological conservatism with political and social conservatism, they have not been particularly comfortable with the radical evangelical position
either. In the first instance, the purely adversarial cultural role assigned to the church by the
radicals has run contrary to the Reformed view of the church as the "transformer" of culture.
They cannot reconcile the radical's wholly negative view of the state with biblical teaching
(e.g., Romans 13) either. In addition, they do not believe that the essentially Manichaean
tone of the radical argument, pitting a small and beleaguered Christian community against
an overwhelmingly evil world system, appropriately reflects God's ability, indicated decisively in Christ's resurrection, to renew his creation. The Reformed intellectuals have also
suggested that radicals might want to go beyond their "prophetic" denunciations and give
some consideration to the practical effectiveness of their actions. And they have criticized
radicals for proposing a secular socialist ideology as the only truly Christian response to the
socioeconomic problems of the modern world. See Nicholas Wolterstorff, "How Does Grand
Rapids Reply to Washington," *Reformed Journal,* October 1977, pp. 10-14; and Isaac Rottenberg, "Dimensions of the Kingdom: A Dialogue with Sojourners," *The Reformed Journal,*
November 1977, pp. 17-21.

68. *The Church and Its Social Calling* (Grand Rapids: Reformed Ecumenical Synod,
1980), p. 107.

69. Chapter 6 of Niebuhr's *Christ and Culture* (New York: Harper & Row, 1951) is
entitled "Christ the Transformer of Culture." There Niebuhr states that "the problem of
culture is . . . the problem of its conversion not of its replacement by a new creation; though

"[our] position at its best represents a radical break with the either/or (Anabaptist) as well as with the both/and (Liberal, Roman Catholic, Lutheran) solutions [to the problem of relating Christ to culture]. The Calvinist perspective seeks to honor an integrally unified, religiously whole view of life, free of all sacred/secular dichotomies. All of life is religion. It is an ongoing response to the Word of God in every sphere of human activity. That response is either obedient or disobedient. All creation is under sin, but all of it has come again under the redeeming work of Christ.[70]

Interestingly, the references in the Synod's affirmation to "spheres of human activity" and "obedient or disobedient" human responses indicate a further refinement of Reformed thought called "neo-Calvinism." Originating in the work of Dutch theologian and statesman Abraham Kuyper (d. 1920) and in the philosophical theology of Hermann Dooyeweerd (d. 1977), neo-Calvinism represents an interesting approach to the modern theological task. As this approach has informed the social and economic thought of many contemporary Christian Reformed intellectuals, it may be helpful to review it briefly before proceeding to our consideration of specific neo-Calvinist appraisals of capitalism.

Abraham Kuyper insisted that Calvinism is a logically consistent "life and world-view" that represents the "completed evolution of Protestantism, resulting in a both higher and richer stage of human development."[71] I cannot go into the support Kuyper offered for this bold claim, but I would note that he appears to have envisioned Calvinism as the only theological system capable of reconciling the characteristically modern understanding of historical development with classical theological notions of ontology. Insofar as theological ontology was concerned, Kuyper stressed the permanence, or fixity, of the creation. The diversity in our experience of the creation, Albert M. Wolters has suggested in a description of the Kuyperian position, is not merely a "product of evolution or the historical process in the sense that any kind of

---

the conversion is so radical that it amounts to a kind of rebirth" (p. 194). James Bratt has suggested that in the Christian Reformed Church the concept of common grace has traditionally "encouraged the redeemed to respect the good remaining in the world and to strive to augment it. Even more, it made many elements of human culture—institutions such as the law and the community, artistic and technical ability, academic disciplines, and scientific methods—not just products but *means* of grace, instruments whereby God restrained sin and enabled men to try to develop creation as he had originally designed. Finally, it legitimized a certain amount of cooperation between the redeemed and unbelievers on the grounds that to some extent they shared a sense of the good and therefore a common purpose" (*Dutch Calvinism in Modern America,* p. 20).

70. *The Church and Its Social Calling,* p. 10.

71. Abraham Kuyper, *Lectures on Calvinism* (Grand Rapids: William B. Eerdmans, 1931), pp. 190, 41.

thing might turn into any other kind of thing in the course of time, but [is] rooted in creation."[72] Kuyper viewed every existing thing—including the forms of social organization that people have ostensibly created—as having been created ultimately by God. And as God's creation, he asserted, they contain within themselves laws, or "creational ordinances," for their continued existence.[73]

Specifically with reference to human culture, Kuyper identified a series of creational "spheres"—principal among them being the state, society, and the church—each of which has its own set of creational ordinances and each of which requires a measure of sovereignty relative to the others. Kuyper advocated this "sphere sovereignty" in contradistinction to "popular sovereignty" (as championed in the French and American Revolutions, for example) and to the Hegelian conception of "state sovereignty." He argued that popular sovereignty locates social authority solely within human nature conceived autonomously and so ignores the authority of God over social life; state sovereignty, on the other hand, concedes too much power to the government, thus making it possible for the state to infringe upon and damage areas of social life not within its jurisdiction. Commenting on the relation of the societal spheres to the state, for example, Kuyper wrote, "in a Calvinistic sense we understand . . . that the family, the business, science, art and so forth are all social spheres, which do not owe their existence to the state, and which do not derive the law of their life from the superiority of the state, but obey a high authority within their own bosom; an authority which rules, by the grace of God, just as the sovereignty of the State does."[74] Further describing Kuyper's position, Wolters has noted that

> the sociological principle that distinct kinds of societal institutions (e.g. state, family, school, church) or cultural sectors (e.g. commerce, scholarship, art) have their proper jurisdictions limited and defined by the specific nature of the "sphere" concerned . . . became the guiding principle for the Christian political party which Kuyper led and provided a rationale for limiting the authority of the state and protecting the distinct rights and responsibilities of institutions like church and family.[75]

On the question of history, Kuyper emphasized that the creation was ordained by God in such a way as to allow for historical development—development called forth from the potentialities that had been created within the

---

72. Wolters, "The Intellectual Milieu," in *The Legacy of Hermann Dooyeweerd: Reflections on Critical Philosophy in the Christian Tradition*, ed. C. T. McIntire (New York: University Press of America, 1985), p. 6.

73. Kuyper, *Lectures on Calvinism*, p. 70.

74. Kuyper, *Lectures on Calvinism*, p. 90.

75. Wolters, "The Intellectual Millieu of Hermann Dooyeweerd," p. 6.

various spheres. Indeed, Kuyper's understanding of human stewardship over creation, often termed mankind's "cultural mandate," suggests the conscious human direction of this ongoing historical development in such a way that it brings glory to God by enabling each created thing, whether natural or social, to conform to the ordinances inhering within it.

> If salvation is really re-creation and if re-creation means a restoration of everything to its proper creational place and function, then, Kuyper thought, there must be a norm, or standard, for each kind of thing to which it must be restored and by which it is distinguished from every other kind of thing. . . . God is sovereign, therefore his word is law for all creatures. That law-word constitutes the normative nature and distinctive identity of every kind of created thing, whether they be oak trees, human rationality, or the body politic. . . . Everything has its own "law of life," the standard to which it must conform if it is to live or function fully and authentically.[76]

Hermann Dooyeweerd, a student of Kuyper's at the Free University of Amsterdam, set himself the task of working out philosophically how it was that created things, both natural and social, actually develop according to their divinely ordained potentialities. An important theme he added to the Kuyperian system in this regard is that of "disclosure," which Wolters has described as follows: "Creation . . . in the neo-Calvinistic world-view was eschatological in an encompassing cultural sense and had implications for a complete philosophy of history. It is this idea which Dooyeweerd worked out in his conception of the 'opening process' [or disclosure] of creation and his theory of historical development. . . . This process means that history involves the differentiation and progressive unfolding of the unique creational nature of each social institution and cultural sector."[77]

Dooyeweerd stressed that the chief barrier to the progressive unfolding or disclosure of creation was well summarized in the theological notion of idolatry—the refusal of fallen humanity to worship its Creator and its choice instead to worship isolated aspects, or spheres, of creation to the detriment of creation as a whole. Indeed, Dooyeweerd felt that the resistance idolatry posed to the stewardly disclosure of creation was what chiefly characterized the human condition.

In recent Christian Reformed appraisals of capitalism, neo-Calvinist analysis has been applied to contemporary social and economic problems in very interesting

---

76. Wolters, "The Intellectual Milieu of Hermann Dooyeweerd," p. 5.

77. Wolters, "The Intellectual Milieu of Hermann Dooyeweerd," p. 8. It is this notion of disclosure, or real historical development, that is missing from the theory of "Christian reconstruction," which in many other respects resembles neo-Calvinism. Indeed, it is the absence of disclosure or its equivalent that accounts for the rather static and ahistorical quality of reconstructionist thought.

ways. Christian Reformed intellectuals have tended to be explicitly antitotalitarian and to argue for the relative autonomy of the various spheres of human activity. They have also been interested in determining the specific creational norms for each of these spheres of activity. Given the fear of communism at mid-century, it was not uncommon for Christian Reformed authors to defend free enterprise, or the sphere of business activity, against the threat of totalitarian Marxism.[78] More recently, however, Christian Reformed scholars have attributed modern social and economic problems to the idolization of the economic sphere over and against the appropriate actualization of other spheres of life.

Capitalism and the Idolization of Progress: Robert Goudzwaard

Robert Goudzwaard, a professor of economics at the Free University of Amsterdam, has written a number of articles and several books on the subject of capitalism that have been quite influential in the American evangelical political-economic debate, especially within the Reformed community.[79] Goudzwaard has argued that the crisis of Western civilization—a crisis characterized by cultural decadence and alienation, increasingly violent conflict, environmental degradation and resource depletion, and the like—has been precipitated by the idolization of progress in the modern period, a problem linked to the institutionalization of modern capitalism.[80] In terms of neo-Calvinist analysis, capitalism, or the economic sphere, has been institutionalized in such a way that it runs roughshod over other spheres of human activity. In short, the economic sphere of modern life has become "absolutized."[81]

> *Capitalism is subject to critique insofar as, for the sake of progress, it is founded on independent and autonomous forces of economic growth and technology, that is, forces which are considered isolated, sufficient, and good in themselves. These economic and technological forces are indeed related to norms of ethics, and social justice, but in such a manner that these norms cannot impede the realization of these forces and the promotion of "progress." These norms are consciously*

78. See Bratt, *Dutch Calvinism in Modern America*, p. 189.

79. The titles include *Economic Stewardship versus Capitalist Religion* (Toronto: Institute for Christian Studies, 1972); *Capitalism and Progress: A Diagnosis of Western Society* (Grand Rapids: William B. Eerdmans, 1979); and *Idols of Our Time* (Downers Grove, IL: InterVarsity Press, 1984).

80. See Goudzwaard, *Capitalism and Progress*, p. xxxiii.

81. Goudzwaard, *Economic Stewardship versus Capitalist Religion*, p. 15. He cites the following examples of the economic sphere's violation of other spheres of human activity: disruptions of the family; commodification of land, labor, and capital; manipulation of consumers via advertising; and subordination of politics to economic interests (pp. 18-19). He further suggests that the concentration of economic power and the internationalization of corporate power in recent years have greatly exacerbated these problems.

viewed as dependent upon and secondary to the forces of progress: they are placed in the service of the expansion of technology and the growth of the economy. The combination of independent and primary factors of progress with dependent and secondary socioethical norms prevents simultaneous and harmonious realization of norms—economic as well as ethical and legal. This combination has made it impossible for capitalism to do justice to the noneconomic norms for human life. Norms of ethics and justice are allowed to play a role only *after* economic production has already occurred. They are permitted to make limited corrections and modest alterations in the process of industrialization, but only *after* this process has autonomously and sovereignly chosen its path through society.[82]

Goudzwaard has traced the historical origins of this problematic development back to a number of sources: (1) the Renaissance proclamation of human autonomy over and against the sovereignty of God, (2) Protestant rationalism's secularization of the notion of providence as reflected, for example, in classical economic theory, and (3) the Enlightenment suggestion that progress in perfecting both man and society can be achieved given the correct application of human reason to the problems of material existence.[83] These philosophical assertions were institutionalized in modern capitalism, a system in which law, morality, and the organization of the economy have granted "unobstructed admission to the forces of economic growth and technological development" in a process resembling natural selection.[84] Hence Goudzwaard has argued that in the modern situation much of what ought to constitute the richness of human existence has been collapsed into the twin categories of economic growth and technological advancement, a process that has resulted in "a persistent narrowing of human relations and purposes to technical and economic achievements as ends in themselves."[85] He has suggested that "unchallenged economic growth, an idol made by our own hands, has become a power which forces its will upon us. Christians and non-Christians alike, *possessed by an end* (material prosperity), have allowed various forces, means and powers in our society (for example, untrammeled economic growth) to rule over us as gods."[86]

The idolization of progress, Goudzwaard has insisted, is reflected in a host of peculiarly modern ideologies, all directed primarily toward legitimating material progress and emphasizing certain limited aspects of human existence to the exclusion of others. Of course, Goudzwaard has contended that the utilitarian apologies for capitalism and free enterprise are ideological in this sense, but he has also suggested that many modern reactions to capitalism are ideological in much the same way. Socialism, for example, pledges allegiance

82. Goudzwaard, *Capitalism and Progress*, p. 66.
83. Goudzwaard, *Capitalism and Progress*, pp. 10, 16, 34.
84. Goudzwaard, *Capitalism and Progress*, p. 34.
85. Goudzwaard, *Capitalism and Progress*, p. 112.
86. Goudzwaard, *Idols of Our Time*, p. 14.

to material progress in a manner essentially identical to that of capitalism.[87] The same is true of nationalistic movements.[88] Even seemingly moderate proposals for the expansion of the welfare state, Goudzwaard has argued, are premised on continued economic growth.[89]

In spite of these many problems, Goudzwaard has refrained from suggesting that there is nothing to be done for our decadent capitalist culture. Indeed, he has insisted that our enslavement to "progress" in the areas of technology and economic growth is only an apparent necessity and that by viewing it as unavoidable we have evaded our historical responsibility as stewards of creation.[90] Goudzwaard has followed Dooyeweerd in arguing that what we need instead is the disclosure of social and economic existence.

> Disclosure implies the recovery of the meaning and value of human life outside of its subjection and service to progress. In the context of our entire discussion it means life's liberation from the closed horizon of a deadly servility to the narrow goals which we have established for ourselves by accepting progress as the essence of western culture. Disclosure, therefore, is first of all a process in which the *norms* for human life—like justice, trust, and truth—regain their original validity for our decisions and acts, also with respect to that broad range of decisions and acts where at the present the criteria of progress are of overwhelming importance. Secondly, in a process of disclosure, cultural *institutions* and societal forms—like governments, trade unions, and economic enterprises—regain opportunities to develop themselves according to their own distinct responsibilities. Finally, a process of disclosure removes the unbridled pressure on the individual *person* to adjust his or her habits and behavior to external demands. . . . Disclosure implies that every day life is intended to have its own meaning; that today's significance is not exhausted in what it may contribute to tomorrow's needs and wants.[91]

The goal of this process of disclosure, then, is the simultaneous realization of the norms of each created sphere of human existence.[92] While the norms for

---

87. Goudzwaard, *Capitalism and Progress,* p. 79; see also chap. 3 of *Idols of Our Time,* pp. 29ff.

88. See chap. 4 of Goudzwaard's *Idols of Our Time,* pp. 39ff.

89. See chap. 5 of Goudzwaard's *Idols of Our Time,* pp. 49ff. He suggests that the "rights of acquisition" granted by the welfare state are linked directly to continued prosperity. Should such prosperity cease, he writes, "it will create a deep crisis of trust in our society as a whole, a crisis putting democracy itself in danger. In all likelihood people will repay the infringement of their 'rights' with bitter accusations against politicians, whose constant promises, sealed in law, cannot be kept. In that 'hour of truth' politicians will feel inclined to postpone the painful outcome for as long as possible. The impulse then to heighten deficits will be even more irresistible until government finances are thrown totally out of gear. If that path is taken—the way of delay—then we must fear for the continued existence of our democratic law state" (pp. 55-56).

90. Goudzwaard, *Capitalism and Progress,* p. 247.

91. Goudzwaard, *Capitalism and Progress,* p. 186; see also *Economic Stewardship versus Capitalist Religion,* p. 2.

92. Goudzwaard, *Capitalism and Progress,* p. 205.

the economic sphere will be realized in this process, so will the norms of such things as family, community, and environment.

Insofar as the norms for economic life are concerned, Goudzwaard has argued on the basis of the presupposition of scarcity that one of these norms is frugality.[93] In addition, he has insisted that economic calculation must not be limited to the consideration of priceable goods but must take all of creation into account—and, he has implied, the future as well.[94] The norms of morality and justice, furthermore, require that laborers be treated as subjects and not merely as commodities, and that fairness must be calculated into business decisions; technological development must be realized as an expression of human creativity for human benefit.[95] All of these norms, Goudzwaard has suggested, are summarized in the ethos of love, an ethos to which capitalism is not necessarily opposed.[96] Indeed, he has argued that, unlike socialism, the market economy is "heteronomous" in the sense that it is able to take its norms and values from outside of itself.[97] The early development of capitalism actually presupposed the kinds of norms just mentioned, Goudzwaard has asserted,[98] and it is only relatively recently in the modern industrial situation that the ethos of love has been expelled from the capitalist system. Goudzwaard maintains that this ethos can be restored to capitalism, however, and in this regard he has advocated moving toward a "maintenance economy" of limited economic growth within which such things as domestic employment and aid to underdeveloped countries take priority over military expenditures.[99]

Goudzwaard has also insisted that the state cannot assume the task of supervising the normative disclosure of the economy. Instead, the reintroduction of the proper norms for economic activity must be undertaken directly by the "production sector of society"—that is, by business and industry.[100] While Goudzwaard has argued that the growth of the modern state may be legitimate given the growth of industry, too much economic cooperation between the state and industry will lead not only to conflicts of interest between the two but also to the violation of the sphere sovereignty of each.[101] Indeed, cooperation between government and industry risks fusing statism, or the "ideology of guaranteed security," with the ideology of nationalism and/or the ideology of material progress, something that could precipitate a "monstrous alliance"

93. Goudzwaard, *Economic Stewardship versus Capitalist Religion,* p. 3.

94. Goudzwaard, *Capitalism and Progress,* p. 212.

95. Goudzwaard, *Capitalism and Progress,* pp. 213-14.

96. Goudzwaard, *Economic Stewardship versus Capitalist Religion,* p. 9.

97. Robert Goudzwaard, "Centrally Planned Economies: Strengths, Weaknesses, and the Future," *Transformation* 4 (June-September/October-December 1987): 55.

98. Goudzwaard, *Economic Stewardship versus Capitalist Religion,* p. 9.

99. Goudzwaard, *Idols of Our Time,* pp. 105-6.

100. Goudzwaard, *Capitalism and Progress,* p. 209.

101. See Goudzwaard, *Economic Stewardship versus Capitalist Religion,* pp. 36-39.

of economic and political power.[102] "We find ourselves at a very critical juncture in the development of Western civilization," Goudzwaard concludes in *Capitalism and Progress.*

> No society or civilization can continue to exist without having found an answer to the question of meaning. The emptiness created by the death of the god of progress must be filled with something else. . . . It seems that we have two choices: either the vacuum will be filled with a new, awe-inspiring myth, possibly built around the leaders of a central and large-scale world authority, who are authorized by their populations to direct all available technical, economic, and scientific means to new objectives with which to assault both heaven and earth; or else there will take place a turnaround of Christians and nonchristians together, a turnaround which directs itself to the Torah or normativity which the Creator of heaven and earth has given to this world as its meaning from the beginning, and which points to a new earth, coming with the return of the crucified One. Without such a turnaround I can hardly imagine a real and permanent disclosure of our western civilization.[103]

Liberation as Disclosure: Nicholas Wolterstorff

In a sense, the neo-Calvinist project hinges on the ability to link traditional theological conceptions of ontology with modern historical understanding. Put differently, the project hinges on the ability to link God's creation of the world with his redemption of it. The neo-Calvinist project also suggests that human responsibility before God necessarily entails the supervision, or stewardship, of the historical disclosure and restoration of creation. For these reasons neo-Calvinists are keenly interested in historical trends and movements, especially those which appear to point toward social renewal. In a study entitled *Until Justice and Peace Embrace,* Nicholas Wolterstorff, formerly a professor of philosophy at Calvin College and now serving as a professor of philosophy for Yale University and Yale Divinity School, reports finding indications of this kind of renewal in contemporary movements of political liberation and hence also in liberation theology.

Wolterstorff suggests that the modern church needs to recover the "world formative" approach to social change that characterized early Calvinism, an approach he contrasts with the "avertive," other-worldly stance of medieval Christendom and a number of more recent Christian movements. "Original Calvinism," he argues, "represented . . . a passionate desire to reshape the social world so that it would no longer be alienated from God. Thereby it would no longer be alienated from mankind, for the will of God is that society be an ordered 'brotherhood' serving the common good."[104]

102. See chap. 7 of Goudzwaard's *Idols of Our Time,* pp. 70ff.
103. Goudzwaard, *Capitalism and Progress,* p. 249.
104. Wolterstorff, *Until Justice and Peace Embrace* (Grand Rapids: William B. Eerdmans, 1983), pp. 21-22.

Wolterstorff contends that in order to eliminate alienation we will need, at the very least, a correct diagnosis of its causes, and he suggests that an "architectonic," or structural, analysis of modern society is necessary in this regard.[105] He lists two theoretical candidates for such a diagnosis: "modernization theory," which suggests that different societies progress toward socioeconomic development along similar paths but independently and at different rates, and "world-systems theory," which asserts that there is only one global economic system at present, in which certain societies benefit at the expense of others.[106] Citing the persistent failure of economic development in many parts of the world and the growing income gap between the First and the Third Worlds, he concludes that modernization theory is "bankrupt" and opts instead for the world-systems theory of Immanuel Wallerstein.[107]

A variation on the theme of economic imperialism similar to Latin American dependency theory, Wallerstein's world-systems theory suggests that there is a single capitalist world economy in which a "core" of advanced industrial nations, including ostensibly "socialist" nations such as the Soviet Union, has systematically exploited both a "semi-periphery" and "periphery" of lesser developed nations. "To oversimplify," Wallerstein says in *The Capitalist World Economy*,

> capitalism is a system in which the surplus value of the proletarian is appropriated by the bourgeois. When this proletarian is located in a different country from this bourgeois, one of the mechanisms that has affected the process of appropriation is the manipulation of controlling flows over state boundaries. This results in patterns of 'uneven development' which are *summarized* in the concepts of core, semi-periphery, and periphery. This is an intellectual tool to help analyze the multiple forms of class conflict in the capitalist world-economy.[108]

The mechanism of this appropriation, Wallerstein stresses, is the price differential between the goods bought by the "core" from the semi-periphery and periphery nations (low-cost raw materials and labor-intensive products) and the goods sold back to the semi-periphery and periphery by core nations (high-priced, finished, capital-intensive products).

Within the framework of world-systems theory, Wolterstorff contends that global capitalism has resulted, at least in the core countries, in the promotion of social and institutional differentiation, which (following Dooyeweerd) he views as part of the ongoing creative process. Capitalism has also resulted in a tremendous expansion of human freedom, both in terms of its mastery of

---

105. Wolterstorff, *Until Justice and Peace Embrace*, p. 23.

106. Wolterstorff, *Until Justice and Peace Embrace*, p. 24. He mentions Talcott Parsons's *Societies: Evolutionary and Comparative Perspectives* (1966) and *The System of Modern Societies* (1971) as representative works in the area of modernization theory.

107. Wolterstorff, *Until Justice and Peace Embrace*, pp. 25-27.

108. Wallerstein, *The Capitalist World Economy* (Cambridge: Cambridge University Press, 1979), p. 293.

nature and in terms of human "self-direction"—and yet only some people enjoy this freedom, and they do so only at the expense of others. "Our deepest dilemma today," writes Wolterstorff, "causing deep rifts within our world-order, is our inability or refusal to devise a social system that comes at all close to satisfying both of these deeply human motivations [i.e., freedom and equality]. The West grasps freedom at the cost of inequality, thereby consigning the economically impoverished to all the constraints of poverty. The East grasps equality at the cost of freedom."[109]

Citing the work of Robert Goudzwaard, Wolterstorff contends that what we need in the contemporary situation is the disclosure of social and economic relationships pointing toward the realization of the richness of each sphere of human activity.[110] Given his adoption of "world-systems" theory, however, Wolterstorff is dissatisfied with Goudzwaard's moderately conservative conclusions and suggests instead that a liberation theology tempered by neo-Calvinism might offer a better model for this process of disclosure than the mere attempt to disclose capitalism. Indeed, he implies that the ongoing creative process is reflected precisely in contemporary movements of political-economic liberation. "Our relation to the Kingdom [of God] is not only obedient waiting, but active contribution," he argues. "Whether one interprets history as a fitful movement toward differentiation or as a fitful movement of liberation, it remains something that we contribute to, not merely something inflicted upon us."[111]

Wolterstorff goes on to suggest that the contribution North American evangelicals can make to the disclosure, or liberation, of history will depend in large part on their recognition of their complicity in the perpetuation of poverty in the Third World by means of world-systems capitalism.[112] He feels that evangelicals have not fully appreciated this, but unlike those on the evangelical left, he does not contend that the evangelical failure in this respect has necessarily been due to ideological entanglement.[113] The workings of the system are, after all, far from obvious. "What must be done is elementary," he

109. Wolterstorff, *Until Justice and Peace Embrace,* p. 39.
110. Wolterstorff, *Until Justice and Peace Embrace,* p. 59.
111. Wolterstorff, *Until Justice and Peace Embrace,* p. 66.
112. "The mass poverty of the Third World is for the most part not some sort of natural condition that exists independently of us," writes Wolterstorff; "quite the contrary, a good deal of it is the result of the interaction of the core of the world-system with the periphery over the course of centuries. In many areas there has been a development of underdevelopment, and we in the core have played a crucial role in that development. Underdevelopment has a history, a history inseparable from ours" (*Until Justice and Peace Embrace,* p. 86).
113. More recently Wolterstorff has argued that the "Anglo-American pattern" of hermeneutics (of which he considers Carl F. H. Henry a good representative) has "spiritualized" the scriptural teaching on issues of social ethics ("The Bible and Economics: The Hermeneutical Issues," *Transformation* 4 [June-September/October-December 1987]: 11-19). In part, he suggests, this is ideological, but it has also been due to evangelical wariness about being associated with the theological and political left.

says: "we must work patiently and persistently to show people the causes of mass poverty, and we must do what we can to convince them that one of the fundamental criteria by which all political and economic institutions and practices must be tested is just this: What do they do to the poor? If they perpetuate poverty, they fail the most important test of legitimacy, and in that case we must struggle to alter them."[114]

Besides advocating this test of legitimacy, which is of course directly linked to his understanding of how the world economy actually functions, Wolterstorff also suggests that Western cultures are ethically ill-equipped to deal with the issue of global poverty because they have not yet developed a notion of "sustenance rights."[115] Elsewhere he has suggested that our Western tradition focuses on abstract entitlements to freedom rather than on entitlements to tangible benefits.[116] Yet by insisting that the right to freedom offers the tangible benefit of being left alone, Wolterstorff has argued for the moral and ethical legitimacy of welfare, or "benefit rights." While such rights do not represent claims on individuals, they do represent claims on society collectively, and "a society is just only when *all agents,* be they individual or social, enjoy their rights."[117] For this reason, and also taking into account modern sociocultural pluralism and human sinfulness, Wolterstorff has argued that the state "has a peculiarly important role to play in forestalling and undoing the violation of rights, including the right to sustenance."[118]

Finally, in terms of actual economic policy, while assuming that much of the left's case against capitalism is correct, Wolterstorff has not been willing to condemn the market system outright. If capitalism is "appropriately regulated," he has suggested (by which he appears to mean regulated in such a way as to guarantee the kinds of benefit rights mentioned above), it represents a tolerable economic arrangement.[119]

The Neo-Calvinist Protest against Conventional Economic Theory

A number of younger neo-Calvinist scholars, elaborating on Robert Goudzwaard's notion that the idolization of economic growth has produced ideologies

---

114. Wolterstorff, *Until Justice and Peace Embrace,* p. 97.

115. Wolterstorff, *Until Justice and Peace Embrace,* p. 81.

116. Nicholas P. Wolterstorff, "Christianity and Social Justice," *Christian Scholar's Review* 16 (March 1987): 211-32.

117. Wolterstorff, "Christianity and Social Justice," p. 215.

118. Wolterstorff, "Christianity and Social Justice," p. 225.

119. Wolterstorff, "Christianity and Social Justice," p. 227. Of course, world-systems theory does not admit to such a solution; it holds that the capitalist world system cannot be reformed, that it must be replaced by a socialist world government. See, for example, Wallerstein, *The Capitalist World Economy,* p. 35.

of various kinds, have recently contended that any distinctively Christian political-economic theory will require replacing the conventional economic theories with an entirely new paradigm, one not founded upon "individualism, autonomy and rationalism."[120] Conventional economic theories, these authors argue (and, while they have tended to focus on neoclassical theory, they would include monetarism, Keynesianism, socialism, and the like in this category), all imply that the economy is an autonomous and self-sustaining system; but the persistence of such things as "stagflation" and high unemployment, problems inexplicable within the frame of reference of these theories, indicate that conventional thinking about economics is seriously flawed. Even the most basic data processed within our present economic system—prices—fail to provide accurate reflections of value.[121] In addition, conventional theories have failed to deal adequately with questions of normativity. In *Notes toward a Critique of Secular Economic Theory*, for example, A. B. Cramp asserts that within the conventional framework "we are left with no principle of judgment on such fundamental matters as the clash between [convictions] that market processes constrain freedom, and . . . equally firm conviction[s] that such processes alone can sustain and preserve freedom. The one group tends to reject the whole system as sinful, the other to embrace it and be unable to perceive its sinful elements."[122]

Following Goudzwaard, neo-Calvinist scholars contend that conventional economic wisdom stems from faulty Enlightenment conceptions of both man and nature, conceptions in which the economy is envisioned as a kind of natural

---

120. W. Fred Graham, George N. Monsma, Jr., Carl J. Sinke, Alan Storkey, and John P. Tiemstra, *Reforming Economics: A Christian Perspective on Economic Theory and Practice*, 2 vols. (Grand Rapids: Calvin Center for Christian Scholarship, 1986), 1: 29. For other work representative of this group, see A. B. Cramp, *Notes toward a Christian Critique of Secular Economic Theory* (Toronto: Institute for Christian Studies, 1975); Alan Storkey, *A Christian Social Perspective* (Leicester: Inter-Varsity Press, 1979), and *Transforming Economics: A Christian Way to Employment* (London: S.P.C.K., 1986); and John P. Tiemstra, "Stories Economists Tell," *Reformed Journal* 38 (February 1988): 14-16.

121. See Graham et al., *Reforming Economics*, 1: 213. Similarly, Paul Marshall has argued that "we continually neglect all sorts of costs in our present 'economic' decision making. Instead of being really economic (stewardly) in our dealings with all things, we focus only on certain things, usually ones which have a price tag, and make a decision *on their basis* only. Consequently we can (and often do) end up, consistently making decisions that are really uneconomic: decisions that consistently have greater real costs than benefits, decisions that make us poorer as people while we maintain the illusion that we are 'growing' economically. The country can fall apart even while economic indicators look good" ("A Christian View of Economics," *Crux* 21 [March 1985]: 5). See also Eugene R. Dykema, "Wealth and Well-Being: The Bishops and Their Critics," in *Prophetic Visions and Economic Realities: Protestants, Jews, and Catholics Confront the Bishops' Letter on the Economy*, ed. Charles R. Strain (Grand Rapids: William B. Eerdmans, 1989), p. 56.

122. Cramp, *Notes toward a Christian Critique of Secular Economic Theory*, p. 28.

process and in which human society is understood simply as the aggregation of atomistic calculations of self-interest.

> This approach has had several major defects. It has tended to isolate economic theory from the broader contexts of life which necessarily enter deeply into normal economic activity. It has also focussed on one unifying motivating theme, namely, rational self-interest, which will integrate the whole body of economic theory. It seeks out a framework of natural order or equilibrium which is mechanical or mathematical, rather than fully human. The net effect is to foreclose the full meaning of people's economic lives in a certain kind of quasimechanicl [*sic*] straightjacket which devalues the economic responsibility of humanity as steward of God's creation by picturing us all as merely pawns within the system.[123]

In addition to pointing out these historical roots, the neo-Calvinists suggest that the crisis in contemporary economic theory has ultimately been caused by idolatry. "Some god or other is made the focus of goals and economic activity," Alan Storkey has written. "Efficiency, growth, competition, profit, consumption, pleasure and technology, have all become at different times the driving force, the authority before which people must bow. Each of these goals induces its own form of slavery."[124]

Yet the recent neo-Calvinist protest against conventional economic theory suggests not simply that it has failed adequately to describe economic activity but also that it has misinformed economic practice and so has itself contributed to the various economic crises we presently face.[125] Conventional theory also serves to block our consideration of newer and perhaps better economic paradigms, and so impedes effective stewardship.[126] The first step toward reforming economic practice, then, is the reformation of economic theory.[127]

Neo-Calvinist authors have suggested that a Christian alternative to conventional economic theory will need to dispense with mechanistic, ostensibly "law-governed" economic modeling.[128] It will need to take environmental

---

123. Graham et al., *Reforming Economics,* 1: 60. See also Cramp, *Notes toward a Christian Critique of Secular Economic Theory,* pp. 36ff.

124. Storkey, *Transforming Economics,* pp. 203-4.

125. The neo-Calvinists have assumed that ideas shape social reality more or less directly, and hence that social reality can be intentionally reshaped if only the correct ideas—theological, economic, and so on—are mustered. Few of them seem to give much credence to the suggestion that ideas may have unintended consequences. Indeed, some of them actually deride this sort of objection as a kind of "fatalism," evidence of an attempt to evade stewardly responsibility. "The control is ours," says Storkey in *Transforming Economics.* "If we have been given responsibility over God's creation, we deny our proper role if we make ourselves pawns of it" (p. 70).

126. See Graham et al., *Reforming Economics,* 2: 457ff. See also Cramp, *Notes toward a Christian Critique of Secular Economic Theory,* p. 23.

127. See Graham et al., *Reforming Economics,* 2: 447ff.

128. See Goudzwaard, *Economic Stewardship versus Capitalist Religion,* p. 32.

factors into account, along with the full range of human motivations.[129] And it will have to take note of and incorporate all of the other academic disciplines "within a coherent overall framework which recognizes the full created complexity of humanity."[130] Economics in this view is "the study of communal stewardship and organization of the creation to meet human needs. Or, to put it in a slightly different way, economics is the study of how people, both individually and institutionally, respond to their calling to be stewards of what God has entrusted to them in the creation."[131]

Reforming economic theory is crucial to the neo-Calvinist notion of mankind's cultural mandate because economics is the discipline that enables mankind collectively to steward the development of creation in such a way that each created thing, natural and social, can realize itself according to the norms inhering within it. In this regard, Alan Storkey has suggested that the primary task of economics is not merely descriptive or even predictive; rather, economics should deal with guiding society toward its appropriate ends. Speaking of the problem of unemployment, for example, Storkey has asserted that "markets can be reshaped. Institutions can be restructured in ways which give a strong, positive valuation to employment. Previously, the naturalistic, mechanical approaches to the problems came up with manipulative techniques. Now we have a more direct appreciation of our responsibilities. And our responses are not pragmatic, but normative. . . . The possibilities and policies for full employment are there if our attitudes are right."[132]

Given this goal of comprehensive and collective human stewardship of creation, neo-Calvinist scholars have had mixed views regarding capitalism. On the one hand, they admit that in our fallen situation we probably do need some system of incentives linking production with consumption, and capitalism has provided such a link. And they generally appreciate the capacity of democratic capitalism to provide opportunity and freedom, as well as its extraordinary ability to produce wealth.[133] But they also believe that it has exhibited several very serious shortcomings. Remarkable as its record of production has been, they say, the market system has been consistently unable to distribute goods and services in such a way as to respond effectively to human need because it operates solely on the basis of effective demand. Commenting on world hunger, for example, George DeVries, Jr., has written, "the problem, experts tell us, is not really a food problem but a money and distribution

129. See Marshall, "A Christian View of Economics," p. 4; and Tiemstra, "Stories Economists Tell," pp. 14-16.

130. Graham et al., *Reforming Economics,* 1: 111.

131. Graham et al., *Reforming Economics,* 1: 114.

132. Storkey, *Transforming Economics,* pp. 179-80.

133. See Eric H. Beversluis, "Backwards Theology," *Reformed Journal* 35 (February 1985): 3-4.

problem. The market mechanism we employ—both domestically and internationally—responds not to real need, but only to demand backed by purchasing power. Designed and institutionalized by rich nations, it shuts out the poor
world."[134] In addition, the market has been unable to provide important public
goods and services—including such "fundamental goods" as education and
health care—in a just and equitable way, and has continually generated externalities (unintended commonly borne costs, such as pollution) because of its
inability to price common goods effectively.[135] The chronic dissatisfaction that
this inequality has caused is yet another issue that the market system seems
incapable of addressing.[136]

In addition, neo-Calvinist observers suggest that in the present situation
the term *market* is somewhat misleading. The concentration of economic power
in large modern corporations is such that they effectively "administer" prices
to consumers who have been manipulated by advertising into desiring the
products they produce. George DeVries, Jr., has suggested that in light of the
considerable amount of political power these huge corporations wield, we
might better describe the present situation in terms of "industrial feudalism"
than industrial capitalism.[137]

Similarly, neo-Calvinist scholars tend to be quite critical of multinational
corporations. While admitting that such enterprises provide employment and
effectively transfer knowledge and skill to developing nations, neo-Calvinist
observers suggest that the influence of multinationals in the Third World has on
balance been largely negative. These firms cause high prices, contribute to
monetary instability by transferring profits out of their host countries, allocate
resources inefficiently, import inappropriate and capital-intensive technologies
into their host countries, and exacerbate the unjust concentration of wealth both
in the host country and back at home.[138] The authors of *Reforming Economics: A*

134. DeVries, "Systems and Hunger," *Reformed Journal* 25 (April 1975): 4. See also
George DeVries, Jr., "The Business of America," *Reformed Journal* 27 (April 1977): 18.
135. See Eric H. Beversluis, "A Critique of Ronald Nash on Economic Justice and the
State," *Christian Scholar's Review* 11 (1981): 343, 345.
136. See Roland Hoksbergen, "The Morality of Economic Growth," *Reformed Journal*
32 (December 1982): 10-13. Hoksbergen quotes the following from an article by Richard
Easterlin: "to the outside observer, economic growth appears to be producing an ever more
affluent society, but to those involved in the process, affluence will always remain a distant,
urgently sought, but never attained goal" ("Does Money Buy Happiness?" *Public Interest*
30 [Winter 1973]: 1-11).
137. See DeVries, "The Business of America," p. 17. See also George N. Monsma, Jr.,
"Vested Interests Survive Another Round," *Reformed Journal* 20 (April 1970): 13-17.
138. See Graham et al., *Reforming Economics*, 2: 533ff. See also George N. Monsma,
Jr., "The Socio-Economic-Political Order and Our Lifestyles," in *Living More Simply:
Biblical Principles and Practical Models,* ed. Ronald J. Sider (Downers Grove, IL: Inter-
Varsity Press, 1980), pp. 194-95.

Christian Perspective on Economic Theory and Practice have suggested that good policy regarding multinational corporations will "enhance their advantages while controlling their problems. This involves 'unbundling the package' of capital, technology, jobs, training profits, and economic control that the multinationals offer to the poor lands. This usually means that the poor country governments must try to obtain the desirable parts of the package, while retaining some control over the enterprise for their own nationals."[139] They also maintain that this control will need to be backed, at the very least, by international agreement and probably by an internationally authoritative governing body.

Neo-Calvinist observers insist that similar regulation needs to be applied on the domestic economic front as well. In the context of a discussion of domestic poverty, George Monsma, Jr., has asked, "can anyone actually believe that a capitalistic system, without any government intervention, will really provide . . . equality of opportunity, even if Christians do more to help the poor?"[140] While neo-Calvinists tend to agree with Kuyper that in theory the state must be limited, in responding to the scale of modern social problems and the negligence they perceive in the private sector, they have in fact advocated an activist role for the state in the economy.[141] Indeed, the authors of *Reforming Economics* argue that the state ought to play a significant role in such areas as the redistribution of wealth and income geared toward material equalization and accomplished via progressive taxation, education and health care, the provision of adequate employment opportunities, the encouragement of worker and public participation in corporate decision making, the correction of problems associated with economic externalities, the regulation of the size of corporations and the extent to which capital may be concentrated, the subsidization of small, worker-owned cooperatives, the setting of wage and price controls, the regulation of matters of health and safety, the provision of consumer information, and the funding of basic scientific research.[142] One of

139. Graham et al., *Reforming Economics,* 2: 537, 538.

140. Monsma, "The Bible and the Free Market," *Reformed Journal* 35 (February 1985): 23.

141. On the one hand the authors of *Reforming Economics* write that the state "must acknowledge the God-given rights of individuals and other institutions . . . to their existence and to what is necessary for them to carry out their God-given callings," and they argue that the imperfect motivations of governments must be taken seriously (2: 403, 409). On the other hand they contend that the state may legitimately take over the functions of these other institutions if "they cannot be induced to end their unjust or wasteful behavior by any other just means" (1: 407). For a justification of this argument based on the gravity of modern social problems, see, e.g., Tony Brouwer, "Poor People and the Economic System," *Reformed Journal* 18 (January 1968): 16-18. On the negligence of the private sector, see Graham et al., *Reforming Economics,* 1: 193; and John Timmerman, "Greed or Gain," *Reformed Journal* 23 (September 1973): 3. For the argument that the state's role needs to be expanded in the present situation, see Storkey, *Transforming Economics,* p. 181.

142. Graham et al., *Reforming Economics,* 2: 298, 354, 404, 405, 417, 426, 428, 429, 430,

the things the state should *not* concern itself with, they insist, is promoting economic growth, and especially not by means of deregulation.[143] In this same vein, responding to the question of why the concept of economic growth is promoted as a solution to inequality, Roland Hoksbergen has written, "One possibility is that people have been led to fear that the only real alternative is direct redistribution of existing income, and to most people this is an un-palatable solution. It is much easier to support aid to the poor through a growing economy (in which all supposedly benefit) than through giving up some of what we already have and have grown accustomed to."[144]

Neo-Calvinist authors legitimate state intervention in the economy theo-logically on the basis of mankind's cultural, or stewardship, mandate. They also explain the necessity of intervention in terms of the state's appropriate sphere responsibility. The authors of *Reforming Economics* imply, for example, that it is the state's responsibility to determine the "true social welfare" and that it is the "special concern of government" both to insure justice for the poor and powerless and to determine maximum standards of consumption.[145] In an attempt to palliate conservative opposition to such suggestions, Alan Storkey has offered the following apology for state-sponsored health care:

> The concept of the welfare state is a misnomer; it really means that there is communal support for various forms of care which have therefore been given a permanent legislative basis. . . . If we regard care in sickness as a part of the love which we ought to have for our neighbor . . . then the formation of a National Health Service is meaningful and natural. It would be wrong for the community to allow health services to be provided on a market exchange basis. . . . However, we also note that the National Health Service is not the *state* health service for to identify with the state is to miss the point; it is not a *political* institution, but an expression of social care.[146]

431, 453, 454, 482. On the matter of taxation, they advocate progressive income taxes for both individuals and corporations, progressive inheritance taxes, luxury taxes, taxes on goods deemed harmful (e.g., cigarettes), and user taxes as appropriate means available to the state for the purposes of redistributing wealth and income (pp. 432ff.). Monsma takes a similar position in "Vested Interests Survive Another Round": "The biblical view of a just distribution of income requires, at the very least, the provision of enough income to each family to provide for its basic needs. In the perfectly just society each would contribute to a society according to his ability, and income would be distributed to each according to his real needs. While this can never be fully achieved in a sinful society . . . , it does provide some standard by which to judge the vertical equity of taxation in a society. . . . This Christian view of justice requires a progressive tax system that reduces the inequality of income" (p. 14). He provides similar arguments in "Nixon's New Economic Policy," *Reformed Journal* 22 (January 1972): 9-11; and "The Need for Tax Reform," *Reformed Journal* 24 (March 1974): 12-15.

143. Graham et al., *Reforming Economics*, 2: 456-57.
144. Hoksbergen, "The Morality of Economic Growth," p. 11.
145. Graham et al., *Reforming Economics*, vol. 2: 399, 182, 400, 420, 434.
146. Storkey, *A Christian Social Perspective*, pp. 376-77.

Neo-Calvinists view justice as entailing more than the simple procedural justice defended by those on the evangelical right.[147] They maintain that justice dictates the equitable distribution of goods and services in society. Evert Van der Heide has listed the following scriptural requirements of a just society:

(1) *All families have access to the basic necessities of life*—creation is adequate for all and has been given for the care of all.

(2) *All people have the opportunity to use and develop their labour resource*— dominion has been given to all to act in the image of God for his glorification, and

(3) *There is a distribution of wealth and income sufficiently equitable to assure that each person can exercise his or her stewardship responsibility.*[148]

"If society is to satisfy [such] standards," Eric Beversluis has asserted, "the state will have to be involved. . . . The free market will not suffice." The necessity for state intervention, he goes on to say, is illustrated not only by present market failures but also by those of the past: "Much of today's inequality of wealth, if we could trace it back, would be found to be based on what Karl Marx called the 'primitive capitalist accumulation' of the early modern period."[149] He assumes that capital accumulates within certain institutions and classes from which it is not subject to dissipation or dispersion, and from which it impedes capital accumulation by other institutions and classes. He also assumes that the market mechanism simply perpetuates this situation and hence that remedial action on behalf of those deprived of resources is necessary if a more equitable distribution of capital is to be restored.[150]

147. In an article entitled "The Socio-Political-Economic Order," for example, George Monsma, Jr., argues that the notion of "equal opportunity" is meaningless unless all persons begin from materially equal starting points. Individual effort and ability, he argues, have only marginal effects on personal income. Similarly, James B. White has suggested that "it is important to note that God's concern for those who are in a socially weak position . . . is spoken of in terms of justice, and not in terms of some paternalistic concept of 'charity.' The paternalistic concept of charity can only exist where the ideology of 'ownerism' exists. . . . But it is clear and certain that Reformed Christianity has utterly failed to present any significant challenge to the ideology of 'ownerism' and the idolizing of the 'successful man' that is at the heart of the spirit of modern American capitalism" ("Jubilee: The Basis of Social Action," *Reformed Journal* 21 [May/June 1971]: 9).
148. Van der Heide, "Justice in International Relations with Less Developed Countries," *Transformation* 1 (April-June 1984): 4. Similar standards are suggested by Beversluis in "A Critique of Ronald Nash," pp. 330-46.
149. Beversluis, "A Critique of Ronald Nash," pp. 336, 338-39.
150. The authors of *Reforming Economics* offer a similar argument: "maintaining and creating a distributed nationwide pattern of ownership requires remedial action. . . . It is therefore necessary to act periodically to restore a more widespread pattern of ownership. This kind of redistribution of wealth and property has largely been ignored in the United States" (1: 216).

While conceding that state-sponsored redistributive efforts have had their problems, Beversluis has suggested that such difficulties are due not to flaws inherent within the welfare system but to the corrupting influence of middle-class vested interests. "Despite these difficulties," he has argued, "the Christian should continue to support political programs that try to increase economic justice."[151] Indeed, Beversluis has contended that if we were to pursue these kinds of programs instead of simply pursuing continued economic growth, the Scriptures indicate that we would achieve not simply justice but prosperity as well: "contrary to the world's appearances, says the Word of God, it makes economic sense to pursue justice before and as a condition of prosperity. Or, better yet, if we pursue justice rather than prosperity, we will be rewarded with both."[152]

Neo-Calvinist authors have also criticized—in some instances severely—the resistance put up by those on the right to the expansion of the welfare state. For example, commenting on the New Religious Right, George DeVries, Jr., recently wrote,

> We are confronted with an ideology that supports the lavishing of our great wealth on the comparative few; that favors reckless use of resources without concern for the future or the environment; that ignores the unemployed, the underemployed, and the farmers; that has no real concern for problems of development in the poor world; that ignores the plight of the homeless and hopeless at home and abroad but is willing to waste billions and billions in its efforts at military security; that defines all problems in terms of a Cold War stance; and that takes pride in our military power and prestige. Such an ideology, popular as it may be, is not one that a Christian, committed to principles God laid down for the governance of this world, can really be comfortable with. . . . We must never forget that the overarching rule of God for the cultural order is justice, for God himself is justice incarnate.[153]

Reformed authors have been concerned to show that simply encouraging economic growth and hoping that some of it will trickle down to the poor, as suggested by advocates of supply-side economic theory, is a poor substitute for actively promoting redistributive social justice. "How, then, does one judge whether economic growth is desirable?" Roland Hoksbergen has asked.

> The central Christian principle upon which to base such judgment is that of service in obedience to God's will. As part of this we must be sure the joint criteria of helping the poor and caring for God's creation are met. . . . If questions such as those above cannot be answered favorably, then it is likely that economic growth will be unnecessary if not actually detrimental. . . . Almost all the rhetoric one

151. Beversluis, "A Critique of Ronald Nash," p. 346.
152. Beversluis, "Backwards Theology," p. 4.
153. DeVries, "The New Old Right," *Reformed Journal* 36 (October 1986): 10.

hears today says we are in dire need of more economic growth. It seems to me, however, that what we really need is a moral and religious awakening to the real purpose of life. Of economic goods we have enough already. What we need to know is how to use them to glorify God.[154]

Hence neo-Calvinist scholars suggest that instead of focusing on the creation of wealth, as those on the evangelical right have been wont to do, contemporary social and economic policy ought to focus on the appropriate distribution and use of existing wealth. In addition, they argue that the distribution and use of existing wealth should not be left to the whim of the market mechanism but should be managed so as to steward society intentionally toward full disclosure.

Excursus: The Contributions of Several British Evangelicals

American evangelical theologians have often benefited from British evangelical scholarship, and the recent American evangelical debate over capitalism and issues of social and economic policy is no exception in this regard. We have already noted the work of British evangelical economist Brian Griffiths in connection with the evangelical right's defense of capitalism. Several other British evangelical scholars have also made substantial contributions to the American debate that are worthy of our consideration here.

One such scholar is John R. W. Stott, a noted author and speaker who helped to frame the Lausanne Covenant in 1974. While his contribution to the social and economic policy debate has been somewhat limited, the work he has done in this area is important and may be indicative of the direction mainstream evangelical thinking is heading.

Stott has suggested that the relation between evangelism and social action is best understood as one of partnership.[155] Social action is not a means to evangelism, nor is it a manifestation of evangelism, he has argued; rather, the two are critical, though independent, aspects of the church's mission. While it remains unclear whether or not this formulation actually resolves the issue, Stott's understanding of the partnership between evangelism and social action does represent something of a move away from the traditional mainstream position (i.e., that social change is the *result* of successful evangelism) and a move toward a more progressive position.

Stott's appraisal of capitalism exhibits a similar move away from the relatively conservative evangelical mainstream. On the one hand, Stott has suggested in a manner similar to Carl Henry that "Christians should oppose in both systems [capitalism and socialism] what they perceive to be incom-

---

154. Hoksbergen, "The Morality of Economic Growth," p. 12.
155. Stott, *Christian Mission in the Modern World* (London: Falcon, 1975), pp. 26-28.

patible with biblical faith which equally emphasizes creativity [i.e., freedom] and compassion, and refuses to foster either at the expense of the other."[156] In addition, while contending that there is a need for a distinctively Christian social and economic policy, Stott has emphasized that neither the gospel nor contemporary economic problems themselves may be reduced to purely material considerations.[157]

When it comes to prescribing social and economic policy, however, Stott's suggestions have again been somewhat to the left of the traditional mainstream. With reference to Third World poverty, for example, he has apparently become convinced that the wealth of the developed North has at least in part accumulated at the expense of the world's poor, and hence he has argued for such things as simpler Northern lifestyles. "The present situation of North-South inequality . . . is not God's fault . . . nor is it the fault of the poor . . . , nor is it necessarily our fault," he has written. "We become personally culpable only if we acquiesce in its continuance."[158] In terms of domestic policy, Stott has insisted that concern for profit should not eclipse the public interest in corporate policy, and he has advocated increased worker participation in corporate decision making.[159] Stott's position on social and economic policy issues, it seems, is something of a combination of conservative theological assumptions and moderately left-of-center policy prescriptions.

Another significant contribution to the American debate has been made by British evangelical economist Sir Frederick Catherwood. While appreciating the market system's economic efficiency, especially as measured against command or socialist alternatives, Catherwood has suggested that capitalism's efficiency rests at the heart of a very serious problem in modern societies—namely, enormous concentrations of economic power. "In the great 17th century breakthroughs—the scientific revolution, the Protestant ethic of hard work, saving, development—and indeed the parallel political breakthrough to representative government, one factor was overlooked. It was overlooked because no one foresaw the huge increase in wealth which these revolutions would bring, and so no one foresaw the problem of dealing with the power which accumulated wealth would bring."[160]

The dangers of concentrated economic and hence political power, Cather-

156. John R. W. Stott, *Involvement,* vol. 2: *Social and Sexual Relationships in the Modern World* (Old Tappan, NJ: Fleming H. Revell, 1985), p. 113.

157. See John R. W. Stott, "The Just Demands of Economic Inequality," *Christianity Today,* 23 May 1980, pp. 30-31.

158. Stott, *Involvement,* vol. 1: *Being a Responsible Christian in a Non-Christian Society* (Old Tappan, NJ: Fleming H. Revell, 1984), p. 185.

159. Stott, *Involvement,* vol. 2, pp. 70, 61.

160. Catherwood, "Christian Faith and Economics," *Transformation* 1 (June-September/October-December 1987): 3.

wood has argued, include the repression of individual freedoms and especially religious freedom: "One has a feeling in reading about past persecutions that they faded out largely through inefficiency and administrative difficulties. In our tightly knit and closely organized society, there would be small hope of this. . . . We owe more than most people will admit to the moral standards of previous generations, largely inspired by Christian teaching. The teaching has been thrown over and the standards of morals and tolerance are visibly deteriorating. We hope that it will go no further, but concentrations of economic power are difficult to pull apart and it seems just as well that they should not be built."[161]

As one might expect given views of this sort, Catherwood's specific policy prescriptions include limiting the size of business enterprises in the hopes of achieving a "genuine diffusion of power" throughout the economy.[162] He has argued that limiting the size of private and public corporations would be preferable to trying to regulate their activities. In addition, he has advocated placing employee and consumer representatives on corporate boards and awarding licenses and/or charters to corporations on the basis of their adoption of acceptable codes of conduct, which would include such things as the maximization of economic performance for the benefit of shareholders, workers, and consumers.[163] Convinced that the economic future of the developing world depends to a large extent on world trade, Catherwood has also called for the elimination of barriers to free trade.[164]

Yet in spite of his willingness to offer specific policy proposals, Catherwood has also warned that "no structural reform . . . can offset the deterioration of moral standards" and hence that the Christian task of encouraging moral reform is crucial to the survival of modern societies.[165] Indeed, he has argued that "given Christian standards, almost any economic system might be able to work. It is not so much the system that really matters as the personal standards which individuals bring to the system."[166]

The American evangelical debate over capitalism has also been influenced by the work of Donald Hay, fellow and tutor of economics at Jesus College, Oxford. Hay's work is more explicitly theological than that of Catherwood and also more technical. His approach involves attempts to "resolve the tension

161. Catherwood, *The Christian in Industrial Society* (London: Tyndale Press, 1966), p. 22.

162. Catherwood, "Christian Faith and Economics," p. 6; see also "The Christian Case for the Diffusion of Economic Power," *Transformation* 9 (October/December 1989): 7-12.

163. Catherwood, *A Better Way: The Case for a Christian Social Order* (London: Inter-Varsity Press, 1975), pp. 122, 124.

164. Catherwood, "Christian Faith and Economics," p. 6.

165. Catherwood, "Christian Faith and Economics," p. 6.

166. Catherwood, *A Better Way*, p. 109.

between God's [scriptural] ideal and what is practicable in a fallen world."[167] "God has a creation plan for mankind," he has written, "but because of the Fall, that plan is not capable of fulfillment. Eden cannot be recreated. We must look for a second best in a sinful world, but at the same time we must continue to affirm God's 'first' best."[168]

Hay has found three economic ideals in Scripture, each of which gives rise to general ethical principles. First, mankind has been given collective dominion over nature and is called to act as a trustee over natural resources. This trusteeship, Hay has suggested, "carries with it an obligation to use resources efficiently. . . . Hence efficiency in production and distribution is a major preoccupation of much economic analysis."[169] Mankind's trusteeship also prohibits the waste and destruction of the created order.[170] Second, mankind (again, understood collectively) has the obligation, and hence the right, to engage in work that is both meaningful and purposeful.[171] Third, Hay has contended that each person has the right to share in God's provision, and thus that all political-economic systems ought to insure a minimum standard of consumption of such things as food, clothing, and shelter.[172] Despite conventional economic wisdom, drawing on the notion of scarcity, Hay has argued that "there can be no pessimism about the ability of the earth to provide adequately for the human race. . . . We would not therefore expect to find that world shortages of resources are the source of international [economic] inequality."[173] Hay has also insisted that there ought to be a maximum standard of consumption corresponding to this minimum standard, and that the Scriptures recognize no absolute right to property or possessions.[174] "The Biblical criterion of fairness," he has stated, "is one of need, not of an income commensurate to the quality of resources supplied."[175]

Hay has subsequently sought to measure capitalist practice against the ideals and principles he has identified. With respect to the dominion mandate, he has suggested that "the market economy has no concept of care for the natural order, and under a wide range of conditions is likely to be destructive of it."[176] And among other ways in which capitalism violates the dominion

167. Hay, *A Christian Critique of Capitalism*, Grove Booklet on Ethics no. 5 (Bramcote, Nottinghamshire: Grove Books, 1977), p. 5.

168. Hay, "The International Socio-Economic-Political Order and Our Lifestyle," in *Lifestyles in the Eighties: An Evangelical Commitment to the Simple Lifestyle*, ed. Ronald J. Sider (Philadelphia: Westminster Press, 1982), p. 85.

169. Hay, "The International Socio-Economic-Political Order and Our Lifestyle," p. 87.

170. Hay, *Economics Today: A Christian Critique* (Leicester: Apollos, 1989), p. 72.

171. See Hay, *A Christian Critique of Capitalism*, p. 8.

172. Hay, "The International Socio-Economic-Political Order," p. 90.

173. Hay, "The International Socio-Economic-Political Order," p. 87.

174. Hay, *Economics Today*, p. 78.

175. Hay, *A Christian Critique of Capitalism*, p. 10.

176. Hay, *Economics Today*, p. 166.

mandate, he has mentioned its tendency toward oligopoly and the problem of natural monopoly (both of which serve to concentrate economic power), its failure to provide certain public goods, and its inability to deal with externalities and investment decisions oriented to the future. He reports "serious doubts about the ability of a pure capitalist system to provide even a tolerably correct pattern of investment" for future economic growth.[177]

In terms of the provision of purposeful work, Hay has contended that capitalism's consistent failure to provide employment for some, and its inability to provide meaningful work for many, constitute very significant problems.

> It is clear that work and the stewardship of resources are linked. Man cannot operate without resources: he must have access to land, capital (tools and machinery) and training in the skills required. . . . Stewards should control production rather than be dominated or merely "hired" by capital. Not only is this a precondition for the exercise of responsible stewardship: it should also provide incentives by insuring that those who work share in the prosperity (or lack of prosperity) of the enterprise. . . . Work is an enterprise in which man cooperates not only with resources but also with his fellow men.[178]

Finally, with reference to the distributional ideals of minimum and maximum standards of provision, Hay has been critical of the selfishness and overconsumption that he sees in capitalist societies.[179] He has suggested that capitalism simply is not capable of either limiting consumption or guaranteeing any kind of minimum standard of distribution. He has argued that in the market system, especially at the international level, one's ability to consume is linked directly to one's ability to pay and to provide the resources necessary for economic participation. Yet many people in today's world simply do not have access to such productive resources. "World distribution of income is in the first place determined by the world distribution of resources—natural resources, human skills, capital equipment, and knowledge. But that distribution is very uneven, and so is the distribution of income. So those who have little to offer must expect to consume very little: that is the essence of the international market system."[180]

Concluding his comparison of capitalism in practice to biblical ideals and principles, Hay asserts that capitalism, "as a system, falls a long way short of satisfying God's creation plan. Surely that is no more than we should expect, given the sinfulness of man? But what is difficult to accept is that a Christian

---

177. Hay, *A Christian Critique of Capitalism,* p. 14.

178. Hay, "The International Socio-Economic-Political Order," p. 90.

179. "It is no exaggeration," Hay writes in *A Christian Critique of Capitalism,* "to say that capitalism accepts human selfishness in the use of resources, and gives it respectability. This is the precise antithesis to the Christian understanding that men are trustees of resources to be put at the service of all mankind" (p. 15).

180. Hay, "The International Socio-Economic-Political Order," p. 105.

could espouse capitalism with any degree of enthusiasm, as many Christians certainly do. . . . *Our ideal must be God's creation standard and nothing less.*"[181]

Unlike those on the evangelical left, however, Hay has not viewed the international socioeconomic-political order as a system in which a wealthy few have consciously exploited the many poor and oppressed. He reports that he has not attributed "malevolent motives to anyone" in reaching his conclusions.[182] Nor does he advocate a socialist or planned economy as a viable alternative.[183] Instead, he has argued for increased state-supervised intervention in economic life aimed at insuring distributive justice. He recently asserted, for example, that it is the responsibility of the state to encourage compliance with the sorts of biblical ideals and principles he has identified and also that political authorities must be ready to redress "perceived" socioeconomic injustices, even if this means exercising bias.[184] In Hay's view, then, the state needs to play an "enabling role," providing an institutional framework for responsible stewardship: "Individuals probably recognize a responsibility to their fellow men . . . , but a sense of benevolence and goodwill is unlikely to be strong enough to lead to a wider responsibility through voluntary cooperation alone."[185] The state, then, must provide the requisite organization for broader economic responsibility.

Domestically, such an organization might include traditional tax and transfer mechanisms, the removal of certain essential goods (e.g., food, housing, education, health care) from the market altogether, a policy of full employment, the regulation of natural monopolies, and a strict antimonopoly program in other areas.[186] Hay has also proposed increased worker participation and ownership of industry and changing corporate shareholder rights in such a way as to eliminate limited liability.[187] At the international level, Hay has suggested that protectionist policies in manufacturing and especially in agriculture should be eliminated.[188] He has also contended that although multinational corporations have aided in the transfer of knowledge and capital to economically underdeveloped regions, they have also tended to produce products only for the existing elites in these regions. "They have little interest in making more appropriate mass produced products," Hay has argued, "since local competition would quickly compete away the profits."[189] And he notes that multinational

181. Hay, *A Christian Critique of Capitalism,* p. 15.
182. Hay, "The International Socio-Economic-Political Order," p. 105.
183. Hay, "The International Socio-Economic-Political Order," p. 125.
184. Hay, *Economics Today,* p. 88.
185. Hay, *Economics Today,* p. 89.
186. See Hay, *A Christian Critique of Capitalism,* pp. 17ff.
187. Hay, *Economics Today,* pp. 173-74.
188. See Hay, "The International Socio-Economic-Political Order," pp. 106ff.
189. Hay, "The International Socio-Economic-Political Order," p. 114.

corporations tend to support right-wing governments as well. For these reasons he has suggested that serious consideration be given to the proposal for a New International Economic Order delivered by a number of Third World delegates to the United Nations in 1974. "While each proposal requires exhaustive and expert analysis . . . , the proposals in the areas of trade liberalization, world food stocks, official development aid and control of the activities of [multi-national corporations] give the most immediate prospects for effective action."[190] More recently he has written that "in practical terms, [this] means continuing aid for the development of the South to give access to resources for poor people, and a willingness to open Northern markets to those products in which the South has a comparative advantage. While such policies may involve costs for the North, these pale into insignificance compared to the immense gap between rich and poor countries that is revealed by international comparisons. The North can and should be able to afford such policies."[191]

Insofar as the responsibility of the church is concerned, in a discussion of the Brandt Commission Report, *North-South: A Program for Survival* (1980), Hay argues that Christians in the North could exhibit a truly prophetic stance by pointing the current political-economic discussion away from domestic economic problems and toward the promotion of economic development in the South.[192] For such a stance to be credible, however, he indicates that an international program of redistribution within the church may well be necessary: "Unless the Christian Church is prepared to implement a radical programme in its own international life, our moral arguments do not even deserve to be heard, and our moral advocacy will fail."[193]

The Evangelical Center and Capitalism: Concluding Remarks

Having discussed the positions of those on the evangelical left and right, I have attempted in this chapter to describe the positions of those evangelicals whose recent appraisals of capitalism are neither wholly positive nor entirely negative and who are attempting to steer a course between the left and the right in the current economic policy dispute. As this review should have made evident, the analyses of many of those in this evangelical "center" are quite sophisticated and their observations of the contemporary political-economic situation astute. Indeed, when it comes to suggesting how capitalism might more adequately be assessed from an evangelical perspective, I will draw upon a number of these observations.

190. Hay, "The International Socio-Economic-Political Order," p. 126.
191. Hay, *Economics Today,* p. 280.
192. Hay, "North and South: The Economic Debate," in *The Year 2000,* ed. John R. W. Stott (Downers Grove, IL: InterVarsity Press, 1983), p. 96.
193. Hay, "North and South," p. 100.

In addition to simply describing the positions of those in the evangelical "center," however, I have also been concerned to see if I could detect which direction this group (which includes the majority of evangelical intellectuals at present) appears to be moving in with respect to the issue of capitalism. As I have already suggested, the existence of left and right wings within American evangelicalism does not tell us very much about the intellectual tendencies of the movement as a whole; it is in the intellectual center of the movement that I would expect these tendencies to be most evident.

Chief among these tendencies, I believe, is a general movement away from the defense of the market economy and toward the advocacy of increased state involvement in economic and social life. There is also a trend away from the "ethic of production" (i.e., a consideration of the rights and obligations associated with producing wealth in an economy) and toward an "ethic of consumption" (i.e., an increasingly exclusive focus on the ways in which society distributes the wealth it has already produced). Many of those in the evangelical center seem to presuppose the existence of wealth, and hence they tend to center their attention not on the critical theological and ethical issues associated with effectively encouraging continued economic growth but rather on the issues associated with allocating existing wealth in a just and equitable fashion.

Insofar as the movement away from defending capitalism is concerned, those in the evangelical mainstream seem to have grown—at least until very recently—increasingly reluctant to support the market system and more ambivalent concerning social and economic policy issues than they were even as recently as the 1950s and 1960s. While Carl Henry and the occasional contributor to *Christianity Today* still defend capitalism, the once generally conservative mainstream has lost not only its position of intellectual preeminence within American evangelicalism but also its certainty with respect to the defense of capitalism. Even when it does offer such a defense, the mainstream tends to approach it in something of an embarrassed and apologetic fashion. Apparently the fear of being labeled conservative or reactionary in the contemporary situation is such that many evangelical intellectuals, and especially many younger scholars, consider it best to avoid too close an association with the defense or advocacy of capitalism. It is true that this hesitancy has diminished in the face of the collapse of European communism and socialism, but it is far from certain that these historical events will push the evangelical center further to the right in the debate over capitalism.

Insofar as the trend toward the advocacy of increased state intervention into economic and social life is concerned, this tendency has been very much in evidence in the work of most of those mentioned in this chapter. The emphasis for those in the evangelical center, it seems, has shifted away from defending capitalism against its critics on the left and toward the defense of a mixed-market or interventionist economy against the critics on the right. This has perhaps been especially true of the positions taken by those in the Christian Reformed community, in which descriptions of the will of God for economic life and of mankind's appropriate cultural mandate have come quite close to mandating something very like the modern welfare state.

Interestingly, while those in the evangelical center have been reluctant to speak of capitalism in terms of freedom, they have not attempted to legitimate expanded state intervention into social and economic life on the basis of capitalist oppression either. Instead, they have argued for expanded state responsibilities by way of an expanded understanding of human rights—rights which they have extended to include such things as employment, housing, and health care. Since the market mechanism obviously cannot provide for such rights, many of those in the evangelical center have seen no alternative but to suggest that the state be empowered to guarantee them.

Lastly, it is important to note that in trying to steer a middle course between the extremes of left and right, the evangelical center is not really concerned to resolve the contest between capitalism and socialism: there are essentially no advocates of socialism per se among those in the center, all of whom take the productive capacity of capitalism as axiomatic. Rather, those in the center are primarily interested in determining just how much state intervention is necessary to correct the market failures that they feel have plagued modern societies and created situations of relative economic inequality and injustice. Those leaning slightly toward the right of center tend to suggest that the welfare state as it currently exists, albeit with minor modifications and with the addition of Christian moral restraints, is adequate to the task of achieving social and economic justice. Those somewhat to the left of center (including, it should be noted, much of the intellectual leadership within the American evangelical movement at present) have tended to feel that such things as social and economic justice will require increased—and in some instances greatly increased—state supervision. In Chapter 4 I will turn to an assessment of the recent conflict over the appropriate role of the modern state in social and economic life—a conflict that focuses ultimately on issues of social power and the appropriate location of social authority, a conflict that has been occurring in virtually all advanced industrial societies in the West for the last half-century.

CHAPTER FOUR

Interpreting the Evangelical Debate
over Capitalism

Having described the range of recent evangelical appraisals of capitalism in some detail, it would be possible to take this discussion in a number of different directions. We could assess the merits of the economic analyses provided by those on the evangelical left, right, and center and their use, or abuse, of the empirical evidence available for such things as economic performance and patterns of income distribution in advanced industrial societies. We could assess the merits of their theological analyses and their use, or abuse, of Scripture. In spite of the importance of these sorts of discussions, however, I have chosen to take a more preliminary approach to the various positions, assessing them not on the basis of their economic and theological merits per se, but rather on the basis of the ways in which they relate to each other in the larger evangelical debate.

As our consideration of the range of positions to this point has made clear, the recent evangelical debate over capitalism takes in a great many issues— issues of economics and politics, ethics and morality, theology and culture. Indeed, it seems clear that capitalism as such is not the only thing at issue in this debate but that the various evangelical factions are contending for entirely different sociocultural visions of American society for which capitalism serves only as a kind of symbol either positively or negatively. Of course, if this is the case, then our understanding of the recent evangelical debate, not to mention our understanding of the many substantive issues raised within the debate, will be well served if we can determine the nature of the conflict that has produced these different visions. In the following, then, I want to try to identify the context within which the recent evangelical debate over capitalism has been taking place.

As I have already noted, the different theories seeking to explain the wealth and poverty of modern nations tend to divide into two competing theoretical camps, one committed to the paradigm of economic imperialism and the other to the paradigm of modernization. While those on the evangelical left approach modern capitalism assuming it to be essentially a system of economic imperialism and oppression, those on the right assume that it is the only system capable of ensuring political freedom and economic development. Both left and right warrant their assumptions by appealing to secular theorists, who are themselves divided along similar lines. Meanwhile, in spite of the fact that those in the center of the evangelical debate repeatedly have called for a middle path between the extremes of left and right, they have not actually managed to develop a third alternative as yet: they stand torn between the two paradigms. For this reason, I will discuss the evangelical conflict largely in terms of two opposing positions—"left" and "right"—in the following. In doing so I am not ignoring the large evangelical "center"; I am simply suggesting that those "in between" the left and right tend to be exactly that—torn between the two competing economic paradigms.

Economic Issues Raised in the Debate

While all of the positions we have reviewed ostensibly address economic issues, it is interesting to note that one of the principal disagreements between left and right concerns just what "economics" is. Those on the right contend that economics must proceed on the basis of the assumption that individual economic agents will invariably act, at least on the aggregate, in a self-interested and rational fashion. Economics in this conservative view is a limited and primarily descriptive science, and its potential for prediction is linked to the assumption that basic human motivations remain relatively constant cross-culturally and over time. Those on the evangelical left, however, argue that the right's position is essentially an act of "bad faith," making needless concessions to human selfishness and completely underestimating the potential for society, with God's help, to progress beyond purely individualistic and self-interested economic behavior. They maintain that economic policies and even economic theories that assume human selfishness a priori constitute an impediment to such progress. Hence those on the evangelical left, and many in the evangelical center with them, conceive of economics as a prescriptive as well as a descriptive discipline with great potential for guiding the social order toward its appropriate normative ends.[1]

---

1. The same debate about the nature of economics has been occurring in the secular community as well. In an essay entitled "Rationalism in Economics," Irving Kristol states that "above all, what radical economics attacks is the basic idea that self-interest, the key

Yet beyond this disagreement about what economics is, the most obvious disagreement between the evangelical left and right has to do with how capitalism functions. Is capitalism a comprehensive sociopolitical-economic system as those on the left tend to argue? Or is it simply a convenient and efficient method for organizing the production and distribution of scarce material resources in society—which would make it just one of many institutions constituting the social order—as those on the right contend? In addition, is capitalism essentially oppressive? Or has it limited oppression by creating a situation in which the voices of both buyers and sellers are heard in the marketplace? More specifically, what is the relation of production to distribution in a capitalist economy? Those on the left focus almost exclusively on issues of distribution, tending to assume a certain level of industrial production and understanding economic growth historically as the result of the transfer of productive resources from one part of society (or from one part of the world) to another. Those on the right stress the unprecedented capacity of modern capitalism to create new wealth, and they understand Western economic growth almost exclusively in these terms. Insofar as distributional problems are concerned, those on the left argue for the mandatory redistribution of existing wealth, while those on the right advocate continued economic growth and the production of new wealth.

Another area of disagreement has to do with who actually makes the important decisions in a capitalist economy. Is the capitalist economy controlled, in spite of all the rhetoric about a "market" to the contrary, by a tiny business elite composed of the owners of capital and various technocrats subservient to them—a group that is almost entirely unaccountable politically and that actively manipulates consumers in order to maximize profit? Assuming this to be the case, those on the left condemn the enormous concentration of capital in modern society and charge that the accumulated wealth and power have not been subject to dissipation and/or redistribution. Those on the right hold that corporations and businesses simply respond to "consumer sovereignty," providing only those goods and services the buying public has deemed appropriate and desirable. They argue that as long as the market mechanism is allowed to function properly, it ensures that capital accrues only to those who most effectively satisfy the demands of consumers. In this regard, I would note that the conflicting positions exhibit completely different understandings of "class" and social mobility. While those on the right assume a

human motive in economics, is an inexpungible aspect of human nature—not necessarily to be admired, but always to be respected and ultimately to be channelled into constructive (or at least harmless) activity. Once you deny this premise, it is easy to dissolve economics into moral and political philosophy" (*The Crisis in Economic Theory*, ed. Daniel Bell and Irving Kristol [New York: Basic Books, 1981], p. 216).

relatively fluid mobility both upward and downward, those on the left tend to believe that social mobility is quite limited in capitalist society. This being the case, it is not difficult to see why those on the left insist on the equalization of economic power—or why those on the right argue that such equalization is unnecessary.

Closely related to the question of who decides, of course, is the question of who benefits from the capitalist economy. Are the beneficiaries of capitalism only the tiny capitalist elite, as those on the left contend (some theorists place only those who own and/or operate the major industrial corporations in this category, while others include all of those living in economically developed Western nations)? Those on the left hold that this small elite benefits at the expense of the vast majority of mankind, and especially at the expense of those in the Third World. Those on the right maintain that in those nations where capitalism is allowed to function properly, the vast middle class is its chief beneficiary, and the benefits do not come at anyone's expense. They believe that capitalism is crucial not only for solving the problems of poverty domestically but for future economic development in the Third World as well. Insofar as Third World development is concerned, the left denounces multinational corporations as villains whereas the right champions them as heroes. Curiously, the data the conflicting camps provide for such things as multinational corporate profits in the Third World are often flatly contradictory; whether these profits are excessive or modest seems to depend only on who is making the argument.

Examples of this sort could be multiplied, but my point here is simply that the disagreement between the evangelical left and right encompasses a number of foundational economic issues. It is also interesting to note that at a foundational level the views of the left and right tend to be mutually exclusive: each position tends to rule the other out by definition.

Political Issues Raised in the Debate

The political issues raised within the evangelical debate over capitalism are closely linked to the economic assumptions entailed in the two conflicting paradigms. The principal point at issue between the left and right, and the question causing the most uncertainty for those in the center, involves the nature of political authority and its location in modern society. Is political power directly linked to economic power, as those on the left believe? Is the American political scene effectively dominated by large corporate interests, making democracy something of an illusion? Or is the situation as those on the right believe it to be, with effective political power residing in several locations, the most threatening of which at present is the relatively small bureaucratic elite that controls the welfare and regulatory apparatus of the modern welfare state? While those on the left maintain that the state is the only institution powerful enough to challenge the political-economic hegemony of business corporations, those on the right argue that the bureaucratic elite that controls the modern state is actually much less accountable to the electorate than those in the business community, who must at least defer to consumer sovereignty. Given their conflicting assessments of the modern state, it is not surprising that the left and right have arrived at completely different understandings of the history of state-sponsored intervention in economic affairs. Those on the left argue that this intervention is crucial and has frequently prevented economic collapse. Those on the right insist that this intervention has precipitated most of the economic problems the nation has faced in the past century.

The conflict between left and right over the issues of capitalist politics is nicely illustrated by the different connotations the two sides attach to the terms *public* and *private*. The left perceives "private" business activity as a direct threat to democracy, in the face of which an increasingly powerful state is needed to defend the "public" interest against the machinations of a corporate elite. On the right, the understanding is exactly the reverse: "private" business activity is viewed as the only effective means to check the increasingly sweeping claims that are made by those in the "public" realm.

Cultural Issues Raised in the Debate

All parties to the evangelical debate concur that there is something desperately wrong with contemporary American culture. There is a sense of urgency, occasionally expressed in apocalyptic terms, in the full range of evangelical appraisals of capitalism. The precise nature of the cultural problem remains, of course, a matter of dispute. The left contends that secularization and cultural decadence are intrinsic to capitalism itself, a system that of necessity encourages and thrives on competitive individualism and consumerism to the detriment of human community and more cooperative forms of behavior. Those on the evangelical right, on the other hand, view capitalism and culture as two distinct entities, and they have attributed cultural decadence to the rise of secular humanism, a philosophical system that undermines religious belief, traditional understandings of work and self-reliance, and the foundation of free enterprise itself.

In addition, those on the left and right have not been able to agree on just who is responsible for the problem of contemporary cultural decadence. While those on the left argue that business interests in collusion with ideologically captive conservative church leaders are chiefly to blame for the cultural problem, those on the right contend that the real culprits are the members of the secular cultural elite—media experts, intellectuals, and liberal religious leaders. The left holds that we can overcome cultural decadence only by progressing beyond unrestrained capitalism and toward a more humane social-ist (or at least heavily interventionist) sociopolitical-economic order. Those on the right contend that the solution to our cultural problems must entail a return to traditional values, including a return to the traditional notions of initiative and achievement exemplified in the free enterprise system.

Interestingly, both left and right appear to be pessimistic about the pros-pects for the future. Those on the left suggest that the projection of military strength required to maintain capitalism internationally may well precipitate a major global war, and those on the right fear that the increasingly heavy burden placed upon the market system by "statist" economic policies may well cause its collapse.

Moral and Ethical Issues Raised in the Debate

In considering the moral and ethical issues raised within the evangelical debate over capitalism, it is very important to note that the normative arguments the various authors make either for or against capitalism depend in large part on which paradigm they choose to work within and which coterie of economic theorists they choose to believe. Thus in spite of the fact that there appear to be very significant differences of opinion between the camps on basic moral and ethical questions, the positions have more in common than appearances might suggest. All parties agree that oppression and exploitation are evil, that justice ought to be the goal of social and economic policy, that freedom is worth preserving, that the problems of poverty ought to be redressed, and so on. The difference between them is not a matter of competing moral and ethical paradigms but of disagreement on the question of whether capitalism promotes or prevents the realization of the norms and values they hold in common.

Still, there are several points of ethical disagreement between the evan-gelical left and right. Perhaps the most interesting has to do with the relation of intentionality to the assessment of the consequences of political-economic policies, a disagreement that ultimately depends on whether one believes that morality is based in a fixed created order or in the movement toward a not-yet-existing ideal society. Those on the left believe that ethical reflection (which they most often express in terms of obedience to the teachings of Jesus) is vitiated by any consideration of the likely consequences of such obedience. Trying to anticipate the consequences of moral behavior ad hoc, they feel, assumes too much continuity between the future and the present and so betrays a basic lack of faith in the ability of God to realize his kingdom in the world.

Those on the right hold that the anticipation of the probable consequences of policy proposals is a crucial task, the good intentions of such proposals notwithstanding. Indeed, those on the right believe that the left's refusal to try to anticipate the likely consequences of the policies they propose represents the height of moral irresponsibility. While we cannot pursue a detailed philosophical discussion of this problem here, it is important to see that the conflicting positions are consonant with the two economic paradigms mentioned above. If the left is correct and the present economic situation is one of oppression and exploitation, then ethical reflection must point entirely beyond it. But if the present economic situation is understood more positively, as it is by those on the right, then a careful assessment of the consequences of policy proposals is necessary in order to ensure that the situation is not made worse.

The evangelical left and right are also divided over the issue of freedom. Those on the left insist that political freedom is ultimately a function of economic power and that economic power is a function of the ownership of, or at least of the control over, capital. The grossly uneven distribution of and control over capital in capitalist societies, they argue, prevents the vast majority of people from exercising economic and hence political freedom. Those on the right link economic and political freedoms as well, but they do not equate political and economic power. Freedom is not so much a function of the ownership of capital as it is of the opportunity to participate freely in market transactions, they say. While some capital is required for such participation, such things as education and skill are at least as important as purely material assets, and the fact that some might possess more of these assets than others does not necessarily imply that they possess more freedom. Those on the right also tend to assume that some degree of inequality characterizes all political-economic systems and that elite groups within such systems will always have access to power and privilege. But by linking the interests of the economic elite with those of consumers, the market system limits the ability of the elite to abuse its power and privilege. In addition, those on the right contend that capitalism serves to prevent totalitarianism by disaggregating political and economic power.

At another level, the debate between the left and right over the issue of freedom reflects a tension between what might be called the "morality of individualism" and the "morality of the collective." Peter Berger has suggested that

> the value conflicts between the two models are clear. There is the primacy of the individual as against that of the collectivity. There is freedom as against belonging. There is acceptance of an "adversary model" of society as against the ideal of "harmony." Now, clearly, the counterposition of these values is rarely absolute. Few who advocate socialism would like to see total eradication of individuality in the collective. Few of even the most enthusiastic advocates of the hurly-burly of free-enterprise competition would carry their enthusiasm as far as a Hobbesian

jungle of the war of all against all. The values are typically posited in relative terms—they are favored, "other things being equal." Yet, even with such relativization, there are many situations in which the alternative presents itself quite sharply.[2]

Of course, in the evangelical debate the alternatives have presented themselves most sharply with respect to the authority of the state. How much should the state, as the representative of the collectivity, be allowed to interfere with individual economic activity? Conversely, how much should individual economic behavior be allowed to impact on the community? Those on the left tacitly equate the public interest with public authority and argue for the moral superiority of the community over that of isolated individuals. Those on the right tend to champion the morality of individualism, assuming that free individuals will naturally form meaningful communities of purpose.

The evangelical left and right also have very different conceptions of justice relative to economic life. Those on the left associate justice primarily with repairing the damage done by capitalism—returning wealth and resources to those from whom they have essentially been stolen. Indeed, the term "social justice" as it is commonly used by those on the left tends to rule out capitalism by definition. And since they closely link the possession of capital with the exercise of freedom, they believe that the goal of justice must be material equality. In addition, they argue that the state must assume the responsibility for implementing a just social policy, for only the state possesses the authority to require the owners of capital to part with it. They contend that voluntary redistribution, or charity, does not fundamentally alter the balance of political and economic power in society and so does not really accomplish justice.

Those on the right reject the assertion that wealth accrues to some individuals only at the expense of others. Because of this, their understanding of justice is somewhat more nuanced than that of the left. In the first instance, they insist that justice does not necessarily require the redistribution of existing wealth. Such wealth may well have been created in a just fashion, and in any event it serves as an incentive toward productive and hence socially useful activity. Instead of focusing the question of justice on distributional problems, many of which they feel could be handled voluntarily at the community and church level, those on the right contend that justice requires ensuring that the procedures for entering and participating in market transactions are fair and that they are properly observed. They admit that exploitation is possible within the capitalist system (though they insist that it is not intrinsic to it), and they hold that justice requires that this exploitation be remedied where feasible. They have noted, however, that remedial action, especially when it is under-

2. Berger, *Pyramids of Sacrifice: Political Ethics and Social Change* (Garden City, NY: Doubleday-Anchor, 1976), pp. 107-8.

taken by the state, requires coercion and so threatens the exercise of freedom. Since freedom is a more fundamental asset than the mere possession of material goods, they argue, when liberty is weighed against justice in social and economic policy, the benefit of the doubt should be left on the side of liberty.

At another level, the evangelical disagreement over the nature of justice may be said to reflect a broader quarrel over the character of society and the nature of social change. Those on the right assert that the just actions of individuals must necessarily add up, in the aggregate, to a just social order. They assume that society consists of the sum total of individual actions. They also assume that individual actions, even when considered in the aggregate, give rise to readily predictable social results. In other words, there are no surprises in history for those on the right, just the more or less logical out-workings of certain presuppositions and/or commitments.

The evangelical left believes very nearly the opposite to be true. They argue that it is possible for even the just actions of individuals to give rise to a *totally* unjust social outcome. Indeed, this is precisely the problem with capitalism; this is why evangelicals must be educated about their complicity in *systemic* injustice. Those on the left imply that our determination of the justice or injustice of the social order must be entirely divorced from our consideration of the justice or injustice of individual actions. In their view, history is full of surprises—so much so that only an analytical "key" (such as that supplied by Marxist analysis) can unlock its meaning for us.

The evangelical left and right are also divided over the issue of human rights. Those on the left tend to conceive of human rights in the context of affluent Western societies. In their view, the fact that some people go without food, shelter, and health care while others have more than they need constitutes a tragedy that demands political redress. If such redress is most effectively legitimated by expanding the notion of "rights" to include the kinds of benefits just mentioned, then this should be done. While those on the evangelical right do not want to deny the importance of human rights, they have been very wary of the left's use of rights language precisely because they see it as a tool being used to legitimate an expanded state, which they believe threatens the most basic human right—the right to freedom from government interference.

Theological Issues Raised in the Debate

It is important to note that the theological issues raised in the evangelical debate over social and economic policy far transcend those of traditional denominational conflict. While evangelicals have ostensibly been united on the principle of *sola Scriptura,* for example, they have exhibited strikingly different opinions about what the Scriptures actually teach. In addition, both left and right have brought extrabiblical sources to bear on social and economic questions, and in an increasingly authoritative fashion. While this is perhaps more noticeable among those on the left, who employ neo-Marxist analysis to assess the world-historical situation, it is also evident among those on the right, who tend to augment the biblical record, albeit implicitly, by reading it through a classical-liberal grid. The theological controversy has extended to questions concerning the nature of God, man, and salvation as well. Does the notion of providence, for example, include history and the social order in such a way as to disallow human attempts to guide them toward their fulfillment? Or does providence lie "behind" human historical-political efforts? Is the so-called "dominion mandate" to be interpreted collectively in such a way as to entail the responsibility of society before God, or should it be understood as relating only to individuals? Is sin a problem primarily at the level of the individual, though with effects on the aggregate, or is it principally a problem at the level of social structures and institutions? Is self-interested individual behavior a declension from a communitarian ideal or is it essential to human rationality? Here again, the answers the left and right give to such questions reflect their conflicting views of the present socioeconomic situation.

The far left, understanding the present sociostructural arrangement in terms of demonically motivated "principalities and powers," subordinates questions of individual evil (and hence also of individual salvation) to those having more directly to do with progressive social reform and redemption. God is at work in history, those on the left maintain, progressively liberating the poor from sociostructural oppression. Indeed, it is precisely this kind of understanding to which one is converted, and this conversion may be subsequently authenticated by one's identification with the poor and oppressed and by certain kinds of left-liberal social and political involvement. Curiously, those on the evangelical far right seem to have arrived at very similar conclusions. Yet instead of neo-Marxist analysis and praxis, advocates of Christian reconstruction have substituted the praxis of laissez-faire in their understanding of historical redemption. Both extremes, in other words, tend to understand salvation and redemption as something realizable in this world, as a process in which conscious sociopolitical striving serves as the instrumental means of eschatological fulfillment. While those on the far left legitimate this kind of understanding in Anabaptist terms, those on the far right argue that this is what postmillennialism has traditionally implied.

Of course, most evangelical intellectuals have not succumbed to the historicization of orthodoxy to the extent that the extremes of the left and right have. The evangelical mainstream still understands history in terms of a basic discontinuity, often construed quite radically, between this world and the next. While the task of social action aimed at the reduction of human suffering is a high priority for those in the mainstream, they tend to be ambivalent about what may actually be achievable in this world and hence contend that social action is not as important as evangelism, which prepares people for the world to come. Admittedly such a position relativizes the importance of sociopolitical activity, and it has drawn rather intense criticism from the extremes of both left and right for its alleged irrelevance and its de facto support of the existing status quo. Indeed, the position of those who would maintain the priority of the task of evangelism over that of social action has become increasingly uncomfortable in a secularized and media-oriented culture in which the pressure to appear concerned about this-worldly social issues has become acute.

Curiously, all parties to the evangelical debate over capitalism tend to agree that the American church is in a state of crisis at present because it has failed to fulfill its proper responsibilities. Yet their ideas of what these responsibilities are and of how the church has actually failed appear to depend again on their choice of economic paradigm. While those on the left contend that the church has succumbed to capitalist ideology, those on the right understand the problem in terms of the church's increasing willingness to advocate a secular humanist sociopolitical agenda and its failure to provide the range of social services now provided by the welfare state. Both left and right agree that the church should model the new humanity made possible by the death and resurrection of Jesus Christ, but they disagree as to whether this means modeling communitarianism or compassionate free enterprise. In addition, all of the various disputants claim continuity with the conservative Protestantism of the eighteenth and nineteenth centuries. Those on the left revere the likes of Wesley and Wilberforce as prophetic social activists who would certainly have supported a radical, or at least a progressive, social agenda. Those on the right consider these same men to have been champions of the cause of evangelism over social action who would surely have contended for free enterprise over and against coercive statism.

There are certainly other theological points at issue within the evangelical debate over social and economic policy, but the few I have mentioned illustrate the breadth of the disagreement. Although some scholars have attempted to interpret the evangelical debate in terms of classical Protestant theological dilemmas—in terms of Anabaptist versus Reformed theology, for example, or in terms of premillennialism versus postmillennialism[3]—the dimensions of the conflict are such that they probably cannot be explained simply on this basis. Of course, it is certainly the case that different theological traditions have had different affinities or predispositions toward one side or the other in the contemporary debate.[4] Anabaptists, for example, are theologically pre-

3. See Robert K. Johnston, *Evangelicals at an Impasse: Biblical Authority in Practice* (Atlanta: John Knox Press, 1979).
4. See Richard J. Mouw, "Thinking about the Poor: What Evangelicals Can Learn from

disposed to criticizing the capitalist status quo. Evangelicals standing in the tradition of American revivalism, on the other hand, are more likely to defend individual freedom and free enterprise. Still, while these theological predispositions may explain why certain people and churches tend toward either the left or the right in the recent conflict, they do not explain how or even necessarily why capitalism is actually attacked or defended. Put differently, the claims that those on both the left and right make about standing in continuity with a centuries-old theological tradition of either the criticism or the defense of capitalism are suspect. The positions are too closely linked to the two contemporary economic paradigms for this to be the case. In addition, were theology actually the decisive factor in the contemporary debate, we would not expect the evangelical positions on either side to resemble their secular counterparts as closely as they do. Certainly it is possible to argue that the secular advocates on either side of the conflict have actually been theologians without realizing it, but it seems more likely that, as they have become increasingly involved in this debate, evangelical advocates on both sides have actually been secularized without recognizing it.

A Few General Observations

Stepping away from these disagreements on issues of political economy, culture, morality and ethics, and theology, it is important to see that the various evangelical appraisals of capitalism also have a number of things in common. Most, for example, are disturbed by the concentration of power in modern society. Most have a paradoxical concern both for the loss of individual freedom in modern society and for the loss of such institutions as family and community which have traditionally constrained individual freedom. In addition, the positions share a concern about the apparently increasing inability of the church to speak and act authentically in the modern situation. Hence it appears that in spite of their radically different estimates of modern capitalism, evangelicals are united in their concern about modernity in general. Indeed, in reviewing the positions at the extremes of left and right, one has the sense that modernization is perhaps one of the chief problems.

According to Peter Berger, "modernization refers to the institutional and cultural concomitants of economic growth under the conditions of sophisticated technology."[5] Variously described and analyzed, the institutional con-

---

the Bishops," in *Prophetic Visions and Economic Realities: Protestants, Jews, and Catholics Confront the Bishops' Letter on the Economy,* ed. Charles R. Strain (Grand Rapids: William B. Eerdmans, 1989), p. 22.

5. Berger, *Pyramids of Sacrifice,* p. 34.

comitants to which he refers are commonly been held to be such things as the large institutions of modern business and government, both of which operate within the enormously complex and pluralistic environment of the modern city. More specifically, capitalism, technology and industrial development, the bureaucratization of both government and business, and social stratification by class all serve to modernize contemporary society. Citing the work of a number of social theorists, James Davison Hunter has listed the following as cultural concomitants of modernization:

> the impulse toward "technical domination" (Ellul), rational "one-dimensionality" (Marcuse), "purposive rationality" (Habermas), "bureaucratization and disenchantment" (Weber), "utilitarian individualism" (Bellah, et al.), etc. A second trend concerns the changing nature of life in the private sphere . . . a tendency toward narcissism (Lash; Sennet), hedonism (Bell), subjectivism (Gehlen), the therapeutic mentality (Rieff), antinomianism (Bell), and expressive individualism (Bellah, et al.).[6]

As Hunter's list indicates, the process of modernization appears to have resulted in the bifurcation of human existence into "public" and "private" spheres. The public sphere is increasingly dominated by the rationalized exigencies of such things as big business and big government. It is a sphere in which the influence of single individuals is, or at least seems to be, negligible. The private sphere, on the other hand, is the sphere of individual fulfillment.[7] People have been left almost completely free to construct their own meaning and structure within this private sphere, but only on an individualistic and hence highly subjective basis. Modernization, then, has paradoxically afforded increased freedom in certain areas of life while at the same time restricting freedom in others. It has been liberating as well as alienating.[8]

The authors of *The Homeless Mind: Modernization and Consciousness* have suggested that in general "the very complexity and pervasiveness of the technologized economy makes more and more social relations opaque to the individual."[9] They also suggest that people have responded to modernization with both ideological apologies and ideological resistance.[10] The apologists tend to construct ethical systems of intense individuation and locate meaning and hope in such things as economic growth and technological progress (often expressed in terms of faith in the market system and technological progress).

6. James Davison Hunter, "America's Fourth Faith: A Sociological Perspective on Secular Humanism," *This World* 19 (Fall 1987): 108-9.

7. Peter L. Berger, *Facing Up to Modernity: Excursions in Society, Politics, and Religion* (New York: Basic Books, 1977), p. 133.

8. See Peter L. Berger, "Western Individuality: Liberation and Loneliness," *Partisan Review* 52 (1985): 323-36.

9. Peter L. Berger, Brigitte Berger, and Hansfried Kellner, *The Homeless Mind: Modernization and Consciousness* (New York: Random House, 1973), p. 182.

10. Berger, Berger, and Kellner, *The Homeless Mind*, p. 188.

The critics locate the problem of modernity precisely in such individualism and call either for a return to the traditional communitarian social patterns of the past or for the realization of communitarian ideals in the near future. While the critics of modernity most commonly identify capitalism as the chief cause of alienation, and so locate hope in a radical curtailment of the market system, resistance to modernity has also been reactionary in the sense that it hearkens back to a cultural situation in which free enterprise was still bounded by the traditional ethical and moral constraints of family, church, and community.

> In the advanced societies of the Western world the protest against individualism is specified in regard to capitalism and bourgeois democracy. Capitalism is perceived as a major fragmenting, "alienating," and ultimately dehumanizing force which pits individuals against each other in a merciless competitive conflict. . . . It is important to see, however, that there are comparable phenomena on the "right." Conservative movements in advanced industrial societies . . . have repeatedly contrasted the dehumanizing individualism of modernity with the safe and reliable collective security of pre-modern society.[11]

Both kinds of responses give evidence of a willingness to sacrifice a certain degree of individual autonomy in exchange for this movement toward communal solidarity, and yet ironically both have been profoundly modernizing in and of themselves in the sense that they both call for the rational manipulation and redirection of the social order.[12]

There are obviously elements of both promodern and antimodern ideologies in many if not all of the recent evangelical appraisals of capitalism. For example, both left and right have exhibited the characteristically modern tendency toward rationalized abstraction and manipulation. The highly individualistic libertarian defense of capitalism made by many of those on the right essentially amounts to an apology for modernity as well. Most of the positions, however, including the libertarian, also evince distinctly antimodern prejudices. The complaints of those on both left and right that political and economic power have become increasingly concentrated and increasingly unaccountable to the democratic process is evidence of this. Further evidence is given in the eagerness with which many of those on both left and right, especially at their extremes, have been willing to exchange individual autonomy for the communal solidarity of either some form of communitarianism or a theonomically governed free enterprise.

But interpreting the range of recent evangelical appraisals of capitalism either as reactions to or apologies for modernization, though instructive, obviously does not tell the whole story. Clearly, the positions are related *to each other* as well as to the abstract process of modernization per se. Historically,

11. Berger, Berger, and Kellner, *The Homeless Mind*, pp. 196-97.
12. Berger, Berger, and Kellner, *The Homeless Mind*, pp. 198, 177.

for example, the defense of free enterprise among the early fundamentalists appears to have been a reaction to the harsh criticism leveled at capitalism by advocates of the Social Gospel. Neo-evangelicals then reacted to fundamentalism's separatism and staunch defense of capitalism. Radical and progressive evangelicalism then renounced what they perceived to be the ideological entanglement of "establishment" evangelicalism within capitalist culture. And the left-liberal tendencies within neo-evangelicalism undoubtedly contributed to the recent rise of neofundamentalism. We have also noted that the two sides use mutually exclusive nonevangelical source material in making their respective cases concerning capitalism, as well as the tendency of both to oversimplify complex social and economic issues and to resort to the passionate rhetorical denunciation of each other. Both sides also make use of critical American "symbols of legitimacy" to rally their respective constituencies— symbols of democracy and populism, of antiauthoritarianism, of America's special mission, of civil rights, and of family, to name just a few.[13] Both sides claim exclusive continuity with nineteenth-century evangelicalism and the classical theological symbols of Protestantism. Both sides exhibit a tendency to abuse Scripture and a disturbing reluctance to engage in detailed exegetical work.[14] Both sides make their cases on behalf of groups they say are socially oppressed—the left on behalf of those exploited and oppressed by capitalism, and the right on behalf of those manipulated and oppressed by taxation and regulation. Both sides depict their opponents as being closely aligned with those responsible for contemporary cultural alienation and oppression—either "business interests" or "secular bureaucrats." In addition, the two sides show no hesitancy to make use of the concept of ideology in debunking each other's positions, and both are quick to make the corresponding claim to cognitive

13. On "symbols of legitimacy," see James Davison Hunter, "American Protestantism: Sorting Out the Present, Looking toward the Future," *This World* 17 (Spring 1987): 62.

14. Describing the exegetical method of the evangelical left, Robert Price has suggested that "most conservative evangelicals have been taught that personal opinions and cultural views are worthless unless they can make direct appeal to a biblical warrant of some sort. Many of the current 'young evangelical' writers grew up in the '60s, and could not resist the perceived cogency of certain cultural trends—for instance, racial and sexual equality, or nonviolence. Their religious upbringing provided no basis or authorization for espousing such views, however. . . . Some renounced their religious backgrounds. Others sought to accommodate their new liberalized stance to the evangelical ethos. The main strategy was an appeal to the Bible that I call 'hermeneutical ventriloquism.' The young evangelical approaches the problem like this: 'Feminism [for example] is true; the Bible teaches the truth; therefore the Bible *must* teach feminism' " ("A Fundamentalist Social Gospel?" *Christian Century*, 28 November 1979, p. 1184). Richard J. Mouw makes a similar observation in "New Alignments," in *Against the World for the World: The Hartford Appeal and the Future of American Religion*, ed. Peter L. Berger and Richard John Neuhaus (New York: Seabury Press, 1976), pp. 99-125. Of course, the same appears to be true of much of the exegetical work done by those on the evangelical right.

privilege for their respective arguments. As a result of all of this, advocates on the two sides are almost incapable of appreciating each other's positions. While those on the evangelical left are unable to comprehend how conservatives can continue to defend the manifestly oppressive sociopolitical-economic system of modern capitalism, those on the right are just as unable to understand how the left can continue to advocate a potentially disastrous form of totalitarian statism.

While some have interpreted this ongoing contest as a manifestation of an irresolvable theological and/or philosophical controversy,[15] the contest between the evangelical left and right, with the evangelical center increasingly torn between the two, also bears the marks of an ideological conflict, a conflict in which the appraisal of capitalism, either negative or positive, has become symbolically important. While I do not want to suggest that the evangelical debate can be reduced to mere ideology, I do believe that there are good reasons to suspect that the conflicting evangelical assessments of capitalism may be functioning ideologically at present. Note, for example, how the two sides tend to make use only of those data that support their respective cases. Note how each side tends to identify only one half of a legitimate ethical and/or theological paradox—either freedom or justice, either equity or equality, either an ethic of responsibility or an absolute ethic, either creation or redemption, either the kingdom of God as a present reality or the kingdom as a future reality, and so on—and then presents that half as the whole truth. Of course, the utility of this kind a procedure is obvious: it enables each side to make a legitimate claim to truth while at the same time delegitimating its opposition. And some legitimate claim to truth is probably necessary for ideology to function properly in motivating people to action (this is perhaps especially true with respect to an evangelical constituency that is committed to the idea of absolute and unchanging truth). Our frank recognition of the ease with which truth may be used ideologically, however, is important—especially if we are interested in trying to resolve any of the substantive issues the recent evangelical conflict

15. Historian Martin Marty, for example, has seen a basic division within American Protestantism between the postmillennial tradition of optimistic social reform and the premillennial tradition of individualism and cultural withdrawal. "So long as the American republic contains people who will be responsive to both sets of symbols, it is probable that there will be two kinds of Protestantism. Neither has been successful at displacing the other, and perhaps neither ever shall be. Both of them have too much tradition going for them. In each generation, both have been blessed with ingenious and dedicated men who could translate their symbols one more time" (*Righteous Empire: The Protestant Experience in America* [New York: Dial Press, 1970], p. 266). Though dealing largely with the "secular" debate over social and economic policy, Thomas Sowell arrives at a similar conclusion in *A Conflict of Visions* (New York: William Morrow, 1987). After a thorough description of the conflicting social "visions," Sowell suggests that they represent two irreconcilable and timeless philosophical positions.

has raised. As Peter Berger has wisely observed, "any attempt at ethical assessment is severely hampered if the ideological function [of truth] remains unperceived."[16]

Of course, the ideological aspects of the evangelical debate over social and economic policy issues have not gone unnoticed. Radical and progressive evangelicals have been accusing those in the conservative mainstream of ideological captivity since the 1960s. Others have suggested that ideology is a problem on both the evangelical left and right. "Liberation theology and the Christian New Right in America are two leading examples of how political ideology can invade Christian theology," Dale Vree commented a few years ago. "Both serve as object lessons in how *not* to do Christian social ethics."[17] But observations like this one have been less instructive than one might hope because they have not been fit into any kind of sociological and/or theoretical framework as yet. By reviewing the so-called "New Class" thesis, I want to try to provide such a framework and identify the sociological context for the evangelical debate over capitalism in the following.

Capitalism and the New Class

Inspired by the failure of Marxist analysis to explain the cultural and ideological dynamics in modern societies, a number of observers have suggested that at least since the end of World War II the predominant class conflict within advanced industrial Western societies has been between two relatively privileged segments of what was once a broadly unified middle class.[18] Peter Berger has suggested, for example, that "contemporary Western societies are characterized by a protracted conflict between two classes, the old middle class (occupied in the production and distribution of material goods and services) and a new middle class (occupied in the production and distribution of sym-

16. Berger, "Ethics and the Present Class Struggle," *Worldview* 21 (April 1978): 9.

17. Vree, "Ideology vs. Theology: Case Studies of Liberation Theology and the Christian New Right," in *Christianity Confronts Modernity,* ed. Peter Williamson and Kevin Perrotta (Ann Arbor: Servant Books, 1931), p. 57. See also Richard J. Mouw, "Toward an Evangelical Theology of Poverty," in *Christian Faith and Practice in the Modern World: Theology from an Evangelical Point of View,* ed. Mark A. Noll and David F. Wells (Grand Rapids: William B. Eerdmans, 1988), pp. 218-38.

18. The term *class* refers to a group of persons who bear a particular relation to the productive process and who exhibit, in part for that reason, common interests and common cultural traits. The term *new class* was apparently first used by Milovan Djilas in *The New Class: An Analysis of the Communist System* (1957), but the idea can also be traced to the writings of Mikhail Bakunin and Leon Trotsky. A more recent discussion of the Eastern European situation appears in Georg Konrad and Ivan Szelenyi's *The Intellectuals on the Road to Class Power* (1978).

bolic knowledge)."[19] While a number of interesting issues have been raised in this conflict between the old and new classes, perhaps the most politically visible concerns the status of modern capitalism. Capitalism, it seems, has become a critical symbolic issue on both sides in this protracted conflict, symbolizing such things as liberty and prosperity for those in the old, or traditional middle class, and elitism and avarice for those in the new class.

Yet in spite of the fact that the conflict has ostensibly focused on the issue of capitalism, it has been suggested that the real point at issue between the old and the new classes concerns the status of the modern welfare state.[20] While the traditional middle class resists the expansion of the welfare state, the New Class tends to favor the continued expansion of the welfare and regulatory apparatus of the modern state. In this regard, the criticism of capitalism serves to legitimate this expansion, and the defense of capitalism serves the opposite purpose. Yet the issue is complicated by the fact that both factions, as relatively privileged segments of the middle class, stand to benefit from welfare-state services. "Two seemingly contradictory tendencies are evident in current think-

---

The idea of the new class has been applied to the Western situation in several different ways. For observations concerning the rise of a technological/managerial elite distinguishable from the capitalist class, see Thorstein Veblen, *Engineers and the Price System* (1932); Adolph Berle and Gardner Means, *The Modern Corporation and the Private Property* (1932); Joseph Schumpeter, *Capitalism, Socialism, and Democracy* (1947); C. Wright Mills, *The White Collar* (1951); John Kenneth Galbraith, *The Affluent Society* (1958), and *The New Industrial State* (1967); and Daniel Bell, *The Coming of Post-Industrial Society* (1973), and *The Cultural Contradictions of Capitalism* (1976).

For observations made by those on the political left concerning the positive political potential of the new class, see David Bazelon, *Power in America: The Politics of the New Class* (1964); Barbara Ehrenreich and John Ehrenreich, "The Professional Managerial Class," *Radical America* 11 (March-April 1977); and Alvin Gouldner, *The Future of Intellectuals and the Rise of the New Class* (1979).

For recent observations made by neoconservative cultural critics, see Daniel Patrick Moynihan, "Equalizing Education: In Whose Benefit?" *The Public Interest* (Fall 1972); Irving Kristol, "About Equality," *Commentary* (1972), and *Two Cheers for Capitalism* (1978); C. Everett Ladd, Jr., "The New Lines Are Drawn: Class and Ideology in America, Part 1," *Public Opinion* (1978); C. Everett Ladd, Jr., and Charles D. Hadley, *Transformations of the American Party System: Political Coalitions from the New Deal to the 1970s* (1978); B. Bruce-Briggs, *The New Class?* (1979); Peter L. Berger, "Ethics and the Present Class Struggle," *Worldview* (1978); and most recently John C. McAdams, *The New Class Struggle: Social Class and Politics in Post-Industrial Society* (Cambridge: Harvard University Press, forthcoming).

A thorough bibliographic essay on the topic appears in an appendix to Gouldner's work, and the introduction to Bruce-Briggs's volume provides a good overview of the recent debate about the new class.

19. Berger, *The Capitalist Revolution: Fifty Propositions about Prosperity, Equality, and Liberty* (New York: Basic Books, 1986), p. 212.

20. Berger, *The Capitalist Revolution,* p. 47.

ing about public policy in America. First, there is a continuing desire for the services provided by the modern welfare state. Partisan rhetoric aside, few people seriously envisage dismantling the welfare state. The serious debate is over how and to what extent it should be expanded. The second tendency is one of strong animus against government, bureaucracy, and bigness as such."[21]

The Structural Basis for the Rise of the New Class

The bifurcation of the middle class is ultimately attributable to technological and economic factors. Recent technological developments have enabled advanced industrial societies to produce an economic surplus such that the vast majority of people in these societies no longer need worry about basic subsistence concerns. These technological developments and the affluence they have afforded have compelled the growth of a "service sector" in modern industrial economies geared toward both "private" and "public" services of various kinds.[22] Of critical importance within this broad service sector is the production and distribution of the knowledge necessary for both continued technological development and the various services themselves. Hence there has been a virtual explosion of what has been called the "knowledge industry" in the advanced industrial or postindustrial situation, an explosion that has dramatically affected such things as education, research and development, media and information services, and health and human services. In a detailed study of the production and distribution of knowledge in American society,

21. Peter L. Berger and Richard John Neuhaus, *To Empower People: The Role of Mediating Structures in Public Policy* (Washington: American Enterprise Institute, 1977), p. 1.

22. On the side of public expenditures, for example, Frederic L. Pryor has provided the following statistics illustrating the tremendous increase of public expenditures since the 1950s: "In the 1950s and early 1960s, the share of public consumption expenditures in the total Gross National Product of nations in East and West Europe was roughly similar. According to the Organization for Economic Cooperation and Development there has been an explosion in this ratio in the West, with non-investment public expenditures rising in the OECD nations from an average of 24.5 percent of G.N.P. in 1955-57 to 36.9 percent in 1974-76 (or from 28.5 to 41.4 percent if all public expenditures are included)" ("The 'New Class': Analysis of the Concept, the Hypothesis, and the Idea as a Research Tool," *American Journal of Economics and Sociology* 40 [October 1981]: 376). Carll Everett Ladd, Jr., has noted that "Public expenditures for health, education, and welfare have grown at an extraordinary rate over the past two decades—from $49.9 billion in 1953 to $410.5 billion in 1975, an increase of over 800 percent in current dollars and just under 400 percent in dollars of constant (1975) purchasing power. (Over the same span, military expenditures jumped 240 percent in current dollars and just about held even in constant dollars)" ("Liberalism Upside Down: The Inversion of the New Deal Order," *Political Science Quarterly* 91 [1976]: 590-91).

Fritz Machlup noted that the share of knowledge-producing occupations in the labor force tripled between 1900 and 1959, while employment in manufacturing declined both relatively and absolutely.[23] In a follow-up study to Machlup's work, Michael Rogers Rubin and Mary Taylor Huber note that this knowledge-producing share doubled again between 1960 and 1980.[24] Similarly, Peter Berger has written that "the knowledge industry (partially as a result of technological innovations, but also because of social changes greatly augmenting the role of bureaucracy and service occupations) has undergone enormous growth since World War II, to the point where its share of the Gross National Product of [the United States] is now estimated at between 30 and 40 percent."[25] In education alone, the number of faculty at institutions of higher education in the United States increased from roughly 86,000 in 1900 to over 344,000 in 1958, and the number of students increased commensurately.[26] By 1980, the number of faculty at such institutions had grown to over one million, and the number of students to over twelve million.[27]

The New Class thesis suggests that the people employed within this new service sector, and particularly those associated with the greatly expanded "knowledge industry," are numerous enough and share the requisite number of common interests to be called a class over and against those still primarily associated with basic material production. In addition, the thesis suggests that the interests of the New Class are just different enough from those of the old class to precipitate a cultural conflict. As John Kenneth Galbraith put it in 1967, "the question remains as to how closely the educational and scientific estate, which owes its modern expansion and eminence to the requirements of the industrial system, will identify itself with the goals of the latter."[28] The rise of such things as the New Left in the late 1960s, the "New Politics" of 1972, and subsequent sociopolitical developments suggest that at least some of those in the "educational and scientific estate" have not been able to identify with the goals of the industrial system very closely at all. "The introduction of cultural conflict into American politics dramatizes the developing cleavages in the society and their social bases," Jeane Kirkpatrick noted recently. "It is

23. Machlup, *The Production and Distribution of Knowledge in the United States* (Princeton: Princeton University Press, 1962), p. 396.

24. Rubin and Huber, *The Knowledge Industry in the United States 1960-1980* (Princeton: Princeton University Press, 1986), p. 197.

25. Berger, "Ethics and the Present Class Struggle," p. 7. In *The Knowledge Industry in the United States*, Rubin and Huber note that while the knowledge industry's share of GNP grew steadily until 1972, it remained relatively constant at roughly 34 percent between 1972 and 1980 (p. 19).

26. Machlup, *The Production and Distribution of Knowledge*, p. 81.

27. Rubin and Huber, *The Knowledge Industry in the United States*, p. 58.

28. Galbraith, *The New Industrial State*, 2d ed. (Boston: Houghton-Mifflin, 1971), p. 293.

now clear that the assault on traditional culture [including capitalism and modern business] was mounted by young and not-so-young representatives of the relatively privileged classes, while the basic institutions of the society were defended by the less-prosperous, less-educated, lower status citizens."[29] And B. Bruce-Briggs has suggested that "in particular the New Class hypothesis tries to account for the prevalence of radical/reformist ideas among members of our society who would appear by any objective measure to be favored in income, status, freedom, power, and other presumed benefits of life."[30]

Objections to the New Class Thesis

The New Class thesis is controversial. While there is substantial agreement that traditional class analysis fails to explain the contemporary cultural dynamic adequately, that the number of people employed in nonmaterial production has expanded considerably in recent years, and that many of these people exhibit left-liberal political orientations, there is considerable disagreement as to just who should be included in the New Class category.[31] As B. Bruce-Briggs has noted, those on the political left tend to include salaried managers, researchers, technicians, and other nonowners of capital in the New Class camp.[32] While such people may conveniently be grouped together as a class over and against the owners of capital, their participation and stake in the private sector raises questions as to how they would stand to benefit from left-liberal, antibusiness political-economic policies. Neoconservatives, on the other hand, tend to limit membership in the New Class to the intellectual and cultural elite—educators, those involved in the media, therapists, professionals, and those employed either directly or indirectly by federal, state, or local governments[33]—and they characterize this group in terms of its adversarial relation to a private-sector elite consisting of both managers

29. Kirkpatrick, "Politics and the New Class," in *The New Class?* ed. B. Bruce-Briggs (New Brunswick, NJ: Transaction Books, 1979), p. 45.

30. Bruce-Briggs, *The New Class?* p. ix. See also Irving Kristol, *Two Cheers for Capitalism* (New York: Basic Books, 1978), p. 17.

31. See Bruce-Briggs, "An Introduction to the Idea of the New Class," in *The New Class?* p. 17. See also Alvin Gouldner, *The Future of Intellectuals and the Rise of the New Class* (New York: Seabury Press, 1979), pp. 6ff.; Robert Wuthnow and Wesley Shrum, "Knowledge Workers as a 'New Class': Structural and Ideological Convergence among Professional-Technical Workers and Managers," *Work and Occupations* 10 (November, 1983): 239-50; and Stephen Brint, " 'New Class' and Cumulative Trend Explanations of the Liberal Political Attitudes of Professionals," *American Journal of Sociology* 90 (July 1984): 34.

32. Bruce-Briggs, "An Introduction to the Idea of the New Class," p. 17; see also Ehrenreich and Ehrenreich, "The Professional-Managerial Class," pp. 11ff.

33. Bruce-Briggs, "An Introduction to the Idea of the New Class," pp. 5, 17.

and owners of capital. Once again, while this would appear to explain the left-liberal orientation of the New Class and its interest in the expansion of the welfare and regulatory apparatus of the modern state, some scholars question whether there really are enough of these people and whether they bear a consistent enough relation to a specifiable means of production to be called a class.[34] In addition, it has been noted that concerted neoconservative opposition to the New Class—opposition which is itself an intellectual phenomenon—cannot be easily accounted for, since the neoconservatives are themselves ostensibly members of this class. Such problems have led observers such as Daniel Bell to conclude that the New Class thesis is at best a "muddled concept."[35] Others have suggested that it simply represents an attack on left-liberal intellectuals by disgruntled neoconservatives.[36] In sum, the connection that proponents of the New Class thesis have drawn between the production and distribution of knowledge per se and a left-liberal political orientation is subject to doubt.[37] Indeed, the whole notion of using "class" as a conceptual tool has itself been questioned.[38]

34. For discussions of this issue, see Irving Louis Horowitz, "On the Expansion of New Theories and the Withering away of Old Classes," *Society* 16 (January/February 1979): 55-62; Andrew Hacker, "Two 'New Classes' or None?" in *The New Class?* p. 167; Brint, " 'New Class' and Cumulative Trend Explanations," p. 44; Pryor, "The 'New Class': Analysis of the Concept," p. 374; and Eva Etzioni-Halevy, *The Knowledge Elite and the Failure of Prophecy* (London: George Allen & Unwin, 1985), p. 15.

35. "If there is any meaning to the idea of a 'new class' as posed by Bazelon, Kristol et al.," Bell has written, "it cannot be located in socio-structural terms [i.e., in terms of 'class' as normally conceived]; it must be found in cultural attitudes. It is a mentality, not a class" ("The New Class: A Muddled Concept," in *The New Class?* p. 186). Following Bell's lead, Stephen Brint has concluded that "this oppositional new class, which inspired so much antagonism and hope among the theorists, is, in the final analysis, a fictional entity made plausible by the conjunction of the following forces: the liberalizing effects of a much expanded higher-education system, the traditional liberalism of a now larger category of social and cultural specialists, and the coming of age of a notably liberal cohort. The incidence of liberalism and dissent in the educated middle class, as in broad sections of the population at large, was fueled for a time by particular historical circumstances that led to a temporarily greater dissatisfaction with conservative outlooks" (" 'New Class' and Cumulative Trend Explanations," p. 60). While Brint is certainly correct about the notably liberal cohort, more commonly known as the "sixties' generation," I wonder if this kind of coincidental conclusion does not raise more questions than it answers.

36. Horowitz, "On the Expansion of New Theories," p. 58.

37. The issue has been further complicated as different researchers have arrived at largely contradictory conclusions on the basis of similar attitudinal surveys. While Brint, for example, has suggested that "very few persons in any of the new-class aggregations" evince a marked distrust of business leadership ("The 'New Class' and Cumulative Trend Explanations," p. 42), John C. McAdams has found a significant difference of opinion on just this matter between "professionals" and what he calls the "traditional middle class," or those associated with "private sector" management (*The New Class Struggle*, p. 72).

38. Horowitz, "On the Expansion of New Theories," p. 62. See also Pryor, "The 'New Class': Analysis of the Concept," p. 369.

I will not attempt to resolve these difficulties here, but I will note that both the advocates and the critics of the New Class thesis are in substantial agreement on several points. First, they agree that there is an identifiable elite within advanced Western societies consisting of intellectuals and educators, media personnel, artists and producers of "high culture," and those involved in public welfare, regulatory activity, and the like that effectively controls the symbolic environment in these societies, an environment consisting of the symbols by which members of these societies understand themselves and their purposes.[39] Second, they agree that this elite has grown tremendously since the turn of the century and especially in the post–World War II period and that although it still constitutes a minority within advanced Western societies, it wields political power disproportionate to its numbers. Third, they agree that this elite is more thoroughly secularized than other social groups. And finally they agree that this elite tends, at least at its extremes, to exhibit explicit hostility to capitalism and business civilization on the one hand and a general advocacy of the expansion of the welfare state on the other.[40] Whether we judge such an elite to constitute a class depends on how we assess the relations between these observations. I feel that they do in fact justify the use of the term *class*, and so I will use the concept in subsequent analysis—but I also grant that B. Bruce-Briggs is probably correct to suggest that these relations cannot be proved in any rigorous sense and are so highly politicized as to make any agreement about them unlikely in the near future.[41]

Among the several characteristics of the New Class mentioned above, those most relevant to our study are its secularity and its general hostility toward capitalism and business activity, both of which I want to consider in more detail.

39. Seymour Martin Lipset has written that "a key function of intellectuals is to provide symbolic formulations for the cultural construction of reality. Hence, they can 'restructure' man's conception of himself and his society. Beyond that, they may be able to motivate others to act toward their favored ends through the threat of withholding needed services, the influence derived from their high prestige, and the values generated by their elaboration of ideology" ("The New Class and the Professoriate," in *The New Class?* p. 79). The services of intellectuals are especially crucial within a liberal-democratic polity, where the sociopolitical agenda must receive popular support. Peter Berger has argued that the category of "intellectuals" in modern societies is not limited to academics per se but includes all those who administer the symbols academics develop—which is to say that it contains a relatively large number of people (*The Capitalist Revolution*, p. 67).

40. B. Bruce-Briggs provides a similar list of points of agreement (though he does not explicitly mention the secularity of the New Class) in "Conclusion: Notes toward a Delineation of the New Class," in *The New Class?* pp. 214-15.

41. See Bruce-Biggs, "Notes toward a Delineation of the New Class," p. 215.

The Secularity of the New Class

Numerous observers have commented on the secularity of those making up the New Class relative to the larger population.[42] If secularization is defined as the process by which sectors of society and culture are withdrawn from the domination and interpretive power of religious symbols and institutions,[43] one might say that the New Class is made up of those people within advanced industrial societies for whom religious symbols and institutions have the least meaning. The reasons for this are not mysterious. Modern higher education, perhaps the most crucial qualification for New Class membership, is inherently secularizing.[44] In addition, the affluence and the rising this-worldly expectations instilled by the process of modernization have served to direct the attentions of the New Class as well as the rest of modern society away from the contemplation of transcendence. And inasmuch as many New Class occupations are directly linked to this-worldly humanistic concerns, the New Class might be said to have a vested interest in actually directing attention away from the contemplation of transcendence.[45] It is also important to note that New Class occupations tend to cluster in or near the institutional centers of modernity which, as noted above, "carry" the rationalized and pluralized attitudes that have so effectively undermined traditional religious certainties for modern people. In fact, the New Class probably qualifies as the most highly secular and modernized group of people in the contemporary world.

The secularity of the New Class can be further specified in terms of what Alvin Gouldner has called the "modern grammar of rationality, or culture of critical discourse."[46] This "culture of critical discourse" is one in which dis-

---

42. Cf. Peter Berger's comments in *The Capitalist Revolution*, p. 199, for example, with those of Alvin Gouldner in *The Future of Intellectuals and the Rise of the New Class*, pp. 1, 47.

43. Peter L. Berger, *The Sacred Canopy: Elements of a Sociological Theory of Religion* (Garden City, NY: Doubleday-Anchor, 1969), p. 107.

44. Howard R. Bowen has reported that "with few exceptions, [attitudinal studies] indicate that [college] students become less favorable to the church, less convinced of the reality of God, less favorable to the observance of the Sabbath, less accepting of religious dogma, less fundamentalistic, less conservative, less orthodox, and more religiously liberal" (*Investment in Learning: The Individual and Social Value of American Higher Education* [San Francisco: Jossey-Bass, 1980], pp. 125-26). Bowen suggests that this heightened secularity tends to stay with students after college as well. Robert Wuthnow makes similar observations in *The Restructuring of American Religion: Society and Faith since World War II* (Princeton: Princeton University Press, 1988), pp. 156ff.

45. See Peter L. Berger, "The Worldview of the New Class: Secularity and Its Discontents," in *The New Class?* p. 53.

46. Gouldner, *The Future of Intellectuals*, pp. 1, 28ff. See also James Davison Hunter, *American Evangelicalism: Conservative Religion and the Quandary of Modernity* (New Brunswick, NJ: Rutgers University Press, 1983), p. 108.

cursive autonomy, or self-groundedness, replaces notions of traditional authority as the central measure of rationality. While it is debatable whether discursive
autonomy can actually be attained, it is not difficult to see how this secularized
culture of critical discourse acts to undermine traditional sources of religious
authority. Appeals to tradition and/or religion are simply ruled out a priori.
Instead, social authority for the New Class has become a function of discursive
sophistication, technical competence, and technical mastery.[47] Noting that this
secular culture of critical discourse rejects all supernatural conceptions of the
universe and asserts that ethical values have no meaning independent of human
experience, its religious adversaries have quite correctly, albeit pejoratively,
labeled it "secular humanism."[48]

Significantly, the secularity of the New Class appears to render its members highly vulnerable to the alienating effects of modernization. Peter Berger
recently commented that "there are good grounds for saying that in most
countries intellectuals have become more estranged from religion and religiously based morality than any other significant population group. Consequently, more than other groups, intellectuals suffer from the 'alienation' and
the *anomie* of modernity. They are ipso facto more susceptible to any secular
messages of redemption from these ills. The socialist myth, especially in its
Marxist version, is unusually well suited to meet these needs."[49] Such "secular
messages of redemption" tend to function as secular theodicies in which a
this-worldly sociopolitical struggle for a better future serves to assuage the
anxiety caused by the recognition of present imperfections within a religiously
closed universe. Hence these messages directly compete with traditional religious affirmations, which have served to relativize sociopolitical striving by
locating ultimacy and hope beyond this world.[50]

Of course, capitalism has historically relied on the legitimation of traditional religion, and just as traditional understandings of such things as provi-

47. See James Davison Hunter, *Evangelicalism: The Coming Generation* (Chicago:
University of Chicago Press, 1987), pp. 194-95.

48. See Donald Heinz, "The Struggle to Define America," in *The New Christian Right:
Mobilization and Legitimation,* ed. Robert C. Liebman and Robert Wuthnow (New York:
Aldine, 1983), pp. 133-34.

49. Berger, *The Capitalist Revolution,* p. 199. Robert A. Nisbet has suggested that "if
we wish to understand the appeal of Marxism, we should do well to pay less attention to its
purely intellectual qualities than to the social and moral values that inhere in it. To a large
number of human beings, Marxism offers status, belonging, membership, and a coherent
moral perspective" (*Community and Power* [New York: Oxford University Press, 1962],
p. 37). In addition, the authors of *The Homeless Mind* suggest that this problem has been
exacerbated by the growth of leisure time in the modern situation—time in which the anomie
of modernity is felt most acutely (p. 191).

50. See Berger, "The Worldview of the New Class," p. 51. See also Kirkpatrick,
"Politics and the New Class," pp. 36-39.

dence have been undermined by the culture of critical discourse of the New Class, so notions of a providentially guided market system have been undermined.[51] Yet the conscious secular assault on traditional religion and notions of transcendence does not, as those on the right tend to believe, wholly account for the legitimation deficit that appears to plague modern capitalism and bourgeois culture. "Unlike any other type of society," Joseph Schumpeter observed some years ago, "capitalism inevitably and by virtue of the very logic of its civilization creates, educates and subsidizes a vested interest in social unrest."[52] Schumpeter argued that the very rationality upon which modern capitalism depends—a rationality tending toward calculated planning and manipulation—serves to undermine not only traditional authorities and institutions but ultimately capitalism itself and the whole system of bourgeois values. This problem is most acute, Schumpeter wrote, among the ranks of intellectuals, or those wielding "the power of the spoken and the written word," who by virtue of their training and skills evince an attitude almost automatically critical of any existing status quo.[53] While intellectuals have historically been relatively few in number, the tremendous increase in the number of people in modern society who either consider themselves intellectuals or identify with the rational/critical intellectual outlook has made the defense of capitalism and bourgeois culture acutely difficult in recent years. Just as education secularizes, so it appears to "liberalize" in the sense that it raises our expectations that all social problems lend themselves to rational and calculated solutions.[54] A sim-

51. It should be noted that some transcendent notion of providence, even if expressed in so thoroughly secularized a fashion as Adam Smith's "invisible hand," has historically been critical to the defense of capitalism. That George Gilder devoted the final chapter of his recent book *Wealth and Poverty* (New York: Basic Books, 1981) to a discussion of the "necessity of faith" is a good indication that this is still the case. A belief in providence, writes Gilder, "will allow us to see the best way of helping the poor, the way to understand the truths of equality before God that can only come from freedom and diversity on earth. It will lead us to abandon, above all, the idea that the human race can become self-sufficient, can separate itself from chance and fortune in a hubristic siege of rational resource management, income distribution, and futuristic planning. Our greatest and only resource is the miracle of human creativity in a relation of openness to the divine. . . . The tale of human life is less the pageant of unfolding rationality and purpose envisaged by the Enlightenment than a saga of desert wanderings and brief bounty, the endless dialogue between man and God, between alienation and providence, as we search for the ever-rising and receding promised land, which we can see most clearly, with the most luminous logic, when we have faith and courage to leave ourselves open to chance and fate" (p. 268).

52. Schumpeter, *Capitalism, Socialism, and Democracy,* 3d ed. (New York: Harper, 1950), p. 146.

53. Schumpeter, *Capitalism, Socialism, and Democracy,* pp. 143, 147.

54. This observation appears to be borne out by Wuthnow and Shrum's analysis of recent survey data, which indicate a "significant positive relationship between college education and liberalism among both professional-technical workers and managers" ("Knowledge Workers as a 'New Class,' " p. 479).

ilar point has been made more recently on the political left by Jürgen Habermas, who has contended that once rational administration, or planning, is extended into the apparently chaotic and irrational market mechanism, the "invisible hand" of liberal capitalism is progressively demystified and economic life becomes politicized in the sense that expanded political intervention in the economy is increasingly viewed as a rational necessity.[55]

Daniel Bell takes a slightly different approach to the problem of capitalism's inherent legitimation deficit in *The Cultural Contradictions of Capitalism* (1976). He suggests that the "institutionalization of envy" in modern capitalism has destroyed its own cultural base in the sense that the cultural disciplines necessary for the proper functioning of capitalism (e.g., the values of hard work, frugality, self-denial, a willingness to delay gratification) have given way, under the pressure of marketing techniques, to a self-indulgent and pleasure-oriented hedonism. An ethic of production, in other words, has given way to a purely consumptive ethic. Thus he argues that the inherent logic of capitalism has rendered it increasingly unable to bear the burden of meaning placed upon it by modern secularized society. "Capitalism does not legitimate itself," Peter Berger has written similarly; "it depends for its legitimation upon traditional values, such as those furnished by religious morality; but the very dynamics of capitalism, its 'creative destruction' (Schumpeter's eloquent phrase), increasingly weakens all traditions and thus pulls away the rug from under its own cultural credibility."[56]

The Anti-Capitalist Animus of the New Class

The comments above concerning the psychological appeal that various secular myths of redemption have for the New Class should not obscure the fact that this class also has more mundane material interests, if not in socialist, then at least in left-liberal political-economic policies.[57] This is simply because the New Class derives its power and prestige not only from its presence in institutions of education, the media, and the like but also in the welfare and regulatory apparatus of the modern state—and hence it stands to benefit from the expansion of this apparatus.[58] The New Class effectively legitimates this

55. Habermas, *Legitimation Crisis* (Boston: Beacon Press, 1975). See also David Held, "Crisis Tendencies, Legitimation, and the State," in *Habermas: The Critical Debate,* ed. John B. Thompson and David Held (Cambridge: M.I.T. Press, 1982), p. 184.

56. Berger, *The Capitalist Revolution,* p. 207.

57. Significantly, this observation is made by those on the political left as well as by those on the right. See, for example, Ehrenreich and Ehrenreich, "The Professional-Managerial Class," p. 24.

58. See Berger, "Ethics and the Present Class Struggle," p. 10; and *The Capitalist Revolution,* p. 69.

expansion by highlighting the role the existing business system has played in causing a variety of social problems and by emphasizing the inability of this system to deal with these problems.

One reason for the development of an anticapitalist animus among members of the New Class is the fact that the competitive business system is simply not designed to appreciate and reward educational attainment per se, and so it undervalues the single most important characteristic distinguishing the New Class from other social groups.[59] Moreover, this comparative disadvantage in the business arena is matched by the comparative advantage members of the New Class have in the modern political arena.[60] Political scientist John McAdams has observed, for example, that government creates a large market for educational credentials and that political activity is more "heavily mediated" than economics in the sense that "the average citizen is almost entirely dependent on the media for the information to function politically."[61] Hence, Irving Kristol has argued that the New Class "tries always to supercede economics with politics—an activity in which it is most competent, since it has the talents and the implicit authority to shape public opinion on all larger issues."[62] It has also been observed that because the public-sector operates with no simple criterion of success—in effect with no "bottom line"—it has become increasingly dependent on New Class experts to define and evaluate its purposes and functions.[63]

In addition, it has been argued that the New Class commonly legitimates its own interests in terms of the "public interest." "Like all rising classes,"

---

59. See Berger, *The Capitalist Revolution,* p. 69. See also Gouldner, *The Future of Intellectuals,* p. 58; and McAdams, *The New Class Struggle,* p. 135. McAdams contends that this has resulted in a situation in which members of the New Class feel deprived of status and power relative to members of the business community, and this fuels their hostility toward business and the market (p. 32). Arguing along similar lines, Berger has suggested that there is a discrepancy "between what intellectuals think they have to offer and what society (at any rate 'bourgeois society') is prepared to offer them by way of power" (*Pyramids of Sacrifice,* p. 77).

60. Berger, "Ethics and the Present Class Struggle," p. 8. McAdams has actually defined the New Class as "consisting of those privileged sectors of society that have, in the struggle for money, power, and prestige, a comparative advantage in politics, as opposed to the market" (*The New Class Struggle,* p. 11).

61. McAdams, *The New Class Struggle,* pp. 28, 14.

62. Irving Kristol, quoted in B. Bruce-Briggs, "An Introduction to the Idea of the New Class," p. 4; see also Kirkpatrick, "Politics and the New Class."

63. McAdams, *The New Class Struggle,* p. 14. The notions of "poverty," "development," "class," "social mobility," and the like—all critical ideas for shaping and legitimating social and economic policy—began as the rather abstract constructions of intellectuals. Andrew Hacker has argued that these ideas have often been reified in such a way as to overshadow the realities they were originally designed to describe ("Two 'New Classes' or None?" p. 164).

Peter Berger has written, "the knowledge class rhetorically identifies its own class interests with the general welfare of society and especially with the downtrodden. . . . This is especially so because the knowledge class has such an interest in the welfare state, which is ostensibly set up on behalf of the poor and of other disadvantaged groups."[64] Corresponding to this equation of the public interest with its own interests, the New Class often portrays the interests of the business class as venal and socially irresponsible.[65] Indeed, Robert L. Bartley has asserted that members of the New Class have defined the "public interest" in such a way as to denote an adversarial relationship to business interests, which is one of the reasons New Class culture has been described as an "adversary culture" vis-à-vis bourgeois, or business culture.[66]

This tendency of the New Class to identify its own interests with those of the larger public has been amplified by the professionalization that characterizes its fields of expertise. First the New Class charges the state with providing substandard services to the public, and then it lobbies for the legislation of increasingly strict standards and levels of certification. If such standards are put in place, they automatically strengthen the monopoly the New Class personnel have over the administration of such services.[67] In addition, members of the New Class tend to insist that welfare and social services, both areas of New Class expertise, are intrinsically more valuable than the other things the government spends its money on. In particular, it is argued that these services are more valuable than military expenditures.

Yet in spite of its anticapitalist animus, it would be a mistake to conclude that the New Class necessarily wishes for the destruction of capitalism and bourgeois civilization.[68] To be sure, a vocal New Class minority may well desire the full implementation of some form of socialism, but the class interests

64. Berger, *The Capitalist Revolution,* p. 70. See also Berger, *Pyramids of Sacrifice,* p. 11. Interestingly, Gouldner and others on the political left have made similar observations (see, e.g., *The Future of Intellectuals,* p. 17). Berger has also suggested that the structure of the welfare state promotes the formation of "distributional coalitions" and makes the rhetoric of "social justice" and redistributive economic policy all the more powerful in the modern situation (*Capitalist Revolution,* p. 88).

65. See Gouldner, *The Future of Intellectuals,* p. 19. See also McAdams, *The New Class Struggle,* p. 393.

66. Bartley, "Business and the New Class," in *The New Class?* p. 64. The term "adversary culture" was coined by Lionel Trilling in the preface to *Beyond Culture* (1965) and is used Norman Podhoretz to describe the New Class in "The Adversary Culture and the New Class," in *The New Class?* pp. 19-31.

67. See Berger and Neuhaus, *To Empower People,* p. 35.

68. James Hitchcock has suggested, for example, that while New Class rhetoric is ostensibly antibourgeois, members of the New Class themselves epitomize the bourgeoisie in the sense that they are rationalized, activistic, antitraditional, achievement-oriented, and individualistic ("The New Class and the Secular City," *Journal of Ecumenical Studies* 6 [Spring 1969]: 220).

of the New Class are better understood simply in terms of the continuation and gradual expansion of welfare-state services. For this reason, New Class interests are most accurately described as "interventionist," with anticapitalist rhetoric serving only to legitimate a permanent place in the social order for New Class services and specialties.[69]

The Social Location of Opposition to the New Class

The New Class thesis suggests that this class stands in conflict with an older segment of the middle class still associated with basic material production and business. Along this line, John McAdams believes he has found indications of opposition to the New Class in his review of the attitudes of the traditional middle class, or business class.[70] Yet even he has suggested that the evidence of business class opposition to the New Class is ambivalent.[71] This opposition appears to be mitigated by several factors. In the first place, both new and old classes are relatively privileged, which takes the edge off their material aspirations (at least as narrowly defined) and complicates the connections between their economic bases and ideologies.[72] In addition, members of the business class, especially those in positions of power, are likely to be highly educated and hence are likely also to have been "liberalized" in the sense mentioned above. This, combined with capitalism's inherent legitimation deficit and the fact that this business class most probably received its education at the hands of New Class personnel, undoubtedly serves to dampen the business community's collective certainty about its interests and attitudes. In addition, since the New Class appears to have a near monopoly on the production and distribution of society's legitimating symbols, effective symbolic opposition to the New Class might be said to be handicapped almost by definition.

Significantly, the principal ideological opposition to New Class aspirations

69. McAdams has suggested that especially in light of the economic failures of existing socialist economies, members of the New Class have come to realize that only a market economy makes many of the services they provide and many of the proposals they advocate possible. "Capitalism generates affluence, and the New Class is very much a product of affluence and the things (widespread education, the welfare state, mass consumption of artistic and intellectual products) that affluence brings. That which threatens affluence threatens the New Class" (*The New Class Struggle,* p. 398).

70. McAdams has asserted that "the T[raditional] M[iddle] C[lass] worldview uniformly involves opposition to government job guarantees, national health insurance, and social services, and favorable attitudes toward 'big business' combined with a coolness toward labor unions" (*The New Class Struggle,* p. 65).

71. McAdams concludes *The New Class Struggle* by suggesting that although the business class will continue to resist the New Class, it ultimately has neither the power nor the will to suppress it entirely (p. 400).

72. See Ladd, "Liberalism Upside Down," pp. 591-92.

has not been voiced by business interests per se, but rather by the lower-middle and working classes. As Stephen Brint has suggested, "The primary social base for New Right conservatism [i.e., anti–New Class sentiment] is to be found, not among the educated middle class, but among blue-collar workers, small-business people, and farmers. . . . New Right conservatives are, in many respects, a poorer and less educated mirror image of traditional conservatives— both tend to be older, white, more religious, and Protestant [and more typically from Western states and rural areas]."[73] Although this lower-middle and working class opposition to the New Class might be interpreted along the lines of purely material interests (e.g., on the grounds that these groups have the least to gain from the expansion of the welfare state),[74] it is perhaps best explained by the fact that these groups are simply less secularized than members of the New Class and so are less receptive to the secular social symbols the New Class has generated. Put differently, the principal ideological opposition to the New Class has not necessarily come from those for whom the expansion of the welfare state per se poses an economic problem but from those who have been most distressed that their symbolic understanding of the social world has been increasingly displaced by the secular formulations of a social and cultural elite. Brint's description of New Right conservatives, for example, coincides almost exactly with James Davison Hunter's recent sociological profile of American evangelicals:

> According to current survey research findings, contemporary American Evangelicalism is a predominantly white, disproportionately female religious phenomenon. Its overall population is generally older than among other religious bodies . . . the largest concentrations of American Evangelicalism are found in the rural, small-town areas of the South and the west central and mid-Atlantic regions, and in medium-size cities in the South and Midwest. Evangelicals are grossly underrepresented in the large cities. They are most greatly represented in the lower echelons of educational achievement, income level, and occupational status; they fall mostly in the lower middle and working classes.[75]

73. Brint, " 'New Class' and Cumulative Trend Explanations," p. 62; see also McAdams, *The New Class Struggle*, p. 394; and Peter L. Berger, "For a World with Windows," in *Against the World for the World*, p. 15.

74. Everett Carll Ladd, Jr., and Charles D. Hadley have asserted that the tax burden of the expanding welfare state is disproportionately borne by the lower-middle classes (*Transformations of the American Party System: Political Coalitions from the New Deal to the 1970s* [New York: W. W. Norton, 1978], p. 221). And elsewhere Ladd has noted that the "major growth in domestic spending has been sustained in part by increases in the effective tax rate. And for those families earning incomes around the national median, the rise has been much steeper than for upper-middle and upper income families. Those at the median experienced a doubling of the proportion of their income going to taxes between 1953 and 1975, compared to a 50 percent increase among families with incomes two to four times the median" ("Liberalism Upside Down," pp. 590-91).

75. Hunter, *American Evangelicalism*, pp. 58-59.

Thus it appears that although the New Class thesis generally suggests a conflict between people employed in the production and distribution of knowledge and people still associated with basic material production and business, the conflict has been most heated between a highly secularized symbolic knowledge elite and a coalition of conservative religious believers upset that their symbolic understanding of social reality has been undermined by that of this elite.[76] Richard John Neuhaus has asserted that a "widespread exclusion of religiously grounded values and beliefs is at the heart of the outraged alienation . . . of millions of Americans. They do not recognize *their* experiences of America in the picture of America purveyed by cultural and communications elites."[77] That this religious outrage has been expressed in terms of sympathy with business interests is ironic but understandable, since traditional religion and business both stand over and against the modern state as apolitical sources of social authority and power.[78]

That said, however, the conflict is scarcely explicable solely in terms of "secular" understandings of social reality having run afoul of religion. As Robert Wuthnow and others have recently noted, the battle has extended into and subsequently split many of the major American religious communities themselves.[79] In many respects it has been most fiercely waged among competing religious elites.[80] Peter Berger has even suggested that the American

76. See Hunter, *American Evangelicalism,* p. 117. See also Heinz, "The Struggle to Define America," pp. 133-48; Nathan Glazer, "Fundamentalism: A Defensive Offensive," in *Piety and Politics: Evangelicals and Fundamentalists Confront the World,* ed. Richard John Neuhaus and Michael Chromartie (Washington: Ethics and Public Policy Center, 1987), p. 250; and Grant Wacker, "Searching for Norman Rockwell: Popular Evangelicalism in Contemporary America," in *The Evangelical Tradition in America,* ed. Leonard I. Sweet (Macon, GA: Mercer University Press, 1984), p. 313. Survey data from the recent "Williamsburg Charter Survey" bear this assertion out. James Hunter has suggested that "there is a chasm between America's 'first faith' (Evangelicalism) and America's 'fourth faith' (secularism). Although only half the number of Evangelicals (roughly 10% of the nation compared with roughly 20%), secularists reflect higher levels of education and stronger national influence because of their predominance in leadership groups" ("The Williamsburg Charter Survey of Religion and Public Life" [Washington: Williamsburg Charter Foundation, 3 February 1988], pp. 41-42).

77. Neuhaus, *The Naked Public Square: Religion and Democracy in America* (Grand Rapids: William B. Eerdmans, 1984), p. 99.

78. See Robert A. Nisbet, *Community and Power*.

79. Wuthnow, *The Restructuring of American Religion,* pp. 163ff. Jeffrey Hadden has observed that in the context of the church, the conflict has been most visible between clergy and laity: "Clergy have challenged the traditional role of the Church in society because they have reinterpreted the theological basis of their faith and in so doing have come to feel that their faith involves a much more vital commitment to the problems of this world. Laity have challenged the authority of clergy because they do not share their understanding of the meaning and purpose of the Church" (*The Gathering Storm in the Churches* [Garden City, NY: Doubleday, 1969], p. 32).

80. See Hunter, "American Protestantism," p. 64.

clergy appear to have assumed the role of "chaplains in the respective class armies."[81] Along this line, it is important to note that the conflict is being fought largely on the level of cultural symbols, with the meaning of a number of traditional American symbols at stake. Modern capitalism is one of these contested symbols and hence has become a critical issue for the competing class armies. Indeed, modern capitalism is a critical symbol not simply in the political and economic conflict between the New Class and the traditional middle class but in the ongoing cultural struggle between religion and secularity in American public life.

Evangelicals, Capitalism, and the New Class Conflict

Having surveyed the recent evangelical debate over capitalism and issues of social and economic policy, I want to suggest that the social context of this debate is that of the conflict described by the New Class thesis. Such an interpretation not only plausibly explains the paradoxical relation of evangelical left, right, and center on a variety of political-economic, cultural, theological, and ethical and moral issues but also explains why so many of these issues have centered in the disagreement over the appropriate location of social and political authority in modern society and over the status of capitalism and business vis-à-vis the modern welfare state.

Of course, by virtue of their involvement in the production and distribution of symbolic knowledge, all of the evangelical authors discussed in this study may be considered members of the New Class. This is perhaps particularly true of those authors who have identified most closely with the neo-evangelical project and who have therefore been especially concerned with educational attainment and with establishing the relevance of evangelicalism within American culture. Yet while the New Class connection may provide insight into the advent of radical and progressive evangelical criticism of capitalism, it does not appear to explain the persistent defense of free enterprise made by evangelical conservatives. In a sense those on the right have become traitors to the New Class. The reasons for this appear to be rooted in the recent history of American evangelicalism.

American Evangelicalism and the Rise of the New Class

In the half century between 1830 and 1880, America was transformed from a predominantly rural, agrarian, and overwhelmingly Protestant society to one

---

81. Berger, "The Concept of Mediating Action," in *Confession, Conflict, and Community,* Encounter Series no. 3, ed. Richard John Neuhaus (Grand Rapids: William B. Eerdmans, 1986), p. 5.

that was much more urbanized, industrialized, and very much less Protestant. As historian Martin Marty has observed, the social transformation of this period was mirrored by a subtle transformation of evangelical theology.

> The earlier clergymen [i.e., prior to 1830] focussed on salvation *after* this life. With that in mind, men were to do their earthly work in part to prove their calling. If they were poor, they were to be content with their status; if they were affluent, they were obliged to show pity and charity to the poor. . . . At the end of the period . a typical Protestant clergyman in the same lineage would focus, without changing his terms, on salvation *in* this life—though, of course, he did not fall entirely silent about eternal rewards and punishments. He simply rendered the temporal fate more vivid than had his predecessors. With that in mind men were to do their earthly work in part to improve their lot and change their calling.[82]

Of course, just how the temporal fate ought to be "rendered more vivid" became the subject of considerable debate. While most Protestant clergymen prior to 1880 simply emphasized *self*-improvement and *individual* enterprise, toward the end of this period the conflict intensified as those associated with theological modernism and the rise of the Social Gospel began to stress the need for *structural* improvement and *social* change. It was toward the end of the nineteenth century, then, that theological conservatism came to be linked to political and economic conservatism, and theological liberalism, as the perspective of the modernists came to be called, coalesced with political and economic left-liberalism.[83]

As things turned out, the liberals carried the day, especially at the level of intellectual discourse, and "conservatives," as the defenders of traditional orthodoxy and/or traditional bourgeois values came to be known, were forced to retreat from the various denominational seminaries. And conservative Protestantism's defeat in the seminaries appears simply to have reflected its defeat within American culture at large. "Within the span of one generation," evangelical historian George Marsden has noted, "between the 1890s and the 1930s, [the] extraordinary influence of evangelicalism in the public sphere of American culture collapsed. Not only did the cultural opinion makers desert evangelicalism, even many leaders of major Protestant denominations attempted to tone down the offenses to modern sensibilities of a Bible filled with miracles and a gospel that proclaimed human salvation from eternal damnation only through Christ's atoning work on the cross."[84]

82. Marty, *The Modern Schism: Three Paths to the Secular* (London: SCM, 1969), pp. 103-4.

83. See Steve Bruce, *The Rise and Fall of the New Christian Right: Conservative Protestant Politics in America, 1978-1988* (Oxford: Clarendon Press, 1988), p. 29. Prior to this time intellectuals alienated from bourgeois culture had been just as likely to move to the political right as to the left.

84. Marsden, *Reforming Fundamentalism: Fuller Seminary and the New Evangelicalism* (Grand Rapids: William B. Eerdmans, 1987), p. 4.   . . .

Significantly, the collapse of evangelical culture coincided almost precisely with the extraordinarily rapid rise of the modern university in the United States.[85] But this was not simply a coincidence, for the development of a greatly expanded system of higher education entailed the removal of restrictive ecclesiastical controls from the new universities. Indeed, it is likely that this institutional secularization contributed to the hostility toward religious fundamentalism that has been characteristic of American intellectual progressivism since the 1920s.[86] Certainly there were other reasons for the rapid disestablishment of conservative Protestantism—such things as the tremendous influx of non-Protestant groups during this period, the secularizing impacts of industrialization and urbanization, the increased privatization of religious faith, and so forth—but the expansion of higher education in America clearly exacerbated the cultural shift. "By the 1920s few respected educational institutions of any sort in the northern United States would even tolerate fundamentalist teaching."[87] Given the close connection between the growth of the knowledge industry and the rise of the New Class, it appears that the rise of this class and the expansion of its "culture of critical discourse" have been inversely related to the fortunes of conservative Protestantism in this century.

Protestant modernism and the development of the Social Gospel appear to be related to the rise of the New Class as well. They may be said to represent early theological accommodations to the increasingly influential "grammar of rationality" of the nascent New Class. Put differently, Protestant modernism represented an early attempt to provide symbolic legitimation for the transformation of the social order signaled by the rise of the New Class. According to Peter Berger, mainline Protestant denominational leadership subsequently became closely allied with the interests and outlook of the New Class: "The religious fall-out of this *Kulturkampf* [i.e., the New Class conflict] is all too visible. The mainline Protestant denominations still contain (probably dwindling) numbers of old middle-class and working-class individuals. But (and this is a decisively important fact) their clergy, officials, and intellectuals have (understandably enough) identified almost completely with the culture and *ipso facto* with the political agenda of the new middle class."[88]

85. See Mark A. Noll, *Between Faith and Criticism: Evangelicals, Scholarship, and the Bible in America* (San Francisco: Harper & Row, 1986), pp. 12ff.

86. See Christopher Lasch, "The Conservative 'Backlash' and the Cultural Civil War," in *Neo-Conservatism: Social and Religious Phenomenon*, ed. Gregory Baum (New York: Seabury Press, 1981), p. 9.

87. Marsden, *Reforming Fundamentalism*, p. 4.

88. Berger, "Different Gospels: The Social Sources of Apostasy," *This World* 17 (Spring 1987): 10. With reference to the "secular theology" of the 1960s, James Hitchcock has suggested that "the theology of the secular city and 'religionless Christianity' can be seen as an attempt of the church to accommodate itself to the emerging new class, the intellectuals and quasi-intellectuals who play an increasingly dominant role in society" ("The New Class and the Secular City," *Journal of Ecumenical Studies* 6 [Spring 1969]: 221).

By the same token, the early fundamentalist movement may be understood as the conservative Protestant response first simply to the shock of cultural disestablishment but later to the threat posed by the New Class. The differences between Charles Erdman's astute criticism of socialism in *The Fundamentals* and Carl McIntire's apocalyptic *Rise of the Tyrant* illustrate this shift quite well. When reasoned theological argument failed, it seems, it became increasingly tempting to bring hyperbolic symbolic rhetoric to the fore in the cultural conflict. In effect, then, the "world" condemned by dispensational premillennialists was the social world perceived to be controlled by an increasingly secularized knowledge elite.

The early fundamentalist coalition of highly educated conservative scholars and popular revivalist leaders proved awkward, however, and while fundamentalist intellectuals were for a time content to abandon the centers of cultural and intellectual influence, already by 1940 they had become restless in exile. Thereafter, the determination of neo-evangelical leaders to reenter and recapture the centers of cultural legitimacy, chiefly by means of advanced scholarship, increasingly thrust evangelical intellectuals back into direct contact with the secular social and cultural knowledge elite, thus reopening the issue of the relation between American evangelicals and the New Class. As this shift has taken place, some evangelical intellectuals have come to identify quite closely with the interests and outlook of the New Class, while others have chosen to adopt an adversarial stance toward it.

The Evangelical Defense of Free Enterprise and the Old Middle Class

As we have seen, the appraisals of capitalism made by those on the evangelical right are to a large extent reactions to the left-liberal positions that radical and progressive evangelicals have voiced. It is also clear that those on the right understand the critical modern problems to be not so much the defense of capitalism per se as the threat that secular humanism poses to religion and the threat that the modern welfare state poses to individual liberty. In terms of the conflict described by the New Class thesis, we could say that those on the evangelical right have chosen to voice the interests of the old, or traditional middle class.

There are obvious affinities between evangelical intellectuals and the traditional middle class. In the first place, the alliance of evangelical intellectuals and the lower-middle and/or working classes has a historical precedent in early fundamentalism, and many of those on the evangelical right have close ties to American fundamentalism—closer at any rate than the more neo-evangelically inclined centrists and leftists. Second, the evangelical constituency is predominantly lower-middle and/or working class. (And it should be noted that the literature produced by many of those on the evangelical right tends to be more obviously directed toward a somewhat less-educated audience than that produced by the progressive and/or radical left.) In addition, conservative businessmen have played and continue to play an important role in funding American evangelical projects of various kinds, which might be expected to render evangelical intellectuals more sympathetic to the concerns of the business class. And finally, it is important to see that the ideology of the traditional middle class, which I have called the "ideology of commerce," includes many classical conservative Protestant themes and has therefore posed much less of a direct threat to evangelical theology than the more explicitly secular ideology of the New Class. Even given the fact that classical liberalism may ultimately be just as secularizing as, say, dialectical materialism, the former does not require, at least on the surface of things, nearly as radical a reinterpretation of orthodoxy as does the latter. Given these sorts of affinities, and given the bitter memories of cultural disestablishment, it is not at all surprising that many evangelical intellectuals have identified more closely with the traditional middle class in the present conflict than with the New Class.

As has already been suggested, the evangelicals who have entered the cultural conflict on behalf of the traditional middle class have attempted to mount a "countermythology" over and against the ideology of secular humanism within which the advocacy of free enterprise serves as the chief intellectual line of defense against the encroachments of the New Class and an expanded welfare state. To this end, conservatives have sought to recapture access to the production and distribution of symbolic knowledge by establishing a network of schools and colleges, television and radio stations, and political associations.[89] The early fundamentalists pursued a similar strategy as they reacted to their disestablishment from what were to become liberal theological institutions. Specifically, the conservative countermythology focuses on issues of family and sexuality, education, and the reestablishment of what might be called a "Christian civilization."[90]

Yet entering the present cultural conflict on the side of the old middle class has not been without its costs, and the advocates of free enterprise on the evangelical right have tended to become just as ideologically entangled within the debate as radicals and progressives have long insisted. Such entanglement is most clearly evident on the far right among those who essentially equate capitalism with the kingdom of God, but it is also evident in the tendency even of moderate defenders of free enterprise to resort to libertarian and/or utilitarian arguments in advocating capitalism. The irony of this situation is illustrated by the fact that the "Christian civilization" many of those on the evangelical right long for is apparently modeled on the cultural hegemony

89. See Heinz, "The Struggle to Define America," p. 137.
90. See Grant Wacker, "Searching for Norman Rockwell," pp. 297-99.

that conservative Protestantism enjoyed just prior to the end of the nineteenth century—and, as we have already seen, while the Protestantism of this period appeared to thrive, it had already been substantially secularized and surrendered its aspirations to Christendom.

> In 1830 the evangelical clergy had regained their place as custodians of the society's spiritual and symbolic lore; after the 1870s they could at best share this role with countless others. During the intervening years they had to change and adapt their views of covenant and community, enterprise and nationhood. They moved from an organismic to pluralistic society; from an organic view of nature to a historic view of environmental mastery. . . . They did all this while invoking the old Biblical texts and credal points and by creating the impression that no great change was occurring. In turn, they were free to save souls, reform individuals, and pronounce the benedictions at public affairs. The churches prospered through the arrangement. But the old dreams of Christendom, of a Christian culture or synthesis, of Protestantism or the Evangelical Empire—these were to evaporate or be crowded with other, newer, more compelling if less ordered visions.[91]

Thus even prior to their rapid disestablishment from the intellectual and cultural centers of American society, conservative Protestants had begun to compromise with an increasingly secular culture. They had already begun to exhibit the calculating rationality, the individualism, and the practical materialism that appear to be the distinctive products of bourgeois capitalist culture. This kind of compromise has simply been exacerbated by the cultural conflict occasioned by the rise of the New Class.

Yet in discussing the ideological captivity of those on the evangelical right, it is important to stress that we would not necessarily expect it to manifest itself in terms of explicit theological compromise. In part this is because the defense of capitalism does not require the wholesale reinterpretation of orthodoxy along explicitly secular lines, but it is also because the theological standards against which we are most likely to measure evangelicalism today have probably been partially secularized already—if the experience of the nineteenth century is any guide. Whatever the reasons, ideological captivity on the evangelical right tends to surface in relatively subtle ways and in terms of what might be called the de facto confession of the ultimacy of economic, or material, existence. While this confession is made theologically explicit on the far right in such things as the "gospel of health and wealth" and in Christian reconstructionism, for the most part it remains largely implicit, reflected only in a thoroughly this-worldly orientation. To be sure, practical materialism is probably just as much the result of material affluence as of identification with the old middle class in the contemporary class conflict, but the this-worldly orientation cannot help but be encouraged by the strident defense of capitalism and free enterprise offered by those on the evangelical right.

91. Marty, *The Modern Schism*, pp. 141-42.

The New Class and Evangelical Concern about Capitalism

If, from the perspective of the cultural conflict described by the New Class thesis, the ardent defense of free enterprise can be interpreted as indicating that evangelical intellectuals have identified with the old middle class, then the harsh denunciation of global capitalist oppression and apologies for a substantially expanded welfare state can be interpreted as indications that others have joined this conflict as allies of the New Class. Indeed, the development of radical and progressive wings within American evangelicalism appears to reflect the growth of New Class influence since mid-century. Speaking of a group roughly equivalent to those I have categorized as belonging to the evangelical left, James Davison Hunter has asserted that "the Young Evangelicals, despite their cognitive minority status, are intricately linked with the New Class and . . . their own growth in numbers and in power is directly related to the growth of the New Class in general. Within the Young Evangelicals, one can find a relatively clear articulation of New Class interests and ideology."[92]

Just as there are affinities between the evangelical right and the traditional middle class, so it is possible to note affinities between evangelical intellectuals and the New Class. By virtue of their involvement in the production and distribution of symbolic knowledge, evangelical intellectuals have a number of concerns in common with members of the secular symbolic knowledge elite, such as a high regard for educational credentials and a need for access to media of various kinds. This has placed evangelical intellectuals in a rather awkward position relative to their largely traditional middle-class constituency. As George Marsden has suggested, evangelical scholars have tried to "have a foot firmly planted in each community, the community of secular scientific academia and the community of fundamentalist-evangelical faith."[93] They have attempted to resolve the tension between the believing and the secular academic communities by carefully balancing the concerns of the two—a balance well summarized by the term "believing criticism."[94] But maintaining this balance has evidently not been easy, for, as James Hunter recently observed in a study of evangelical higher education, evangelical faculty overall are even

92. Hunter, "The New Class and the Young Evangelicals," *Review of Religious Research* 22 (December 1980): 166. Describing a 1979 *Sojourners* readership survey, Hunter notes that "roughly 86 percent of their readership has a college degree and roughly 66 percent had either a graduate degree or some graduate/professional school training. A full 70 percent had what can be considered 'New Class' occupations: 33 percent, clergy; 16 percent, professional services; 12 percent, education; 8 percent, social services; 1 percent, journalism. An additional 1 percent were students who had not yet entered occupations. Interestingly, of the remaining percent, only 4 percent claim to be involved in business and 3 percent had blue collar occupations." For a similar discussion, see Hunter, *American Evangelicalism*, pp. 111-12.

93. Marsden, *Reforming Fundamentalism*, p. 250.

94. On this, see Mark A. Noll, *Between Faith and Criticism*.

less committed to the theological and cultural traditions of evangelicalism than their students.[95] Thus it appears that for a number of evangelical intellectuals, and perhaps especially for those concerned with educational attainment, the ideological pull in the direction of the New Class has been quite strong.

It is possible to distinguish an additional affinity between evangelical intellectuals and the New Class by recalling that one of the chief goals of the neo-evangelical movement has been to reestablish an evangelical presence within the public policy arena, an arena which as we have noted has been increasingly dominated by New Class personnel since mid-century. Indeed, since members of the New Class generally control access to the public policy debate, they may be said to hold the keys to the cultural legitimacy and recognition that neo-evangelicals have sought since the late 1940s. Though they obviously have not thought of it in these terms, it has been the New Class with which neo-evangelicals have been seeking to "cooperate without compromise." Their emphases on educational attainment and use of the media indicate that they have intuitively recognized this. Thus it is perhaps not coincidental that Carl F. H. Henry was a journalist before he became a theologian.

Of course, neo-evangelicals initially used the phrase "cooperation without compromise" to refer to cooperation with nonevangelical Christians in the service of evangelism. But over time the phrase came to mean cooperation with secularists and others on issues of social and economic import while refusing to compromise conservative Protestant theology. Originally, neo-evangelicals wanted to participate fully in the cultural debate and at the same time reinject the message of redemption within it—a strategy they pursued well into the 1950s and 1960s. The evangelical stance was exemplified in Carl Henry's insistence on active individual participation in "Caesar's kingdom" while maintaining the priority and transcendence of the kingdom of God as modeled in the church. This strategy is still advocated within what I have called the evangelical mainstream.

Yet Henry's refusal to draw the church *as* church into the public policy arena drew severe criticism from a younger generation of radical and progressive evangelical intellectuals. In their opinion, Henry's establishment stance simply represented an implicit legitimation of the existing sociopolitical-economic status quo and reflected the ideological captivity of evangelicalism within bourgeois culture. In terms of the New Class thesis, the conflict between the radical and progressive evangelical left and the conservative mainstream signaled the younger generation's having begun to adopt the New Class as a primary reference group. Serious cooperation with the New Class, in other words, appeared to require more than just dialogue: it required advocacy of the New Class agenda in the cultural conflict.

95. Hunter, *Evangelicalism: The Coming Generation*, p. 175.

Yet perhaps the most obvious affinity between evangelical intellectuals and the New Class lies in a common sociopolitical agenda. The expressed concern of the New Class for the rights of the downtrodden in the face of their oppressors is consistent with and has its origins in the Judeo-Christian tradition and even more specifically in Christian social teaching. Indeed, there is no question but that the Scriptures teach that God desires justice for the poor and reserves wrath and judgment for those who oppress them. Given the relatively limited number of other points where cooperation with the secular New Class is possible without theological compromise, the coincidence of ostensible New Class concerns for the poor and oppressed and Christian social ethical themes is quite significant. In essence, adopting the sociopolitical agenda of the New Class has provided younger evangelicals with what has seemed an ideal opportunity to reestablish the cultural relevance of conservative Protestant theology. Far from compromising this theology, the New Class agenda has actually seemed to authenticate it. From the perspective of the members of the largely secular New Class, on the other hand, the alliance with Protestant liberalism and subsequently with evangelicalism has provided them with a degree of religious credibility they simply could not have generated for themselves.[96] Hence it appears that the evangelical desire for legitimacy within an increasingly politicized culture has come together in a kind of symbiotic relationship with the New Class's need to enhance the legitimacy of its sociopolitical agenda.

Undoubtedly there are those who will argue that the left-liberal drift of radical and progressive evangelical intellectuals does not in and of itself constitute sufficient evidence to indict them of ideological collaboration with the New Class. But I believe that this collaboration is confirmed by their drift to the left not only politically but theologically as well. As suggested above, the New Class's "culture of critical discourse" has tended to shift the locus of authority decisively away from traditional sources such as religion and toward sophisticated rational discourse that is judged on the merits of its autonomy, or self-groundedness. Indeed, for those on the political left such as Alvin Gouldner, this is one of the most promising elements of New Class ideology. Were evangelical intellectuals to align themselves with the New Class, then, we might expect theological compromise to surface first in a weakening of their commitment to traditional notions of theological authority. In addition, since the sociopolitical agenda of the New Class is commonly expressed and legitimated in terms of secular myths of redemption such as the socialist, we might also expect theological compromise to surface in the reinterpretation of orthodoxy along the lines of these myths. Although one finds these myths addressing many of the same basic questions as Christian

96. See Hunter, "The New Class and the Young Evangelicals," p. 166.

orthodoxy, the answers they give are predictably limited along the lines of anthropocentrism and immanence. Thus when traditional orthodoxy is compromised by these myths, it is usually evident in the translation of transcendence into immanence,[97] a process epitomized recently in the various theologies of liberation.

Of course, there is a considerable amount of evidence that the kinds of theological changes we would expect to result from continuous dialogue with the secularized New Class have indeed begun to occur for those on the evangelical left. While they have by no means abandoned their commitment to Scripture, they have in effect expanded their conception of theological authority to include neo-Marxist socioeconomic analysis. Furthermore, they have tended to shorten the eschatological horizon to the merely historical, if not explicitly then at least in terms of emphasis. In addition, they increasingly speak of sociopolitical activity as the instrumental means by which God is progressively moving history forward toward a this-worldly liberation. Indeed, those on the left have effectively placed social action, conceived largely in left-liberal political terms, on a par with evangelism in the church's mission. Radicals have even gone so far as to suggest that it is principally a sociopolitical agenda to which one is converted, and they define the boundaries of the church on the basis of resistance to or advocacy of this agenda.

Yet although it is most visible on the radical left (and right), the process of immanentization is also evident in progressive and mainstream circles. That neo-Calvinists have expanded the notion of stewardship to include the "guidance" of history and the self-conscious creation of human culture provides some indication of this. It seems that providence is either relegated only to those areas in which human knowledge and skill have not yet become sufficient for mastery, or it is said to lie "behind" human rationality and historical striving. Even more subtly, however, the process of immanentization is evident in the shift of evangelical interests increasingly away from the world to come and increasingly toward this-worldly political and economic concerns. Like their mid-nineteenth-century forebears, contemporary evangelicals have become primarily concerned with "rendering the temporal fate" more and more vivid. Indeed, an increasing number of evangelical intellectuals have come to view a concern for other-worldliness as evidence of social irresponsibility and even apostasy. While the trend toward this-worldliness is apparent across the entire political-economic spectrum and is, to a large extent, probably attributable to the effects of affluence and the heightened material expectations affluence generates, where it is expressed in terms of "social action" and/or "social responsibility" it appears to reflect involvement within the present cultural conflict on the side of the New Class.

97. See Berger, "For a World with Windows," p. 16.

Recent Evangelical Appraisals of Capitalism and the New Class Conflict

Based on their recent appraisals of capitalism, it appears that a number of evangelical intellectuals have fallen out to either side of the contemporary cultural conflict described by the New Class thesis. The high visibility of economic policy issues combined with the impatience of evangelicals to display their cultural relevance make this tendency understandable, but the results are disturbing nonetheless. Both the evangelical left and right have succumbed to an ideological abuse of Scripture and a de facto (and occasionally explicit) confession of the ultimacy of economic life. Meanwhile, those in the evangelical center, torn between the extremes of left and right, have themselves begun subtly to modify Christian orthodoxy simply by shifting their attention increasingly away from eternal concerns and increasingly toward temporal political and economic concerns.

Of course, I realize that my attempt to link the recent evangelical appraisals of capitalism to the cultural conflict described by the New Class thesis is provocative, to say the least. No one appreciates being told that his or her opinions are functioning ideologically, least of all intellectuals. But I am not suggesting that the kind of sociology-of-knowledge perspective I have employed "explains" the positive content of the positions evangelicals have taken; I am simply suggesting that it helps to explain why certain matters have become so important within the debate and why the debate has become polarized in the peculiar ways that it has. In this regard, it is very important to remember that religious, moral, and even empirical affirmations never occur in a social vacuum but in contexts that are, at least in principle, specifiable. As sociologist Robert Nisbet observed a number of years ago, "neither personal freedom nor personal achievement can ever be separated from the contexts of community. . . . This is not to deny the role of the individual, nor the reality of personal differences. It is assuredly not to accept the argument of crude social determinism—which asserts that the creative works of individuals are but the reflection of group interests and group demands. It is merely to insist on the fundamental fact that the perspectives and incentives of the free creative mind arise out of communities of purpose."[98] The New Class thesis simply suggests that in the contemporary American situation, two "communities of purpose" are at odds with each other over the status of the welfare state and ultimately over the appropriate location of social and political authority in modern society. As a result of this conflict, modern capitalism has become a key symbolic issue for two competing definitions of social reality, on the one hand symbolizing oppression and avaricious private interests and on the other hand symbolizing traditional values and freedom from governmental interference. The best way to understand the symbolic use of

98. Nisbet, *Community and Power,* p. 235.

capitalism on either side of the contemporary conflict is in terms of the notion of "elective affinity." The criticism of capitalism is "elected" by those who have an "affinity" with shifting the locus of social authority away from business and the so-called "private" sector and toward the regulatory and welfare apparatus of the modern state. Conversely, the defense of capitalism (and the corresponding criticism of the state) is elected by those whose interests, whether or not they are located in business as such, are not served by further enhancing the power of the so-called "public" sector.

This much said, several important questions remain. The first has to do with the impact of recent political-economic developments in Eastern Europe and elsewhere which highlight the economic bankruptcy of capitalism's chief alternatives. Have not these developments rendered the left's criticism of capitalism untenable? The recent convergence of evangelical opinion exemplified by the "Oxford Declaration on Christian Faith and Economics" might be interpreted as evidence that recent political-economic events are leading to new thinking. Doesn't this suggest that ideological entanglement on both sides of the contemporary conflict can be overcome? Indeed, doesn't this convergence indicate that the evangelical debate is really a free intellectual debate after all? The answers to such questions, of course, are both Yes and No. On the one hand, it is certainly possible for people to overcome ideological entanglement and to change their minds in the face of new empirical evidence. After all, even Ronald Sider recently stated that "a market economy and private ownership . . . is the direction in which biblical values and experience seem to point."[99] On the other hand, even empirical evidence is subject to interpretation. Most scholars on the evangelical left, for example, have continued to denounce capitalism almost as if nothing had happened. Wesley Granberg-Michaelson recently argued in *Sojourners* that one of the real problems posed by the recent political-economic developments in Eastern Europe is that people may be deceived into thinking that capitalism offers a better alternative, when politically, culturally, and environmentally it does not.[100]

Thus it appears that while a convergence of evangelical opinion may have begun to develop with respect to capitalist *economics,* this has not yet translated into a convergence of opinion with respect to capitalist politics or capitalist culture or the appropriate economic role of the welfare state. In this regard, it is significant that the recent Oxford conference did not address the question of appropriate limits to political intervention in economic life. Ronald Sider has suggested that this was one of the weaknesses of the declaration: "I would have said several things more strongly. For example, I think government needs to play

99. Sider, "A Trickle-up Response to Poverty," *Advocate* (March 1990): 2.
100. Granberg-Michaelson, "Economics: Searching for Alternatives," *Sojourners* 19 (July 1990): 4-5.

a substantial role in correcting the gross inequalities and injustices that the free market sometimes produces."[101] Of course, such comments are not likely to make those on the evangelical right very happy. In fact, they are likely to leave conservatives scratching their heads wondering just what kind of victory they have really won. Yet Sider's comments make perfect sense in the context of the contemporary conflict, for, as noted above, the interests of the New Class—of which I would argue that Sider is a representative—are best served not by the elimination of the market economy but simply by its continued politicization. Perhaps especially given the demise of European communism and socialism, future New Class interests may be most effectively expressed *apart from* the harsh criticism of capitalism. Along this line, we might expect New Class apologists to legitimate the curtailment of the market and the expansion of the regulatory and welfare apparatus of the modern state on the basis of democracy and/or human rights. Gar Alperowitz recently suggested in *Sojourners,* for example, that "the central idea of reform—liberalism or social democracy—is that the institutions of corporate capitalism exist and, in practice, should not be considered for fundamental change. But if 20th-century experience teaches us anything, it is that despite the gains of the civil rights movement, the feminist movement, the New Deal, and the Great Society, progress toward reducing real world inequality of fundamental economic circumstance has been virtually nil."[102] Alperowitz's solution to this problem, then, is to suggest a fundamental "reconstruction" of capitalist society in which the principle of equality is seen as a matter of right.[103] Such a reconstruction will require, among other things, community-owned business firms, guaranteed employment, guaranteed income, and a substantial increase in economic planning.

So it would seem that suggestions that the evangelical debate over capitalism is finally over are probably premature. I suspect that the political-economic "Revolution of '89" will not make nearly as much difference to those on the evangelical left as those on the right think it should. While some of those on the left may join Ronald Sider in praising the market economy for its economic efficiencies, my guess is that they will continue to have a great deal of trouble with the market for any number of reasons and chiefly for its inability to distribute social goods equitably. The evangelical left will probably find plenty of excuses, in other words, for keeping such things as health care, housing, employment, education, and the environment off the market. Those on the evangelical right, meanwhile, may well react to this resistance by becoming even more defensive of capitalism and the market and even less

101. Sider, "A Trickle-up Response to Poverty," p. 2.

102. Alperowitz, "Building a Living Democracy: A Whole New Way of Thinking about Politics and Economics," *Sojourners* 19 (July 1990): 22.

103. Alperowitz, "Building a Living Democracy," p. 15.

critical of business enterprise. For, as remarkable as the political-economic events of the past few years have been, they have not fundamentally altered the class dynamics in the postindustrial situation—and as we have seen, these dynamics have a great deal to do with how modern capitalism is assessed.

Hence the conflict over capitalism is likely to continue in intellectual circles. If the contest should cease to focus on capitalist economics, it will undoubtedly shift to the issues of capitalist politics and perhaps especially to the issues of capitalist culture. Whether or not the evangelical debate continues to mirror this larger intellectual conflict will depend, at least in part, on how well (or poorly) evangelicals are able to assess the ideological pitfalls that continue to surround the debate. In this regard, I hope that this study has shed some useful light. It has been intended to provide a starting point for further evangelical discussion about the relation of evangelical theology to the various social, economic, and political problems we face in the contemporary situation—not so much in the sense of making this theology "relevant" to these problems as in the sense of enabling evangelicals to arrive at more theologically *balanced* appraisals of public policy issues. For the ideological "pull" toward either side in the contemporary cultural conflict simply must be appreciated if balance is ever to be achieved.

Toward an Evangelical Reappraisal of Capitalism

Clearly, capitalism has become a problem for American evangelical intellectuals in recent decades. At the extremes of left and right, evangelicals have become either *very* critical or *very* defensive of capitalism and bourgeois culture. Less extremely they have been torn on the one hand by the tendency to become quite critical of private enterprise and not at all critical of public administration, or on the other hand to become harshly critical of the state and not at all critical of business. As we have seen, these twin tendencies can be interpreted sociologically in terms of the contemporary cultural conflict between the New Class and the traditional middle class, a conflict that involves, among other things, the status of the modern welfare state. Apparently an increasing number of evangelical authors have fallen out on either side of this conflict, providing a kind of chaplaincy for the competing class factions.

It is probably true that evangelical criticism of capitalism has been muted of late by recent political-economic developments in Eastern Europe and elsewhere—events that conservatives have understandably interpreted as a resounding vindication of their defense of capitalism. Yet as the contemporary conflict centers ultimately on the appropriate location of social and political authority in modern society, I think it likely that suspicion of business (or alternatively of government) will continue to plague the evangelical debate over social and economic policy for some time to come. For while the capitalism versus socialism debate may be over economically speaking, the cultural split between the New Class and the traditional middle class will continue to be reflected in the social and economic policy debate, and each of the factions will probably continue to attract its share of evangelical support.

Of course, the kind of ideological entanglement we have noted, coupled with the tendency of evangelical disputants to anathematize one another, has

207

been and will continue to be disturbing. Antagonism of this sort not only undermines the credibility of conservative Protestant orthodoxy but also leads to a great deal of confusion concerning the issues associated with the political-economic debate, many of which are very real and call for serious reflection. At the same time, it is precisely the seriousness with which evangelicals have approached these issues that has, ironically, proven so theologically problematic, for the political-economic debate appears to be one of the more significant points at which evangelical theology has been secularized.

Yet simply to leave the matter here would be both misleading and unhelpful: misleading because it might seem to imply that debilitating ideological entanglement on either side of the contemporary cultural conflict is the inevitable price of entry into this arena, and unhelpful because it might thereby encourage evangelicals to retreat from involvement in the political-economic arena and hence to neglect the important social problems the contemporary political-economic debate has centered upon.

To avoid such mistakes, it might be helpful to recall that the kind of sociological perspective I have employed necessarily exaggerates the inevitability of ideological entanglement. The sociology-of-knowledge perspective assumes that ideas are socially "locatable" in the sense that their success (though not necessarily their content) can be explained in terms of their social utility. Such a perspective is predisposed, then, to understanding things like the recent evangelical debate as reflections of underlying social conflicts and/or processes. After all, ideas don't argue with each other, people do; and people invariably have real material and ideal interests in promoting or preventing social change.

But there are other perspectives from which to consider our participation in public life, perspectives that do not exclude the possibility of intelligent self-criticism and objective assessment of economic realities, perspectives that can point beyond the kind of stalemate that has characterized evangelical opinion of late. Indeed, my intent in this analysis of the ideological pitfalls that currently surround the political-economic debate has simply been to help evangelicals better understand the nature of the contemporary debate and recognize the possible theological costs of advocacy within it. I hope that it will serve as a kind of lens to correct ideologically distorted vision, for we will need clear vision before we can proceed toward effective participation in public life on questions of political economy or toward the important task of developing a coherent evangelical economic ethic. In an effort to point the evangelical discussion constructively forward toward such a development, I offer the following suggestions as to how modern capitalism might be assessed from an evangelical perspective that transcends the recent ideological impasse.

The Contemporary Intellectual Context

In Chapter 4 I suggested that there are elements of the political-economic proposals on both the evangelical left and right that are characteristically modern and modernizing and that also tend to be secularizing. As James Hunter and others have noted, contemporary evangelical intellectuals appear to be following in the footsteps of earlier Protestant modernists in the sense that they, too, are modernizing orthodoxy—but with an important difference: evangelicals do not, for the most part, intend to do this, and so they do not see it happening. Modernization is slipping in the evangelical back door, as it were, through various *adiaphora*—including the political-economic debate—that on the surface do not appear to threaten evangelical theology. The radical evangelical left has become secularized, for example, not because the radicals have become convinced of such things as the Marxist philosophical anthropology but simply because they have found it much easier to talk to others who share their concerns for "peace and justice" and their particular understanding of modern society when they deemphasize or leave unmentioned certain evangelical theological propositions. The same has been true of those on the evangelical far right as they have reacted to those on the left. And something similar has been true of progressive evangelical intellectuals who have been concerned to display the relevance of evangelical theology in the contemporary situation.

Along this line, it is important to stress that the contemporary marketplace of ideas is dominated by very secularized merchants. While evangelicals are allowed to buy and sell there, the rules for exchange—for example, the guidelines for determining what is and is not "relevant" in the political-economic arena—are for the most part set by others. Relevance, in other words, is socially constructed and comes at a price. For evangelical theology, the price of relevance in the modern situation appears to involve some measure of immanentization, a modification commonly justified in that it facilitates concern for and participation in public life. In developing an evangelical economic ethic, then, perhaps the first thing that needs to be discussed is the intellectual context within which this ethic is likely to be developed.

The sociostructural process of modernization has a concomitant in what might be called "modern consciousness," a consciousness characterized, among other things, by an intense individuation, a "functionally rational" or problem-solving orientation, and a practical materialism or this-worldliness. Indeed, the rationally manipulative hubris of modern consciousness is matched only by its deep-seated insecurity and acute sense of alienation. Just as its aspirations have been heightened by technological mastery and affluence, so these aspirations have transcended the world that modern consciousness has created for itself and enclosed itself within. Seeking an outlet for its heightened expectations, modern consciousness has turned its attention toward manipulating history and engineering the future social order, a social order which it is hoped will transcend the present either by moving progressively beyond it or by moving backward "behind" it in a kind of conservative reaction.[1] The increasingly exclusive emphasis on historical social change has been rendered particularly plausible of late by the fast-paced and radical way in which the process of modernization has transformed our world.

Although the aspirations of modern consciousness are located in the abstract, in "history" and "progress," they have translated practically into sociopolitical activism. As Julien Benda observed a number of years ago, this is particularly true for modern intellectuals who, Benda argued, have essentially become the "spiritual militia" of the material and political.[2] Of those modern institutions capable of shaping history, it seems, the modern state has been deemed the most powerful and the most "rational" candidate for directing historical development. In the political-economic context of capitalism, the sociopolitical aspirations of modern consciousness have commonly been expressed in terms of dissent against the bourgeois "sociopolitical-economic order." This protest, however, has not been against the state mechanism per se but against the irrationality of the capitalist state, which has found itself in the position of having continually to adjust to an apparently chaotic market mechanism. While conservatives ostensibly defend bourgeois culture and the irrationality of the market against any kind of planned alternative, their defense often takes on the appearance of being little more than an attempt to delegitimate a left-liberal political status quo—and hence of being a part of their own quest for political power. Evangelicals have not been immune to these tendencies. Noting the nostalgia with which many contemporary evangelicals have tended to regard the nineteenth century, evangelical historian Douglas Frank recently remarked,

> both the left and the right in evangelicalism today would, I suspect, like to run the [cultural and political] show. Each believes it knows what the country needs, and each craves the influence to implement its vision. The rapid and highly visible emergence of evangelicalism during the 1970s and '80s gives each faction the hope that perhaps this influence is within its grasp. It is significant, I think, that the *Sojourners* community moved from Chicago to Washington, D.C., the seat of national power, and that the Moral Majority has aligned itself with the leading

1. The "traditionalist" defense of capitalism, for example, focusing as it has on the wisdom embedded within the political-economic tradition, has really not been any less "historicist" than the radical critique of capitalism and bourgeois culture. The two have differed only in their assessments of the present historical moment. While radicals call for revolution, traditionalists contend that the present moment calls for conservation. Both understand historical social change either explicitly or implicitly as being subject to conscious human manipulation.

2. Benda, *The Treason of the Intellectuals* (New York: W. W. Norton, 1969).

nonreligious but conservative political action groups. . . . The evangelicals of the left and the evangelicals of the right may not share political platforms, but they do seem to share a desire to remake America according to their own version of Christian principles, and they like the fact that at one time in our history evangelicals had the opportunity to do exactly that.[3]

The sociopolitical aspirations of modern consciousness are also commonly expressed in terms of the "public" interest or on behalf of those "poor and oppressed" by the political-economic status quo. This appears to be the case regardless of the kind of political economy the existing status quo is perceived to represent. When measured against ideal sociopolitical standards, all existing systems are judged to fall decisively short, and while such a judgment might be a cause of despair, in practice it is mitigated by faith and hope in the movement of the historical process toward some kind of immanent fulfillment. Indeed, "faith" in this political-historical sense is at the heart of the notion of theodicy held by modern consciousness, and in fact serves as the standard against which all faith is measured.

When modern consciousness comes into contact with traditional religion, it demands that attention be shifted away from God and an objectively given moral order and increasingly toward the human historical project and the human subject.[4] Modern consciousness exerts tremendous pressure toward the translation of notions of transcendence into purely immanent and historical categories. As is evident from the surveys of the evangelical left and right, this translation process has extended to the immanentization of theological orthodoxy. Where it is successful, the process of immanentization transforms the universe of traditional religion, once the dominion of the transcendent, into an exclusively human universe, a universe in which God, if his existence is granted at all, is conceived as simply standing "behind" or "within" the conscious human manipulation of history, meaning, and value. "To use a term which has become popular in some theological circles," evangelical theologian Oliver O'Donovan has commented, describing this process, "the end of history is the 'hominization' of the world: all events are to fall under the conscious direction of human culture, so that the world itself becomes, so to speak, a human artefact."[5] In classical theological terms, modern consciousness trans-

3. Frank, *Less Than Conquerors: How Evangelicals Entered the Twentieth Century* (Grand Rapids: William B. Eerdmans, 1986), p. 5.
4. See Peter L. Berger, "A Sociological View of the Secularization of Theology," *Journal for the Scientific Study of Religion* 6 (Spring 1967): 4.
5. O'Donovan, *Resurrection and Moral Order: An Outline for Evangelical Ethics* (Grand Rapids: William B. Eerdmans, 1986), p. 68. William Garrett has expressed similar views: "Reformers commenced by translating their doctrine of God into some theological category of immanence, wherein God either revealed Himself solely through the world, or God and the world become inextricably one. Although the vehicle for perceiving Divine

lates traditional understandings of creation into emanation, traditional notions of sin into sociopolitical failure, traditional conceptions of redemption into sociopolitical evolution, traditional understandings of eschatology into "realizable" historical scenarios, and so on. Transcendence, in short, becomes wholly subsumed under the heading of immanence conceived anthropocentrically.[6]

Of course, conservative orthodoxy is capable of resisting the process of immanentization. Indeed, the reinterpretation required by modern consciousness is radical and extensive enough that it has often raised the suspicions of the orthodox, especially when it has been pressed all at once or too quickly. The early fundamentalist reaction to Protestant modernism illustrates this resistance quite well. For this reason, immanentization usually takes places only when the orthodox remain in dialogue with modern consciousness over a number of years or even generations. Sociologically speaking, sustained dialogue of this kind requires the speakers to share a common social location—that is, they must be socially positioned in such a way as to be able to converse. In addition, some point of contact, issue, or concern common to both the modernized and the orthodox is necessary to keep the conversation going. This issue or concern must be capable of bearing the historical aspirations of modern consciousness while not threatening doctrinal orthodoxy too directly.

Insofar as these sociological requirements are concerned, it is not difficult to see that with the movement of neo-evangelicalism, and more recently of neofundamentalism, back into the social and cultural centers of modern society, and especially with their movement back into the centers of modern higher education, neo-evangelical and neofundamentalist intellectuals have moved into direct and sustained contact with what is perhaps the most thoroughly modernized group of people in the contemporary world: the New Class. It also appears that the debate over questions of social ethics is one of the principal points at which the dialogue between modern consciousness and traditional orthodoxy has been initiated. Matters of social ethics are eminently well-suited

---

immanence might be as varied as Natural Law, Nature, history, or politics, social reformers have consistently tended to recast Divinity in immanent terms. . . . However, the irony is—and this is the crucial point—that total sacralization is absolutely indistinguishable from total secularization" ("Politicized Clergy: A Sociological Interpretation of the 'New Breed,'" *Journal for the Scientific Study of Religion* 12 [December 1973]: 387-88).

6. In a discussion of the "secular theology" movement, Thomas J. J. Altizer has asserted that "the death of God abolishes transcendence, thereby making possible a new and absolute immanence, an immanence freed of every sign of transcendence" (*The Gospel of Christian Atheism* [Philadelphia: Westminster Press, 1966], p. 154). Of course—and this may well have been Altizer's underlying concern—theology is also secularized if divine transcendence is emphasized to the extent that God is effectively removed from this world altogether. But obviously no one involved in the political-economic debate has fallen into this characteristically pietist error.

to bear the concerns for social existence of traditional orthodoxy and the political-historical aspirations of modern consciousness at the same time.

While it is conceivable that the the dialogue between orthodoxy and modern consciousness over questions of social ethics could result in the conversion of the latter back to a confession of transcendence, in fact the reverse has occurred in the past and appears to be occurring at present. "As religious traditions and the sociohistorical realities of the modern world order confront each other," James Davison Hunter has suggested, "there is little question as to which of the two gives way to the other. Almost invariably the former yields to the latter."[7] The advent of the Social Gospel at the turn of the century and the recent conversion of many mainline Protestant intellectuals to the various theologies of liberation provide telling illustrations of Hunter's assertion. The increasing attraction liberation theology has had for many evangelical intellectuals, along with the proclivity of others to place social action on a par with proclamation of the gospel in the church's mission, provides further confirmation that the dialogue between modern consciousness and orthodoxy has, at least at the level of intellectual discourse, been weighted heavily in favor of modernity. Modernity's advantage is further strengthened in the context of a media-oriented culture in which the pressure to appear socially relevant is at least as important as actually contending with social problems. "The lure of left-wing politics is understandable enough," Alan Gilbert has suggested. "Not only does it offer the prospect of high moral commitment in the interests of social justice for the poor, powerless and dispossessed, but it also becomes a *raison d'être* for a Church highly secularized. It promises that Christians who are no longer pilgrims looking for another world can regard themselves nevertheless as 'the salt of the earth.' "[8]

In making these brief comments on the character of modern consciousness and its relation to conservative Protestant orthodoxy, I do not mean to suggest that evangelicals should not pursue higher education or that they should not attempt to formulate a social ethics. Indeed, to the extent that the term *social ethics* reflects a reaction to the characteristically modern process of privatization in which ethical considerations are increasingly relegated to the private or personal sphere, the evangelical concern for social (or public) ethics represents a vital theological development. Still, it is important to stress that just as power tends to corrupt, so the striving for social and political influence tends to corrupt the ideals that lie behind the striving, even if these ideals are good.[9]

7. Hunter, *Evangelicalism: The Coming Generation* (Chicago: University of Chicago Press, 1987), p. 48.

8. Gilbert, *The Making of Post-Christian Britain: A History of the Secularization of Modern Society* (London: Longman, 1980), p. 125.

9. See Robert A. Nisbet, *Community and Power* (New York: Oxford University Press, 1962), p. 215.

It is also important to note that the neo-evangelical attempt to recapture the symbolic environment in modern culture by means of such things as higher education (an attempt that has been emulated recently by neofundamentalists) inherently threatens the preservation of orthodoxy. For in placing its intellectual leadership in a position of sustained and isolated conversation with the most modernized people in society, the neo-evangelical strategy has virtually ensured that its leadership will suffer some degree of cognitive contamination and that this contamination will find expression in varying degrees of theological immanentization. Given the nature of the contemporary debate, it is not surprising that the modernization of traditional orthodoxy has begun with and been channeled through issues of social ethics.

Social Change and Historical Expectations

In spite of the dangerous nature of the social ethics debate, however, there is no question that evangelicals should be concerned with a number of pressing social and economic problems. The task at hand, then, is to develop an evangelical social ethic in general, and an evangelical economic ethic in particular, and to address these problems without succumbing to theological immanentization. Put differently, evangelicals must find a way to take historical sociopolitical change seriously but not ultimately seriously, as modern consciousness is prone to do. It is very important to stress here that such a position would not entail an evasion of historical responsibility. After all, we cannot make history, and hence sociopolitical change, the sole locus of human aspirations without rendering it meaningless as history. As O'Donovan has noted,

> When we think of the church's faith and hope . . . we think of dispositions which are quite without point if they are viewed in isolation from the end [of history]. Faith and hope have no validity apart from what is believed and hoped in. The church believes and hopes throughout its historical pilgrimage, and yet no possible extension or development of that pilgrimage can make faith and hope sensible historical projects. If the Son of man were not to come in great glory, the very words 'faith' and 'hope', which already presuppose a positive answer to the question about what is believed and hoped in, would be inappropriate to describe the church's pointless expectancy: 'If Christ has not been raised, then our preaching is in vain and your faith is in vain' (1 Cor. 15:14). Only as the pilgrimage reaches the end which God has destined for it can the faith and hope of the church be validated and justified.[10]

Thus the evangelical understanding refuses to take history (at least history in the sense of "sensible historical projects") with ultimate seriousness. In the

10. O'Donovan, *Resurrection and Moral Order,* pp. 245-46.

first place it refuses to do so because the evangelical understanding appreciates history's *end*. Yet it also refuses to do so because the evangelical understanding appreciates history's *beginning* in that it affirms the existence of a created moral order not subject to sensible historical change. By virtue of the clarification of the nature of both creation and history provided by Scripture, the evangelical understanding is able to recognize what history really is and where it is ultimately going. At the same time, the evangelical understanding does not expect the immanent realization of history's goal, because the Redeemer of creation and history must decisively and surprisingly *end* both to realize this goal. At present, we are in the position of awaiting his coming in glory.

Thus an evangelical understanding is idealistic and yet profoundly realistic, radical and yet conservative. It is an understanding shaped by three kinds of affirmations, each gleaned from Scripture: (1) the affirmation of the creational ideal for human life, (2) the affirmation that certain allowances must be made for the frustration of this ideal prior to the restoration of all things, and (3) the affirmation that the restoration of all things will both restore and yet will also exceed the original creational ideal in ways that we cannot yet comprehend. All of these affirmations find a single focus in the Christ—not in "Christ" as a kind of transhistorical principle, but concretely in Jesus of Nazareth. Conceiving of the "love of Christ" apart from the person of Jesus Christ who "became flesh and lived for a while among us" only leads again to the confusion of God's activity in history with our own, a situation in which what really elicits our devotion is the idea of a deified humanity.[11] God's redemptive activity in Christ, in other words, does not just "happen" in the natural historical course of events, in a way that might be described by the formula "God is always at work in history liberating the poor and the oppressed." Karl Löwith has argued that the theological understanding of history "cannot be translated into world-historical terms and worked out into a philosophical system. World-historical establishments and upheavals hopelessly miss the ultimate reality of the Christian hope and expectation. No secular progress can ever approximate the Christian goal if this goal is the redemption from sin and death to which all worldly history is subjected."[12]

Instead, God's redemptive activity in Christ happens as a surprising gift, as amazing grace. While this activity decisively redeems "world-historical" events, it remains largely hidden from us at present and is recognized only with the eyes of faith. Thus while an evangelical understanding of history does not posit a radical disjunction between "sacred" and "secular" histories, it does insist that we cannot at present know just what the relation between these two is. We trust that there is

11. See O'Donovan, *Resurrection and Moral Order*, p. 242.
12. Löwith, *Meaning in History: The Theological Implications of the Philosophy of History* (Chicago: University of Chicago Press, 1949), p. 189.

a relation, just as we trust that our individual histories are "hidden in Christ," but we must wait along with the rest of creation for the meaning of history to be revealed. Redemption is not unambiguously evident, as those on both the evangelical left and right have mistakenly asserted. For this reason the "prophetic" nature of the evangelical understanding of history is given not in assertions that God is working visibly in historical movements of sociopolitical change but rather in a relativization of all political-historical projects. This is an essential part of the gospel at the individual level, for it prevents us from damning either ourselves or particular others for the injustice and suffering in the world.[13] Yet this relativization of world-historical events also has profound effects at the level of politics, and hence at the level of political economy.

> Western theology starts from the assertion that the kingdoms of this world are *not* the kingdom of our God and of his Christ, not, at any rate, until God intervenes to make them so at the end. . . . This does not mean (as it has sometimes come to mean in degenerate forms of the tradition) that the secular state can be independent from God and his claims, or that the pious individual can cultivate a private existence without regard for the claims of his society. It means simply that earthly politics, because they do not *have* to reconcile the world, may get on with their provisional task of bearing witness to God's justice. And it means that the individual, because he is not absorbed by the claims of his earthly community, can contribute to its good order that knowledge of man's good which he learns from his heavenly calling.[14]

"It may be worth observing," Reinhold Niebuhr commented similarly, "that it is not the Christian faith, but secular idealism, which expresses itself naturally in terms of utopianism and imagines that there will be, or that there ought to be, a perfect society of universal justice on the other side of a war or a revolution. . . . It is at this point that the much despised Christian 'other worldliness' becomes a resource for historical striving. . . . It gives us a faith by which we can seek to fulfill our historic tasks without illusions and without despair."[15] Indeed, it is precisely its other-worldly hope that keeps the evangelical ethic from becoming hardened to the suffering of the world and also prevents it from lapsing into the kind of irresponsibility that results from the fear of becoming hardened to this suffering.[16]

---

13. As Glenn Tinder has written, "the idea that man is fundamentally good and innocent is surprisingly treacherous. This is because it leads almost inevitably to an effort to identify those responsible for the evil all around us. Since the world is filled with injustice and suffering, if man generically is innocent, then a few must be peculiarly culpable" ("Community: The Tragic Ideal," *The Yale Review* 65 [Summer 1976]: 558).

14. O'Donovan, *Resurrection and Moral Order,* p. 72.

15. Niebuhr, quoted by Richard John Neuhaus, in *The Religion and Society Report* 5 (July 1988): 7-8.

16. See Emil Brunner, *The Divine Imperative: A Study in Christian Ethics* (Philadelphia: Westminster Press, 1947), p. 482.

Along this line it has been argued that the loss of evangelical other-world-liness, and specifically the loss of any sense of personal immortality, has been the most important political fact of this last century.[17] For again, when historical sociopolitical change is made the sole locus of human aspirations, the political task is fundamentally altered and tends to lapse into the kind of utopian absurdity—Stalin's Russia, Hitler's Germany, Pol Pot's Cambodia—of which this century has witnessed more than its share.

Returning to our discussion of modern consciousness, it is important to understand that by ascribing ultimacy to immanent historical social change and by rejecting any notion of a fixed normative moral order, modern consciousness effectively forfeits its ability to understand what such things as justice and morality are. While the rhetoric of justice and morality remains in the contemporary cultural context, it is increasingly devoid of any real moral force.[18] This problem has a specific history. According to Emil Brunner, the idea of justice began to disintegrate at the Enlightenment:

> The *divine* law of nature, the objective, superhuman standard of justice, became the subjective standard of human reason, its substance soon being narrowed down into the individualistic notion of subjective rights of man. Later, following the trend of the time, the element of "nature" in law was reinterpreted in a naturalist sense. The historicism of the Romantic period then declared war on a timelessly valid justice, replacing it by the conception of justice as a historical growth. It was, however, the positivism of the nineteenth century [indicated, e.g., in the separation of fact from value], with its denial of the metaphysical and superhuman, which dissolved the idea of justice by proclaiming the relativity of all views of justice.[19]

It should also be noted that the attribution of ultimacy to historical sociopolitical change has made it very difficult to adjudicate between the claims of individuals and those of the community. While there has on the one hand been a tendency to narrow the notion of justice down to the "rights" of individuals, there has on the other hand been a tendency to reduce justice to the requirements of the community. This is why the contemporary debate tends to oscillate between an entirely individualistic understanding of justice, in terms of "human rights," and an exclusively sociological understanding of

17. Irving Kristol, "About Equality," *Commentary* 54 (November 1972): 42.

18. Alasdair MacIntyre has suggested that the confusion plaguing the moral and ethical discussion of late stems from our continuing failure successfully to replace the religiously grounded moral order destroyed at the Enlightenment: "Both the utilitarianism of the middle and late nineteenth century and the analytical moral philosophy of the middle and late twentieth century are alike unsuccessful attempts to rescue the autonomous moral agent from the predicament in which the failure of the Enlightenment project of providing him with a secular, rational justification for his moral allegiances had left him" (*After Virtue: A Study in Moral Theory,* 2d ed. [Notre Dame, IN: University of Notre Dame Press, 1984], p. 68).

19. Brunner, *Justice and the Social Order* (London: Lutterworth Press, 1945), p. 15.

justice as a social construction. In addition, Oliver O'Donovan has suggested that the modern historicist understanding inevitably confuses "the goodness of natural structures with sin and disorder . . . [because] actual good and evil alike stand together under the judgment of historical fulfilment, as 'imperfect.' "[20] Expressed theologically, the effect of taking historical social change too seriously leads to the elimination of any distinction between the Creator and the creature, and ultimately to the elimination of any distinction between God and ourselves.[21] Richard John Neuhaus has argued that in practice this is manifested in public policy that effectively surrenders the normal to the abnormal and the dominant to the deviant.[22] Thus, it must be stressed that pinning our aspirations to history and hence to historical sociopolitical change—something both the evangelical left and right have shown an increasing tendency to do—is not only bound to lead to disappointment but is also likely to make the present consideration of justice difficult if not impossible. There is no immanent solution to the problem of history.[23] History does not reveal its own meaning. Instead its meaning and "solution" (and with it the meaning of such things as justice) must be *revealed* to us from outside of the historical flux.

Informed by this unique understanding of history, an evangelical social ethic, and with it an evangelical economic ethic, *defer* the realization of perfect political community to the eschaton. As Glenn Tinder has suggested, the decisive feature in the evangelical understanding "is that community is affirmed (in the standard of love) but postponed; it becomes the anticipated climax, and end, of history. In leading to such a climax history is meaningful and calls for human participation. Yet, since the conflict between man's essence and condition is historically unresolvable, participants are freed from the demand that strains civility so acutely, the demand for perfect community here and now."[24] For this reason, the evangelical social and economic ethic understands and allows for compromise and for what has been called the "polity of imperfection."[25] Unlike revolutionary ideologies, it is not willing to risk the destruction of the present imperfect community in an attempt to realize a community of perfection.[26] Of course, this is precisely why Marx and others have insisted that the criticism of religion must precede political-economic criticism. Marx recognized quite accurately that notions of religious transcen-

20. O'Donovan, *Resurrection and Moral Order,* p. 63.

21. See Löwith, *Meaning in History,* p. 185.

22. Neuhaus, *The Naked Public Square: Religion and Democracy in America* (Grand Rapids: William B. Eerdmans, 1984), pp. 144ff.

23. See Löwith, *Meaning in History,* p. 191.

24. Tinder, "Community: The Tragic Ideal," p. 563.

25. John Murray Cuddihy, *No Offense: Civil Religion and Protestant Taste* (New York: Seabury Press, 1978), p. 209.

26. See Cuddihy, *No Offense: Civil Religion and Protestant Taste,* p. 210.

dence decisively undermine the motivation to look for the realization of perfect political community *in* history.

Still, the evangelical understanding does not justify either a separatist attitude toward political involvement or an attitude of *Realpolitik*. The separatist position is ruled out by the evangelical contention that the political order, as a part of creation, is divinely ordained and hence intrinsically valuable. The attitude of *Realpolitik* is ruled out by the evangelical affirmation that although the political order is marred by sin, God both desires and will effect its redemption in Christ.

In addition, just as the evangelical social and economic ethic postpones the realization of perfect community, so it also defers the historical realization of perfect justice. Here again, this does not mean that Christians should avoid participation in the world of economic exchange or that they may rest satisfied with a kind of *Realeconomik* presumed to lie beyond ethical comment. What the postponement of perfect justice does mean is that we recognize that the systems of justice we create are at best only approximately just and that they will inevitably embody both justice and injustice.[27] To say that institutionalized justice is at best only approximate is not to suggest that justice is therefore relative. Such a suggestion, as Emil Brunner has noted, is "as unreasonable as to maintain that the notion of the straight line is a relative one because no human being has yet been able to draw a straight line."[28] The evangelical social ethic aspires to perfect justice but does not presume that this perfect standard can be politically engineered or implemented. It expects ignorance and sin to vitiate even the most sincere efforts to implement just social policy. Indeed, nowhere does the truth of the doctrine of original sin become so painfully evident as in the economic sphere of life.[29]

All of this means that even though it is quite permissible to criticize existing political-economic structures in the light of biblical ideals, we must not allow ourselves to suppose that these ideals are historically realizable. For this reason an evangelical economic ethic must exhibit a kind of prescriptive humility. It must resist the temptation to attach the name of Christ to particular political-economic programs, for he stands above all of them in judgment. Similarly, we must not attach the name of Christ to any particular critique of the economic status quo, for such critiques inevitably assume specific political-economic paradigms and thus imply specific policy alternatives. In short, we have to maintain a minimum critical distance between the gospel and political-economic advocacy. For as Brunner has noted, "the economic order is always like the drunken peasant whom Luther describes, who when he is

27. See O'Donovan, *Resurrection and Moral Order,* p. 74.
28. Brunner, *Justice and the Social Order,* p. 27.
29. See Brunner, *The Divine Imperative,* p. 399.

helped on to his horse on one side promptly falls off on the other; it oscillates continually between an individualism which destroys community, and a collectivism which destroys freedom."[30]

Because it is prescriptively humble, an evangelical economic ethic is likely to appear conservative in practice. To appreciate why this is the case, recall that one of the points at issue between the evangelical left and right is whether obedience to Christ entails trying to anticipate the likely consequences of our actions. Those on the left view any suggestion that political-economic policy must be "realistic"—in the sense that it must be feasible within the confines of present realities—as an act of bad faith that grossly underestimates the ability of God to realize his kingdom in history. Those on the right view the failure—and indeed refusal—of the left to try to anticipate the likely consequences of their policy proposals as the height of moral irresponsibility. In an attempt to resolve this dispute, it is important to note that the two positions reflect two moral languages, both of which are present in Scripture and both of which must be correlated in ethical reflection rather than set against each other.

On the one hand, we must never use the actualities of fallen human existence as the sole standards for determining ethical feasibility. The scriptural demand that we "be holy as God is holy" obviously suggests an objective standard against which actions can be measured in spite of the fact that our performance at present must always fall short of this standard. On the other hand, the language of unconditional obedience and "absolute ethics" must give way to an "ethic of responsibility" if ethical reflection is to have an impact on the ordering of actual human existence.[31] "It is impossible to define the task of the Christian within the economic sphere," Emil Brunner has argued, "if we do not know this economic sphere in its specific historical form. . . . Failure to perceive this fact is one of the main causes for the almost incredible remoteness of traditional Protestant ethics from actual life."[32]

This suggestion that ethical reflection on economic practice both requires and is bounded by an understanding of how the political-economic status quo actually functions—and thus by an understanding of what constitutes the range of realistic possibilities for reform—is not an indication of a lack of moral courage or of a failure of obedience. Rather, it indicates a refusal to give in to the essentially narcissistic temptation to rest content with good intentions and wishful thinking.[33] In this regard, it may be helpful to recall that great social evils have not uncommonly resulted from genuinely well-intended policy proposals. As

30. Brunner, *The Divine Imperative*, p. 406.

31. The terms are those of Max Weber, but O'Donovan develops this point with reference to evangelical ethics in *Resurrection and Moral Order*, p. 143.

32. Brunner, *The Divine Imperative*, p. 416.

33. See Brunner, *Justice and the Social Order*, p. 96.

Reinhold Niebuhr warned, "There is . . . no problem of history and no point in society from which one may not observe that the same man who touches the fringes of the infinite in his moral life remains embedded in finiteness, that he increases the evil in his life if he tries to overcome it without regard to his limitations. Therefore it is as important to know what is impossible as what it possible in the moral demands under which all human beings stand."[34]

In addition, we need to recall that the normative prescriptions issued by those on both the left and right tend to reflect their prior commitments to one or the other of the competing political-economic paradigms. Their conflicting understandings of what *ought* to be done rest on conflicting understandings of how capitalism actually functions. It needs to be stressed, however, that many of the specific points of disagreement in this respect remain open either to empirical verification or falsification, and they should be investigated on this basis. Any adequate social ethic, in other words, must rest on an accurate assessment of how the modern capitalist economy actually operates. It is obviously not enough simply to presume that a certain set of theorists is necessarily correct on such matters. Even if we are not in a position actually to do empirical research ourselves, we must at the very least be willing to evaluate the research that has been done by others, even if—*especially* if— such research threatens our own understanding.

In summary, an evangelical economic ethic will need to be grounded first in a scriptural understanding of both creation and redemption. An under- standing of this sort is essential if such terms as *goodness, justice,* and ulti- mately *history* itself are to have any positive content. Second, an evangelical economic ethic must insist that our political-economic expectations are bounded by an eschatology that does not permit us to look for an immanent solution to the problems of the human condition. Finally, an evangelical economic ethic must insist that while ethical reflection on economic systems and policies must keep biblical ideals in view, this reflection must also allow these ideals a purchase in real, actual, concrete situations. In practice, then, an evangelical ethic will compare the existing political-economic alternatives not only with the biblical ideals themselves but also with each other. Our task is not simply to state what kind of economic order biblical ideals might ultimately point to but to determine which of the existing alternatives most nearly ap- proximates biblical ideals "in the mean time."

As we have seen, the two biblical ideals that surface most often in the evangelical political-economic debate are liberty and justice, and they are characteristically pitted against each other. While the evangelical right tends to subsume justice under the heading of liberty, the evangelical left seems

34. Niebuhr, *An Interpretation of Christian Ethics* (San Francisco: Harper & Row, 1935), p. 83.

willing to sacrifice liberty in the service of justice. A logical place to employ the kind of ethical analysis just outlined, then, will be in trying to determine just what "liberty" and "justice" are from a biblical perspective and how well the capitalist political economy, as compared with its reasonable alternatives, is able to approximate these ideals.

The Question of Liberty

On the question of liberty, recall that evangelical intellectuals have not been able to decide whether freedom ought to be defined in terms of the exercise of relative economic power or in terms of the ability of individuals to participate at any given level in the economic order. In addition, evangelicals have not been able to decide whether the freedom of the individual ought to take precedence over that of the collective or vice versa. There is considerable confusion, in other words, as to just what freedom is.

I have no presumptions of entering into a detailed philosophical or theological treatise on freedom here, but I would like to suggest at the very least that freedom cannot be made an end in itself without becoming meaningless as freedom. Freedom must be *for* something, and in an evangelical understanding freedom is ultimately *for* the expression of love toward God and neighbor. This being the case, the church would do well to revive the understanding of economic activity as a form of service and the idea that we are each responsible for one another in our economic activity. As Brunner has written, "all the natural orders point to the same truth, whether it be the relation between old and young, [parent] and child, leader and followers, the productive and the receptive, or the natural inequalities which determine the living character of economic life. Everywhere life is permeated by a characteristic, natural inequality, which makes one human being stand in need of another."[35]

An evangelical understanding of freedom must also insist, however, that although freedom is essential to our humanity, we have in large part surrendered our freedom, and so also our humanity, to the oppression of sin and death. Thus while an evangelical ethic will uphold the ideal of freedom *for* love, it will also recognize that our actual experience will be frustrated by various kinds of oppression inflicted upon us both externally and internally. In many respects, the crucial social-ethical questions are not how freedom can be perfectly realized or how oppression can be entirely eliminated. An evangelical understanding defers the realization of perfect freedom to the eschaton and turns its attention instead to questions of how our limited freedoms can be enhanced and how oppression can be minimized.

35. Brunner, *The Divine Imperative,* p. 212.

Wisdom suggests that oppression will be minimized to the extent that the potential sources of oppression—which is to say, the sources of social, political, and economic power—are diffused or at least balanced over and against each other. In this regard, it is very important to realize that one of the most remarkable features of the capitalist political-economy, especially as compared to its reasonable alternatives, is its ability to diffuse and to balance both economic and political power. While this diffusion and balancing is inefficient in a strictly economic sense, it appears to account for the observation that under modern conditions capitalism is a necessary (albeit not sufficient) condition for democracy.[36]

> The modern state, even in its democratic form, represents the greatest agglomeration of power in human history—not because of any malign totalitarian ideology somehow inherent in modernity but because of the immense technological resources available to governments for purposes of control. Conversely, a capitalist economy, even when subjected to all sorts of governmental interventions, creates its own dynamic that confronts the state as a relatively autonomous reality. Whatever else the government then controls, it does not fully control this zone, which ipso facto limits state power. The "fit" between capitalism and democracy is the consequence of this.[37]

Recent political-economic developments around the world would seem to attest that there is also a "fit" between socialism and political oppression. Not only does a planned or "command economy" eliminate economic freedom by failing to produce adequate goods and services, but its reliance on centralized economic planning necessarily eliminates political and eventually religious freedoms as well.[38] Sociologist of religion David Martin has asserted that "none of the societies which have banned individual economic activity have succeeded in nourishing individual selfhood and the rights of conscience."[39]

Furthermore, suggestions that the centralized planning mechanism will eventually give way to truly "participatory democracy," however much we might desire such a development, need to be taken with several grains of salt.[40] Societies are always run by elites and, in concentrating both political and economic power in the hands of a single elite, the command economy simply gives way to new and even more extreme forms of political inequality and

36. See Peter L. Berger, *The Capitalist Revolution: Fifty Propositions about Prosperity, Equality, and Liberty* (New York: Basic Books, 1986), p. 212.

37. Berger, *The Capitalist Revolution,* p. 79.

38. See Berger, "Human Development and Economic Alternatives," *Crisis* (November 1987): 22.

39. Martin, "The Clergy, Secularization, and Politics," *This World* 6 (Fall 1983): 139-40.

40. Berger, "The Serendipity of Liberties," a lecture delivered at the I.S.E.C./C.R.S. conference, Boston University, October 1987).

oppression.[41] Hence, it is somewhat ironic that evangelical intellectuals would attempt to provide religious legitimation for the socialist project in terms of the so-called theologies of liberation.[42] As Michael Novak has suggested, the question to raise with respect to these theologies is "Will they actually liberate?" And the answer appears to be "No, in all likelihood, they will not."[43] Relative to its nonmarket alternatives, capitalism is preferable both in terms of economic and political liberty, for it diffuses economic decision making and institutionalizes the separation of economic and political power.

The connection between capitalism and freedom should not be taken to imply that there is no legitimate place in an evangelical economic ethic for the state, however. Understanding the state as an aspect of the created order ordained for the purpose of preserving community, at least as considered externally or publicly, an evangelical economic ethic will recognize that the state is able to make legitimate (though only partial) claims on the public activities of individuals. Such claims are not based merely on the consent of individuals within a so-called social contract, as classical liberalism has suggested. Nor are these claims based solely on the modern state's de facto monopoly over the means of coercion. While the state's use of coercive force incurs real guilt by impinging on freedom and love, it still represents God's chosen means of maintaining public order, as Paul argues in Romans 13. Hence, the state may be said to represent community, even if this community is somewhat artificial at present.[44]

While the state is able to make legitimate claims on the economic activities of individuals, however, it is important to note that it is by no means the only order of creation ordained for the preservation of community. Indeed, as communities necessarily grow increasingly impersonal and coercive the larger they become, the state is actually the communal order least able to foster love in freedom. After all, true fellowship can occur only in the interaction of free and reasonable people, and the bureaucratic apparatus of the modern state is not known for fostering either freedom or reasonableness. Consequently, relative to the smaller communal orders of family, friendship, church, local community, and the like, the state may be said to be the least important, at least with respect to the preservation of fellowship in community.[45] This affirmation of a hierarchy of communal orders, arranged on the basis of their ability to

41. Edward R. Norman, "Denigration of Capitalism: Current Education and the Moral Subversion of Capitalist Society," in *The Denigration of Capitalism: Six Points of View*, ed. Michael Novak (Washington: American Enterprise Institute, 1979), p. 13.

42. Berger, *Capitalist Revolution*, p. 192.

43. See Novak, *Will It Liberate? Questions about Liberation Theology* (New York: Paulist Press, 1986).

44. See Brunner, *The Divine Imperative*, pp. 444ff.

45. See Brunner, *Justice and the Social Order*, p. 122.

encourage love and community, is elaborated in Roman Catholic social teaching under the heading of the "principle of subsidiarity," and something like it is implied in Protestant thought with the notion of different "kingdoms" of divine activity. A very similar affirmation is also implied in the neo-Calvinist notion of "sphere sovereignty" and has been discussed by recent neo-Calvinist thinkers in terms of "principled structural pluralism."[46] This affirmation has significant policy implications, for the state exceeds the other communal orders only in its ability to maintain the stability and continuity of external or public order, and any attempt on the part of the state to absorb the functions of these smaller and more personal communal orders is essentially totalitarian, betraying the erroneous assumption that all personal and communal existence ultimately finds its fulfillment in the state.

In this regard, it is important to see that in addition to the existence of autonomous economic activity, the existence of the church also relativizes the importance of the state—not only because the church refuses, or ought to refuse, to concede ultimacy to the political-historical project but also because the church represents a kind of community that the larger political community aspires to but cannot realize. Thus the church's most important contribution to the polity is simply to *be* the church. As Stanley Hauerwas has argued, "this does not involve a rejection of the world, or a withdrawal from the world; rather it is a reminder that the church must serve the world on her own terms. We must be faithful in our own way, even if the world understands such faithfulness as disloyalty. But the first task of the church is not to supply theories of governmental legitimacy or even to suggest strategies for social betterment. The first task of the church is to exhibit in our common life the kind of community possible when trust, and not fear, rules our lives."[47] While conflict between the church and the state is likely in any case, given the propensity of modern consciousness to locate its aspirations exclusively in the political-historical project, conflict between them in the contemporary situation is almost certain.

Thus insofar as liberty is concerned, an evangelical economic ethic will be interested in diffusing and limiting oppression by balancing the sources of social, political, and economic power. Since capitalism manages to diffuse and balance these sources of power better than its reasonable alternatives, it may be viewed favorably from an evangelical perspective, although the size of modern business corporations is cause for concern, since this increasing size does indicate a concentration of economic power. Similarly, the increasing size

46. See James W. Skillen, "Going beyond Liberalism to Christian Social Philosophy," *Christian Scholar's Review* 19 (March 1990): 220-30.

47. Stanley Hauerwas, *A Community of Character: Toward a Constructive Christian Social Ethic* (Notre Dame, IN: University of Notre Dame Press, 1981), p. 85.

of the modern state is cause for concern from an evangelical perspective, for although the evangelical ethic will recognize the state's place in the created order and its legitimate claims, it will also recognize that by virtue of its size and its effective monopoly over the means of coercion, the modern state will inevitably and in spite of the best intentions of policymakers abet injustice and foster alienation even as it tries to implement justice and to maintain civil order.

The Problem of Justice

In addition to disagreeing about the nature of liberty, evangelicals are also divided on the issue of justice. Does social justice require the redress of capitalist expropriation and the establishment of distributional equality, as those on the left insist? Or is justice primarily a procedural matter and a question of ensuring that the rules of economic acquisition and transfer are fair and properly observed, as those on the right insist? In other words, do the principles of just distribution take precedence over the principles of just acquisition and entitlement, or vice versa? What is the nature of justice? Who is responsible for maintaining justice? If an evangelical economic ethic defers or postpones the realization of perfect justice, what is it that is being deferred?

Unfortunately there simply aren't any conclusive answers to these kinds of questions, for there is not at present any agreement on exactly what justice is, nor is there likely to be anytime soon. Indeed, it has been suggested that the contemporary moral debate is plagued by *competing* definitions of justice, definitions that appeal to entirely different moral paradigms and are therefore logically incompatible. "When claims invoking rights are matched against claims appealing to utility or when either or both are matched against claims based on some traditional concept of justice," Alasdair MacIntyre has written, "it is not surprising that there is no rational way of deciding which type of claim is to be given priority or how one is to be weighed against the other."[48] MacIntyre goes on to argue that this present state of confusion is the logical consequence of the characteristically modern notion that things like justice are socially and historically relative. Yet, as I have already asserted, justice can have no practical meaning unless it is grounded in something that transcends history. Any serious use of the term *justice* ipso facto presupposes a supreme standard against which all human laws, contracts, and customs are measured.[49] But even among those who agree that justice ought to be grounded in revelation there has been considerable disagreement as to just what justice is.

48. MacIntyre, *After Virtue*, p. 70.
49. Brunner, *Justice and the Social Order*, pp. 47ff.

Instead of attempting to redefine justice here, then, it may be more helpful simply to summarize the kinds of concerns represented by the various, and at times competing, theories of justice and then to ask how well modern capitalism—again, as compared to its reasonable alternatives—is able to address these concerns. While such a procedure is no substitute for a careful philosophical and theological definition of justice, it may serve to move this discussion forward, for, as we have seen, the disagreement over the definition of justice is very much at the heart of the modern debate over capitalism.

As Karen Lebacqz has suggested in her interesting comparative study *Six Theories of Justice* (1986), justice has been variously defined in terms of human rights, as a matter of social utility, as having to do with the equal distribution of social goods, as guaranteeing freedom of exchange, as requiring participation in political and economic decision making, and as a matter of balancing social, economic, and political power. Such concerns may be summarized in the following three propositions: (1) justice respects certain individual rights but aims also at certain beneficial social outcomes, (2) justice seeks the equal distribution of social goods but respects the freedom of exchange, and (3) while justice is best determined democratically, we should be careful not to overestimate the ability of a democracy to determine what justice is, and we should be prepared to admit that injustice may well result from even the most well-intentioned social policy.

How well does modern capitalism fare with respect to these three propositions? With respect to the first it fares quite well: the market economy has exhibited an extraordinary and historically unparalleled ability to generate prosperity. Modern capitalism comprises a unique combination of entrepreneurial imagination (an imagination largely freed from the economically inefficient constraints of tradition), an infinitely nuanced market mechanism, and the practical genius of modern science and technology.[50] No other political-economic system in human history has come close to matching capitalism's productive capacity. According to Peter Berger, "Advanced industrial capitalism has generated, and continues to generate, the highest material standards of living for large masses of people in human history."[51] If we judge higher standards of living for large masses of people to be a good thing, then capitalism obviously scores quite high with respect to social utility.

Insofar as individual human rights are concerned, the cultivation of such rights has been a virtual hallmark of bourgeois society, for, as we have seen, personal and political rights appear to depend in practice on the right of free economic exchange. It is true that the West has shown a tendency to abstract and universalize the concepts of "right" and "entitlement" and therefore to

50. See Berger, "Human Development and Economic Alternatives," 20.
51. Berger, *The Capitalist Revolution,* p. 43.

look only to the modern state to provide and guarantee such rights and entitlements. After all, it is the responsibility of the state to ensure that these rights
and entitlements—precisely because they are universal—do not vary from
place to place and from region to region. But this tendency to look only to the
the modern state to provide and guarantee an increasing number of rights and
entitlements has resulted in the dramatic growth of government in recent
decades, both in terms of expenditures and employees and in terms of responsibilities.

> During the past fifty years, the federal government (in particular) has expanded
> its activities in and control over the economic system. The various governments
> within the political system now employ some 15.6 million civilian workers (1978).
> By contrast, the top five hundred industrial corporations listed by *Fortune* mag-
> azine employ 15.8 million workers. . . . The politicization of moral and cultural
> issues now extends to the role of women, homosexuality, marriage, family, abor-
> tion, renting and selling real estate, busing, educational experiments, and the like.
> The "new politics" has expanded the reach of the political system.[52]

While this trend has almost certainly been exacerbated by the ideology of the
New Class, it also appears to be the political legacy of classical liberalism and
so presents a distinct problem in the Western context in the sense that those
on both the left and right are likely to be blind to it.[53] Proponents of the welfare
state argue that the welfare and regulatory apparatus of the modern state is
capable of representing the interests of minority groups over and against the
interests of the majority. At the same time, however, active political mediation
on behalf of such groups tends to compete with and even destroy the delicate
and nuanced infrastructure of those institutions—family, community, church,
voluntary association, and so forth—which serve to mediate between the
individual and the large institutions of public life in modern society.[54] This
essentially renders these groups defenseless in the face of the kind of alienation
and anomie that characterize modern public life.

Now, while it is unclear just what the solution to this problem is, at the
very least it will require a frank recognition of the fact that there may well be
a conflict between the interests of the state and those of the lesser institutions
that help to provide individuals with meaning and purpose, as well as material
support, in a highly abstract society. Similarly, it may be necessary to draw a
distinction between government's ability to spread unavoidable social risks

52. Michael Novak, *The Spirit of Democratic Capitalism* (New York: Simon & Schuster,
1982), p. 179.

53. See Peter L. Berger and Richard John Neuhaus, *To Empower People: The Role of
Mediating Structures in Public Policy* (Washington: American Enterprise Institute, 1977),
pp. 4ff.

54. See Peter L. Berger, *Facing Up to Modernity: Excursions in Society, Politics, and
Religion* (New York: Basic Books, 1977), pp. 130-41.

and its ability to solve social problems. While the modern state may well be able to accomplish the former, it is simply too blunt an instrument to accomplish the latter. Thus while any number of evangelical intellectuals have stressed recently that expanding the authority of the state is a morally legitimate means toward the end of protecting human rights, it may be worth recalling that rights language was originally intended to limit the state's authority, and for good reason. Even in a democracy, individual human rights are threatened very directly by the exercise of political power. Intellectuals have grown accustomed to applying critical theory to the operations of modern business; perhaps it is time for them to take a much more critical look at the actual workings of the modern state. I am not suggesting that we should adopt the traditional conservative position, in which criticism of the state amounts to de facto support for the large institutions of modern business; rather, I would urge that we view both state and business as potential threats to the institutions that are best able to meet both material and spiritual needs. But regarding these two threats, I will grant that managing if not limiting the growth of the modern welfare state seems to me the more critical social ethical task in coming years. As Daniel Bell commented in 1976,

> Above all, the basic allocative power is now *political*, rather than *economic*. And this raises a fundamental question of restraints. The economic constraint on private wants is the amount of money that a man has, or the credit he is able to establish. But what are constraints on political demands? . . . Today the public household is more than a third sector [i.e., in addition to the economic and cultural sectors]; increasingly in the modern polity it absorbs the other two. And the major aspect of the public household is the centrality of the budget, the level of government revenues and expenditures, as the mechanism for reallocation and redress. How much government shall spend, and for whom, obviously is the major political question of the next decades.[55]

With respect to the second proposition—that justice seeks equality but respects the freedom of exchange—capitalism fares somewhat less well. For while the market economy does permit relatively free economic exchange— indeed, a "market" is defined by such exchange—the market does not distribute prosperity equally, and relative inequality characterizes even the most prosperous capitalist societies. But the failure of capitalism to produce social equality must be put into perspective, for while capitalism does not distribute prosperity equally, neither does socialism or any other presently existing or plausibly imagined political-economic arrangement.[56] Thus while capitalism remains open to the criticism that it fosters inequality and therefore undermines

---

55. Bell, *The Cultural Contradictions of Capitalism* (New York: Basic Books, 1976), pp. 226-27.

56. Berger, *The Capitalist Revolution*, p. 219.

participation, no alternative has proven any better at distributing wealth and income, and many have proven worse.

To say this is not to advocate a kind of laissez-faire approach to justice, however, or to suggest that an "invisible hand" will somehow use the unjust actions of some to correct the unjust actions of others.[57] But I do think we need to reject the kind of egalitarianism that demands perfect equalization at present. The egalitarian project may be plausible in a modern context in which social stratification has increasingly become a function of the simple possession of money, but the redistribution of wealth and income would not eliminate stratification; it would simply make it subject to other criteria.

If capitalism requires us to compromise with respect to the ideal of equality, then, it only illustrates the importance of combining justice with mercy, *both* of which must be elements of any humane society. Providing the norm for institutional behavior, justice renders to each his or her due, while mercy compensates for the impersonality of institutions and the accidents of birth and circumstance. And of course mercy is not limited to acts of charity per se. Indeed, a wonderful illustration of a kind of institutionalized combination of justice and mercy is given in the scriptural injunction to landowners not to completely glean their fields (Lev. 19:9-10; 23:22; Deut. 24:19-21). In its original context, this prescription was meant to give the poor a chance to find enough food to eat. More generally, it suggests that we should not pursue our own legitimate economic self-interest to its logical conclusion, that we should not necessarily act to maximize our own satisfaction. Instead, those less able to meet their needs are to enter into our calculations—and not simply as an afterthought, but in the midst of our production of wealth. They should be given a chance to glean some of the product that we would otherwise have a perfectly legitimate claim to.

Finally, with respect to our third proposition—that although justice is best determined democratically, the ability of even a democracy to determine and to implement justice is fraught with problems—capitalism again fares quite well. Along the lines of the "fit" that exists between capitalism and democracy, and even in spite of the fact that decisions in the modern capitalist economy are increasingly concentrated in the hands of those who manage large business corporations, these decisions are still relatively more diffuse than they would be if they were made subject to political control, and they are still subject to the relatively autonomous decisions of a multitude of consumers.

Perhaps even more importantly, modern capitalism fosters incessant social change, change which insures that however unjust we might judge existing social and economic arrangements to be, these arrangements are not likely to last very long. Economist Joseph Schumpeter has argued that "the fundamental

57. On this, see Brunner, *Justice and the Social Order,* p. 138.

impulse that sets and keeps the capitalist engine in motion comes from the new consumers' goods, the new methods of production or transportation, the new markets, the new forms of industrial organization that capitalist enterprise creates. . . . This process of Creative Destruction is the essential fact about capitalism."[58] While capitalism's process of "creative destruction" has admittedly led to disruptions and dislocations in the labor force, we need to remember that it has also led to disruptions and dislocations of capital and the economic power that capital represents.

Thus, just as there seems to be a fit between capitalism and liberty, so there seems to be a fit between modern capitalism and the kinds of concerns people typically have when they use the word *justice*. Relative to its reasonable alternatives—alternatives that simply cannot equal capitalism's economic utility, alternatives that in spite of their promises are not able to respect individual human rights or produce social equality, alternatives that inevitably exacerbate the concentration of economic and political power—capitalism comes closest to approximating the central concerns of the most common modern theories of justice.

But of course it is important to stress that, however we define it, justice must not be seen as an end in itself.

> Even should it be possible to create a just order in every realm of life, what would be gained by it? It lies in the very nature of justice that it cannot touch the deepest depths in man. It is concerned with the person in the institution, not with the person *qua* person. Hence it comes that the most perfect organization, the best of orders, in the last resort provides no guarantee of a truly humane life. The evil in the human heart is so deep-seated that it can transform the most just of institutions into injustice. And personal freedom belongs so profoundly to the God-created nature of man that not the best of institutions can satisfy him. That should not prevent us from doing our utmost to create a just order, but it should safeguard us from the illusion that the problem of human life will be solved by it.[59]

Thus the gospel of Jesus Christ must never be entirely collapsed into the quest for political-economic justice, for this quest itself stands in need of redemption and must ultimately be overcome by love. Those on both the left and the right who imply that the gospel is principally a matter of establishing a particular kind of social order are gravely mistaken, even when they herald this order under that banner of justice.

---

58. Schumpeter, *Capitalism, Socialism, and Democracy*, 3d ed. (New York: Harper, 1950), p. 83.
59. Brunner, *Justice and the Social Order*, p. 229.

The Culture of Capitalism

The foregoing largely positive political and economic assessment of modern capitalism does not mean that there are no faults in the system, however. Although modern industrial capitalism has changed our world for the better, it has also changed it for the worse. While it has created fantastic affluence, this affluence has not been evenly distributed, and it has come at the price of a frightening and almost unbelievably rapid depletion of a number of natural resources. Similarly, although modern capitalism has thoroughly revolutionized our temporal life expectations, it has not necessarily brought us joy. And while it has fabulously expanded the realm of human mastery and freedom, its "creative destruction" has also undermined traditional solidarities and so expanded individual freedom that this freedom frequently overwhelms the ability of individuals to create form and meaning within it. In addition, although capitalism has fostered the institutional and attitudinal prerequisites for modern democracy, it has also given rise to institutions and organizations so large as to completely dwarf the individuals involved in and confronted by them. Capitalism's substantial material benefits, in other words, have entailed a number of significant costs, costs that are perhaps best discussed under the heading of capitalism's peculiar *culture*.

It is important to realize that although the critique of capitalism is typically expressed largely in economic terms, it is never simply an economic critique. In fact, the energy that the critics of capitalism bring to the debate is probably generated less by their dissatisfaction with the economic and political features of the market economy per se than by their dissatisfaction with capitalist culture, a culture often characterized by secularization and anomie, by ceaseless acquisitiveness and narcissism and excessive individualism. And while it is true that some critics have exaggerated these kinds of cultural indictments of capitalism, it is equally true that these indictments have some warrant.

That capitalism is secularizing, for example, is beyond dispute. On the one hand, this is simply because capitalism produces affluence, and affluence fosters spiritual insensitivity. Only the affluent can afford to locate the sum total of their aspirations in temporal reality. But secularity may be more than just accidental to the capitalist process in this way. In their recent study *How the West Grew Rich* (1986), Nathan Rosenberg and L. E. Birdzell, Jr., argue that it is the relative autonomy of the economic sphere in the capitalist political economy—its freedom *from* religion and politics—that accounts for the remarkable productivity the West has experienced in recent centuries. If secularization is defined as the process by which sectors of society become freed from the decisive influence of religion,[60] it can be argued not merely that the

60. Peter L. Berger, *The Sacred Canopy: Elements of a Sociological Theory of Religion* (Garden City, NY: Doubleday-Anchor, 1969), p. 107.

market economy is secularized but that it appears to work precisely *because* it is secularized.[61] Ironically, the logic of the marketplace appears to undermine the very cultural and religious values upon which bourgeois civilization—and capitalism itself—depends.

In the absence of religious and political benchmarks, the market economy has institutionalized a new kind of standard against which success and failure in economic life are measured: capital accumulation. This was one of Karl Marx's central contentions, and Max Weber sought to explain the peculiar spirit of this accumulation in terms of the Protestant ethic. There is a great deal that could be said about the spirit of capitalism, but suffice it to say here that it gives rise to a particular kind of rationality, the character of which is perhaps best illustrated by its attitude toward money. Describing the modern "habit of rationality," Schumpeter has written that

> it exalts the monetary unit—not itself a creation of capitalism—into a unit of account. That is to say, capitalist practice turns the unit of money into a tool of rational cost-profit calculations, of which the towering monument is double-entry bookkeeping. Without going into this, we will notice that, primarily a product of the evolution of economic rationality, the cost-profit calculus in turn reacts upon that rationality; by crystallizing and defining numerically, it powerfully propels the logic of enterprise. And thus defined and quantified for the economic sector, this type of logic or attitude or method then starts upon its conqueror's career subjugating—rationalizing—man's tools and philosophies, his medical practice, his picture of the cosmos, his outlook on life, everything in fact including his concepts of beauty and justice and his spiritual ambitions.[62]

Of course, this has given rise to comments on the "one dimensionality" of bourgeois culture,[63] and also to the observation that only those things that can be priced—that is, only those things that can be "rationalized"—are valued in a capitalist society. And to a degree this is true. The market mechanism does in fact reward those goods and activities that are easily measured by means of price. It is very easy to overstate this point, but it must be conceded that the market is able to reward such things as profit more easily than such things as wisdom or virtue. We may hope that socially beneficial business practices will result in profitability, but this is obviously not always the case. At the very least this is because the market's time horizon is quite short and there is not always enough time for sound business practices to translate into profitability—that is, into an easily measurable index of success. Another reason is that

61. This is one of the central "cultural contradictions" of capitalism according to Daniel Bell in *The Cultural Contradictions of Capitalism.*

62. Schumpeter, *Capitalism, Socialism, and Democracy,* pp. 123-24.

63. See, for example, Herbert Marcuse, *One Dimensional Man: Studies in the Ideology of Advanced Industrial Society* (Boston: Beacon Press, 1964).

easily measurable indices of success such as profit are relatively easily manipulated. To the extent that we equate profitability with social utility, then, we may be fooled; we should not make the mistake of equating success in the market with virtue.

> We are all acquainted with the facile identification of acting economically and efficiently, that is, acting in such a way as to acquire the greatest possible result in terms of goods or money. But it is not difficult to discern that in this way the economic norm for human life is both narrowed and distorted. It is narrowed into something which is limited to the creation of material or financial surplus, and it is distorted into something which is primarily a matter of self-interest. Such a conception of economics has been emptied of almost everything which might be reminiscent of a response to God and to one's neighbor.[64]

The problem with capitalist culture may be summarized by saying that although modern capitalism is profoundly liberating, it is also profoundly alienating. The thrusts of the messages of both evangelical left and right reflect just this paradox. While those on the right tend to dissociate secularization and cultural decadence from modern capitalism, those on the left blame capitalism for these problems in their entirety and drastically discount the relation of capitalism to economic and political freedom. In this connection it is not difficult to see that both right and left are partially mistaken, but for different reasons.

Those on the right neglect the fact that modern capitalism, as a principal carrier of modernization, helps to create not only a number of cultural problems but also the very coercive statism they protest. In the first place this is because modern secularization and decadence are not entirely attributable to "secular humanism." Indeed, the nineteenth-century cultural pattern to which many of those on the evangelical right would have us return—a pattern in which capitalism was more firmly bounded by the constraints of family, church, and community—was at least in part destroyed by capitalism itself. In addition, those on the right fail to recognize that the capitalist political economy naturally requires a relatively high degree of social stability and predictability—two things that only a large, bureaucratically administered, and relatively interventionist state is able to provide.

Those on the left, meanwhile, wrongly believe that we can overcome modern cultural decadence simply by overcoming capitalism. Capitalism may well contribute to the problems of modern culture, but it is by no means the only contributor. Modern technology, industrial production, urbanization, and perhaps most importantly the bureaucratization of both business and government all carry the habit of rationality as well. So the discussion of modern

64. Robert Goudzwaard, *Capitalism and Progress: A Diagnosis of Western Society* (Grand Rapids: William B. Eerdmans, 1979), p. 211.

capitalism needs to be disaggregated from the discussion of modernizatio
se,[65] the latter of which can by definition take into account the contribu
of other social institutions to the problems of rationalization, alienation,
the like. Similarly, the problems of Third World development probably ne
to be distinguished from the quite different problems of cultural decadence
the First World. Western intellectuals need to avoid the temptation to use th
Third World's plight for what may be narcissistic ends.[66]

What appears to be needed in the context of modern capitalism, then, is
a strategy for preserving the market economy's liberating economic and political benefits while at the same time minimizing its cultural costs. Along this
line, it has been observed that secularization, rationalization, alienation, and
the like are most acute at the level of the largest modern institutions, including
modern business and the modern state. As those on both the left and right have
observed, each with their characteristic emphases, these are the institutions
that most dwarf individuals and most actively compete and interfere with the
collectivities of family, church, and community in the modern situation. This
being the case, attempts to address the problem of alienation at the level of
these large institutions are probably misdirected.[67] These institutions are simply
too large and their workings too abstract and impersonal to provide the kind
of community we seek. Our efforts might more usefully be focused on strength-
ening the lesser structures of family, church, and community themselves. These
are the institutions that most effectively mediate between the large impersonal
institutions of modern business and government on the one hand and individuals on the other, and hence they are the most crucial for eliminating the isolation
and anomie prevalent in advanced industrial society.[68] Of course, this kind of
strategy is already suggested by a social ethic that prioritizes communal orders
on the basis of their ability to foster community and love.

Ironically, both the modern state and the capitalist economy require the
healthy functioning of these mediating institutions for their success and survival.[69] As Robert Nisbet observed a number of years ago, "capitalism is either
a system of social and moral allegiances, resting securely in institutions and
voluntary associations, or it is a sand heap of disconnected particles of human-

65. "One of the recurrent errors in contemporary social thought (on the Right as much
as on the Left) is to confuse the consequences of modernization with the consequences of a
particular means of production," Peter Berger has suggested. "Modernization is a global
process brought on by technology, and it has certain consequences regardless of the manner
in which economic life is organized" ("The Serendipity of Liberties").

66. On this, see Jacques Ellul, *The Betrayal of the West* (New York: Seabury, 1978).

67. See Berger, *Pyramids of Sacrifice: Political Ethics and Social Change* (Garden
City, NY: Doubleday-Anchor, 1976), p. 198.

68. See Berger and Neuhaus, *To Empower People*, p. 2; see also Berger, *Pyramids of
Sacrifice*, p. xiii.

69. See Berger, *Capitalist Revolution*, p. 113.

ity. If it is, or is allowed to become, the latter, there is nothing that can prevent the rise of centralized, omnicompetent political power. Lacking a sense of political participation in economic society, men will seek it . . . in the servile State." He went on to suggest that we do indeed need to foster laissez-faire, but rather than conceiving of it in terms of autonomous individuals per se, we need to think about the conditions under which relatively autonomous groups of individuals are enabled to form communities of meaning and purpose.[70]

Finally, it is important to stress that the complexity of the contemporary context is such that there will inevitably be disagreements over specific problems and policies. Evangelical opinion must allow room for these disagreements. While the problems we face are urgent, little if anything can be accomplished by condemning those who differ with us. The urgency of the situation, in other words, is no excuse for neglecting careful study, indulging in conceit, or harboring bitterness. Indeed, we would expect wisdom in this area to be clothed in humility and patience.

Concluding Meditation: The Sabbath as a Limit to Economic Rationality

It is interesting and probably instructive that the one commandment in the Decalogue modern consciousness is least able to appreciate is the commandment to observe the Sabbath (Exod. 20:8-11; Deut. 5:12-15). That modern consciousness understands the other commandments, even those in the so-called "first table," is given if only in the fact that it is able self-consciously to rebel against them. Yet beyond such trivial things as intentionally playing golf or working on Sunday, the modern mind has difficulty even imagining what rebellion against the Sabbath commandment would entail. We do not understand it.

Yet even a cursory review of the Old and New Testaments reveals the Sabbath commandment to be of vital significance.[71] Indeed, for the nation of Israel it could be said that the battle for the Sabbath was the battle for the covenant itself (see Jer. 17:19ff.); and in the new covenant, the Sabbath, with Jesus as its Lord, is a primary symbol of justification and of eternal life (Heb. 4:9). The Sabbath symbolizes, and seems institutionally to have been intended to reinforce, a sharp distinction between God's creative activity and mankind's. The people of Israel, for example, were prophetically urged to keep from doing "as they pleased" on the Sabbath (Isa. 58:13), to put aside their own goals and projects, and to rest instead in their knowledge of God's goals and projects for

70. Nisbet, *Community and Power,* pp. 241, 278.
71. On this matter of the Sabbath, I am particularly indebted to the insights of the late Klaus Bockmuehl, professor of systematic theology and ethics at Regent College (Vancouver, B.C.) until his death in 1989.

them. Thus the Sabbath erected a fence around Israel's legitimate creative activity. It was a reassertion of creation and of Israel's createdness, and hence of the nation's contingency and dependence on God.

Significantly, business and commerce formed one of the principal threats to Sabbath observance in the Old Testament. With an eye toward the preservation of Israel's recently renewed covenant, Nehemiah wrote,

in those days I saw men in Judah treading winepresses on the Sabbath and bringing grain and loading it on donkeys, together with wine, grapes, figs and all other kinds of loads. And they were bringing all this into Jerusalem on the Sabbath. Therefore I warned them against selling food on that day. Men from Tyre who lived in Jerusalem were bringing in fish and all kinds of merchandise and selling them in Jerusalem on the Sabbath to the people of Judah. I rebuked the nobles of Judah and said to them, "What is this wicked thing you are doing—desecrating the Sabbath day? Didn't your forefathers do the same things, so that our God brought all of this calamity upon us and upon this city? Now you are stirring up more wrath against Israel by desecrating the Sabbath. When evening shadows fell on the gates of Jerusalem before the Sabbath, I ordered the doors to be shut and not opened until the Sabbath was over. I stationed some of my own men at the gates so that no load could be brought in on the Sabbath day. Once or twice merchants and sellers of all kinds of goods spent the night outside of Jerusalem. But I warned them and said, "Why do you spend the night by the wall? If you do this again, I will lay hands on you." From that time on they no longer came on the Sabbath. Then I commanded the Levites to purify themselves and go and guard the gates in order to keep the Sabbath holy. (Neh. 13:15-22)

Indeed, business and commerce not only threatened the observance of the Sabbath, but often became the object of idolatrous devotion and worship. Isaiah warned that

The LORD Almighty has a day in store
    for all the proud and lofty,
    for all that is exalted
    (and they will be humbled),
for all the cedars of Lebanon, tall and lofty,
    and all the oaks of Bashan,
for all the towering mountains,
    and all the high hills,
for every lofty tower
    and every fortified wall,
for every trading ship
    and every stately vessel.
The arrogance of man will be brought low
    and the pride of man humbled;
the LORD alone will be exalted in that day,
    and the idols will totally disappear. (Isa. 2:12-18, NIV)

In the minds of the prophets, then, there appears to have been something profoundly destructive and culpable about Israel's tendency toward unrestrained commercial activity. While mankind had been commanded to "work" and to "take care" of creation (Gen. 2:15), the covenant also required the regular and periodic cessation of this activity in Sabbath observance. Failure to observe the Sabbath, furthermore, seemed inevitably to lead to the oppression of the poor, to the dehumanizing absurdity of idolatry (i.e., the absorption of the worshiper into the object of worship), and to a provocation of the wrath of God against the nation, which ultimately led to judgment.

Strikingly similar observations have been made about the process of modernization and the nature of modern industrial society. Technologically driven economic growth and the rationalization of human existence have become, as Max Weber suggested, something of an "iron cage" for us. While we have reaped previously unimaginable material rewards from our engineering of this world, one wonders if we are not like the rich fool in Jesus' parable (Luke 12:13-21), unaware that this world in general and our lives in particular are rapidly passing away. The rationalization of modern life all but prevents us from appreciating this. Modern capitalism is one of the principal carriers of rationalization and of our engineering mindset. Yet the fact that most proposals for the elimination or reform of the modern capitalist system are equally rationalizing illustrates the seemingly ineluctable force of this process and underscores the irony of our situation.

While it would be naive, and perhaps even theologically mistaken, to suggest that the simple observance of the Sabbath would solve these modern problems, fruitful consideration of the political-economic dilemmas posed by modern capitalism might well require the adoption of a Sabbath *attitude*. At the very least, such an attitude would help us to put political-economic problems in perspective by relativizing them. Such an attitude would shudder, for example, at assertions that we create ourselves through labor or that we can somehow usher in the kingdom of God by our own conscious sociohistorical effort. The god of any kingdom thus fashioned would simply be a shadow of man and a human projection. The Sabbath attitude would also look with horror on the modern preoccupation with the pursuit of *temporary life* at the expense of any consideration of *eternal life*.[72] It would reject the spirit of endless accumulation and acquisition and concentrate instead on what accumulation is *for*. In addition, the Sabbath attitude would shudder at the commodification of human labor and at the notion that the created order is valuable only insofar as humanly constructed prices can be attached to it. Instead, the Sabbath attitude would affirm the goodness of creatureliness as such and, by encourag-

72. See Abraham Joshua Heschel, *The Earth Is the Lord's: The Sabbath* (New York: Harper & Row, 1966), p. 45.

ing us to rest in God, would break open the "iron cage" of rationalized material progress which, while instrumentally valuable, cannot ultimately satisfy us. The Sabbath attitude would understand the concept of *limit* and recognize that certain boundaries are part and parcel of the created order and hence not subject to human cultural negotiation. As Abraham Joshua Heschel has noted, "The Sabbath is the day on which we learn the art of surpassing civilization."[73] Indeed, it appears that a rediscovery of Sabbath and of a Sabbath attitude may be the only way of preventing our civilization from surpassing us.

Jesus' admonition that we cannot serve both God and mammon (Matt. 6:24; Luke 16:13, RSV) does not leave us with the option of serving neither but only of choosing between the two. Mammon promises us material blessings, but only at the cost of ceaseless acquisitive activity, and there is considerable doubt as to its continuing ability to keep its promises. Our Father, meanwhile, promises us both material blessing and rest for our souls. He requires only that we periodically cease from our acquisitive activity, activity that otherwise tends to prevent us from understanding justice, mercy, and humility.

Essential to the development of an evangelical economic ethic, then, is a rediscovery of the meaning of Sabbath. For the contemporary situation cries out not only for the positive definition of such things as liberty and justice but also for a perspective that puts political-economic questions into a larger context, a perspective that seeks to balance the harmful and beneficial elements of modern industrial capitalism. The idea of Sabbath provides just such a perspective, and in taking it seriously we may be better able to steer a course between the ruthless efficiencies of laissez-faire and the debilitating inefficiencies of an endlessly expanding welfare state.

73. Heschel. *The Earth Is the Lord's*, p. 27.

Bibliography

Adeney, Miriam. *God's Foreign Policy: Practical Ways to Help the World's Poor.* Grand Rapids: William B. Eerdmans, 1984.

Adeymo, Tokunbok; Vinay Samuel; and Ronald J. Sider. "Introducing Transformation." *Transformation,* March 1984, pp. 1-2.

Alexander, John. "Back at the Family Farm: Economics as if God Mattered." *The Other Side,* September 1987, pp. 14-15.

_____. *Your Money or Your Life: A New Look at Jesus' View of Wealth and Power.* San Francisco: Harper & Row, 1986.

Alperovitz, Gar. "Building a Living Democracy: A Whole New Way of Thinking about Politics and Economics." *Sojourners,* July 1990, pp. 11-23.

_____. "Economics: Putting a Value on Values." *Sojourners,* November 1985, pp. 18-22.

Ammerman, Nancy Tatom. *Bible Believers: Fundamentalists in the Modern World.* New Brunswick, NJ: Rutgers University Press, 1987.

Amstutz, Mark R. "The Bishops and Third World Poverty." In *Prophetic Visions and Economic Realities: Protestants, Jews and Catholics Confront the Bishops' Letter on the Economy,* ed. Charles R. Strain, pp. 61-80. Grand Rapids: William B. Eerdmans, 1989.

_____. "The Churches and Third World Poverty." *Missiology* 17 (October 1989): 453-64.

Antonides, Harry. *Multinationals and the Peaceable Kingdom.* Toronto: Clark & Irwin, 1977.

_____. *Stones for Bread: The Social Gospel and Its Contemporary Legacy.* Jordan Station, Ont.: Paideia Press, 1985.

Armerding, Carl E. "Exodus: The Old Testament Foundation of Liberation." In *Evangelicals and Liberation,* ed. Carl E. Armerding. Nutley, NJ: Presbyterian & Reformed, 1977.

Arthur, John, and William H. Shaw, eds. *Justice and Economic Distribution.* New Jersey: Prentice Hall, 1978.

240

Bacciocco, Edward J., Jr. *The New Left in America: Reform to Revolution.* Stanford, CA: Hoover Institution Press, 1974.

Bahnsen, Greg L. "Christ and the Role of Civil Government: The Theonomic Perspective, Part 1." *Transformation,* April-June 1988, pp. 24-31.

_____. "Christ and the Role of Civil Government: The Theonomic Perspective, Part 2." *Transformation,* July-September 1988, pp. 24-28.

Baker-Shenk, Charlotte. "Breaking the Shackles: Liberation Theology and the Day Community." *Sojourners,* March 1985, pp. 30-32.

Baldwin, Stanley C. "A Case against Waste and Other Excesses." *Christianity Today,* 16 July 1976, pp. 10-14.

Barnet, Richard, and Ronald Muller. *Global Reach: The Power of the Multinational Corporations.* New York: Simon & Schuster, 1974.

Barnett, Jake. *Wealth and Wisdom: A Biblical Perspective on Possessions.* Colorado Springs: Navpress, 1987.

Bartel, Robert J. "A Response to Peter Hill." *Transformation,* June-September/October-December 1987, pp. 52-53.

Bartley, Robert L. "Business and the New Class." In *The New Class?* ed. B. Bruce-Briggs, pp. 57-66. New Brunswick, NJ: Transaction Books, 1979.

Batey, Richard. *Jesus and the Poor.* New York: Harper & Row, 1972.

Bauer, P. T. *Dissent on Development.* Cambridge: Harvard University Press, 1972.

_____. *Equality, The Third World and Economic Delusion.* London: Herdenjild & Nicholson, 1981.

_____. *Reality and Rhetoric: Studies in the Economics of Development.* London: Herdenjild & Nicholson, 1984.

Bazelon, David T. *Power in America: The Politics of the New Class.* New York: New American Library, 1964.

Beckman, David M. *Where Faith and Economics Meet: A Christian Critique.* Minneapolis: Augsburg, 1984.

Beisner, E. Calvin. "Biblical Incentives and Economic Systems." In *Biblical Principles and Economics: The Foundations,* Christians in the Marketplace Series no. 2, ed. Richard C. Chewning, pp. 168-86. Colorado Springs: Navpress, 1989.

_____. *Prosperity and Poverty: The Compassionate Use of Resources in a World of Scarcity,* Turning Point Christian Worldview Series no. 5, ed. Marvin Olasky. Westchester, IL: Crossway Books, 1988.

Bell, Daniel. *The Coming of the Post-Industrial Society.* New York: Basic Books, 1973.

_____. *The Cultural Contradictions of Capitalism.* New York: Basic Books, 1976.

_____. "The New Class: A Muddled Concept." In *The New Class?* ed. B. Bruce-Briggs, pp. 169-90. New Brunswick, NJ: Transaction Books, 1979.

Bell, Nelson, "The Church and Poverty," *Christianity Today,* 27 March 1970, p. 27.

_____. "A Guaranteed Income?" *Christianity Today,* 5 July 1969, pp. 29-30.

Bellah, Robert, "The Normative Framework for Pluralism in America," *Soundings* 61 (Fall 1978): 355-71.

Bellah, Robert; Richard Madsen; William M. Sullivan; Ann Swidler; and Steven M. Tipton. *Habits of the Heart: Individualism and Commitment in American Life.* Berkeley and Los Angeles: University of California Press, 1985.

Benda, Julien. *The Treason of the Intellectuals*. New York: W. W. Norton, 1969.

Benjamin, Walter W. "Liberation Theology: European Hopelessness Exposes Latin Hoax." *Christianity Today*, 5 March 1982, pp. 21-23.

Benne, Robert, and Philip Hefner. *Defining America*. Philadelphia: Fortress Press, 1974.

Berger, Brigitte, and Peter L. Berger. *The War over the Family: Capturing the Middle Ground*. Garden City, NY: Doubleday-Anchor, 1983.

Berger, Peter L. "American Religion: Conservative Upsurge, Liberal Prospects." In *Liberal Protestantism: Realities and Possibilities*, ed. Robert S. Michaelson and Wade Clark Roof, pp. 19-36. New York: Pilgrim Press, 1986.

_____. "A Call for Authority in the Christian Community." *Princeton Seminary Bulletin*, December 1971, pp. 14-24.

_____. *The Capitalist Revolution: Fifty Propositions about Prosperity, Equality, and Liberty*. New York: Basic Books, 1986.

_____. "The Concept of Mediating Action." In *Confession, Conflict, and Community*, Encounter Series no. 3, ed. Richard John Neuhaus, pp. 1-11. Grand Rapids: William B. Eerdmans, 1986.

_____. "Different Gospels: The Social Sources of Apostasy." *This World*, Spring 1987, pp. 6-17.

_____. "Ethics and the Present Class Struggle." *Worldview*, April 1978, pp. 6-11.

_____. *Facing Up to Modernity: Excursions in Society, Politics, and Religion*. New York: Basic Books, 1977.

_____. "For a World with Windows." In *Against the World for the World: The Hartford Appeal and the Future of American Religion*, ed. Peter L. Berger and Richard John Neuhaus, pp. 8-19. New York: Seabury Press, 1976.

_____. *The Heretical Imperative: Contemporary Possibilities of Religious Affirmation*. Garden City, NY: Doubleday-Anchor, 1980.

_____. "Human Development and Economic Alternatives." *Crisis*, November 1987, pp. 18-23.

_____. "Moral Judgment and Political Action." University Lecture. Boston University, 26 October 1987.

_____. *Pyramids of Sacrifice: Political Ethics and Social Change*. Garden City, NY: Doubleday-Anchor, 1976.

_____. *A Rumor of Angels: Modern Society and the Rediscovery of the Supernatural*. New York: Doubleday-Anchor, 1970.

_____. *The Sacred Canopy: Elements of a Sociological Theory of Religion*. Garden City, NY: Doubleday-Anchor, 1969.

_____. "The Serendipity of Liberties." Paper delivered at I.S.E.C./C.R.S. conference. Boston University, October 1987.

_____. "A Sociological View of the Secularization of Theology." *Journal for the Scientific Study of Religion* 6 (Spring 1967): 3-16.

_____. "Western Individuality: Liberation and Loneliness." *Partisan Review* 52 (1985): 323-36.

_____. "The Worldview of the New Class: Secularity and Its Discontents." In *The New Class?* ed. B. Bruce-Briggs, pp. 49-55. New Brunswick, NJ: Transaction Books, 1979.

Berger, Peter L.; Brigitte Berger; and Hansfried Kellner. *The Homeless Mind: Modernization and Consciousness.* New York: Random House, 1973.

Berger, Peter L., and Richard John Neuhaus. *To Empower People: The Role of Mediating Structures in Public Policy.* Washington: American Enterprise Institute, 1977.

Berger, Peter L., and Thomas Luckmann. *The Social Construction of Reality: A Treatise in the Sociology of Knowledge.* New York: Pelican, 1984.

Berkhof, Hendrik. *Christ and the Powers.* Scottsdale, PA: Herald Press, 1962.

Berkhof, L. *The Church and Social Problems.* Grand Rapids: Eerdmans & Sevensma, 1913.

Berthoud, Pierre. "Prophet and Covenant." In *Freedom, Justice, and Hope: Toward a Strategy for the Poor and Oppressed,* Turning Point Christian Worldview Series no. 3, ed. Marvin Olasky, pp. 19-39. Westchester, IL: Crossway, 1988.

"A Better Way to Confront Poverty." *Christianity Today,* 13 January 1969, pp. 24-26.

Beversluis, Eric H. "Backwards Theology." *Reformed Journal,* February 1985, pp. 3-4.

_____. "A Critique of Ronald Nash on Economic Justice and the State." *Christian Scholar's Review* 11 (1981): 330-46.

Billingsley, Lloyd. "First Church of Christ Socialist." *National Review,* 28 October 1983, p. 139.

Bloesch, Donald G. *The Evangelical Renaissance.* Grand Rapids: William B. Eerdmans, 1973.

_____. *The Future of Evangelical Christianity: A Call for Unity amid Diversity.* New York: Doubleday, 1983.

Bockmuehl, Klaus. "After Lausanne—What?" *Christianity Today,* 14 March 1975, pp. 67-68.

_____. "Destroyer or Provider." *Christianity Today,* 6 June 1975, pp. 49-50.

_____. *Evangelicals and Social Ethics: A Commentary on Article 5 of the Lausanne Covenant.* Downers Grove, IL: InterVarsity Press, 1979.

_____. "Evangelical Assertions on Social Change." *Christianity Today,* 21 May 1976, pp. 45-46.

Bookser-Feister, John. "The Struggle for Work Place Justice." *The Other Side,* April-May 1985, pp. 46-49.

Boonstra, Harry. "The Poor You Always Have with You (Unfortunately)." *Reformed Journal,* March 1977, pp. 6-7.

Bower, Howard R. *Investment in Learning: The Individual and Social Value of American Higher Education.* San Francisco: Jossey-Bass, 1980.

Branson, Mark Lau. "Striving for Obedience, Haunted by Dualism: The Consultation on the Relationship between Evangelism and Social Responsibility." *TSF Bulletin,* September-October 1982, pp. 10-12.

Bratt, James D. *Dutch Calvinism in Modern America: A History of a Conservative Subculture.* Grand Rapids: William B. Eerdmans, 1984.

Brint, Stephen. " 'New Class' and Cumulative Trend Explanations of the Liberal Political Attitudes of Professionals." *American Journal of Sociology* 90 (July 1984): 30-71.

Brouwer, Tony. "Poor People and the Economic System." *Reformed Journal,* January 1968, pp. 16-18.

Brown, Dale W. *The Christian Revolutionary.* Grand Rapids: William B. Eerdmans, 1971.

Brown, Harold O. J. *Christianity and the Class Struggle.* New Rochelle, NY: Arlington House, 1970.

_____. "What Is Liberation Theology? A Hermeneutical Battlefield." In *Liberation Theology,* ed. Ronald H. Nash, pp. 5-16. Milford, MI: Mott Media, 1984.

Bruce, Steve. *The Rise and Fall of the New Christian Right: Conservative Protestant Politics in America, 1978-1988.* Oxford: Clarendon Press, 1988.

Bruce-Briggs, B. "Conclusion: Notes toward a Delineation of the New Class." In *The New Class?* ed. B. Bruce-Briggs, pp. 191-216. New Brunswick, NJ: Transaction Books, 1979.

_____. "An Introduction to the Idea of the New Class." In *The New Class?* ed. B. Bruce-Briggs. New Brunswick, NJ: Transaction Books, 1979.

_____. "Is There a New Class?" *Society* 16 (January/February 1979): 14.

Brunner, Emil. *The Divine Imperative: A Study in Christian Ethics.* Philadelphia: Westminster Press, 1947.

_____. *Justice and the Social Order.* London: Lutterworth Press, 1945.

Burkett, Larry. "Is Welfare Scriptural?" *Fundamentalist Journal,* April 1985, pp. 21-23.

Campolo, Anthony. *We Have Met the Enemy and They Are Partly Right.* Waco, TX: Word Books, 1985.

"Capitalism: Basically Unjust?" *Christianity Today,* 24 October 1975, pp. 31-32.

"Capitalism vs. Communism." *Christianity Today,* 12 February 1971, pp. 34-35.

Carpenter, Joel A. "From Fundamentalism to the New Evangelical Coalition." In *Evangelicalism and Modern America,* ed. George Marsden, pp. 3-16. Grand Rapids: William B. Eerdmans, 1984.

_____. "The Fundamentalist Leaven and the Rise of an Evangelical United Front." In *The Evangelical Tradition in America,* ed. Leonard I. Sweet, pp. 257-88. Macon, GA: Mercer University Press, 1984.

Catherwood, Sir Frederick. *A Better Way: The Case for a Christian Social Order.* London: Inter-Varsity Press, 1975.

_____. "The Christian Case for the Diffusion of Economic Power." *Transformation,* October-December 1989, pp. 7-12.

_____. *The Christian in Industrial Society.* London: Tyndale Press, 1966.

_____. "Christian Faith and Economics." *Transformation.* June-September/ October-December 1987, pp. 1-6.

Chewning, Richard C. "Human Nature and Economic Exchange." In *Biblical Principles and Economics: The Foundations,* Christians in the Marketplace Series no. 2, ed. Richard C. Chewning, pp. 11-22. Colorado Springs: Navpress, 1989.

Chilton, David. *Productive Christians in an Age of Guilt Manipulators: A Biblical Response to Ronald J. Sider.* Tyler, TX: Institute for Christian Economics, 1981.

Christensen, James L. "What America Stands For." *Christian Economics,* 17 November 1953, pp. 1-4.

Christiansen, Larry. *Social Action: Jesus Style.* Minneapolis: Dimension, 1976.

"Christian Social Action." *Christianity Today,* 14 March 1969, pp. 24-25.

The Church and Its Social Calling. Grand Rapids: Reformed Ecumenical Synod, 1980.

Clapp, Rodney. "Democracy as Heresy." *Christianity Today,* 20 February 1987, pp. 17-23.

_____. "Where Capitalism and Christianity Meet." *Christianity Today,* 4 February 1983, pp. 22-29.

Claydon, David. "On Being a Christian Radical." *Christianity Today,* 8 November 1974, pp. 6-7.

Clouse, Robert G. "The Evangelical Christian, Social Concern, and a Theology of Hope." *Evangelical Quarterly* 44 (April-June 1972): 68-75.

Clouse, Robert G., ed. *Wealth and Poverty: Four Christian Views of Economics.* Downers Grove, IL: InterVarsity Press, 1984.

Clouse, Robert G.; Robert Linder; and Pierard Richard, eds. *The Cross and the Flag.* Carol Stream, IL: Creation House, 1972.

Coleson, Edward. "The Coming of Christian Capitalism." *Journal of Christian Reconstruction* 1 (Summer 1974): 115-25.

Coleson, Edward, and Richard V. Pierard. "Is There a Christian Economic System?" *Journal of the American Scientific Affiliation* 29 (March 1977): 13-18.

Collins, Gary, ed. *Our Society in Turmoil.* Carol Stream, IL: Creation House, 1970.

Collum, Danny. "Assault on the Poor." *Sojourners,* July 1981, pp. 12-16.

_____. "Assumptions from on High: The Assaults of Capitalism." Review of *The Spirit of Democratic Capitalism,* by Michael Novak. *Sojourners,* May 1983, pp. 40-42.

_____. "The Big Picture: Where We Are and How We Got Here." In *The Rise of Christian Conscience,* ed. Jim Wallis, pp. 3-16. San Francisco: Harper & Row, 1987.

_____. "The Crash of '87." *Sojourners,* January 1988, pp. 4-5.

_____. "Economics: The Way America Does Business." *Sojourners,* November 1985, pp. 12-17.

Colson, Charles. "Budget Cuts and Self-Denial." *Christianity Today,* 20 September 1985, p. 56.

Conn, Harvie M. "Contextualization: Where Do We Begin?" In *Evangelicals and Liberation,* ed. Carl E. Armerding, pp. 90-119. Nutley, NJ: Presbyterian & Reformed, 1977.

_____. "The Mission of the Church." In *Evangelicals and Liberation,* ed. Carl E. Armerding, pp. 60-89. Nutley, NJ: Presbyterian & Reformed, 1977.

"A Conversation with Young Evangelicals." *Post American,* January 1975, pp. 4-13.

Costas, Orlando. *The Church and Its Mission: A Shattering Critique from the Third World.* Wheaton, IL: Tyndale, 1974.

_____. *The Integrity of Mission.* New York: Harper & Row, 1979.

Cotham, Perry C. *Politics, Americanism, and Christianity.* Grand Rapids: Baker Book House, 1973.

"Counting the Cost of Giving." *Christianity Today,* 30 January 1976, pp. 21-22.

Cramp, A. B. *Notes towards a Christian Critique of Secular Economic Theory.* Toronto: Institute for Christian Studies, 1975.

Cuddihy, John Murray. *No Offense: Civil Religion and Protestant Taste.* New York: Seabury Press, 1978.

Curry, Dean C. "Michael Novak." *Eternity,* July-August 1986, p. 23.

"The Danger of Christian-Marxist Dialogue." *Christianity Today,* 27 October 1967, pp. 26-27.

Davids, Peter H. "God and Mammon: Part 1." *Sojourners,* February 1978, pp. 11-17.

_____. "God and Mammon: Part 2." *Sojourners,* March 1978, pp. 25-29.

Davis, John Jefferson. *Christ's Victorious Kingdom: Postmillennialism Reconsidered.* Grand Rapids: Baker Book House, 1986.

_____. "The New Information Age," *The Freeman,* March 1986, pp. 102-7.

_____. "Poverty: Justice, Compassion, and Personal Responsibility." *Fundamentalist Journal,* April 1985, pp. 27-30.

_____. "Profits and Pollution," *The Freeman,* June 1982, pp. 323-31.

_____. *Your Wealth in God's World: Does the Bible Support the Free Market?* Phillipsburg, NJ: Presbyterian & Reformed, 1984.

Dayton, Donald W. *Discovering an Evangelical Heritage.* New York: Harper & Row, 1976.

DeBoer, Cecil. *The Ifs and Oughts of Ethics: A Preface to Moral Philosophy.* Grand Rapids: William B. Eerdmans, 1936.

DeKoster, Lester. "Liberation Theology Adopts Marxism." *Family Protection Scorecard,* special edition, pp. 14-17. Costa Mesa, CA: National Citizens Action Network, 1989.

DeMar, Gary. *Ruler of the Nations: Biblical Principles of Government,* Biblical Blueprint Series no. 2. Ft. Worth: Dominion, 1987.

DeVries, George, Jr. "The Business of America." *Reformed Journal,* April 1977, pp. 15-19.

_____. "Our Latin Neighbors." *Reformed Journal,* May-June 1976, pp. 4-6.

_____. "The New Old Right." *Reformed Journal,* October 1986, pp. 8-10.

_____. "Systems and Hunger." *Reformed Journal,* April 1975, pp. 4-6.

_____. "Trade on the High Seize." *The Other Side,* January-February 1976, pp. 59-62.

DeVries, Robert C. "In the Market Place: Covenants and Contracts." *Reformed Journal,* November 1976, pp. 20-23.

Diehl, William E. "The Guided Market System." In *Wealth and Poverty: Four Christian Views of Economics,* ed. Robert G. Clouse. Downers Grove, IL: InterVarsity Press, 1984.

_____. "A Theology for a Competitive Society?" *Centering,* Spring 1988, pp. 14-17.

Dollar, Truman. "Can Fundamentalism Survive?" *Fundamentalist Journal,* December 1985, p. 74.

_____. "A Theology of the Poor." *Fundamentalist Journal,* October 1985, p. 74.

Doner, Colonel V. *The Samaritan Strategy: A New Agenda for Christian Activism.* Brentwood, TN: Wolgemuth & Hyatt, 1988.

Dooyeweerd, Hermann. *In the Twilight of Western Thought: Studies in the Pretended Autonomy of Philosophical Thought.* Phillipsburg, NJ: Presbyterian & Reformed, 1960.

Douglas, J. D., ed. *Let the Earth Hear His Voice: The International Congress on World Evangelization.* Minneapolis: World Wide Publications, 1975.

Dykema, Eugene R. "Wealth and Well-Being: The Bishops and Their Critics." In

Prophetic Visions and Economic Realities: Protestants, Jews and Catholics Confront the Bishops' Letter on the Economy, ed. Charles R. Strain, pp. 48-60. Grand Rapids: William B. Eerdmans, 1989.

Ehrenreich, Barbara and John. "The Professional-Managerial Class." *Radical America,* March-April 1977, pp. 7-31.

Eidsmoe, John. *God and Caesar: Christian Faith and Political Action.* Westchester, IL: Crossway, 1984.

Eller, Vernard. *The Simple Life: The Christian Stance toward Possessions.* Grand Rapids: William B. Eerdmans, 1973.

Ellul, Jacques. *The Betrayal of the West.* New York: Seabury Press, 1978.

_____. *The Presence of the Kingdom.* New York: Seabury Press, 1967.

Elzinga, Kenneth G. "A Christian View of the Economic Order." *Reformed Journal,* October 1981, pp. 13-16.

_____. "The Demise of Capitalism and the Christian's Response." *Christianity Today,* 7 July 1972, pp. 12-16.

Erdman, Charles R. "The Church and Socialism." In *The Fundamentals: A Testimony,* vol. 12, pp. 108-19. Chicago: Testimony Publishing, 1914.

Escobar, Samuel, and John Driver. *Christian Mission and Social Justice.* Scottdale, PA: Herald Press, 1978.

_____. "Evangelism and Man's Search for Freedom, Justice, and Fulfillment." In *Let the Earth Hear His Voice: The International Congress on World Evangelization,* ed. J. D. Douglas, pp. 303-18. Minneapolis: World Wide Publications, 1975.

_____. "The Hermeneutical Task in Global Economics." *Transformation,* June-September/October-December 1987, pp. 7-10.

_____. "The Social Impact of the Gospel," In *Is Revolution Change?* ed. Brian Griffiths, pp. 84-105. Downers Grove, IL: InterVarsity Press, 1972.

Etzioni-Halevy, Eva. *The Knowledge Elite and the Failure of Prophecy.* London: George Allen & Unwin, 1985.

Evangelism and Social Responsibility: An Evangelical Commitment (The "Grand Rapids Report"), Lausanne Occasional Paper no. 21. Wheaton, IL: Lausanne Committee for World Evangelization & World Evangelical Fellowship, 1982.

Falwell, Jerry. *Listen America.* Garden City, NY: Doubleday, 1980.

Falwell, Jerry; Ed Dobson; and Ed Hindson, eds. *The Fundamentalist Phenomenon: The Resurgence of Conservative Christianity.* Garden City, NY: Doubleday, 1981.

Faw, Bill. "Our Daily Bread: Biblical Themes of Economics." *Sojourners,* January 1980, pp. 22-24.

Finger, Thomas. "Christians and Marxists: The Debate Goes On . . ." *Sojourners,* April 1977, pp. 33-36.

"Flesh-and-Blood Priorities." *Christianity Today,* 13 January 1989, pp. 18-19.

Flynn, Charles P. "Competition and Christian Ethics." *Journal of the American Scientific Affiliation* 33 (December 1981): 220-24.

Fowler, Robert Booth. *A New Engagement: Evangelical Political Thought, 1966-1976.* Grand Rapids: William B. Eerdmans, 1982.

Frame, Randy. "The Theonomic Urge." *Christianity Today,* 21 April 1989, pp. 38-40.

Frank, Douglas W. *Less Than Conquerors: How Evangelicals Entered the Twentieth Century.* Grand Rapids: William B. Eerdmans, 1986.

Friedman, Milton. *Capitalism and Freedom.* Chicago: University of Chicago Press, 1962.

"From Berlin to Lausanne." *Christianity Today,* 5 July 1974, p. 28.

Frykenberg, Robert E. "World Hunger: Food Is Not the Answer." *Christianity Today,* 11 December 1981, pp. 36-39.

Fuller, Reginald, and Brian K. Rice. *Christianity and the Affluent Society.* Grand Rapids: William B. Eerdmans, 1966.

Furness, Charles Y. *The Christian and Social Action.* Old Tappan, NJ: Fleming H. Revell, 1972.

Galbraith, John Kenneth. *The Affluent Society.* 2d ed. Boston: Houghton Mifflin, 1971.

_____. *The New Industrial State.* Boston: Houghton Mifflin, 1971.

Gallaway, Ira. "Liberation and Revolution." *Christianity Today,* 25 August 1972, p. 20.

Garrett, William R. "Politicized Clergy: A Sociological Interpretation of the 'New Breed.' " *Journal for the Scientific Study of Religion* 12 (December 1973): 383-99.

Garrison, Stephen. "Liberation Theology: A Challenge to the Church." *Crux,* June 1980, pp. 20-23.

Geisler, Norman L. "Dispensationalism and Ethics." *Transformation,* October-December 1989, pp. 7-14.

Gerth, H. H., and C. Wright Mills. *From Max Weber: Essays in Sociology.* New York: Oxford University Press, 1946.

Gilbert, Alan P. *The Making of Post-Christian Britain: A History of the Secularization of Modern Society.* London: Longman, 1980.

Gilbreath, W. J. S. "The Political Economy of the Disclosed Society: A Response to Bob Goudzwaard." *Crux,* June 1986, pp. 22-24.

Gilder, George. *Wealth and Poverty.* New York: Basic Books, 1981.

Gish, Arthur G. "Decentralist Economics." In *Wealth and Poverty: Four Christian Views of Economics,* ed. Robert G. Clouse, pp. 131-59. Downers Grove, IL: InterVarsity Press, 1984.

_____. *The New Left and Christian Radicalism.* Grand Rapids: William B. Eerdmans, 1970.

Glazer, Nathan, "Fundamentalism: A Defensive Offensive." In *Piety and Politics: Evangelicals and Fundamentalists Confront the World,* ed. Richard John Neuhaus and Michael Chromartie, pp. 245-58. Washington: Ethics and Public Policy Center, 1987.

Goldfrank, Walter L., ed. *The World System of Capitalism: Past and Present,* vol. 2. Beverly Hills: Sage Publications, 1979.

Goudzwaard, Bob. *Capitalism and Progress: A Diagnosis of Western Society.* Grand Rapids: William B. Eerdmans, 1979.

_____. "Centrally Planned Economics: Strengths, Weaknesses, and the Future." *Transformation,* June-September/October-December 1987, pp. 54-59.

_____. *Economic Stewardship versus Capitalist Religion.* Toronto: Institute for Christian Studies, 1972.

_____. *Idols of Our Time.* Downers Grove, IL: InterVarsity Press, 1984.

Gouldner, Alvin. *The Future of Intellectuals and the Rise of the New Class.* New York: Seabury Press, 1979.

_____. "The New Class Project, I and II." *Theory and Society* 5-6 (1978): 153-203, 343-89.

Graham, Billy. "Why Lausanne?" In *Let the Earth Hear His Voice: The International Congress on World Evangelization,* ed. J. D. Douglas, pp. 22-26. Minneapolis: World Wide Publications, 1975.

_____. "Why Lausanne?" *Christianity Today,* 13 September 1974, pp. 4-14.

Graham, W. Fred; George N. Monsma, Jr.; Carl J. Sinke; Alan Storkey; and John P. Tiemstra. *Reforming Economics: A Christian Perspective on Economic Theory and Practice.* 2 vols. Grand Rapids: Calvin Center for Christian Scholarship, 1986.

Gran, Guy. "Is Poverty Really Inevitable? A Short Guide to the World Economy Debate." *Sojourners,* April 1977, pp. 29-32.

Granberg-Michaelson, Wesley. "Economics: Searching for Alternatives." *Sojourners,* July 1990, pp. 4-5.

Grant, George. *Bringing in the Sheaves: Transforming Poverty into Productivity.* Brentwood, TN: Wolgemuth & Hyatt, 1988.

_____. *The Changing of the Guard: Biblical Principles for Political Action,* Biblical Blueprint Series no. 8. Fort Worth: Dominion, 1987.

_____. *In the Shadow of Plenty: Biblical Principles of Welfare and Poverty,* Biblical Blueprint Series no. 4. Fort Worth: Dominion, 1986.

Greaves, Percy L. Jr. "Christianity and Economics." *Christian Economics,* 2 December 1952, pp. 1-3.

_____. "Economic Equality." *Christian Economics,* 27 January 1953, pp. 1-3.

Griffiths, Brian, "Conclusion: The Christian Way." In *Is Revolution Change?* ed. Brian Griffiths, pp. 106-11. Downers Grove, IL: InterVarsity Press, 1972.

_____. *The Creation of Wealth: A Christian Case for Capitalism.* Downers Grove, IL: InterVarsity Press, 1984.

_____. "The Law and Order Issue." In *Is Revolution Change?* ed. Brian Griffiths, pp. 9-30. Downers Grove, IL: InterVarsity Press, 1972.

_____. *Morality and the Market Place: Christian Alternatives to Capitalism and Socialism.* London: Hodder & Stoughton, 1982.

Grounds, Vernon. *Evangelicalism and Social Responsibility.* Scottdale, PA: Herald Press, 1969.

_____. *Revolution and the Christian Faith.* Philadelphia: J. B. Lippincott, 1971.

_____. "Scripture in Liberation Theology: An Eviscerated Authority." In *Challenges to Inerrancy: A Theological Response,* ed. Gordon Lewis and Bruce Demarest, pp. 317-46. Chicago: Moody Press, 1984.

Gruber, Alan R. "Poverty." In *Our Society in Turmoil,* ed. Gary R. Collins, pp. 113-21. Carol Stream, IL: Creation House, 1970.

Grudem, Wayne A. "How an Economic System Can Be Compatible with Scripture." In *Biblical Principles and Economics: The Foundations,* Christians in the Marketplace Series no. 2, ed. Richard C. Chewning, pp. 27-52. Colorado Springs: Navpress, 1989.

Gutiérrez, Gustavo. "A Spirituality for Liberation." *The Other Side*, April/May 1985, pp. 40-43.

_____. *A Theology of Liberation: History, Politics, and Salvation*. Maryknoll, NY: Orbis Books, 1973.

Gwartney, James D. "A Christian Speaks Up for Capitalism," *The Freeman*, August 1986, pp. 284-85.

_____. "Human Freedom and the Bible." Paper prepared for "Biblical Perspectives on a Mixed Market Economy" conference. Wheaton College, 18-20 September 1987.

Haan, Roelf L. "Christian Belief, Marxism, and Rich and Poor Countries." In *The Challenge of Marxist and Neo-Marxist Ideologies to Christian Scholarship*, ed. John C. Vander Stelt, pp. 111-48. Sioux Center, IA: Dordt College Press, 1982.

Habermas, Jürgen. *Legitimation Crisis*. Boston: Beacon Press, 1975.

Hacker, Andrew. "Two 'New Classes' or None?" In *The New Class?* ed. B. Bruce-Briggs, pp. 155-168. New Brunswick, NJ: Transaction Books, 1979.

Hadden, Jeffrey. *The Gathering Storm in the Churches*. Garden City, NY: Doubleday, 1969.

Hall, Eddy, "Living Cooperatively in a Competitive World." *The Other Side*, January 1983, pp. 10-14.

Halsey, A. H. "Universities in Advanced Industrial Societies." In *Readings in Economic Sociology*, ed. Neil J. Smelser, pp. 46-53. Englewood Cliffs, NJ: Prentice Hall, 1965.

Halteman, Jim. *Market Capitalism and Christianity*. Grand Rapids: Baker Book House, 1988.

Hamilton, Kenneth. "Liberation Theology: An Overview." In *Evangelicals and Liberation*, ed. Carl E. Armerding, pp. 1-9. Nutley, NJ: Presbyterian & Reformed, 1977.

_____. "Liberation Theology: Lessons Positive and Negative." In *Evangelicals and Liberation*, ed. Carl E. Armerding, pp. 120-27. Nutley, NJ: Presbyterian & Reformed, 1977.

Hammersmark, Judy. "Grandmother Was a Capitalist." *Fundamentalist Journal*, September 1985, pp. 32-33.

Hammond, Phillip E. "In Search of a Protestant Twentieth Century: American Religion and Power since 1900." *Review of Religious Research* 24 (June 1983): 281-94.

Hanks, Thomas P. "The Evangelical Witness to the Poor and Oppressed." *TSF Bulletin*, September-October 1986, pp. 11-20.

_____. *God So Loved the Third World*. Maryknoll, NY: Orbis, 1983.

_____. "Why People Are Poor." *Sojourners*, January 1981, pp. 19-22.

Hansen, Kristen. "Corporate Cult: A Christian Views the New Managerial Emphasis on Corporate Culture." *Crux*, March 1985, pp. 7-9.

Hargrove, Barbara. *The Emergence of the New Class and Its Implications for Church and Society*. New York: Pilgrim Press, 1986.

Harper, Charles, and Kevin Leicht. "Religious Awakenings and Status Politics: Sources of Support for the New Religious Right." *Sociological Analysis* 45 (Winter 1984): 339-53.

Harrington, Michael. "The New Class and the Left." *Society* 16 (January/February 1979): 24-30.

Hart, Hendrik. "The Marxist Challenge to Christians in Education." In *The Challenge of Marxist and Neo-Marxist Ideologies to Christian Scholarship*, ed. John C. Vander Stelt, pp. 251-58. Sioux Center, IA: Dordt College Press, 1982.

Hatfield, Mark. *Between a Rock and a Hard Place*. Waco, TX: Word Books, 1976.

_____. "Celebrating the Year of Liberation." *Christianity Today*, 26 March 1976, pp. 12-14.

_____. "An Economics for Sustaining Humanity." *Post American*, January 1975, pp. 14-19.

Hauerwas, Stanley. *A Community of Character: Toward a Constructive Christian Social Ethic*. Notre Dame, IN: University of Notre Dame Press, 1981.

Hay, Donald. *A Christian Critique of Capitalism*. Grove Booklet on Ethics no. 5. Bramcote, Nottinghamshire: Grove Books, 1977.

_____. *Economics Today: A Christian Critique*. Leicester: Apollos, 1989.

_____. "The International Socio-Economic-Political Order and Our Lifestyle." In *Lifestyles in the Eighties: An Evangelical Commitment to the Simple Lifestyle*, ed. Ronald J. Sider. Philadelphia: Westminster Press, 1982.

_____. "North and South: The Economic Debate." In *The Year 2000*, ed. John R. W. Stott, pp. 72-102. Downers Grove, IL: InterVarsity Press, 1983.

Hedstrom, James Alden. "Evangelical Program in the United States, 1945-1980: The Morphology of Establishment, Progressive, and Radical Platforms." Ph.D diss., Vanderbilt University, 1982.

Heilbroner, Robert L. *The Nature and Logic of Capitalism*. New York: W. W. Norton, 1985.

Heinz, Donald, "The Struggle to Define America." In *The New Christian Right: Mobilization and Legitimation*, ed. Robert C. Liebman and Robert Wuthnow, pp. 133-48. New York: Aldine, 1983.

Heisler, James B. "Social Responses to the Problem of Scarcity." In *Counting the Cost: The Economics of Christian Stewardship*, by Robin Kendrick Klay, pp. 13-31. Grand Rapids: William B. Eerdmans, 1986.

Hemmingson, A. Robert. "The American Economic System in the Light of Christian Teachings." *Journal of the American Scientific Affiliation* 13 (March 1961): 6-11.

Henderson, Robert T. "Ministering to the Poor: Our Embarrassment of Riches," *Christianity Today*, 8 August 1980, pp. 16-18.

Henry, Carl F. H. "Christian Perspective on Private Property." In *Property in a Humane Economy*, ed. Samuel L. Brumenfeld, pp. 23-45. La Salle, IL: Open Court, 1974.

_____. *The Christian Mindset in a Secular Society: Promoting Evangelical Renewal and National Righteousness*. Portland: Multnomah Press, 1984.

_____. "Christian Personal and Social Ethics in Relation to Racism, Poverty, War and Other Problems." In *Let the Earth Hear His Voice: The International Congress on World Evangelization*, ed. J. D. Douglas, pp. 1163-82. Minneapolis: World Wide Publications, 1975.

_____. "Church and State: Why the Marriage Must Be Saved." *Christianity Today*, 19 April 1985, pp. 9-13.

_____. *Confessions of a Theologian: An Autobiography*. Waco, TX: Word Books, 1986.

_____. *Evangelicals in Search of Identity*. Waco, TX: Word Books, 1976.

_____. "Evangelicals in the Social Struggle." *Christianity Today*, 8 October 1965, pp. 3-11.

_____. *God, Revelation, and Authority*. 6 vols. Waco, TX: Word Books, 1976-83.

_____. "The Gospel and Society." *Christianity Today*, 13 September 1974, pp. 66-67.

_____. "Interview." *Sojourners*, April 1976, pp. 27-32.

_____. "The Judgement of America." *Christianity Today*, 8 November 1974, pp. 22-23.

_____. "Liberation Theology and the Scriptures." In *Liberation Theology*, ed. Ronald H. Nash, pp. 187-202. Milford, MI: Mott Media, 1984.

_____. "Perspective for Social Action: Part 1," *Christianity Today*, 19 January 1959, pp. 9-11.

_____. "Perspective for Social Action: Part 2," *Christianity Today*, 2 February 1959, pp. 13-16.

_____. *A Plea for Evangelical Demonstration*. Grand Rapids: Baker Book House, 1971.

_____. "The Resurgence of Evangelical Christianity." *Christianity Today*, 30 March 1959, pp. 3-6.

_____. "Revolt on Evangelical Frontiers." *Christianity Today*, 26 April 1974, pp. 4-8.

_____. "The Tension between Evangelism and the Christian Demand for Social Justice." *Fides et Historia*, Spring 1972, pp. 3-10.

_____. *The Uneasy Conscience of Modern Fundamentalism*. Grand Rapids: William B. Eerdmans, 1947.

_____. "Where Will Evangelicals Cast Their Lot?" *This World* 18 (Summer 1987): 3-11.

Henry, Paul B. *Politics for Evangelicals*. Valley Forge, PA: Judson Press, 1974.

Herberg, Will, "Religious Group Conflict in America." In *Religion and Social Conflict*, ed. Robert Lee and Martin E. Marty, pp. 143-58. New York: Oxford University Press, 1964.

Heschel, Abraham Joshua. *The Earth Is the Lord's: The Sabbath*. New York: Harper & Row, 1966.

Heyne, Paul. "Christianity and 'the Economy.'" *This World*, Winter 1988, pp. 26-39.

_____. "The Concept of Economic Justice in Religious Discussion." In *Morality and the Market: Religious and Economic Perspectives*, ed. Walter Block, Geoffrey Brennan, and Kenneth Elzinga, pp. 463-82. Vancouver, B.C.: Fraser Institute, 1982.

Hill, Peter J. "An Analysis of the Market Economy: Strengths, Weaknesses, and the Future." *Transformation*, June-September/October-December 1987, pp. 40-47.

_____. "Appropriate Intervention in a Market System: A Critique of the Literature." Paper prepared for conference entitled Biblical Perspectives on a Mixed Market Economy. Wheaton College, 18-20 September 1987.

_____. "The Christian and Creation." *Chronicles*, February 1988, pp. 19-25.

Hill, Peter J., and Randall Oyler. "Educational Reform: A Christian Perspective." Unpublished paper, 1989.

Hitchcock, James. "The New Class and the Secular City." *Journal of Ecumenical Studies* 6 (Spring 1969): 218-26.

Hoksbergen, Roland. "The Morality of Economic Growth." *Reformed Journal*, December 1982, pp. 10-13.

Hollander, Paul. "Alienation and the Adversary Culture." *Society,* May-June 1988, pp. 40-48.

_____. *Political Pilgrims: Travels of Western Intellectuals to the Soviet Union, China, and Cuba, 1928-1978.* New York: Oxford University Press, 1981.

Hollinger, Dennis P. "American Individualism and Evangelical Social Ethics: A Study of *Christianity Today,* 1956-1976." Ph.D. diss., Drew University, 1981.

Horowitz, Irving Louis. "On the Expansion of New Theories and the Withering Away of Old Classes." *Society,* January-February 1979, pp. 55-62.

_____. *Philosophy, Science, and the Sociology of Knowledge.* Springfield, IL: Charles C. Thomas, 1961.

Hote, Donald E. "Evangelicals Face the Future." In *Consultation on Future Evangelical Concerns.* Pasadena: William Carey Library, 1978.

House, Wayne H., and Thomas Ice. *Dominion Theology—Blessing or Curse: An Analysis of Christian Reconstructionism.* Portland: Multnomah Press, 1988.

Howard, Irving E. "Christ and the Libertarians." *Christianity Today,* 17 March 1958, pp. 8-10.

_____. "Christian Approach to Economics." *Christianity Today,* 18 August 1958, pp. 7-9.

_____. "Christianity: Parent of Modern Capitalism." *Christian Economics,* 17 May 1966, p. 4.

_____. "The Mission of America." *Christian Economics,* 13 January 1953, pp. 1-4.

_____. "The Piety of Materialism." *Christian Economics,* 16 November 1965, p. 4.

_____. "The Providence of God and Economics." *Christian Economics,* 22 February 1966, p. 4.

"How Did We Get There?" *Christianity Today,* 24 November 1972, pp. 28-29.

Hubbard, David Allan. *What Evangelicals Believe.* Pasadena: Fuller Theological Seminary, 1979.

Hundley, Raymond C. "Dangers of Liberation Theology." *Family Protection Scorecard,* special edition, 7. Costa Mesa, CA: National Citizens Action Network, 1989.

Hunt, Angela Elwell. "Hungry Strangers: Whose Responsibility Are They?" *Fundamentalist Journal,* November 1984, pp. 25-26.

Hunt, Norman C. "Christians and the Economic Order." *Christianity Today,* 2 September 1959, pp. 5-8.

Hunter, James Davison. *American Evangelicalism: Conservative Religion and the Quandary of Modernity.* New Brunswick, NJ: Rutgers University Press, 1983.

_____. "American Protestantism: Sorting Out the Present, Looking toward the Future." *This World,* Spring 1987, pp. 53-76.

_____. "America's Fourth Faith: A Sociological Perspective on Secular Humanism." *This World,* Fall 1987, pp. 101-10.

_____. "Culture Wars: The Struggle to Define America." Unpublished manuscript, 1988.

_____. *Evangelicalism: The Coming Generation.* Chicago: University of Chicago Press, 1987.

_____. "The Liberal Reaction." In *The New Christian Right: Mobilization and*

Legitimation, ed. Robert C. Liebman and Robert Wuthnow, pp. 149-63. New York: Aldine, 1983.

_____. "The New Class and the Young Evangelicals." *Review of Religious Research* 22 (December 1980): 155-69.

_____. "The Perils of Idealism: A Reply." *Review of Religious Research* 24 (March 1983): 267-76.

_____. "Subjectivization and the New Evangelical Theodicy." *Journal for the Scientific Study of Religion* 20 (1982): 39-47.

_____. "The Williamsburg Charter Survey of Religion and Public Life." Washington: Williamsburg Charter Foundation, 3 February 1988.

"Ideology Succumbs to Unity in Oxford." *Christianity Today,* 19 March 1990, p. 52.

Inch, Morris A. *The Evangelical Challenge.* Philadelphia: Westminster Press, 1978.

"Is Christian-Marxist Dialogue Possible?" *Christianity Today,* 6 January 1967, pp. 26-27.

James, Hugh. "Free Will in a Free Market: Christian Constraints on Capitalism." *Reformed Journal,* May 1987, pp. 9-12.

"Jesus, Marx and Co." *Christianity Today,* 8 June 1973, p. 28.

Johnston, Arthur P. *The Battle for World Evangelism.* Wheaton, IL: Tyndale House, 1978.

_____. "The Kingdom in Relation to the Church and the World." In *In Word and Deed,* ed. Bruce J. Nichols, pp. 109-34. Grand Rapids: William B. Eerdmans, 1985.

Johnston, Robert K. *Evangelicals at an Impasse: Biblical Authority in Practice.* Atlanta: John Knox Press, 1979.

Jones, Rufus, "The Problem of Poverty." *United Evangelical Action,* November 1967, pp. 19-21.

Kantzer, Kenneth S. "Unity and Diversity in Evangelical Faith." In *The Evangelicals: What They Believe, Who They Are, Where They Are Changing,* ed. David Wells and John D. Woodbridge, pp. 58-87. Grand Rapids: Baker Book House, 1975.

_____. "Summing Up: An Evangelical View of Church and State." *Christianity Today,* 19 April 1985, pp. 9-13.

Kelly, Douglas. "The Present Struggle for Christian Reconstruction in the United States." *Journal for Christian Reconstruction* 9 (1982-83): 15-23.

Kershner, Howard E. "The Role of the Church in Social Problems." *Christian Economics,* 5 October 1965, pp. 1-3.

_____. "The Church and Social Problems." *Christianity Today,* 4 March 1966, pp. 34-35.

Kirk, Andrew. *The Good News of the Kingdom Coming: The Marriage of Evangelism and Social Responsibility.* Downers Grove, IL: InterVarsity Press, 1983.

Kirkpatrick, Jeane J. "Politics and the New Class." In *The New Class?* ed. B. Bruce-Briggs, pp. 33-48. New Brunswick, NJ: Transaction Books, 1979.

Klay, Robin Kendrick. *Counting the Cost: The Economics of Christian Stewardship.* Grand Rapids: William B. Eerdmans, 1986.

Knapp, Stephen C. "The Economic Crisis: Blessing in Disguise?" *Eternity,* February 1975, pp. 10-23.

_____. "A Preliminary Dialogue with Gutiérrez' *A Theology of Liberation.*" In

Evangelicals and Liberation, ed. Carl E. Armerding, pp. 10-42. Nutley, NJ: Presbyterian & Reformed, 1977.

Krass, Alfred. "The Land of Angel Food Cake: Adam Smith and the Biblical Jubilee." *The Other Side,* September 1988, pp. 41-42.

Kraus, C. Norman. "Evangelicalism: The Great Coalition." In *Evangelicalism and Anabaptism,* ed. C. Norman Kraus, pp. 39-61. Scottdale, PA: Herald Press, 1979.

Kristol, Irving. "About Equality." *Commentary,* November 1972, pp. 41-47.

_____. "Rationalism in Economics." In *The Crisis in Economic Theory,* ed. Daniel Bell and Irving Kristol, pp. 201-18. New York: Basic Books, 1981.

_____. " 'When Virtue Loses Her Loveliness': Some Reflections on Capitalism and 'The Free Society.' " *Public Interest,* Fall 1970, pp. 3-14.

Kuhn, Harold B. "Obstacles to Evangelism in the World." *Christianity Today,* 28 October 1966, pp. 18-24.

_____. "Twentieth Century Evangelism." *Christianity Today,* 14 October 1966, pp. 61-62.

Kuyper, Abraham. *Lectures on Calvinism.* Grand Rapids: William B. Eerdmans, 1931.

Lacey, Hugh. "The Harsh Choice: Resisting Systematic Violence." *The Other Side,* November 1986, pp. 24-25.

Ladd, Carll Everett, Jr. "Liberalism Upside Down: The Inversion of the New Deal Order." *Political Science Quarterly* 91 (1976): 577-600.

_____. "Pursuing the New Class: Social Theory and Survey Data." In *The New Class?* ed. B. Bruce-Briggs, pp. 101-22. New Brunswick, NJ: Transaction Books, 1979.

Ladd, Carll Everett, Jr., and Charles D. Hadley. *Transformations of the American Party System: Political Coalitions from the New Deal to the 1970s,* 2d ed. New York: W. W. Norton, 1978.

Lasch, Christopher. "The Conservative 'Backlash' and the Cultural Civil War." In *Neo-Conservatism: Social and Religious Phenomenon,* ed. Gregory Baum, pp. 8-11. New York: Seabury, 1981.

Lebacqz, Karen. *Six Theories of Justice.* Minneapolis: Augsburg, 1986.

"Liberation." *Christianity Today,* 19 January 1973, pp. 26-27.

Lichter, S. Robert; Stanley Rothman; and Linda S. Richter. *The Media Elite.* Bethesda, MD: Adler & Adler, 1986.

Lindbeck, Asar. *The Political Economy of the New Left: An Outsider's View.* New York: Harper & Row, 1971.

Linder, Robert D. "Modern Evangelical Christianity, Social Concern, and Hope: An Historical Perspective." *Evangelical Quarterly,* April-June 1972, 76-83.

_____. "The Resurgence of Evangelical Social Concern, 1925-1975." In *The Evangelicals: What They Believe, Who They Are, Where They Are Changing,* ed. David F. Wells and John D. Woodbridge, pp. 209-30. Grand Rapids: Baker Book House, 1975.

Linder, Robert D., and Richard V. Pierard. *Twilight of the Saints: Biblical Christianity and Civil Religion in America.* Downers Grove, IL: InterVarsity Press, 1978.

Lindsell, Harold. *The Battle for the Bible.* Grand Rapids: William B. Eerdmans, 1976.

_____. *Free Enterprise: A Judeo-Christian Defense.* Wheaton, IL: Tyndale House, 1982.

_____. "Lausanne '74: An Appraisal." *Christianity Today,* 13 September 1974, pp. 21-26.

Lipset, Seymour Martin. "The New Class and the Professoriate." In *The New Class?* ed. B. Bruce-Briggs, pp. 67-87. New Brunswick, NJ: Transaction Books, 1979.

Lorentzen, Louise J. "Evangelical Life-Style Concerns Expressed in Political Action." *Sociological Analysis* 41 (Summer 1980): 144-54.

Löwith, Karl. *Meaning in History: The Theological Implications of the Philosophy of History.* Chicago: University of Chicago, 1949.

Lum, Ada. *Jesus the Radical.* Downers Grove, IL: InterVarsity Press, 1970.

MacDonald, Angus. "God and Economics." *Christian Economics,* December 1972, pp. 25-28.

Machen, J. Gresham. *Christianity and Liberalism.* Grand Rapids: William B. Eerdmans, 1972.

Machlup, Fritz. *The Production and Distribution of Knowledge in the United States.* Princeton: Princeton University Press, 1962.

MacIntyre, Alasdair. *After Virtue: A Study in Moral Theory,* 2d ed. Notre Dame, IN: University of Notre Dame Press, 1984.

"Man in Search of Answers." *Moody Monthly,* February 1965, pp. 16-21.

Mannheim, Karl. *Ideology and Utopia: An Introduction to the Sociology of Knowledge.* New York: Harcourt, Brace & World, 1968.

Marcuse, Herbert. *One Dimensional Man: Studies in the Ideology of Advanced Industrial Society.* Boston: Beacon Press, 1962.

Marsden, George. "The Evangelical Denomination." In *Evangelicalism and Modern America,* ed. George Marsden, pp. vii-xix. Grand Rapids: William B. Eerdmans, 1984.

_____. "From Fundamentalism to Evangelicalism: A Historical Analysis." In *The Evangelicals: What They Believe, Who They Are, Where They Are Changing,* ed. David F. Wells and John D. Woodbridge, pp. 142-62. Grand Rapids: Baker Book House, 1975.

_____. *Fundamentalism and American Culture: The Shaping of Twentieth Century Evangelicalism, 1870-1925.* New York: Oxford University Press, 1980.

_____. "The Gospel of Wealth, the Social Gospel, and the Salvation of Souls in Nineteenth Century America." *Fides et Historia,* Spring 1973, pp. 10-21.

_____. *Reforming Fundamentalism: Fuller Seminary and the New Evangelicalism.* Grand Rapids: William B. Eerdmans, 1987.

_____. "The State of Evangelical Christian Scholarship." *Reformed Journal,* September 1987, pp. 12-16.

_____. "Understanding Fundamentalist Views of Society." In *Reformed Faith and Practice,* ed. Ronald H. Stone, pp. 65-76. Washington: University Press of America, 1983.

Marshall, Paul. "Calling, Work, and Rest." In *Christian Faith and Practice in the Modern World,* ed. Mark A. Noll and David F. Wells, pp. 199-217. Grand Rapids: William B. Eerdmans, 1988.

_____. "A Christian View of Economics." *Crux,* March 1985, pp. 3-6.

Martin, David. "The Clergy, Secularization, and Politics." *This World,* Fall 1983, pp. 131-42.

Marty, Martin E. "Fundamentalism as a Social Phenomenon." In *Evangelicalism and Modern America,* ed. George Marsden, pp. 56-68. Grand Rapids: William B. Eerdmans, 1984.

_____. "Interpreting American Pluralism." In *Religion in America: 1950 to the Present,* ed. Jackson W. Carroll, Douglas W. Johnson, and Martin E. Marty, pp. 78-90. San Francisco: Harper & Row, 1979.

_____. *The Modern Schism: Three Paths to the Secular.* London: SCM Press, 1969.

_____. *Righteous Empire: The Protestant Experience in America.* New York: Dial Press, 1970.

_____. "Tensions within Contemporary Evangelicalism: A Critical Appraisal." In *The Evangelicals: What They Believe, Who They Are, Where They Are Changing,* ed. David F. Wells and John D. Woodbridge, pp. 190-208. Grand Rapids: Baker Book House, 1975.

"The Marxist Never-Never Land." *Christianity Today,* 20 December 1974, pp. 19-20.

Mathews, M. R. "The Implications of Western Theologies of Development for Third World Countries and Churches." In *Evangelicals and Development: Toward a Theology of Social Change,* ed. Ronald J. Sider, pp. 89-101. Philadelphia: Westminster Press, 1981.

Mavrodes, George I. "Jubilee—A Viable Model?" *Reformed Journal,* January 1978, pp. 15-19.

_____. "On Helping the Hungry." *Christianity Today,* 30 December 1977, pp. 46-50.

McAdams, John C. *The New Class Struggle: Social Class and Politics in Post-Industrial Society.* Unpublished manuscript, 1988.

McAuliffe, Joseph R. "Economic Oppression." *Chalcedon Report* no. 277, August 1988, pp. 14-15.

McClain, George. "Money Trouble." *The Other Side,* March 1978, pp. 17-21.

McGavran, Donald C. "Is Social Action Evangelism?" *Eternity,* November 1966, pp. 23-44.

McIntire, Carl T. "Dooyeweerd's Philosophy of History." In *The Legacy of Hermann Dooyeweerd: Reflections on Critical Philosophy in the Christian Tradition,* ed. Carl T. McIntire, pp. 81-118. New York: University Press of America, 1985.

McIntire, Carl. *The Rise of the Tyrant: Controlled Economy vs. Private Enterprise.* Collingswood, NJ: Christian Beacon Press, 1945.

McLellan, Barbara Lenes. "Milton Friedman and His Ethics of the Free Market: A Critical Appraisal." *Crux,* June 1986, pp. 27-35.

McMaster, R. E., Jr. "Common Grace in a Free Market." *Chalcedon Report* no. 278, September 1988, pp. 8ff.

Meadows, Gary T. "John R. W. Stott on Social Action." *Grace Theological Journal,* Fall 1980, pp. 129-47.

Middelman, Udo. "A Response to Stephen Mott." *Transformation,* June-September/ October-December 1987, pp. 36-40.

Míguez Bonino, José. *Christians and Marxists: The Mutual Challenge to Revolution.* Grand Rapids: William B. Eerdmans, 1976.

Miller, Donald L. "How We Can Defeat Communism without War." *United Evangelical Action,* January 1962, pp. 11-12.

Miller, Elizabeth McEachern. "Money, Inheritance, and the Family." In *The Roots of Inflation,* by Rousas John Rushdoony, pp. 91-96. Vallecito, CA: Ross House Books, 1982.

Moberg, David O. *The Great Reversal: Evangelism and Social Concern.* Philadelphia: J. B. Lippincott, 1977.

_____. *Inasmuch: Christian Social Responsibility in Twentieth Century America.* Grand Rapids: William B. Eerdmans, 1965.

Monsma, George N. "The Bible and the Free Market." *Reformed Journal,* February 1985, pp. 21-26.

_____. "Love and the National Economy." *Reformed Journal,* October 1968, pp. 12-15.

_____. "The Need for Reform." *Reformed Journal,* March 1974, pp. 12-15.

_____. "Nixon's New Economic Policy." *Reformed Journal,* January 1972, pp. 9-11.

_____. "The Socio-Economic-Political Order and Our Lifestyles." In *Living More Simply,* ed. Ronald J. Sider, pp. 173-202. Downers Grove, IL: InterVarsity Press, 1980.

_____. "Vested Interests Survive Another Round." *Reformed Journal,* April 1970, pp. 13-17.

Monsma, Stephen V. *Pursuing Justice in a Sinful World.* Grand Rapids: William B. Eerdmans, 1984.

_____. "Should the Poor Earn Their Keep?" *Christianity Today,* 12 June 1987, pp. 28-31.

_____. *The Unraveling of America.* Downers Grove, IL: InterVarsity Press, 1974.

Montgomery, John Warwick. "Evangelical Social Responsibility in Theological Perspective." In *Our Society in Turmoil,* ed. Gary R. Collins, pp. 13-23. Carol Stream, IL: Creation House, 1970.

_____. "Neither Marx nor Jesus." *Christianity Today,* 8 October 1971, pp. 60-61.

Mooneyham, W. Stanley. *What Do You Say to a Hungry World?* Waco, TX: Word Books, 1975.

Moore, Stanley W., and Fred Jappe. "Christianity as an Ethical Matrix for No-Growth Economics." *Journal of the American Scientific Affiliation* 32 (September 1980): 164-68.

Moorecroft, Joseph C. "Liberation Criticisms of Capitalism." *Family Protection Scorecard,* special edition, pp. 12-13. Costa Mesa, CA: National Citizens Action Network, 1989.

Morris, Leon. "Objections to Evangelism." *Christianity Today,* 13 March 1970, pp. 58-59.

Mott, Stephen C. *Biblical Ethics and Social Change.* New York: Oxford University Press, 1982.

_____. "How Should Christian Economists Use the Bible? A Study in Hermeneutics." Paper prepared for conference entitled Biblical Perspectives on a Mixed Market Economy. Wheaton College, 18-20 September 1987.

_____. "The Contribution of the Bible to Economic Thought." *Transformation,* June-September/October-December 1987, pp. 25-33.

_____. "The Politics of Jesus and Our Responsibilities." *Reformed Journal,* February 1976, pp. 7-10.

Mouw, Richard J. "The Call to Holy Worldliness." *Reformed Journal*, January 1989, pp. 8-14.

_____. "New Alignments." In *Against the World for the World: The Hartford Appeal and the Future of American Religion*, ed. Peter L. Berger and Richard John Neuhaus, pp. 99-125. New York: Seabury Press, 1976.

_____. *Political Evangelism*. Grand Rapids: William B. Eerdmans, 1973.

_____. *Politics and the Biblical Drama*. Grand Rapids: William B. Eerdmans, 1976.

_____. "The Task of 'Christian Social Ethics'." *Christianity Today*, 5 January 1968, pp. 3-5.

_____. "Thinking about the Poor: What Evangelicals Can Learn from the Bishops." In *Prophetic Visions and Economic Realities: Protestants, Jews and Catholics Confront the Bishops' Letter on the Economy*, ed. Charles R. Strain, pp. 20-34. Grand Rapids: William B. Eerdmans, 1989.

_____. "Toward an Evangelical Theology of Poverty." In *Christian Faith and Practice in the Modern World*, ed. Mark A. Noll and David F. Wells, pp. 218-38. Grand Rapids: William B. Eerdmans, 1988.

Mulford, John E. "The War on Poverty: A Christian Economist on the Bible and State Involvement." *Christianity Today*, 14 June 1985, p. 30.

Murch, James Deforest. *Cooperation without Compromise: A History of the National Association of Evangelicals*. Grand Rapids: William B. Eerdmans, 1956.

Nash, George H. *The Conservative Intellectual Movement in America since 1945*. New York: Basic Books, 1979.

Nash, Ronald H. "Biblical Efforts and Economic and Political Freedom." *Fundamentalist Journal*, July-August 1985, pp. 25-27.

_____. "The Christian Choice between Capitalism and Socialism." In *Liberation Theology*, ed. Ronald H. Nash, pp. 45-67. Milford, MI: Mott Media, 1984.

_____. "Does Capitalism Pass the Moral Test?" *Evangelical Journal* 5 (1987): 35-45.

_____. *Dooyeweerd and the Amsterdam Philosophy: A Christian Critique of Philosophic Thought*. Grand Rapids: Zondervan, 1962.

_____. "The Economics of Justice: A Conservative's View." *Christianity Today*, 23 March 1979, pp. 24-30.

_____. *Evangelicals in America: Who They Are, What They Believe*. Nashville: Abingdon Press, 1987.

_____. *Freedom, Justice, and the State*. Lanham, MD: University Press of America, 1980.

_____. "Liberation Theology." *Eternity*, July-August 1986, pp. 15-21.

_____. "Liberation Theology: Will It Liberate or Enslave?" *Family Protection Scorecard*, special edition, pp. 4ff. Costa Mesa, CA: National Citizens Action Network, 1989.

_____. *Poverty and Wealth: The Christian Debate over Capitalism*. Westchester, IL: Crossway Books, 1986.

_____. "A Reply to Eric Beversluis." *Christian Scholar's Review* 11 (1981): 347-58.

_____. *Social Justice and the Christian Church*. Milford, MI: Mott Media, 1983.

_____. "Some Questions about Benefit-Rights." *Christian Scholar's Review*, March 1987, pp. 229-32.

_____. "The Subjective Theory of Economic Value." In *Biblical Principles and Economics: The Foundations,* Christians in the Marketplace Series no. 2, ed. Richard C. Chewning, pp. 80-96. Colorado Springs: Navpress, 1989.

Neff, David. "When Economists Pray," *Christianity Today,* 9 April 1990, p. 13.

Neuhaus, Richard John. *The Naked Public Square: Religion and Democracy in America.* Grand Rapids: William B. Eerdmans, 1984.

_____. "Why Wait for the Kingdom? The Theonomist Temptation." *First Things,* May 1990, pp. 13-21.

Newfield, Jack, and Jeff Greenfield. *A Populist Manifesto: The Making of a New Majority.* New York: Warner Paperback Library, 1972.

_____. *A Prophetic Minority.* New York: New American Library, 1966.

Newland, E. V. "The Economy and Resources." In *Evangelicals Face the Future,* ed. Donald E. Hoke, pp. 61-68. Pasadena: William Carey Library, 1978.

Nicholls, Bruce, ed. *In Word and Deed: Evangelism and Social Responsibility.* Grand Rapids: William B. Eerdmans, 1985.

Nichols, Alan. *An Evangelical Commitment to Simple Life-Style: Exposition and Commentary,* Lausanne Occasional Papers no. 20. Wheaton, IL: Lausanne Committee for World Evangelization, 1980.

Niebuhr, H. Richard. *Christ and Culture.* New York, Harper & Row, 1951.

_____. "The Doctrine of the Trinity and the Unity of the Church." *Theology Today,* October 1946, p. 371.

_____. *The Nature and Destiny of Man.* 2 vols. New York: Scribner's, 1941, 1943.

Niebuhr, Reinhold. *An Interpretation of Christian Ethics.* San Francisco: Harper & Row, 1935.

Nisbet, Robert A. *Community and Power.* New York: Oxford University Press, 1962.

Noll, Mark A. *Between Faith and Criticism: Evangelicals, Scholarship, and the Bible in America.* San Francisco: Harper & Row, 1986.

_____. "Christian Thinking and the Rise of the American University." *Christian Scholar's Review* 9 (1979): 3-16.

Norman, Edward R. "Denigration of Capitalism: Current Education and the Moral Subversion of Capitalist Society." In *The Denigration of Capitalism: Six Points of View,* ed. Michael Novak, pp. 7-23. Washington: American Enterprise Institute, 1979.

North, Gary. "Free Market Capitalism." In *Wealth and Poverty: Four Christian Views of Economics,* ed. Robert G. Clouse. Downers Grove, IL: InterVarsity Press, 1984.

_____. *Inherit the Earth: Biblical Principles for Economics,* Biblical Blueprint Series no. 7, ed. Gary North. Fort Worth: Dominion Press, 1987.

_____. *An Introduction to Christian Economics.* Nutley, NJ: Craig Press, 1974.

_____. *Liberating Planet Earth: An Introduction to Biblical Blueprints,* Biblical Blueprint Series no. 1. Fort Worth: Dominion Press, 1987.

_____. "Pollution Control and Biblical Justice." *The Freeman,* September 1986, pp. 338-44.

_____. *The Sinai Strategy: Economics and the Ten Commandments.* Tyler, TX: Institute for Christian Economics, 1986.

_____. "Trickle-Down Economics." *The Freeman,* May 1982, pp. 268-81.

_____. *Unconditional Surrender: God's Program for Victory.* Tyler, TX: Institute for Christian Economics, 1988.

Novak, Michael. "Democratic Capitalism: A North American Liberation Theology." *Transformation,* January-March 1985, pp. 18-23.

_____. *The Spirit of Democratic Capitalism.* New York: Simon & Schuster, 1982.

_____. "The Revolution That Wasn't." *Christianity Today,* 23 April 1990, pp. 18-20.

_____. "A Theology of Development for Latin America." In *Liberation Theology,* ed. Ronald H. Nash, pp. 21-44. Milford, MI: Mott Media, 1984.

_____. *Will It Liberate? Questions about Liberation Theology.* New York: Paulist Press, 1986.

Ockenga, Harold J. "The Economy and Resources: Response." In *Evangelicals Face the Future,* ed. Donald E. Hoke, pp. 69-74. Pasadena: William Carey Library, 1978.

_____. "From Fundamentalism, through New Evangelicalism, to Evangelicalism." In *Evangelical Roots,* ed. Kenneth Kantzer, pp. 35-46. Nashville: Thomas Nelson, 1978.

_____. "Resurgent Evangelical Leadership." *Christianity Today,* 10 October 1960, pp. 11-14.

O'Donovan, Oliver. *Resurrection and Moral Order: An Outline for Evangelical Ethics.* Grand Rapids: William B. Eerdmans, 1986.

Olasky, Marvin N. "Unholy Alliance." *Eternity,* June 1985, pp. 19-23.

Owensby, Walter L. *Economics for Prophets: A Primer on Concepts, Realities, and Values in Our Economic System.* Grand Rapids: William B. Eerdmans, 1988.

Packer, J. I. "How to Recognize a Christian Citizen." *Christianity Today,* 19 April 1985, pp. 4-8.

Padilla, C. René. "Evangelism and Social Responsibility: From Wheaton '66 to Wheaton '83." In *The Best of Theology,* vol. 1, ed. Paul Fromer, pp. 239-52. Carol Stream, IL: Christianity Today, 1988.

_____. "Evangelism and the World." In *Let the Earth Hear His Voice: The International Congress on World Evangelization,* ed. J. D. Douglas, pp. 116-33. Minneapolis: World Wide Publications, 1975.

_____. "Liberation Theology." In *The Challenge of Marxist and Neo-Marxist Ideologies for Christian Scholarship,* ed. John C. Vander Stelt, pp. 86-103. Sioux Center, IA: Dordt College Press, 1982.

_____. "Liberation Theology." *Reformed Journal,* June 1983, pp. 21-23.

_____. "Liberation Theology Is Remarkably Protestant." *Christianity Today,* 15 May 1987, p. 12.

_____. *Mission between the Times: Essays on the Kingdom.* Grand Rapids: William B. Eerdmans, 1985.

_____. *The New Face of Evangelicalism: An International Symposium on the Lausanne Covenant.* Downers Grove, IL: InterVarsity Press, 1976.

_____. "The Theology of Liberation." *Christianity Today,* 9 November 1973, pp. 69-70.

_____. "Revolution and Revelation." In *Is Revolution Change?* ed. Brian Griffiths, pp. 70-83. Downers Grove, IL: InterVarsity Press, 1972.

Pannell, William E. "A Call to Simpler Life-Style." In *Living More Simply,* ed. Ronald J. Sider, pp. 17-26. Downers Grove, IL: InterVarsity Press, 1980.

_____. "Evangelism and the Struggle for Power." In *Mission Trends no. 4: Liberation Theologies,* ed. Gerald H. Anderson and Thomas F. Stransky, pp. 150-60. Grand Rapids: William B. Eerdmans, 1979.

Pearson, Fred. *They Dare to Hope: Student Protest and Christian Response.* Grand Rapids: William B. Eerdmans, 1969.

Perkins, John. "Liberation Theology: A Case Study U.S.A." In *The Challenge of Marxist and Neo-Marxist Ideologies for Christian Scholarship,* ed. John C. Vander Stelt, pp. 104-10. Sioux Center, IA: Dordt College Press, 1982.

_____. "Preaching the Gospel of the Kingdom of God." *Radix,* Fall 1986, pp. 8-9, 28.

_____. "With Justice for All." *Fundamentalist Journal,* February 1988, pp. 14-16.

_____. *With Justice for All.* Ventura, CA: Regal Books, 1982.

Pew, J. Howard. "Faith and Freedom." *Christian Economics,* 3 August 1965, pp. 1-3.

_____. "The Mission of the Church." *Christian Economics,* 6 February 1968, pp. 1-2.

Pierard, Richard V. "Billingsly and Billingsgate." *Reformed Journal,* August 1986, pp. 7-8.

_____. *Evangelical Christianity and Political Conservatism.* Philadelphia: J. B. Lippincott, 1970.

_____. "Evangelical Christianity and the Radical Right." In *The Cross and the Flag,* ed. Robert Clouse, Robert Linder, and Richard Pierard, pp. 99-118. Carol Stream, IL: Creation House, 1972.

_____. "Floundering in the Rain." *Reformed Journal,* October 1975, pp. 6-8.

_____. "Needed: An Evangelical Social Ethic." *Evangelical Quarterly,* April-June 1972, pp. 84-90.

_____. *The Unequal Yoke: Evangelical Christianity and Political Conservatism.* Philadelphia: J. B. Lippincott, 1970.

_____. "Where America Missed the Way." *Journal of the American Scientific Affiliation* 29 (March 1977): 18-21.

Pinnock, Clark H. "A Call for the Liberation of North American Christians." In *Evangelicals and Liberation,* ed. Carl E. Armerding. Nutley, NJ: Presbyterian & Reformed, 1977.

_____. "The Christian Revolution." *Post American,* Fall 1971, pp. 10-11.

_____. "Liberation Theology: The Gains, the Gaps." *Christianity Today,* 16 January 1976, pp. 13-15.

_____. "A Pilgrimage in Political Theology." In *Liberation Theology,* ed. Ronald H. Nash, pp. 101-20. Milford, MI: Mott Media, 1984.

_____. "The Pursuit of Utopia." In *Freedom, Justice, and Hope: Toward a Strategy for the Poor and the Oppressed,* Turning Point Christian Worldview Series no. 3, ed. Marvin Olasky, 65-83. Westchester, IL: Crossway, 1988.

_____. "Pursuit of Utopia, Betrayal of the Poor." *Crux,* December 1987, pp. 5-14.

_____. *The Scripture Principle.* San Francisco: Harper & Row, 1984.

"The Place to Start." *Christianity Today,* 27 September 1974, pp. 36-37.

Podhoretz, Norman. "The Adversary Culture and the New Class." In *The New Class?* ed. B. Bruce-Briggs, pp. 19-31. New Brunswick, NJ: Transaction Books, 1979.

"The President's Poverty Plan." *Christianity Today,* 12 December 1969, pp. 34-35.

Price, Robert. "A Fundamentalist Social Gospel?" *Christian Century,* 28 November 1979, pp. 1183-86.

"Provoking to Good Works." *Christianity Today,* 21 December 1973, p. 23.

Pryor, Frederic L. "The 'New Class': Analysis of the Concept, the Hypothesis and the Idea as a Research Tool." *American Journal of Economics and Sociology* 40 (October 1981): 367-79.

Pyles, Volie E. "Bruised, Bloodied, and Broken: Fundamentalism's Internecine Controversy in the 1960's." *Fides et Historia,* October 1986, pp. 45-55.

Quebedeaux, Richard. *The New Charismatics II: How a Christian Renewal Movement Became a Part of the Evangelical Mainstream.* San Francisco: Harper & Row, 1976.

_____. *The Worldly Evangelicals.* New York: Harper & Row, 1978.

_____. *The Young Evangelicals: Revolution in Orthodoxy.* New York: Harper & Row, 1974.

Ramm, Bernard L. *The Evangelical Heritage.* Waco, TX: Word Books, 1973.

Rauschenbusch, Walter. *A Theology for the Social Gospel.* New York: Abingdon Press, 1945.

Rawls, John. *A Theory of Justice.* Cambridge: Harvard University Press, 1971.

Reese, Boyd. "Christ and Capitalism: Evangelicals Look at the Free Market System." *Sojourners,* May 1984, pp. 36-37.

_____. "Is *Sojourners* Marxist?: An Analysis of Recent Charges." *TSF Bulletin,* November-December 1984, pp. 14-17.

Richardson, J. David. "Christian Doubts about Economic Dogmas." In *Christianity Challenges the University,* ed. Peter Wilkes, pp. 51-61. Downers Grove, IL: InterVarsity Press, 1981.

_____. "Frontiers in Economics and Christian Scholarship." *Christian Scholar's Review,* June 1988, pp. 381-400.

Ritchie, Daniel. "Churches and the Wealth of Nations." *Eternity,* July-August 1985, p. 8.

Roberts, Payton N. "Liberation Theologies: Looking at Poverty from the Under Side." *Christianity Today,* 17 May 1985, pp. 14-16.

_____. "Where Has Liberation Theology Gone Wrong?" *Christianity Today,* 19 October 1979, pp. 26-28.

Robertson, Pat. *The Secret Kingdom: A Promise of Hope and Freedom in a World of Turmoil.* Nashville: Thomas Nelson, 1982.

Roche, George. "Capitalism and the Future of America." *Imprimus,* special edition. Hillsdale, MI: Hillsdale College, 1988.

Ropke, Wilhelm. *A Humane Economy: The Social Framework of the Free Market.* Chicago: Henry Regnery, 1960.

Rose, Tom. "Anarchy: Fruit of Government 'Charity.'" *Christian Economics,* May 1971, pp. 1-5.

_____. *Economics: The American Economy from a Christian Perspective.* Mercer, PA: American Enterprise Publications, 1985.

_____. "Economics from a Christian Perspective?" *Journal of Christian Reconstruction,* Summer 1975, pp. 10-27.

_____. *Economics: Principles and Policy from a Christian Perspective.* 2d ed. Mercer, PA: American Enterprise Publications, 1986.

_____. *Free Enterprise Economics.* Mercer, PA: American Enterprise Publications, 1988.

_____. "The Free Market." *Christian Economics,* 17 March 1970, pp. 1-3.

Rose, Tom, and Robert M. Metcalf. "Inflation Is Immoral." *Journal of Christian Reconstruction,* Summer 1980, pp. 31-39.

Rosenberg, Nathan, and L. E. Birdzell, Jr. *How the West Grew Rich: The Economic Transformation of the Industrial World.* New York: Basic Books, 1986.

Rottenberg, Isaac. "Dimensions of the Kingdom: A Dialogue with 'Sojourners'." *Reformed Journal,* November 1977, pp. 17-21.

_____. "The Shape of the Church's Social-Economic Witness." *Reformed Journal,* May 1977, pp. 16-21.

Rubin, Michael Rogers, and Mary Taylor Huber. *The Knowledge Industry in the United States, 1960-1980.* Princeton: Princeton University Press, 1986.

Rushdoony, Rousas John. "Capitalism is the Product of Work and Thrift." *Comments in Brief.* Vallecito, CA: Chalcedon.

_____. *The Flight from Humanity: A Study of the Effects of Neoplatonism on Christianity.* Fairfax, VA: Thoburn Press, 1973.

_____. *The Foundations of Social Order: Studies in the Creeds and Councils of the Early Church.* Fairfax, VA: Thoburn Press, 1978.

_____. *The One and the Many: Studies in the Philosophy of Order and Ultimacy.* Fairfax, VA: Thoburn Press, 1971.

_____. *Politics of Guilt and Pity.* Fairfax, VA: Thoburn Press, 1978.

_____. *The Roots of Inflation.* Vallecito, CA: Ross House Books, 1982.

_____. "Wealth and the City." *Chalcedon Position Paper* no. 28. Vallecito, CA: Chalcedon.

_____. "Wealth and the State." *Chalcedon Position Paper* no. 30. Vallecito, CA: Chalcedon.

Russell, Kirk. *The Conservative Mind: From Burke to Santayana.* Chicago, 1953.

Rutschman, LaVerne. "Anabaptism and Liberation Theology." *The Mennonite Quarterly Review,* July 1981, pp. 255-70.

Sabath, Bob. "The Bible and the Poor." *Post American,* February-March 1974, pp. 4-5, 14.

Samuel, Vinay, and Chris Sugden. "Evangelism and Social Responsibility: A Biblical Study on Priorities." In *In Word and Deed,* ed. Bruce J. Nicholls, pp. 189-214. Grand Rapids: William B. Eerdmans, 1985.

_____. "A Just and Responsible Lifestyle: An Old Testament Perspective." In *Lifestyle in the Eighties: An Evangelical Commitment to Simple Lifestyle,* ed. Ronald J. Sider, pp. 42-53. Philadelphia: Westminster Press, 1982.

_____. "Theology and Development: A Guide to the Debate." In *Evangelicals and Development: Toward a Theology of Social Change,* ed. Ronald J. Sider, pp. 19-42. Philadelphia: Westminster Press, 1981.

_____. "Toward a Theology of Social Change." In *Evangelicals and Development:*

Toward a Theology of Social Change, ed. Ronald J. Sider, pp. 45-68. Philadelphia: Westminster Press, 1981.

Sapp, W. David. "Southern Baptist Responses to the American Economy, 1900-1980." *Baptist History and Heritage,* January 1981, pp. 3-12.

Sauer, James L. "The Myth of Social Justice." *Chalcedon Report* no. 273 (April 1988): 2-3.

Schaeffer, Francis A. "Race and Economics." *Christianity Today,* 4 January 1974, pp. 18-19.

Schaeffer, Franky. Introduction to *Is Capitalism Christian?* ed. Franky Schaeffer, pp. xv-xxix. Westchester, IL: Crossway Books, 1985.

Schall, James V. "Religion and the Demise of Capitalism." In *The Denigration of Capitalism: Six Points of View,* ed. Michael Novak, pp. 32-38. Washington: American Enterprise Institute, 1979.

Schlossberg, Herbert. "The Cultural Roots of Economic Growth." Paper presented at the Oxford Conference on Christian Faith and Economics, Oxford, U.K., 3-9 January 1990.

_____. *Idols for Destruction: Christian Faith and Its Confrontation with American Society.* Nashville: Thomas Nelson, 1983.

_____. "Imperatives for Economic Development." In *Freedom, Justice, and Hope: Toward a Strategy for the Poor and the Oppressed,* Turning Point Christian Worldview Series no. 3, ed. Marvin Olasky, pp. 99-117. Westchester, IL: Crossway, 1988.

_____. "A Response to Nicholas Wolterstorff." *Transformation,* June-September/ October-December 1987, pp. 20-24.

Schumpeter, Joseph A. *Capitalism, Socialism, and Democracy.* 3d ed. New York: Harper & Brothers, 1950.

Scott, Waldron. *Bring Forth Justice: A Contemporary Perspective on Mission.* Grand Rapids: William B. Eerdmans, 1980.

Sider, Ronald J. "Abortion Is Not the Only Issue." *Christianity Today,* 14 July 1989, pp. 28-32.

_____. *The Chicago Declaration.* Carol Stream, IL: Creation House, 1974.

_____. *Cry Justice: The Bible on Hunger and Poverty.* New York: Paulist Press, 1980.

_____. *Evangelicals and Development: Toward a Theology of Social Change.* Philadelphia: Westminster Press, 1981.

_____. "An Evangelical Theology of Liberation." *The Christian Century,* 19 March 1980, pp. 314-18.

_____. "An Evangelical Vision for American Democracy: An Anabaptist Perspective." In *The Bible, Politics and Democracy,* Encounter Series no. 5, ed. Richard John Neuhaus, pp. 32-54. Grand Rapids: William B. Eerdmans, 1987.

_____. "Evangelism, Salvation, and Social Justice." *International Review of Missions,* July 1975, pp. 251-67.

_____. "Introduction to *Transformation.*" *Transformation,* January-March 1984, p. 2.

_____. "Is God Really on the Side of the Poor?: Heeding the Biblical Evidence," *Sojourners,* October 1977, pp. 11-14.

_____. "The Great Economic Debate: Towards a Spirit and Agenda for Dialogue." *Transformation,* April-June 1984, p. 1.

_____. *Living More Simply: Biblical Principles and Practical Models.* Downers Grove, IL: InterVarsity Press, 1980.

_____. "Living More Simply for Evangelism and Justice." In *Lifestyle in the Eighties: An Evangelical Commitment to Simple Lifestyle,* ed. Ronald J. Sider, pp. 23-41. Philadelphia: Westminster Press, 1982.

_____. "Mischief by Statute: How We Oppress the Poor," *Christianity Today,* 16 July 1976, pp. 14-19.

_____. "A Plea for Conservative Radicals and Radical Conservatives." *Christian Century* 103 (1986): 834-38.

_____. *Rich Christians in an Age of Hunger.* Downers Grove, IL: InterVarsity Press, 1977.

_____. "Toward a Biblical Perspective on Equality: Steps on the Way to Christian Political Engagement." *Interpretation,* April 1989, pp. 156-69.

_____. "A Trickle-up Response to Poverty," *Advocate,* March 1990, pp. 1-2.

Simon, Arthur, *Bread for the World.* Grand Rapids: William B. Eerdmans, 1975.

Sine, Tom. "Development: Its Secular Past and Its Uncertain Future." In *Evangelicals and Development: Toward a Theology of Social Change,* ed. Ronald J. Sider, pp. 71-86. Philadelphia: Westminster Press, 1981.

_____. *The Mustard Seed Conspiracy.* Waco, TX: Word Books, 1981.

Skillen, James W. "Going beyond Liberalism to Christian Social Philosophy." *Christian Scholar's Review,* March 1990, pp. 220-30.

_____. "Human Freedom and Social Justice: A Christian Response to the Marxist Challenge." In *The Challenge of Marxist and Neo-Marxist Ideologies for Christian Scholarship,* ed. John C. Vander Stelt, pp. 23-53. Sioux Center, IA: Dordt College Press, 1982.

_____. "Politics and Justice and Peace." *Reformed Journal,* December 1984, pp. 17-22.

Skinner, Tom. *Black and Free.* Grand Rapids: Zondervan, 1970.

Sleeman, John. *Economic Crisis: A Christian Perspective.* London: SCM Press, 1976.

Smith, Timothy L. "Evangelical Christianity and American Culture." In *The Believable Futures of American Protestantism,* Encounter Series no. 7, ed. Richard John Neuhaus, pp. 1-17. Grand Rapids: William B. Eerdmans, 1988.

Sowell, Thomas. *A Conflict of Visions.* New York: William Morrow, 1987.

Stackhouse, Max L. *Public Theology and Political Economy: Christian Stewardship in Modern Society.* Grand Rapids: William B. Eerdmans, 1987.

Stark, Rodney, and Charles Glock. *American Piety: The Nature of Religious Commitment.* Berkeley and Los Angeles: University of California Press, 1968.

St. Clair, Robert James. "Now It's the Social Welfare Gospel." *United Evangelical Action,* January 1962, pp. 8-10.

Storkey, Alan. *A Christian Social Perspective.* Leicester: Inter-Varsity Press, 1979.

_____. *Transforming Economics: A Christian Way to Employment.* London: SPCK, 1986.

Stott, John R. W. *Christian Mission in the Modern World.* London: Falcon, 1975.

_____. "Economic Equality among Nations: A Christian Concern?" *Christianity Today*, 2 May 1980, pp. 36-37.

_____. *Evangelism and Social Responsibility: An Evangelical Commitment.* Exeter: Paternoster Press, 1982.

_____. *Involvement.* Vol. 1: *Being a Responsible Christian in a Non-Christian Society.* Old Tappan, NJ: Fleming H. Revell, 1984.

_____. *Involvement.* Vol. 2: *Social and Sexual Relationships in the Modern World.* Old Tappan, NJ: Fleming H. Revell, 1985.

_____. "The Just Demands of Economic Inequality." *Christianity Today*, 23 May 1980, pp. 30-31.

_____. *The Lausanne Covenant: An Exposition and Commentary,* Lausanne Occasional Papers no. 3. Wheaton, IL: Lausanne Committee for World Evangelization, 1975.

Stringfellow, William. *An Ethic for Christians and Other Aliens in a Strange Land.* Waco, TX: Word Books, 1973.

_____. "Jesus the Criminal." *Christianity and Crisis*, 8 June 1970, p. 119.

Sundet, John. "Understanding Unemployment." *Eternity*, February 1985, p. 14.

Sweeting, George. "America, Right or Wrong?" *Moody Monthly*, July-August 1974, p. 3.

Tabb, Bill. "The Demise of Our Free Enterprise System." *The Other Side*, December 1979, pp. 44-49.

Tarr, Leslie K. "Are Some Electronic Preachers Social Darwinists?" *Christianity Today*, 21 October 1983, p. 50.

Taylor, Richard K. *Economics and the Gospel.* Philadelphia: United Church Press, 1973.

Thompson, John B., and David Held. *Habermas: The Critical Debate.* Cambridge: MIT Press, 1982.

Tiemstra, John. "Stories Economists Tell." *Reformed Journal*, February 1988, pp. 14-16.

Timmerman, John. "Greed or Gain?" *Reformed Journal*, September 1973, p. 3.

Tinder, Glenn. "Community: The Tragic Ideal." *Yale Review*, Summer 1976, pp. 550-64.

Toland, Eugene; Thomas Fenton; and Lawrence McCulloch. "World Justice and Peace: A Radical Analysis for American Christians." *The Other Side*, January-February 1976, pp. 50-58.

Towns, Elmer L. "How Social Is the Gospel?" *Fundamentalist Journal*, April 1985, pp. 24-26.

Turner, Carlton B. "A New Man." *Post American*, Fall 1971, pp. 4-5.

Turner, James. *Without God, without Creed: The Origins of Unbelief in America.* Baltimore: The Johns Hopkins University Press, 1985.

Tygart, Charles E. "The Role of Theology among Other 'Belief' Variables for Clergy Civil Rights Activism." *Review of Religious Research*, Spring 1977, 271-78.

Van Dahm, Thomas E. "The Christian Far Right and the Economic Role of the State." *Christian Scholar's Review* 12 (1982): 17-36.

_____. "A Theology of Economic Life." *Reformed Review*, December 1964, pp. 18-27.

Van der Heide, Evert. "Justice in International Relations with Less Developed Countries." *Transformation*, April-June 1984, pp. 2-8.

Vandezande, Gerald. *Christians in Crisis: Toward Responsible Citizenship.* Toronto: Anglican Book Center, 1983.

Van Til, Cornelius. *A Christian Theory of Knowledge.* Phillipsburg, NJ: Presbyterian & Reformed, 1969.

"Villars Statement on Relief and Development." In *Freedom, Justice, and Hope: Toward a Strategy for the Poor and the Oppressed,* Turning Point Christian Worldview Series no. 3, ed. Marvin Olasky, pp. 141-48. Westchester, IL: Crossway Books, 1988.

Vogt, Virgil. "Economic Koinonia." *Post American,* June-July 1975, pp. 22-27.

Von Drimmelen, Rob. "Christian Reflections on Economics." *Transformation,* June-September/October-September 1987, pp. 66-84.

Von Mises, Ludwig. *The Free and Prosperous Commonwealth: An Exposition of the Ideals of Classical Liberalism.* New York: D. Van Nostrand, 1962.

Vree, Dale. "Ideology vs. Theology: Case Studies of Liberation Theology and the Christian New Right." In *Christianity Confronts Modernity,* ed. Peter Williamson and Kevin Perrotta, pp. 57-85. Ann Arbor: Servant Books, 1981.

Wacker, Grant. "Searching for Norman Rockwell: Popular Evangelicalism in Contemporary America." In *The Evangelical Tradition in America,* ed. Leonard I. Sweet, pp. 289-315. Macon, GA: Mercer University Press, 1984.

_____. "Uneasy in Zion: Evangelicals in Post-Modern Society." In *Evangelicalism and Modern America,* ed. George Marsden, pp. 17-28. Grand Rapids: William B. Eerdmans, 1984.

Wagner, C. Peter. "Evangelism and Social Action in Latin America." *Christianity Today,* 6 January 1966, pp. 10-12.

_____. *Latin American Theology: Radical or Evangelical?* Grand Rapids: William B. Eerdmans, 1970.

Wallerstein, Immanuel. *The Capitalist World Economy.* Cambridge: Cambridge University Press, 1979.

Wallis, Jim. *Agenda for a Biblical People.* New York: Harper & Row, 1976.

_____. *The Call to Conversion.* San Francisco: Harper & Row, 1981.

_____. "Counting the Cost: A Sermon on Discipleship." In *The Rise of Christian Conscience,* ed. Jim Wallis, pp. 147-53. San Francisco: Harper & Row, 1987.

_____. "The Invisible Empire." *Post American,* November-December 1973, pp. 1, 14.

_____. "Liberation and Conformity." In *Mission Trends no. 4: Liberation Theologies,* ed. Gerald H. Anderson and Thomas F. Stransky, pp. 51-56. Grand Rapids: William B. Eerdmans, 1979.

_____. "Of Rich and Poor." *Post American,* February-March 1974, pp. 10, 13.

_____. "Post American Christianity." *Post American,* Fall 1971, pp. 2-3.

_____. "Revolt on Evangelical Frontiers: A Response." *Christianity Today,* 21 June 1974, pp. 20-21.

_____. "The Rise of Christian Conscience." In *The Rise of Christian Conscience,* ed. Jim Wallis, pp. xix-xxx. San Francisco: Harper & Row, 1987.

_____. "A View From the Evangelical Left." *Christianity Today,* 19 April 1985, pp. 26-27.

_____. "What Does Washington Have to Say to Grand Rapids?" *Sojourners,* July 1977, pp. 3-4.

Walton, Rus. *Biblical Solutions to Contemporary Problems: A Handbook.* Brentwood, TN: Wolgemuth & Hyatt, 1988.

Ward, Benjamin. *The Ideal Worlds of Economics.* New York: Basic Books, 1979.

Wauzzinski, Robert Alan. "God and Mammon: The Interrelationship of Protestant Evangelicalism and the Industrial Revolution in America, 1820-1914." Ph.D. dissertation, University of Pittsburgh, 1985.

Webber, Robert E. *Common Roots: A Call to Evangelical Maturity.* Grand Rapids: William B. Eerdmans, 1978.

_____. *Evangelicals on the Canterbury Trail: Why Evangelicals Are Attracted to the Liturgical Church.* Waco, TX: Word Books, 1985.

Westphal, Merold. "Sing Jubilee." *The Other Side,* March 1978, pp. 28-35.

"The Wheaton Declaration." *International Review of Missions* 55 (October 1966): 458-76.

"Where Is Tomorrow's Food?" *Christianity Today,* 13 September 1974, pp. 52-53.

White, Charles E. "Charles White Responds." *Christianity Today,* 14 July 1989, p. 32.

White, James B. "Jubilee: The Basis of Social Action." *Reformed Journal,* May-June 1971, pp. 8-11.

"Why Are People Starving?" *Christianity Today,* 25 October 1974, p. 35.

Wigglesworth, Chris. "Evangelical Views of the Poor and Social Ethics Today." *Tyndale Bulletin* 35 (1984): 161-84.

Wilber, Charles K., and Laura Grimes. "The Moral Defense of Market Capitalism: A Critique of the Literature." Paper prepared for conference entitled Biblical Perspectives on a Mixed Market Economy, Wheaton College, 18-20 September 1987.

Wildavosky, Aaron. "Using Public Funds for Private Interests." *Society* 16 (January-February 1979): 39-41.

Wink, Walter. *Naming the Powers: The Language of Power in the New Testament.* Philadelphia: Fortress Press, 1984.

_____. "The Powers behind the Throne." *Sojourners,* September 1984, pp. 22-25.

_____. "Unmasking the Powers: A Biblical View of Roman and American Economics." *Sojourners,* October 1978, pp. 9-15.

_____. *Unmasking the Powers: The Invisible Forces That Determine Human Existence.* Philadelphia: Fortress Press, 1986.

Wirt, Sherwood Eliot. *The Social Conscience of the Evangelical.* New York: Harper & Row, 1968.

Wogaman, J. Philip. *The Great Economic Debate.* Philadelphia: Westminster Press, 1977.

Wolters, Albert M. "The Intellectual Milieu of Hermann Dooyeweerd." In *The Legacy of Hermann Dooyeweerd: Reflections on Critical Philosophy in the Christian Tradition,* ed. C. T. McIntire, pp. 1-19. New York: University Press of America, 1985.

Wolterstorff, Nicholas P. "How Does Grand Rapids Reply to Washington?" *Reformed Journal,* October 1977, pp. 10-14.

_____. "Reply by Nicholas Wolterstorff." *Reformed Journal,* December 1984, pp. 23-29.

_____. "Christianity and Social Justice." *Christian Scholar's Review,* March 1987, pp. 211-32.

_____. "Why Care about Justice?" *Reformed Journal,* August 1986, pp. 9-14.

_____. "The Bible and Economics: The Hermeneutical Issues." *Transformation,* June-September/October-December 1987, pp. 11-19.

_____. *Until Justice and Peace Embrace.* Grand Rapids: William B. Eerdmans, 1983.

Woudstra, Marten H. "A Critique of Liberation Theology by a Cross-Culturalized Calvinist." *Journal of the Evangelical Theological Society,* March 1980, pp. 3-12.

Wurmbrand, Richard. "Karl Marx's Ties with Satanism." *Family Protection Scorecard,* special edition, pp. 26ff. Costa Mesa, CA: National Citizens Action Network, 1989.

Wuthnow, Robert. "The Church in the World: The Current Moral Climate, What Pastors Think." *Theology Today,* July 1979, pp. 239-50.

_____. "The Moral Crisis in American Capitalism." *Harvard Business Review,* March-April 1982, pp. 76-84.

_____. *The Restructuring of American Religion: Society and Faith since World War II.* Princeton: Princeton University Press, 1988.

_____. *The Struggle for America's Soul: Evangelicals, Liberals, and Secularism.* Grand Rapids: William B. Eerdmans, 1989.

Wuthnow, Robert, and Wesley Shrum. "Knowledge Workers as a 'New Class': Structural and Ideological Convergence among Professional-Technical Workers and Managers." *Work and Occupations* 10 (November 1983): 471-87.

Yinger, J. Milton. *Religion, Society and the Individual: An Introduction to the Sociology of Knowledge.* New York: Macmillan, 1957.

Yoder, John Howard, "A Critique of North American Evangelical Ethics." *Transformation,* January-March 1985, pp. 28-31.

_____. *The Politics of Jesus.* Grand Rapids: William B. Eerdmans, 1972.

Zingaro, John, and Philip Harnden. "Since Steel Went Down." *The Other Side,* April-May 1985, pp. 30-36.

Zorilla, C. Hugo. "Repression and Revolution in Central America." *The Mennonite Quarterly Review* 58 (August 1984): 335-44.

Zylstra, Bernard. "Marxism and Education: Some Observations." In *The Challenge of Marxist and Neo-Marxist Ideologies for Christian Scholarship,* ed. John C. Vander Stelt, pp. 245-50. Sioux Center, IA: Dordt College Press, 1982.

Index

271

Vree, Dale, 177

Wallerstein, Immanuel, 141
Wallis, Jim, 22, 23, 24, 25, 29n.36, 31, 31n.44, 32, 35, 39, 47, 49, 50, 52
Wealth and poverty: biblical teaching on, 41-61, 88-94, 119, 155, 230, 236-39. *See also* Economic growth (development): theories of; Stewardship
Welfare programs, 78-79, 81, 122, 124, 128-29. *See also* Economic policy
White, James B., 150n.147
Wilber, Charles K., 130

Wink, Walter, 34n.58, 43n.93, 48-49, 49n.123
Wirt, Sherwood, 15-16
Wolters, Albert M., 133, 134
Wolterstorff, Nicholas, 140-43
World Evangelical Fellowship, 19, 59
"World-systems theory," 141, 143n.119
Wuthnow, Robert, 192

Yoder, John Howard, 24, 48, 50, 52n.139, 53n.142, 60

Zylstra, Bernard, 62, 110